The hidden alternative

The hidden alternative

Co-operative values, past, present and future

Edited by
Anthony Webster, Alyson Brown,
David Stewart, John K. Walton and Linda Shaw

MANCHESTER
1824

Manchester University Press

United Nations
University Press

TOKYO • NEW YORK • PARIS

Published by Manchester University Press in the UK, Europe, Australia and New Zealand
Oxford Road, Manchester M13 9NR, UK
www.manchesteruniversitypress.co.uk

A catalogue record for this book is available from the British Library

ISBN 978 07190 8655 7 hardback
ISBN 978 07190 8656 4 paperback

Published by United Nations University Press in North America and its Dependancies, Japan and Geneva, Switzerland
United Nations University Press
United Nations University, 53-70, Jingumae 5-chome,
Shibuya-ku, Tokyo 150-8925, Japan
Tel: +81-3-5467-1212 Fax: +81-3-3406-7345
E-mail: sales@unu.edu general enquiries: press@unu.edu
http://www.unu.edu

United Nations University Office at the United Nations, NewYork
2 United Nations Plaza, Room DC2-2062, NewYork, NY 10017, USA
Tel: +1-212-963-6387 Fax: +1-212-371-9454
E-mail: unuony@unu.edu

United Nations University Press is the publishing division of the United Nations University.

The views expressed in this publication are those of the authors and do not necessarily reflect the views of the United Nations University.

Printed in Great Britain

ISBN 978-92-808-1212-1 hardback
ISBN 978-92-808-1213-8 paperback

A catalog record for this book is available from the Library of Congress

Typeset by Action Publishing Technology Ltd, Gloucester
Printed in Great Britain by TJ International Ltd, Padstow

Contents

Figures, tables and boxes

Box

Contributors

Patrizia Battilani is Professor of Economic History at the University of Bologna. She has published many books and several essays, mainly concerning the history of tourism, the economic history of Italy and the history of co-operative enterprises. She sits on the Advisory Board of the Journal of Tourism History. Her recent publications include, amongst others, *Cooperation, Networks, Service. Innovation in Outsourcing* (Preston: Carnagie Publishing, 2010) and 'The Bel Paese and the Transition to a Service Economy', *Journal of Modern Italian Studies*, 15 (2010).

James Beecher is a PhD student based at the Cardiff Institute for Co-operative Studies and funded by the University of Wales Institute, Cardiff. The title for his PhD project is *Risk Society: Exploring the Resilience of Mutual Financial Institutions in Times of Crisis*. He has been interested in co-operatives since joining a member-run social centre in Brighton (the Cowley Club) while studying for his under-graduate degree in International Relations and Development Studies at the University of Sussex. James is a member of the Stroud Pound Co-operative that promotes an alternative local currency in his home town, and one of twelve directors of the local environmental initiative Transition Stroud.

Alyson Brown is a Reader in History at Edge Hill University. Her specialism is crime history and she has published *English Society and the Prison* (2003) as well as numerous articles and chapters on this subject area. She is currently working on a monograph for Palgrave Macmillan on the Dartmoor Prison Riot, 1932 and Inter-war Penal Policy. However, she also has a long-held interest in co-operative ideals and practice, which has involved acting in elected positions within the movement and work for a credit union.

Dr Jenny Clegg is a Senior Lecturer at the University of Central Lancashire, Preston. Her work on co-operatives in China, past and present experiences, builds on research carried out over a number years. She has been a member of the Beijing-based International Committee for the Promotion of Chinese Industrial Co-operatives since 1998. She also has a specialist interest in the implications of China's rise for the world order and her book *China's Global Strategy: Towards a Multipolar World* was published by Pluto Press in 2009. Other recent publications include work on Sino-European relations and Western stereotypes of the Chinese 'Yellow Peril'.

Ian G. Cook is Emeritus Professor of Human Geography, Liverpool John Moores University. He has been variously Head of Geography, Head of the Centre for Pacific Rim Studies, and Chair, Faculty of Media Arts and Social Science Faculty Graduate Research Committee. Apart from co-operatives, his main research interests are on the linkages between ageing, urbanisation, health and environment in China, and related aspects of social gerontology globally. Recent publications include co-edited volumes entitled *New Perspectives on China and Aging* (2007) and *Aging in Asia* (2009), both for Nova Science Publishers, New York, plus articles in such journals as *Health Policy, Social Science and Medicine* and the *International Journal of Sociology and Social Policy*. He is theme editor for a Special Issue of the *International Journal of Society Systems Science* on 'Health, Environment, Disease and Longevity', in press, and is currently working on a book on comparative ageing for Springer Press, New York.

Dr Katarina Friberg is a Swedish historian who recently finished a post-doctorate project entitled *From Moral Economy to Fair Trade: A Comparative Historical Study of Swedish and British Consumer Co-operation Related to International Trade and Development Aid*, sponsored by the Swedish Research Council, at Södertörn University, Stockholm. She completed her PhD, *Workings of Co-operation: A Compartive Study of Consumer Co-operative Organisation in Britain and Sweden 1860 to 1970*, in 2005. She is involved in several academic and co-operative networks producing anthologies, contributing with articles on the relation between vision and organisation and international co-operative trade in theory and practice. Apart from co-operatives, her research interests are in town and country planning. She completed a project entitled *The Purpose of a Plan – A History of Regeneration and the Case of Middlesbrough* as a Leverhulme Trust Visiting Research Fellow at Teesside University, Middlesbrough in October 2008.

Elizabeth Hicks is a Chartered Accountant and an Associate Professor in the Business and Tourism Department of Mount Saint Vincent University. She currently sits on the boards of the Centre of Excellence for Accounting and Reporting for Co-operatives (CEARC) and the Association of Nonprofits and Social Economy Research (ANSER). Elizabeth's research interests are in the area of environmental, social and ethical accounting and reporting. Currently she is working with two research teams: one to develop understanding of co-operative businesses through the creation of an accounting tool and system that better reflects the true nature of the business and the other to develop a Statement of Recommended Practice for Co-operatives to guide co-operatives in applying generally accepted accounting principles that meet their unique characteristics and incorporate the 'co-operative difference' into their reports.

Samantha Lacey works for the Commonwealth Development Corporation in London. She previously worked at the Co-operative College as a researcher into co-operatives and international development particularly in East and Southern Africa. She has worked in Kenya on Fair Trade and co-operative development for smallholder farmers and written on the wider relationships between co-operatives and Fair Trade. Prior to this, she worked for the Co-operative Asset Management and managed engagement projects with investee companies on specific issues including palm oil and biofuels.

Marzia Maccaferri is a Research Fellow at the Faculty of Humanities, University of Modena and Reggio Emilia. She completed her PhD in Comparative Political History at the University of Bologna, and she was Visiting Researcher at the LSE and Goldsmiths, University of London. Her main research interests are on the interconnections between intellectual and political history. Her recent work was 'Spostare avanti la soglia dei diritti. Contrattazione, conflittualità e cittadinanza nell'esperienza sindacale di Claudio Sabattini', in *Operai e sindacato a Bologna* (Roma: Ediesse, 2010).

Ian MacPherson, Professor Emeritus of History, is a former Department Chair, Dean of Humanities, and Director of the British Columbia Institute for Co-operative Studies at the University of Victoria. His writings have focused primarily on the Canadian and international co-operative movements and on Co-operative Studies as a distinct field of enquiry. An elected co-operative official for forty years, he chaired the process and wrote the documents whereby the International Co-operative Alliance developed its Identity Statement for the Twenty-First Century at its Manchester Congress, 1995.

John Maddocks is Technical Manager: Third Sector and Sustainability, at the Chartered Institute of Public Finance and Accountancy (CIPFA), and is an accountant with over twenty-five years' experience of working with member-based organisations. Prior to joining CIPFA

John was Director of Research at the Centre of Excellence in Accounting and Reporting for Co-operatives (CEARC), Saint Mary's University, Nova Scotia. He is still involved with the centre's research activities including development of a draft statement of recommended practice on co-operative accounting and reporting. John is also a member of the Cardiff Institute for Co-operative Studies.

Ed Mayo is Secretary General of Co-operatives UK, the membership network for co-operative enterprise, and a Board Member of Co-operatives Europe. He is a long-term co-operator and has a track record of innovation around economic justice, including as one of the team that helped to start the Fairtrade Mark, as Chair of the Jubilee 2000 campaign and as Director of the New Economics Foundation. His writing includes *Consumer Kids*, on the commercialisation of childhood, co-written with Agnes Nairn and published by Constable in 2009. Ed has been awarded an honorary doctorate from the London Metropolitan University for his work to build an ethical economy.

Dr Fernando Molina is 'Ramon y Cajal' Fellow at the Department of Contemporary History, University of the Basque Country (Spain). He has written a number of books and articles on Mondragón co-operation and the Basque social economy. His English publications on this topic include an article (with Antonio Miguez) in *Social History* (Vol. 33/3, 2008), and a chapter in *Basque Cooperativism* (Center for Basque Studies, Reno, Nevada, 2011). He has also written (in Spanish) a historical biography of the founder of Mondragón, Jose María Arizmendiarrieta (2005), and histories of the co-operative Fagor Electrodomésticos (2006), and Lantegi Batuak, a Basque Foundation for disabled workers (2008). Another recent publication is a historical survey of the Basque Centre for Co-operative Promotion, the Consejo Superior de Cooperativas de Euskadi (2009).

Dr Jan Myers is a Senior Lecturer and researcher at Cardiff School of Management, UWIC and the Cardiff Institute of Co-operative Studies (CICS). She has considerable experience of working in and with non-profit and member-based organisations and is part of the Social Economy and Sustainability Research Network (Atlantic Canada) researching policy impacts on social economy organisations. Her work with CICS colleagues includes a recent review of Welsh credit unions on behalf of the Welsh Assembly Government and an evaluation project with the Plunkett Foundation and Farmers Retail and Markets Association.

Alan Robb was appointed an Adjunct Professor at Saint Mary's University, Halifax, Nova Scotia, in March 2006. He has taught at the University of Canterbury, New Zealand where he served two terms as

Head of the Department of Accountancy, Finance & Information Systems. He was responsible for introducing a postgraduate paper on co-operatives and mutual organisations. His academic specialisations include financial accounting, fraud and company failure, business ethics, co-operatives and mutual businesses.

Dr Vishwas Satgar is a Senior Lecturer in the International Relations Department at the University of Witwatersrand, Johannesburg, South Africa. He is the former Executive Director of the Co-operative and Policy Alternative Center (COPAC) and is currently on the Board. He has published widely on co-operatives, South Africa, and Africa's international relations. He is finishing a book with Michelle Williams entitled *Humanizing History: Cooperatives and the Solidarity Economy Alternative.*

Linda Shaw is Vice-Principal at the Co-operative College in Manchester. Currently responsible for research and international work, she has also worked on educational programmes for UK co-operative members drawing on many years of experience in adult and continuing education. Her current focus is on co-operative education in the UK and internationally, especially in Africa. Linda has also written and researched on gender and ethical trade issues.

David Stewart is a Senior Lecturer in history at the University of Central Lancashire (UCLAN) and joint UCLAN–People's History Museum Research Fellow. His research interests traverse modern political history, labour history and Scottish history. His publications include *The Path to Devolution and Change: A Political History of Scotland under Margaret Thatcher* (London: I. B. Tauris, 2009) and *The British Labour Movement and Imperialism* (Newcastle: Cambridge Scholars, 2010).

Dr L. K. Vaswani is Director of KIIT School of Rural Management, KIIT University, Bhubaneswar and Orissa, India. Prior to joining KSRM he was Acting Director of the Institute of Rural Management (IRMA), Anand, National Bank for Agriculture and Rural Development (NABARD) Professor and CEO, Indian Coffee Marketing Cooperative Ltd. (COMARK). His research and writings have primarily focused on management issues confronting Indian co-operatives. Apart from co-operatives his research interests include improving viability of smallholder agriculture, and market linkages for farm and non-farm produce from rural areas.

Keith Vernon is Principal Lecturer in History at the University of Central Lancashire, teaching modern British history. He has researched and written on the history of education and the history of science in Britain in the nineteenth and twentieth centuries. His book,

Universities and the State in England, 1850–1939, was published by Routledgefalmer in 2004.

John K. Walton is an IKERBASQUE Research Professor in the Department of Contemporary History, University of the Basque Country, Bilbao. A historian of tourism, sport and popular culture, he has worked intermittently on the British co-operative movement and on Basque social history for nearly twenty years. He edits the *Journal of Tourism History* (Routledge), and his most recent book (with Keith Hanley) is *Constructing Cultural Tourism: John Ruskin and the Tourist Gaze* (Bristol: Channel View, 2010).

Tom Webb is Adjunct Professor at Saint Mary's University, Halifax, Nova Scotia and the Program Manager of the Master of Management – Co-operatives and Credit Unions programme in the Sobey School of Business. He is a former adviser to the Prime Minister of Canada, and other federal ministers. He has held management and board positions in co-operative businesses including Manager of the Corporate Services Division of Co-op Atlantic. He has also worked extensively as a consultant on co-operative business and has been a speaker at co-operative meetings in Canada, the USA, the UK, Australia and New Zealand. His writing has appeared in journals, the popular press and in several books. The focus of his work has been on the adaptation of management issues and skills for co-operative business including people development, marketing, economics and financial issues. His most recent publication is *Co-operative Capital: What it is and Why Our World Needs It*, published in the proceedings of the EURICSE conference on Financial Co-operative Approaches to Local Development Through Sustainable Innovation, Trento, Italy.

Anthony Webster is Reader and Head of History at Liverpool John Moores University. A historian of business and the economics of British imperialism, he is currently working with John Wilson and Rachael Vorberg-Rugh on a major new business history of the Co-operative Group of the UK. His most recent book was *The Twilight of the East India Company: The Evolution of Anglo-Asian Commerce and Politics 1790–1860* (Woodbridge: Boydell, 2009).

Dr Michelle Williams is a Senior Lecturer in the Department of Sociology at the University of Witwatersrand, Johannesburg, South Africa. She is the author of *The Roots of Participatory Democracy: Democratic Communists in South Africa and Kerala, India* (Palgrave, 2008). She is also completing a book with Vishwas Satgar entitled *Humanizing History: the Solidarity Economy Alternative*. She is the Chairperson of the Global Labour University-Wits programme.

John F. Wilson is Professor of Strategy and Director of Programmes at the University of Liverpool Management School. He has written extensively about British and international business and management history, more recently concentrating on a study of the CWS/Co-operative Group for its 150th anniversary.

Tom Woodin is a Senior Lecturer in education at the Institute of Education, University of London. For many years he has researched co-operative and community organisations and previously worked for the Co-operative College. Publications include *Community and Mutual Ownership – A Historical Review* for the Joseph Rowntree Foundation and a number of articles on working-class writing and community publishing. He is currently writing two books on community publishing and on the school leaving age in historical perspective, a project funded by the Economic and Social Research Council (ESRC). Other research interests include the life and work of the educationist Brian Simon. He is co-editor of the *History of Education Researcher*.

1

The hidden alternative?

Anthony Webster, Linda Shaw, David Stewart
John K. Walton & Alyson Brown

The proclamation by the UN of 2012 as the International Year of Co-operatives represents a milestone in the history of the international co-operative movement. It marks an important recognition within the international community of the role of co-operatives in promoting the 'fullest possible participation in the economic and social development of all people', including women and peoples of all ages, creeds, ethnicities and disabilities.[1]

It reflects the growth and renewal of co-operatives globally during the early part of the twenty-first century. Whether we focus on the rapid growth of financial co-operatives[2] or the increase in the numbers of co-operatives across Africa,[3] the evidence of a co-operative revival is becoming impossible to ignore. The International Labour Organization (ILO), the lead UN agency on co-operatives, developed the only international government instrument on co-operatives in its Recommendation on the Promotion of Co-operatives (2002).[4] Furthermore, co-operatives have proved to be more resilient in the wake of the global financial crisis of 2008–09 than many mainstream commercial organisations.[5] In 2010, for example, the European Commission recognised co-operatives as a mainstream development actor alongside non-governmental organisations (NGOs) and trade unions.[6] Crucially the Recommendation includes a definition of co-operatives based on the movement's own core values and principles – an unusual and perhaps unique occurrence.[7] A systematic re-focusing on core values has also been critical to the process of co-operative renewal as many of the articles in this collection demonstrate.

This international acclaim for co-operation was mirrored by some startling developments in UN member states. Perhaps most notably in Britain, following its victory in the May 2010 election, David Cameron's Conservative–Liberal Democrat coalition government identified co-operatives and other forms of mutual enterprise as integral to its strategy for reducing public expenditure and public sector employment through the development of non-state structures to deliver essential public services.[8] This idea was mooted in the Conservative election manifesto and in a special policy document published in March 2010, which coined the phrase 'Big Society'. This has become the cornerstone of coalition policy presentation, despite criticism that it lacks definition.[9] At the time of writing, in light of the absence of any clearly articulated strategy or resources to establish the new co-operatives which are supposed to 'take up the slack' left by massive public expenditure cuts, it is hard not to conclude that the 'Big Society' is little more than cosmetic political 'spin' to placate deepening anxieties caused by the deepest cuts in public services in living memory. Nonetheless, even this dubious nod in the direction of co-operation shows that co-operatives are beginning to become part of the mainstream political economy. As such they are experiencing an unexpected surge of political and intellectual approval and celebration, even as doubts intensify about the coalition government's seriousness about the 'Big Society'.[10] Nevertheless, it is clear that, in some circles and some senses, at least, co-operatives are in fashion.

It was not always so. As recently as the late twentieth century, the global prospects for co-operation were gloomy indeed. By 1990, co-operatives were in decline in many parts of the developed world – especially in Europe. Nowhere was this more apparent than among the great consumer co-operative movements of Western Europe, most of which were in full retreat, losing market share to formidable investor-owned corporate retailing chains of supermarkets and department stores. By 1990, the main consumer co-operative organisations of Austria, Germany, France and Belgium were either dead or dying, while in Britain the future of co-operation looked perilous indeed.[11] In Britain , the social democratic model for managing the economy was abandoned in favour of a neo-liberal, 'free' market one. Advocates of the new orthodoxy tended to idealise the investor-led model of business organisation over alternatives such as co-operatives, which were associated with left-wing ideas and the previous social democratic approach to economic development. Co-operative associations also conflicted with the neo-conservative model of individualised 'classless' consumerism and the New Right's desire to disempower organised labour. This negativity towards co-operatives was exacerbated by the failure of the Soviet socialist model, completed by the regime's collapse in 1991. This was widely represented as not only a victory for the Western liberal 'democratic' political model, but also of the Western investor-led corporate capitalist system, as exemplified by the USA, much of Western Europe and Japan.[12] Co-operation tended to be seen by the neo-conservative orthodoxy which emerged from the Cold War as an adjunct of socialism and therefore almost equally discredited. The emergence of state-controlled 'co-operatives' in the Soviet bloc during the Cold War period, though strongly criticised by Western elements within the international co-operative movement itself, served to reinforce this perception of co-operation as a questionable quasi-socialist experiment, as did the left-leaning political credentials of some Western movements. Triumphalist advocates of Western corporate capitalism consequently believed that co-operatives would, in due course, be consigned with the rest of the left's economic ideas to the dustbin of history.[13] Even among those economic thinkers resistant to such ideological stereotyping, there was, and still is, a tendency to see co-operation as a 'stop-gap' response to the rare cases where markets are temporarily unable to respond to the needs of groups in society. Such failures are, it is argued, short-lived, as are the co-operatives which address such failures, before more efficient investor-led firms soon emerge to meet the group's needs. As Robert Grott, a particularly strong supporter of this view, puts it:

> In summary, the consumer co-op structure is a useful one which can offer many things to individuals and a community. However, it seems that, for the structure to be appropriate, certain environmental conditions must be present. These include a real need for a product or service and the presence of an active desire for social/economic change. History has repeatedly shown that when those conditions change, the movement that they engendered begins to diminish.[14]

A wave of demutualisations across the developed and developing world, together with a rejection of co-operatives in the former Soviet bloc countries, largely because of the association of the model with Communist oppression, seemed to point the way to the probable extinction of co-operative models of economic organisation within a generation. In short, co-operation was being measured for its shroud.

This introduction will return to the reasons for the intriguing upturn in co-operative fortunes, but first the theme, aims and provenance of this book should be explained. In July 2009 the Co-operative College in Manchester and a consortium of universities in the north-west of England, aware of evidence of co-operative revivals in the UK and elsewhere, held a major conference of academics and co-operative practitioners to consider the question: 'Can values make a difference? Moving from the Rochdale Pioneers to the Twenty-first century'. The aim was to share the varied ways in which the values of co-operation have been interpreted and translated into action at different times and

in different places and contexts; how the basic philosophy which
underpins the movement has been adapted to meet a diversity of
circumstances and to overcome a wide range of obstacles and
problems. Over a hundred delegates from 32 countries attended the
two-day event, at which case studies were presented and discussed,
highlighting the interpretation and application of co-operative values
and principles in a wide variety of contexts. The remit of the conference was wide. Papers were invited and presented on a broad spectrum
of themes, encompassing social, cultural and political aspects of
co-operative practice as well as business and economic activity.
Themes included education, politics, environmental sustainability,
ethical trade and development, finance and international law, governance and economic performance, and relationships between co-operatives and the state, as well as the history of co-operatives in different
national contexts. There were also discussion sessions on the development of co-operation in particular countries. So thought-provoking
were the contributions, and stimulating and fruitful the debates, that
the conference organisers decided to publish this edited volume of
expanded versions of some of the papers, with the addition of two
significant contributions which have been offered subsequently. It is a
book which seeks to present the many different ways in which co-
operative values and principles have been developed, re-interpreted
and adapted to meet the diverse challenges faced by women and men
seeking to put them into practice.

In the light of the decision to make 2012 the UN International Year
of Co-operatives, and the recent growth and renewal of co-operatives
globally, the title *The Hidden Alternative* might be regarded as unnec-
essarily pessimistic about popular appreciation of the importance of
the movement. It is true that the early twenty-first century has seen
something of a revival of historical interest in co-operatives as
important actors in the development of consumerism and voluntarist
social traditions, especially in Britain. Birchall, Gurney, Purvis,
Ekberg, Friberg and others have all made important contributions in
these fields. But this flowering of academic writing on co-operatives
has been largely confined to historians working in specialist fields of
social and economic history, and so far has made limited wider impact
in other disciplines. In particular, it has yet to substantially change the
curriculum or challenge the hegemony of the investor-led business
model in economics and business studies.[15] A brief glance at most
university undergraduate and postgraduate programmes in business,
history and the social sciences reveals a startling lack of awareness of
and curiosity about co-operation and co-operatives, even within the

academic community. Nor are co-operatives any more visible on school syllabuses or on the shelves of the big bookselling chains. In Britain, the movement is almost absent from GCSE syllabuses. Where it does appear, on the AQA and EDEXCEL syllabuses, it is as an after-thought in options covering social problems, popular politics and radical movements between 1815 and 1851. AQA offers a sample question on 'What was the Co-operative movement, and why did it succeed?' But this is for a module whose time-frame ends in 1851.[16] Courses on later periods of British history, when the movement was at its most dynamic and influential between the late nineteenth century and the Second World War, ignore it completely. Much the same applies to textbooks and popular surveys, where Richard Tames and A.N. Wilson are unusual in giving even a page of coverage to the movement in its late Victorian pomp, while Eric Evans's widely used survey is briskly dismissive.[17] In similar publications on the twentieth century the co-operative movement is almost invisible: to gain a purchase on its importance it is necessary to be able to access more specialised texts, and historians with a strong research focus on co-operation are a tiny minority who command little attention outside particular circles in labour and social history. Perhaps even more significant is the creeping collective amnesia about co-operatives among economists. Kalmi has tracked the slow but inexorable fading and disappearance of co-operative models from economics textbooks since the Second World War.[18] The incorporation of citation indices and measures of research 'impact' into academic management systems have also tended to marginalise co-operatives, especially in economics, where the dominant journals have imposed a neo-classical monocul-ture which consigns work on co-operatives to niche areas which carry little professional weight.[19] Little wonder that many, if not most, academics with expertise in disciplines for which co-operation has much to offer, possess little awareness of and less expertise in what has been, and still should be, a major field of human thought and practical endeavour.

In the UK, even with the deployment of Bob Dylan's 'Blowin' in the Wind' to front a major 2009 television campaign to trumpet the successes of the Co-operative Group, what little popular awareness there is of co-operation tends to oscillate between rose-tinted memories of a family 'divi' number, and a general assumption that the 'Co-op' is a rather outdated shopping chain, on the brink of extinction. Media blindness towards the movement does not help. A recent BBC reality series which claimed to bring to life the retail history of a notional British High Street over several generations from the Victorian period onwards, simply ignored the existence of the local co-operative stores, in a display of complacent historical ignorance which should have had Lord Reith spinning in his grave.[20] The historic Somerset town of Shepton Mallet was used as a guinea pig for the BBC's experiment, and the series was associated with a full package of educational activities for use by teachers, schools and the general public – all of which testify to the serious historical intent which underpinned the project.[21] For the record, in 1882 Shepton Mallet had its own co-operative society, with 380 members, and sold produce to the value of £6,832 during that year – making it by value sold the second most successful co-operative society in Somerset for that year.[22] Formed originally in 1861, by 1944 the society boasted over 1,100 members, sales in excess of £27,000 for a 34-week period and 26 employees.[23] Astonishingly it was simply ignored by the producers of the programme, regardless of the fact that they had set for themselves serious educational objectives. Internationally, notwithstanding the UN's 2012 initiative, the spectacular failure of flagship co-operative businesses in Germany, France, Austria and Belgium in the later twentieth century had contributed to a widespread perception that this was a business form which had had its day. From such perspectives, the editors remain convinced that the co-operative alternative remains, to a large extent, hidden.

Of course, the theme of the book begs the question: what *are* co-operative values and principles? Given the diverse international origins of the movement, and the different types of co-operatives which have been formed in different contexts, the answer is not as straightforward as one might expect. A good starting point perhaps is the definition of co-operative values and principles offered by the International Co-operative Alliance (ICA), the organisation which represents co-operatives and co-operators on the global stage. Following its major conference in Manchester in 1995, the ICA published a 'Co-operative Identity Statement' which set out values and principles which guide most if not all co-operatives.[24] In the introduction to this, the ICA statement defines a co-operative as: 'an autonomous association of persons united voluntarily to meet their common economic, social, and cultural needs and aspirations through a jointly owned and democratically controlled enterprise'. It goes on to identify seven main principles which define co-operative organisation and practice: voluntary membership open to all; independence from state control, or by other bodies; autonomous decision-making by democratic structures which allow for democratic control of the co-operative by its members; participation based on membership in the economic benefits of the co-operative, rather than the size of share-ownership in the co-operative; and a commitment to work collaboratively towards common goals with other co-operatives, generally define the political and governance principles which underpin how co-operatives should be organised. In addition, co-operatives work more generically towards the common good, through education both within and beyond the co-operative movement, and through the promotion of the general well-being of the societies within which co-operatives exist and operate. This recognises and affirms that although co-operatives are economic organisations – businesses, in many cases, in the commonly understood meaning of that term – they embrace and promote defined moral obligations based upon equity, participation and an overt commitment to the wider welfare of society.

The 1995 statement by its nature was the product of compromise between the highly diverse traditions and forms of organisation which make up the global co-operative movement. As MacPherson's chapter shows, it was the product of a long debate within the International Co-operative Alliance about the common values of a varied global co-operative movement, and how these values interacted with notions of community and individuality. It is worth identifying a few of the component traditions of the international movement, and their intellectual and ideological origins, in order to get a sense not only of the roots of some of these core values, but also of the underlying tensions between the different strands in the movement. Perhaps the most celebrated of these is the 'Rochdale model', which emerged from the consumer co-operatives movement in the UK during the nineteenth century. This provided probably the first attempt at a definition of co-operation, in the form of the 'Rochdale principles' based on open membership, democratic control, limited and fixed return on capital invested, education for the membership and distribution of surplus *pro rata* upon members' purchases.[25] But during the nineteenth century a separate co-operative tradition emerged in Germany, influenced by the ideas of Friedrich Raiffeissen, the leader of the rural credit union movement which emerged in the 1860s. At the same time in Germany, but separately, Hermann Schulze-Delitzsch established a similar credit union movement, but one aimed at helping handicraft workers and artisans. Both of these movements stressed the need for self-help and a substantial commitment to the co-operative. Schulze-Delitzsch emphasised the importance of self-reliance and rugged independence in the movement, together with vigorous resistance to external interference, a stance which precluded state involvement in the promotion of co-operatives. Charles Gide, the French economist, stressed the flexibility of co-operative models, and their usefulness in meeting a wide range of human needs. Gide argued that so useful were the models that they transcended political philosophies of the right and left, arguing that:

> conservatives or revolutionists, bourgeois or workmen, collectivists or anarchists, Protestants or Catholics preach co-operation in turn, although with very different objects.[26]

Gide rejects the idealism of such early advocates of co-operation as Robert Owen or some of the early Christian Socialists, who saw in co-operation the basis of a new society organised on collective, co-operative and socialist lines. For Gide, co-operation is fundamentally a practical economic philosophy which is adaptable to many socio-economic circumstances, including co-existence with private, free market capitalism. Indeed Gide argues that political neutrality is the ideological position of 'true co-operation'; as it allows for such adaptation to a wide range of contexts, and a flourishing and varied range of versions of the co-operative model.[27]

The varied contexts in which co-operatives have arisen, and the differing ideological strands in co-operation, tend to confirm Gide's notion that the development of co-operation is based at least as much on instrumental practicability, as it is on adherence to a coherent co-operative ideology. Take, for example, Battilani's chapter in this volume, which identifies late nineteenth-century Italian co-operatives emerging from separate liberal, religious and socialist traditions, albeit sharing some common notion of an 'ideal of community happiness'. She argues that co-operation flourished in a wide range of regional, social and cultural contexts in Italy because it offered practical advantages such as strengthened bonds of trust and stronger commonalities between different socio-cultural groups which reduced conflict and built consensus around collective political and economic decisions. In some instances, the specific intellectual traditions from which particular co-operative movements sprang provided practical assistance for survival and growth in what seemed highly inauspicious contexts. For example, Molina and Walton's study of Mondragón, in the Spanish Basque Country, illustrates how the religious origins and connections of that co-operative initiative helped to secure it against Franco's rabidly centralising, anti-leftist, and conservatively Roman Catholic regime.

This plurality of co-operative origins, ideological positions and practical adaptations to specific socio-economic and political contexts also prompts careful reflection on the notion of co-operation as an alternative to the business and social models offered by mainstream capitalism. It is fair to say that the aspirations of co-operators to displace or offer something different to mainstream capitalist business and social relations vary between national movements, types of co-operation (producer, consumer and other forms of co-operative enterprise) and even within the same bodies of co-operators over time. At one extreme the British co-operative movement in its earliest phase of development during the early and mid nineteenth century unequiv-ocally aspired to the gradual replacement of privately owned capitalist business by co-operatives in all fields of economic activity. At the other, the supporters of Mondragón during the Franco period could not afford to antagonise the regime by offering such lofty ambitions even had they wished to do so. In many contexts, co-operatives (especially producer ones) are seen as alternative modes of business organisation *within* a predominantly capitalist economy and society. Indeed it is fair to say that this has become the prevailing sense of the way in which co-operation offers an alternative to capitalism; as an alternative option within capitalism rather than an alternative to the system itself. Thus the British Co-operative Group, notwithstanding the recent revival of its fortunes, sees itself continuing and developing in the twenty-first century as an important player in a market of predomi-nantly capitalist competitors. But what appears at first sight to be a scaling down of co-operative ambition, a surrender to the notion that capitalism will forever be the dominant form of economic organisa-tion, on closer scrutiny arguably offers an effective and nuanced role for co-operation in shaping the world of the twenty-first century. This is arguably more realistic than a project to completely replace global capitalism, for which there appears as yet to be little widespread support. However, co-operatives, with their suspicion of speculative activity and their emphasis upon commercial accountability and wealth distribution, may yet shape capitalist organisations, prompting the adoption by investor-led firms of practices more normally found in co-operatives. Certainly the recent global economic crisis has exposed many of the inherent problems of investor-led corporate capitalism, including its propensity to rampant and perilous financial speculation, its lack of accountability to shareholders and governments, its dubious morality and its tendency to exacerbate social and economic inequali-ties. It is perhaps significant that many supporters of the investor-led model who supported the demutualisation drives of the 1980s and 1990s, are beginning to think again, especially in the wake of spectac-ular failures in the banking sector such as in the case of the demutu-alised building societies in Britain (Northern Rock, HBOS). Such reassessments of co-operative and other alternatives may also be encouraged by the tendency for co-operatives to develop new, 'hybrid' modes of organisation, which blend co-operative forms of ownership and control with elements of 'command and control' structures more commonly found in investor-led firms. Such strategies have emerged where co-operatives have moved into new areas of commercial activity, in which collaboration with other co-operatives, or even with non-co-operative organisations, has been necessary. The work of Chaddad and Cook, on the development of 'New Generation Co-operatives' in US agriculture since the 1980s, has been important in highlighting the adaptability of co-operatives when faced with a fast-evolving capitalist environment.[28] How such developments will shape the trajectory of co-operation in the twenty-first century is of course uncertain, and speculation is perhaps unwise; the history of global co-operation has been, after all, quite volatile.

The global co-operative movement experienced dramatic shifts in fortune during the twentieth century. The demise of major co-operative organisations in Western Europe by the 1980s, and the subsequent rejection of the model in much of the former Eastern Communist bloc, seemed to presage its demise. Yet within twenty years co-operatives were flourishing again, not just in the developing world, but also in advanced economies such as the UK. Several of the chapters in this book highlight the severity of some of these challenges, and also some of the reasons for the durability of co-operation, occasionally against the odds. Cook and Clegg's study of the 'Gung Ho' co-operatives in China demonstrates both the adaptability of that specific model of co-operation to the extremes of war and socio-political collapse, and its attraction for people living through such dire times. Myers, Maddocks and Beecher focus upon the durability of building societies and financial co-operatives during the recent global economic crisis, stressing the importance of such co-operative principles as proximity and accessibility to clients, strong community links and an emphasis upon stability and security in preference to profit maximisation, as explanations for their success in weathering the fluctuations caused by global financial meltdown. This resilience has been evident in the face of international institutions and assumptions which have rarely been congenial to co-operative needs. As Maddocks, Hicks, Robb and Webb show in their chapter on co-operatives and global accounting, even in the face of global accounting standards set by an International Accounting Standards Board steeped in the ideology of the 'free' market and the investor-led business organisation, co-operatives adapt and survive.

A theme common to many stories of co-operative demise and

survival is the question of co-operative values – how they are interpreted in the light of prevailing conditions, and the extent to which
they sustain real and continuing purchase on the moral and commercial judgements of key decision-makers within co-operatives. Wilson's
chapter on the infamous attempt in 1997 by Andrew Regan's Lanica
organisation to take over the Co-operative Wholesale Society shows
that the revival of belief in core values amongst a new generation of
leaders was crucial in defeating the attack, and setting the scene for a
comprehensive reform and renaissance of the co-operative movement
in the UK. Crucially this meant reinterpreting co-operative values for
the demands of a post-industrial consumer society, shifting the
emphasis away from direct democracy and localist co-operative independence to notions of ethical trading, and the application of the
market power of the consumer for socially and morally desirable ends.
Conversely, many of the demutualisations which occurred across the
world from the 1980s were made possible by a 'hollowing-out' of the
values of those organisations, as belief in core co-operative ideas was
abandoned by their leaders. Here of course lies one of the great
dilemmas faced by co-operatives the world over, confronted by
powerful multinational corporations and a fast-changing market environment. How far should co-operative principles be compromised in
the battle to survive and flourish? To what extent should co-operatives
mimic their capitalist rivals in order to defend and enhance their
positions? How far should they recruit key personnel from beyond the
culture of the movement? As alluded to earlier, much recent work on
the commercial strategies of co-operatives emphasises the proliferation
of organisational variations and innovations to meet the challenges of
a fast-evolving global market. Many of these organisational variants
have involved the adoption of practices and structures more commonly
found outside the original core of the movement, as 'hybrid' co-
operative models emerged, such as the 'New Generation Co-operatives' in US agriculture.[29] More recently, the decision by the
Co-operative Group in the UK to transfer its travel business to a joint
venture with Thomas Cook might be viewed as the creation of a hybrid
model, and has not been without controversy, as it is seen by some as
a compromise too far for the principles of the organisation.[30]

The manifestation of co-operative values in fields other than
commerce is also an important theme of this book. In the British
movement a mission to educate was enshrined in the original
'Rochdale principles', and other national movements followed similar
paths. Woodin's chapter provides a useful overview of the evolution of
co-operative education in the UK, with a particular focus on the Co-

operative College, and its role in both the development of wider understanding of co-operative principles and in furnishing the movement
with staff equipped technically to run its wide spectrum of businesses.
The latter theme is taken up by Vernon, whose chapter on the training
of co-operative managers and personnel brings home just how far
ahead of the private sector the British co-operative movement was in
this field during the inter-war period. Shaw's chapter takes the debate
about co-operative education onto the global stage, with an overview
of the varying strategies adopted by co-operative educators across the
world, particularly in Africa.

Co-operation is, by its nature, an all-encompassing approach not
only to business, but to the full spectrum of human endeavour and
experience. Its philosophy has implications for global economic
relations, the moral codes which underpin social interaction, how
power is distributed and exercised and even how the human environment is shaped and planned. All of these themes are addressed in the
chapters of this volume. Co-operative politics are brought into focus
by Stewart's chapter on the British Co-operative Party, the only co-
operative political party in the world. Focusing on the Co-operative
Party's role in the formation of the Social Democratic Party during the
early 1980s, Stewart explores the complex and contentious relationships between the British co-operative movement, the trade unions and
the Labour Party. In perhaps the most unusual examination of the
social impact of co-operation, Maccaferri shows how in post-war Italy,
a unique 'co-operative of intellectuals' (*Caire*) influenced urban
planning in several cities.

Yet another important theme in the book is the role of co-operation
and co-operatives in international economic development. The rise
towards the end of the twentieth century of the Fair Trade movement
is the focus of chapters by Friberg and Lacey. Friberg explores the
problems involved in negotiating equitable international relationships
between producers and consumers through co-operative organisations,
by linking historical developments and debates in Sweden and Britain
with modern problems of Fair Trade. Lacey provides a contemporary
assessment of co-operative involvement in the Fair Trade movement,
and offers some important options for future strategies in this field.
These general explorations of Fair Trade are supplemented by chapters
that provide insights into specific national contexts. Vaswani's chapter
addresses the challenge for co-operative revival in India in the context
of continuing government interference. Greater autonomy is needed to
enable co-operatives to align their governance structures more closely
to member need and democratic control. In South Africa, as Satgar and

Willams' chapter demonstrates, co-operatives were placed at the centre of the post-apartheid regime's strategy for reconstruction, albeit with mixed success.

It would be impossible in a volume of this length to explore the multiplicity of fields in which co-operatives have shaped the modern world. Only a partial overview can be presented of the huge global impact that this movement, in its many manifestations, has enjoyed. The editors are aware that co-operation has received insufficient attention from both academia and the media, and the main purpose of this volume is to begin to remedy this impoverishing oversight. A key aim of the book is to stimulate further research and both academic and public debate about co-operative solutions to the pressing global problems of the twenty-first century. Since the end of the Cold War, and the steady retreat of state-led alternatives to free market capitalism, the investor-led, corporate model has been in the ascendant, and at times has seemed unchallengeable. The global financial catastrophe of 2008 confirmed the suspicions of many that this neo-conservative orthodoxy was inherently flawed, and that a new vision was needed of how the global economy might operate. At the heart of all of the contributions in this collection is the belief that co-operation offers a real and much-needed alternative for the organisation of human economic and social affairs. This alternative should no longer remain hidden.

Notes

1 Resolution adopted by the General Assembly of the UN, on the report of the Third Committee, 64th session, Agenda item 61 (b).
2 C. Cuevas and K. Fischer, *Cooperative Financial Institutions: Issues in Governance, Regulation and Supervision* (World Bank Working Paper No. 82, 2006).
3 I. Pollet, *Co-operatives in Africa: The Age of Reconstruction – Synthesis of a Survey in Nine African Countries* (CoopAfrica Working Paper No. 9, Dar Es Salaam: ILO, 2009).
4 Full text available at www.ilo.org/ilolex/cgi-lex/convde.pl?R193.
5 J. Birchall and L. Ketilson, *The Resilience of the Co-operative Business Model in Times of Crisis* (Geneva: ILO, 2009).
6 See ec.europa.eu/europeaid/who/partners/civil-society/structured-dialogue _en.htm.
7 International Labour Organization, *Report of the Committee on Co-operatives 2002*, available at www.ilo.org/public/english/standards/relm/ilc /ilc90/pdf/pr-23.pdf (accessed 22 December 2010).
8 *Building the Big Society* (Cabinet Office, May 2010).
9 *Big Society, Not Big Government: Building a Big Society* (The Conservative Party, March 2010).

10 An important source for these new ideas is Philip Blond, founder of the
    Conservative-leaning think tank *ResPublica*. See P. Blond, *Red Tory: How
    Left and Right Have Broken Britain and How We Can Fix it* (London:
    Faber, 2010) for some of Blond's thoughts on the use of mutuals in the
    Post Office and in lieu of other state agencies. For a powerful critique of
    the book, and its arguments, see Jonathan Raban's review, 'Cameron's
    Crank' in the *London Review of Books* April 2010 at www.lrb.co.uk
    /v32/n08/jonathan-raban/camerons-crank.

11 For work on some of these failures, see R. Schewidy, 'The Decline and Fall
    of Konsum Austria', *Review of International Co-operation* 89:2 (1996),
    62–68; J. Brazda, 'The Consumer Co-operatives in Germany' and F.
    Muller, 'Consumer Co-operatives in Great Britain' in J. Brazda and R.
    Schewidy (eds), *Consumer Co-operatives in a Changing World Volume 1*
    (Geneva: ICA, 1989) pp. 139–228 and pp. 45–128.

12 F. Fukuyama, *The End of History and the Last Man* (New York: Avon
    Books Inc, 1992).

13 A useful summary of the criticisms of co-operation offered during the 1980s
    and 1990s can be found in E. Furlough and C. Strikwerda, 'Economics,
    Consumer Culture and Gender: An Introduction to the Politics of Consumer
    Co-operation', in E. Furlough and C. Strikwerda, *Consumers Against
    Capitalism: Consumer Co-operation in Europe, North America and Japan,
    1840–1990* (Lanham: Rowman and Littlefield, 1999), pp. 29–30.

14 Robert Grott, 'Why Co-ops Die', *Cooperative Grocer No. 9*, Feb-March
    1987, available at www.cooperativegrocer.coop/articles/2004–01–09
    /why-co-ops-die.

15 J. Birchall, *Co-op: The People's Business* (Manchester: Manchester
    University Press, 1994); P. Gurney, *Co-operative Culture and the Politics
    of Consumption in England, 1870–1930* (Manchester: Manchester
    University Press, 1996); M. Purvis, 'Stocking the Store: Co-operative
    Retailers in North East England and Systems of Wholesale Supply circa
    1860–1877', *Business History* 40:4 (1998), 55–78; K. Friberg, *The
    Workings of Co-operation: A Comparative Study of Consumer Co-
    operative Organisation in Britian and Sweden, 1860 to 1970* (Växjö
    University, 2005); E. Ekberg, *Consumer Co-operatives and the
    Transformation of Modern Food Retailing: A Comparative Study of the
    Norwegian and British Consumer Co-operatives, 1950–2002* (University
    of Oslo, 2008); L. Black and N. Robertson, *Consumerism and the Co-
    operative Movement in Modern British History: Taking Stock*
    (Manchester: Manchester University Press, 2009); N. Robertson, *The Co-
    operative Movement and Communities in Britain, 1914–1960, Minding
    Their Own Business* (Farnham: Ashgate, 2010).

16 See *http://store.aqa.org.uk/qual/renogese/pdf/AQA-4040–W-TRB-SWU2BB.PDF* and
    www.edexcel.com/migrationdocuments/Current%20GCSE/139079_uk
    _quals_gcse_history_1335_17802.PDF (both accessed 5 December 2010).

17 R. Tames, *Economy and Society in Nineteenth-Century Britain* (London:

Taylor and Francis, 2006), pp. 107–108; A.N. Wilson, *The Victorians* (London: Arrow, 2003), pp. 564–565; E.J. Evans, *The Forging of the Modern State*, 3rd edn (Harlow: Longman, 2001), pp. 209, 357.

18 P. Kalmi, 'The Disappearance of Co-operatives from Economics Textbooks', *Cambridge Journal of Economics* 31:4 (2007), 625–647.

19 F.S. Lee, 'The Research Assessment Exercise, the State and the Dominance of Mainstream Economics in British Universities', *Cambridge Journal of Economics* 31 (2007), 309–325. Lee makes clear that this is an international phenomenon.

20 'Turn Back Time: The High Street', screened on BBC, Autumn 2010.

21 Hands on History website at www.bbc.co.uk/history/handsonhistory /download_turnbacktime.shtml.

22 *Co-operative Congress Report* for 1883, p. 101.

23 Statistics for 34 weeks' trading; *Co-operative Congress Report* (1945), pp. 554–555.

24 The essence of this statement is laid out at the ICA's website. See: www.ica.coop/coop/principles.html.

25 See A. Bonner, *British Co-operation: The History, Principles and Organisation of the British Co-operative Movement* (Manchester: Co-operative Union, 1961) pp. 48–49.

26 C. Gide, *Consumer's Co-operatives Societies* (London: T. Fishser Unwin, 1921), p. 3.

27 Ibid., pp. 232–236.

28 F.R. Chaddad and M.L. Cook, 'Understanding New Cooperative Models: An Ownership-Control Right Typology', *Review of Agricultural Economics* 26:3 (2004), 348–360.

29 Ibid.

30 See www.telegraph.co.uk/finance/newsbysector/retailandconsumer/leisure /8051945/Thomas-Cook-ties-up-with-Co-op-to-create-travel-giant-jobs-to-go.html.

2

Co-operativism meets City ethics: the 1997 Lanica take-over bid for CWS[1]

John F. Wilson

One of the most traumatic events in recent British co-operative history was the attempted take-over in 1997 of the Co-operative Wholesale Society (CWS) by Lanica Trust Ltd. Coming at a time when CWS was struggling with substantial challenges, this represented a full-scale assault on its independence, just when some of the equally old mutual building societies were being converted into public limited companies by a wave of 'carpetbaggers'. Described by the *Sunday Times* as 'one of the boldest takeover attempts the City has ever seen',[2] the two factions could not have been more different: the predator was a thirty-one-year-old entrepreneur, Andrew Regan, backed by 'blue-chip' City names such as Hambros, Schroder and Nomura; while in contrast the 134–year-old CWS was showing weaknesses that critics claimed were fatal. Much to the surprise of these critics, however, under the imaginative leadership of its chief executive, Graham Melmoth, CWS not only saw off Regan and his backers, but emerged from the experience in much better shape to tackle its challenges. While others have written about this episode,[3] and contemporary newspapers offered copious commentary, providing useful insights into the people and issues involved, it is fascinating to assess the longer-term implications of an event that prompted decisive changes across CWS and associated organisations.

This chapter will start by providing the essential context to the take-over bid, focusing initially on the commercial, organisational and managerial challenges facing CWS, at a time when market share was falling and an 'image' problem was limiting the organisation's ability to respond effectively to these pressures. The second part of the chapter will evaluate the institutions and personalities involved in the take-over bid, examining in greater detail the attitude of Britain's leading financial institutions, prevailing corporate ethics, and the

1990s 'demutualisation' movement that sparked a frenzy of speculative activity in certain quarters. It will then be possible in the third section to assess how Graham Melmoth and his team laid the foundations for the achievement of a radical reorganisation capable of underpinning a commercial revival of considerable proportions, overcoming the residual organisational resistance to this mission in a series of moves that resulted in much greater integration across what came to be known as the 'co-operative family'. Using extensive primary archival resources, including board minutes, newspaper coverage and interviews with key personnel, this chapter will offer original insights into a crucial era in the history of CWS. It will be especially interesting to analyse what we might call the 'Regan Paradox', because while he set out to acquire and asset-strip CWS, thereby undermining the British co-operative movement, he actually achieved exactly the opposite effect, sparking a revival that accelerated over the following fifteen years.

CWS in the 1990s

Although few in senior management were willing to accept it, by the 1990s CWS and regional co-operative societies were struggling to cope with the fierce competition they had been encountering for several decades from much more aggressive and ambitious retailing operations.[4] Of course, as we shall see later, other parts of CWS – banking, insurance, travel agency and funerals – were performing extremely well, generating improved returns that kept CWS afloat. Nevertheless, as food represented 70% of total turnover, not to mention the driving force behind the creation and evolution of many co-operative societies, with market share falling dramatically from its formerly dominant position of the 1960s, commentators were quick to condemn performance. Seth and Randall were especially scathing, summarising the problems as 'no capital, no strategy, no store profile, in essence no co-operation'.[5] They especially highlighted how CWS was not working with Co-operative Retail Services (CRS), stating boldly that this lack of co-operation denoted an 'undeniable death wish'.[6] As Figure 2.1 indicates, during the 1990s CWS turnover (at current prices) stagnated, while in real terms (deflated at 2005 price levels) there was a significant decline. Although Figure 2.2 reveals that apart from 1993 CWS generated a surplus, most regarded these results as wholly inadequate for an organisation with such a substantial turnover (recorded in Figure 2.1). Moreover, without the contributions of the Co-operative Bank, CWS would have made heavy losses, further substantiating the critics' claims that the business model was fatally flawed. In addition, it must be noted that debts of over £300 million had been accumulated by CWS, indicating the scale of the internal challenges facing senior management.

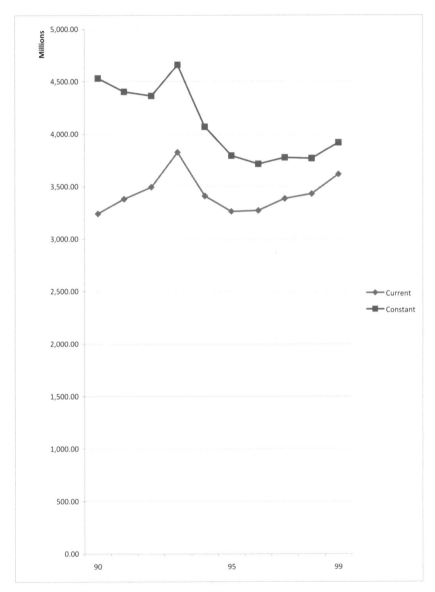

Figure 2.1 CWS turnover in constant (2005 prices) and current prices (£million), 1990–99

At the root of CWS's poor financial performance was a calamitous decline in its share of the retail grocery trade. While it is difficult to break the data down into individual components of the co-operative trading operations, in 1965 co-operative trading societies had the largest single share of this market (35%), but by 2000 this had fallen to just 4.4%, while the large-scale multiple traders such as Tesco, Sainsbury, Asda and Safeway increased their combined share to 65%, compared to 30% in 1965.[7] A range of factors can be identified to explain this trend, not least among which was the image of the typical Co-op retail outlet. In spite of several attempts to upgrade the Co-op brand since the 1960s, to an increasing number of consumers the Co-op image was associated with drab facilities that were resonant of an earlier age, especially compared to the shiny retail 'palaces' of the independent multiple retailers. It was to the latter that consumers preferred to drive, rather than visit the cramped and poorly organised Co-op convenience stores, reflecting a decisive switch in retail consumption behaviour. There was also conclusive evidence of a failure to match the multiples on productivity, with sales per square foot in Co-op outlets at just one half of those achieved in the multiple retailers.[8] Even though a greater emphasis on 'ethical retailing' was being developed, with Fair Trade products featuring prominently in advertising campaigns,[9] the abiding impression of that era was a struggling, demoralised business empire that lacked the collective drive to engineer a recovery.

Having highlighted the depressing scenario that was unfolding during the 1990s, it is also vital to stress the fundamental issue that handicapped CWS, namely, the dysfunctional nature of a business organisation that was built around local autonomy. Formed in 1863 to supply co-operative retail societies through an integrated distribution system, CWS was originally a wholesaler owned by its member societies. At no stage, however, were these members obliged to buy all of their goods from CWS; indeed, local retail societies continued to use a range of suppliers with whom they had built up effective relationships.[10] Even though a predominantly working-class membership was enormously supportive of the annual dividend, and CWS had almost from the start extended its activities into manufacturing and international buying-points, from the mid-twentieth century local autonomy developed into a commercial weakness, especially compared to the rapidly expanding multiples that were sourced and organised centrally. This independent streak was not only manifested in relations between CWS and local societies, but also in territorial disputes and rivalries within regions, significantly limiting the prospects of merger and ratio-

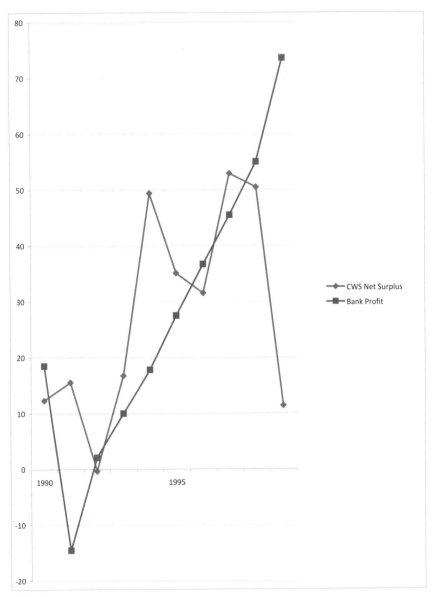

Figure 2.2 CWS net surplus and Co-operative Bank surplus (£million), 1990-99

nalisation. While built on the democratic principle that lay at the heart of what were generally known as the 'Rochdale Principles', the dysfunctional nature of the co-operative wholesale and retail operations increasingly came to be regarded as the major obstacle to integration and cohesive decision-making. Moreover, a series of scandals in various regional trading societies during the early 1990s placed an enormous question mark over corporate governance across the movement, a situation only resolved in 1994 by the introduction of a fresh Code of Practice that reasserted members' rights and the essentially democratic nature of co-operativism.

There were naturally many attempts to change this mindset, while as a result of mergers the number of retail co-operative societies fell from over 1,400 in 1903 to just fifty-five by 1994. Although as we shall see later in 1993 a Co-operative Retail Trading Group (CRTG) was established, to co-ordinate buying across a significant proportion of the co-operative movement, by the mid-1990s decision-making in the co-operative retail network was still dispersed across a series of local and central bodies, none of which would appear to have been willing to work collectively in coping with the competitive challenges they faced. Symptomatic of these problems was the lack of collaboration between CWS and CRS. The latter had been established in 1934 as CWS Retail Services, largely as a refuge for failing co-operative societies, changing its name to CRS in 1957. In the decades which followed its creation, however, CRS acquired an identity and existence which was increasingly separate from, and independent of, CWS. Indeed, by 1990 CRS had built its own headquarters in Rochdale, away from CWS's Manchester complex, while the Registrar of Friendly Societies had insisted on the creation of separate boards to run the two organisations. These developments inevitably limited the prospects of collaboration, with successive merger talks having stalled at least four times, indicating how the potential economies of scale and scope available in such an arrangement were largely wasted.

Having stressed the organisational and commercial weaknesses inherent in the British co-operative movement, it is vital to remember that to a business predator the various branches represented an enormous opportunity. In the first place, not only was CWS the largest farmer in the UK (with 80,000 acres), but it also possessed a huge property portfolio worth £104 million. As we noted earlier, the travel agency (256 shops) and funeral care businesses (359 outlets) were also extremely well placed in the domestic market, generating sound returns that justified the continued investment in these sectors.[11] Above all, the bank and insurance businesses were highly profitable operations that could well be described as the organisation's most lucrative assets. Although the insurance business had been hived off into the Co-operative Insurance Service, organised as a separate business serving 3.5 million customers, the Co-operative Bank (with assets worth £3.9 billion) was fully integrated into CWS, providing the bulk of the organisation's profits throughout the 1990s (see Figure 2.2) and extending the ethical marketing drive that was attracting an increasing number of customers.

Regan and the City

It is consequently no surprise that at a time when British business in general was indulging in intensive merger and acquisition activity, and prominent mutual societies were being converted into public limited companies, CWS would become the unwilling victim of a predatorial take-over bid. The Conservative governments of 1979–97 had been intent on deregulating the British financial system, introducing a range of liberalising measures that undoubtedly fuelled the rapid expansion of what is euphemistically called 'the City'.[12] These measures included deregulating international financial transactions (1979–81), eradicating restrictive practices and computerising London Stock Exchange activities ('Big Bang' in 1986), while the privatisation of many public sector utilities added considerably to the City's prosperity. Another innovation was the 1986 Building Society Act, which permitted these financial institutions to demutualise, as long as 75% of the membership voted in favour.[13] While a clause was inserted into this Act which prescribed a qualifying period of two years before members could benefit from the process, in 1989 the courts overruled this safeguard, resulting in a group of what have passed into the vocabulary as 'carpetbaggers' who activated in favour of demutualisation. As a result, starting with the Abbey National Building Society in 1989, by 2000 ten major building societies had demutualised, accounting for two-thirds of this sector's assets.[14]

While demutualisation was clearly a major theme of the 1990s, this must be seen within the context of an aggressively buoyant City that was booming over this period. Crucially, there were intense waves of 'merger mania' that soaked up significant quantities of capital: over the period 1985–89 the value of British merger expenditure averaged £19.1 billion (at 1987 prices), compared to the previous peak of £9.5 billion during the early 1970s, while by the mid-1990s this had risen to £30.1 billion per annum.[15] The intensity of this activity also enhanced the growing impression that British business was driven more by the struggle for corporate control, rather than improving performance and competitiveness; that retaining shareholder loyalty was more important to senior management than innovation and productivity, placing the prime emphasis on money-making, as opposed to organisational culture and loyalty to employees. Several high-profile scandals also revealed some of the murkier aspects of City activities. While these incidents represented only a small fraction of the booming range of City transactions, when the public read about the illegal operations of people such as Robert Maxwell, Ernest Saunders and James Guerin,[16] this significantly tarnished the City's reputation at a time when successive governments proved unwilling to introduce stronger corporate governance regulations.

It was in this milieu that Andrew Regan operated, using impeccable contacts with blue-chip City institutions and entrepreneurs linked to household and food products to build a flourishing business empire.[17] As a schoolboy in Macclesfield, he had allegedly been puzzled by the sight of a chauffeur-driven Jaguar dropping off a friend every morning, especially as the car was owned by a CWS manager who enjoyed yachting. This anecdote was later used as part of his publicity drive when bidding for CWS, implying that its executives were somehow no longer sticking to the socialist principles that underpinned their movement.[18] Regan's first venture into business had been in 1985, when at the age of just eighteen he had established Cadismark Household Products. Using his close contacts with David Thompson, the chief executive of the leading food processor Hillsdown Holdings, he merged Cadismark into one of its former subsidiaries, Hobson, and proceeded to recruit a management team capable of building a flourishing business.[19] It was as chief executive of Hobson that in 1994 Regan came to prominence, when he borrowed £30 million from Lloyds Bank and floated £80 million worth of shares, underwritten by the Swiss Banking Corporation, to purchase for £111 million CWS's food manufacturing operations, including the subsidiary trading as F.E. Barber.[20] Part of this deal was a three-year agreement to continue to supply CWS customers, worth £220 million per year, providing Hobson with a sound business model. Even though he had assured CWS executives that existing employees would not be affected by the acquisition,[21] Regan immediately closed two factories (making 3,600 people redundant) and sold off a further two operations, reflecting a desire to improve productivity across his new business. Crucially, in 1995 he paid £2.85 million for a two-year extension to the original deal to supply CWS, significantly enhancing the value of his streamlined operation.

One should stress that this extension had been negotiated with Allan Green, Deputy Head of Food at CWS, but without the involvement of CWS board members, who were only informed of the deal in 1997, by which time it was apparent that this executive had been supplying Regan with considerable quantities of confidential data about CWS. It was also later discovered that Hobson had paid £2.4 million into a private Swiss bank account to Ronald Zimet of Trellis International, a company registered in British Virgin Islands, who it was claimed had acted as an intermediary on the extension agreement. We shall return to these issues later, because Zimet's mysterious role was used as ammunition against Regan when he launched an assault on CWS. The failure to provide an adequate explanation for this payment had also persuaded Swiss Banking Corporation to withdraw its services to Regan's business, resulting in the latter starting an ill-fated relationship with Hambros Bank.[22] Crucially, though, Hobson was such a highly attractive proposition that in December 1995 Hillsdown Holdings paid £121 million for the business, reportedly making Andrew Regan £3 million on his original investment, after paying off his financial supporters.[23]

These deals consequently established Regan's City reputation as that of somebody capable of raising large sums of money and generating appreciable returns within a short period of time, characteristics that were regarded as highly attractive to a financial community driven by short-term imperatives. As one contemporary noted: 'Regan is one of an elite band of young City dealmakers whose recent adventures have set the world of high finance alight ... They all play the business world like a roulette wheel and so far their numbers have come up.'[24] In order to exploit this reputation further, in October 1996 Regan made a successful £4 million hostile bid to acquire New Guernsey Securities as his vehicle to launch further acquisitions, renaming it Lanica Trust Ltd and spinning off a subsidiary called Galileo to handle acquisitions. Counting amongst his supporters such prestigious City names as Hambros Bank, Schroders, Jupiter Tyndall and Killik & Co, Regan also recruited a formidable management team, including David Lyons, the Rea Brothers financier who had advised CWS on the sale of its food manufacturing activities. The City clearly responded favourably to these developments, because Lanica's share price rose from 58p to 1950p within four months, in anticipation of more lucrative deals.[25] Not wanting to disappoint his backers and admirers, using the Galileo subsidiary Regan put together a bold £500 million bid for CWS's non-food businesses, including its opticians, funeral parlours, garages and travel agencies. As we shall see later, it is now known that a large quantity of CWS data had been illegally acquired to inform Galileo's bid, leading to several court cases that trundled on for a further six years. Nevertheless, after the *Sunday Times* produced a sensational revelation on 9 February 1997 that Regan was about to launch this bid,[26] the business world was aghast at the scale and audacity of his intentions. Even though the London Stock Exchange was immediately obliged to suspend Lanica's shares, in order to suppress any further speculation, Regan stood astride the City as the epitome of its ethos and attitudes, with support from highly prestigious institutions that were anticipating another financial bonanza.

Melmoth and CWS

Prior to the *Sunday Times* exposé on 9 February about Regan's intentions, CWS chief executive, Graham Melmoth, had already been tipped off by his City contacts about Regan's intentions, providing him with invaluable time to initiate a robust riposte. It was not in this person's character to accept such an assault without offering a response that would shake the City establishment to its roots. Melmoth had joined CWS as co-operative secretary in 1975, after having been trained in several London firms as a company secretary.[27] As he had always sympathised with left-of-centre political views, espousing an ideological commitment to co-operative principles, the Manchester job reflected his own social democratic tendencies. Initially, though, he was sorely disappointed by the culture of an organisation that had become a 'monastery', with intense internal rivalries undermining the co-operative principle and a board totally dominated by successive chief executives who rarely consulted others on strategy. Indeed, Melmoth almost left CWS within a year of securing the post, but persevered in the hope that opportunities might arise to change this self-defeating culture. Over the following two decades he worked effectively to impose greater co-ordination across CWS and local retail societies, successfully placing the co-operative secretary's office at the heart of an organisation that had traditionally allowed the retail executives to control strategy and structure. In the early 1990s, he also played a leading role in the drive of the International Co-operative Alliance (ICA) to reaffirm and modernise the '1844 Rochdale Principles'. This culminated in the publication of *Co-operative Values in a Changing World*, first published in 1992 and implemented after the 1995 ICA conference that was chaired by Graham Melmoth. It was primarily as a result of this influential role that in November 1996 Melmoth became CWS chief executive, defeating his principal rival, John Owen, the head of retail.[28]

While Melmoth's rise to prominence over that period deserves more detailed analysis, it is clear that apart from his strong commitment to co-operative values and principles, he had demonstrated considerable organisational talent in pulling together a business empire which, as noted above, had traditionally been internally divided and dysfunctional. Crucially, it was the secretary's department that negotiated the assimilation of local co-operative societies into CWS, providing Melmoth and his team with the opportunity to effect greater co-ordination over the disparate movement. Crucially, he had assembled a team – Bill Shannon (corporate affairs), Roger Jones (co-operative secretary), Allan Green (controller of retailing), Alan Prescott (production and property), Martin Weir (operations), David Chambers (supply chain), John Owen (regional retailing), and David Jackson (financial controller) – that shared both his strong belief in co-operative principles and the desire to build an organisation capable of converting these principles into commercial success. Of course two of the team – Green and Chambers – were also involved in the corruption scandal surrounding the 1997 take-over bid, but this did not undermine the commitment of Melmoth's team to pursue the chief executive's vision.

One of Melmoth's first actions as chief executive, reflecting his belief that a strong commitment to the philosophical principles and values of co-operation should come from the top, was to publish a booklet entitled *Managing Change through People*.[29] This outlined his commitment to co-operative values and explained that the organisation should 'work for the long-term success of the co-operative sector'. Although the chief executive acknowledged that CWS had been undergoing 'a metamorphosis' in the past decade, he felt that to build on these foundations and cope with the increasingly competitive marketplace it was necessary to place an especial emphasis on four key dimensions, *Performance – People – Communication – Planning*. It was a radical manifesto that left nobody in any doubt about how and why Melmoth and his team would drive CWS forward, not least because it was followed by the introduction of an extensive training programme, initially for the top 200 managers and later for over 1,000, conducted by the Co-operative College, inculcating the message into the very fabric of the organisation. Externally, Melmoth offered the prospect of much closer collaboration between CWS and CRS,[30] as relations between these two organisations had deteriorated to such an extent that they were almost 'warring factions'.

Melmoth had clearly given himself an ambitious agenda in attempting to overcome toxic historical features of a movement that was at the same time struggling to compete with the major multiple retailers, forming the essential context in which to study Regan's bid; even though Melmoth had been tipped off about the bid, it still came as a massive shock. Business editors of broadsheet newspapers, notably the *Sunday Times* and *Sunday Telegraph*, devoted many column inches to highlighting CWS weaknesses, implicitly supporting Regan's bid. Melmoth was consequently obliged to counter this adverse publicity by commissioning CWS's merchant bank, S.G. Warburg, and solicitors, Linklater Paine, to build a defence against Regan. While this formidable team boosted CWS's chances of repelling Regan, not least because of the creative work of Warburg's Brian Keelan, it is nevertheless vital to stress that the predator was also the victim of his own tactics, in that it rapidly became apparent that Lanica executives were being fed information of a highly confidential nature to support the bid. For example, one Sunday newspaper published CWS's financial results before they had been officially released,[31] while Green later admitted that he had provided board minutes, property valuations and profit forecasts.[32] The feeling that confidential information was being leaked to Regan sparked a forensic internal investigation of executive activities, including expenses claims and telephone records, revealing that Green and Chambers were most likely to be responsible. A firm of corporate investigators, Control Risks Group, was also hired, securing photographic evidence of Regan meeting these CWS executives in the car park of a Buckinghamshire hotel,[33] during which boxes of CWS documents were being ferried from one car to another. Apart from showing a film of this incident to a high court judge, CWS was able to use this ammunition in a highly subtle way, by privately alerting Regan's backers to the highly dubious nature of his business practices. Melmoth likened the strategy to isolating a battleship by attacking its supporting flotilla, thereby rendering it vulnerable to counter-attacks and negating its offensive potential.[34]

Before explaining how all of this was played out in a blaze of publicity, it is vital to explain the three key stages through which the bid passed. As we have already seen, the first stage was Galileo's plan to bid £500 million for CWS's non-food businesses. Once Lanica's shares had been suspended on 10 February 1997, however, it is clear that over the following six weeks Regan and his advisers started to hatch an even more ambitious bid, estimated at approximately £1.2 billion, for the whole of CWS, with Nomura Securities (the world's largest financial trader) providing the bulk of the capital. Using confidential information supplied by Green and Chambers, Regan had calculated that if the organisation was broken up into palatable portions on which his business contacts could gorge, an estimated £1.8–2.0 billion could be generated, making him a substantial fortune on a single deal.[35] To expedite matters, Allied Irish Bank was lined up to buy the Co-operative Bank, while Sainsbury was going to be offered the retail network, achieving the kind of financial synergy to which

City denizens aspired. The rumour machine was also cranked up to inform opinion-makers of the plans, further enhancing Regan's reputation as one of the City's emerging stars.

Before explaining how all of this unravelled for Regan and his City supporters, it is important to stress that in spite of the advice emanating from David Lyons and the illicit material coming from Green and Chambers, the predators were guilty of pursuing a misdirected strategy. This error was based on a fundamental misinterpretation of CWS's membership structure, because Regan thought that if he offered £1,000 to each of its 500,000 active members, this would facilitate the transfer of ownership into Galileo. It was a strategy that had handsomely rewarded the 'carpetbaggers' converting mutual building societies into public limited companies. Indeed, the Alliance & Leicester Building Society was going through exactly this process in April 1997. As various commentators explained, however, this strategy was flawed, in that CWS's active members merely elected either members of corporate bodies (retail societies) or regional committees, which in turn elected CWS board members.[36] CWS executives also noted that while Galileo was receiving some support from members, the total membership was in excess of two million (even if some of this figure resulted from the failure of CWS to delete member names at the time of their death), and the predator would need 75% to vote in favour before ownership could be transferred, as well as approval of the Registrar of Friendly Societies. Furthermore, as the board represented 70% of the membership, its rejection of Regan's request to engage in talks would make it impossible for Galileo to succeed with its strategy. Regan had made a fatal error, albeit one that was never tested in practice because of his other failings.

Of course, while the second stage was unfolding Melmoth and his team were by no means inactive, because it was in this period that an internal audit team headed by Paul Smedley was filtering through expenses claims and telephone logs, as well as following Green and Chambers to their secret rendezvous with Regan and advisers.[37] As a result of certain early 1990s corporate governance scandals in regional co-operative societies, Smedley's team had developed a series of techniques that uncovered a host of illegal activities. By the time Regan was ready to launch his bid for the whole of CWS, Melmoth was consequently well armed to forestall the process with a series of lethal strikes that destroyed the predatorial 'flotilla' with devastating speed and ruthlessness. The first of these strikes was fired before Regan had officially placed his bid, when on 17 April not only were Green and Chambers suspended from their CWS positions, on the grounds of what a CWS press release claimed was a 'suspected recent serious breach of trust',[38] but Melmoth also wrote to Lord Hambro (head of Hambros Bank) enquiring about the £2.4 million payment to Ronald Zimert in 1995. This certainly destabilised Regan's team, especially as it was followed the day after by CWS requesting an injunction blocking the use of the confidential information that Green and Chambers had leaked to the predators and requiring its return to CWS. The full extent of the accusations against Green, Chambers, Regan, Lyons and Hambros Bank was revealed at a second hearing on 25 April, when Mr Justice Lightman concluded that the bid had patently been based on 'iniquitous conduct'.[39] This view was reached after CWS's QC, Christopher Clarke, explained how almost all of the documents passed by Green and Chambers to Regan had been given to Hambros Bank, which in turn had provided copies to seventeen organisations that wished to benefit from the bid (including HSBC, Lloyds Bank, Goldman Sachs, JP Morgan and Price Waterhouse). Lightman was consequently in no doubt that the actions of Regan, Lyons, Green and Chambers had been 'clearly dishonest', extending the ban on using all information to Hambros Bank and Travers Smith Braithwaite. In a forlorn attempt to rescue the situation, on 24 April Lyons wrote to all twenty-eight CWS directors, including a copy of the 72–page Galileo bid, encouraging them to convene a special general meeting of all members to consider a sale. The CWS chairman, Lennox Fyffe, refused to entertain the document, insisting that all directors return it 'unopened and unread', effectively terminating the process on the day that Galileo returned seven boxes of CWS material.[40] Melmoth also continued to write to both Hambros Bank executives and Regan, requesting explanations about the veracity of documentation used in compiling the bid and hinting at criminal prosecutions, further embarrassing the City establishment at a time when its less scrupulous activities were coming under closer scrutiny.[41]

Apart from killing the Regan bid, Mr Justice Lightman's ruling was clearly a serious indictment of what Melmoth described as 'illegal activity that strikes at the heart of the City'. Even the key executive at CWS's investment bank, Brian Keelan of Warburg's, was willing to concede that: 'It has not been a good week for the City. It's been ugly.'[42] This sparked the third and longest stage in the bid process, because while Regan had been soundly defeated, CWS announced that it would not only pursue its predators for appropriate compensation, but also prosecute all parties involved in the bid. Information relating to the mysterious payment to Ronald Zimet of Trellis International had already been passed to the Serious Fraud Office (SFO), given that CWS was convinced it was a bribe paid to Green and Chambers to extend the Hobson supply contract in 1995, both men having denied that any intermediary had been involved in the negotiations.[43] Green and Chambers were formally dismissed from CWS on 27 April, while entreaties were made to the relevant authorities to investigate possible insider trading in Lanica's shares, given their rapid increase in value prior to February 1997 from just £2 to almost £20. Although Sir Chips Keswick, chairman of Hambros Bank, was obliged to issue a public apology to CWS, as well as sharing with Travers Smith Braithwaite a compensation package of approximately £1 million to cover CWS legal and other costs,[44] in 1998 this institution was fined £270,000 (plus £80,000 costs) by the Securities and Futures Authority for using confidential information.[45] CWS also dropped its private case against Green, Chambers, Regan and Lyons when on 12 May they paid an estimated £750,000 to cover legal and other costs,[46] leaving all actions in the hands of the SFO.

It was September 1999 before the SFO charged Green and Chambers with corruption, and the following month it issued a warrant for Regan's arrest (as he was by then living in Monaco), having finally decided that the mysterious £2.45 million payment to Trellis International was a bribe to secure an extension of the Hobson–CWS supply agreement.[47] In the interim, the SFO investigated not only this payment and the actions of Regan and Lyons, but also County Produce, a bogus farming co-operative set up by Lanica as a means of convening a special CWS meeting to vote on the bid. Such was Regan's status by May 1997 that he had resigned from all of his other directorships,[48] while Galileo was placed in voluntary liquidation and the Stock Exchange refused to refloat Lanica's shares. At that point, Regan moved his family to Monaco, from where he ran an investment syndicate that by the end of 1999 had made him an estimated £50 million.[49] Finally, after a trial that lasted almost six months, in April 2002 Green and Chambers were convicted of each receiving a £1 million bribe, crimes for which they were given jail sentences of three-and-a-half years and a £50,000 fine. In addition they were forced to refund the bribe (including interest). To the amazement of many, the jury failed to reach a verdict on Regan, who had been accused of stealing £2.45 million from F.E. Barber plc for the purposes of bribing Green and Chambers. At a subsequent retrial in January 2003, the judge ordered yet another trial with a fresh jury, but in August 2003 this resulted in a 'not guilty' verdict, allowing him to return to his Monaco investment business.

Conclusions and implications

There was widespread recognition of the resounding nature of the victory achieved by Graham Melmoth and his team in April 1997, with prolific newspaper coverage announcing how the 'Knightsbridge whizz-kid'[50] had been humbled by the Manchester-based CWS.[51] Apart from defeating Regan, Melmoth was anxious to stress that: 'We have uncovered much evidence of activity that does strike at the heart of the City.' Speaking immediately after the decisive court hearing, he was also convinced that:

> We are not here to celebrate. It's the end of a chapter in the life of the society that is part of the fabric of British society. It's 135 years old, and it's been doing good for all that time and intends to carry on doing so.[52]

Two weeks earlier, Melmoth had described CWS as 'a third division player', when compared to 'first division' firms such as Tesco, Sainsbury and Asda, stressing the need to gain promotion as quickly as possible.[53] The 1997 CWS annual meeting also proved difficult for the senior management, because many corporate members used the opportunity to highlight how Regan's bid had emerged because of widely acknowledged weaknesses in both structure and strategy.[54] Melmoth responded by arguing that he wanted to forestall future bids by developing 'a successful co-operative business', with the emphasis placed on all three words.[55] Above all, CWS management wanted to avoid the implications of one headline, 'Funeral postponed',[56] because if Regan had achieved anything, it was revealing the inherent weaknesses in a rambling, unco-ordinated organisation that possessed some highly valued assets worth approximately £2 billion. Indeed, in April 1999 the US take-over specialist Babcock & Brown tabled a £2 billion offer for CWS. One must stress, though, that this bid faded as rapidly as it had emerged from the City rumour-mill once the Americans realised that they faced a defence based on strength, rather than perceived weaknesses.

This highlights what we can regard as the 'Regan Paradox', because while he assembled his bid on the premise that CWS was in decline, the decisive leadership demonstrated by Melmoth and his team both during the bid and over the following five years provided the foundations for a recovery in fortunes. Again, it is essential to stress that one can easily exaggerate the significance of the 1997 bid, given that through mergers and rationalisation CWS had been pursuing a more integrated structure since the 1980s. Indeed, many would stress essential importance of an active membership and the bulk of the managers at every level across the movement, in stark contrast to the situation in building societies which were succumbing to the 'carpet-baggers'.[57] Moreover, in 1997 Melmoth was merely implementing the core elements of a document that the ICA had published five years earlier, *Co-operative Values in a Changing World*. On the commercial front, the introduction of a loyalty card in 1997 and revival of the co-operative dividend in 2005, allied with the rapid adoption of the 'ethical trader' brand, had also been instrumental in fuelling sales growth.[58] Crucially, many executives in the Co-operative Group would also argue that essential changes to the commercial structure of CWS still needed to be made by the time Melmoth retired as chief executive in 2002. Nevertheless, Melmoth's status in April 1997 as the 'defender of co-operative values' provided him with the momentum to press forward with even more radical changes. He was also able to appoint his right-hand man during the Lanica bid, Alan Prescott, to the position of deputy chief executive in May 1997, strengthening the team as key agents of change[59] and prefacing significant organisational and strategic changes over the following five years.

To many, the key issue facing CWS was co-ordinating the disparate, sprawling business empire, and in particular merging with CRS to exploit the potentially enormous economies of scale and scope across the two organisations. As we noted earlier, co-operation between these two bodies had been minimal for decades; indeed, the relationship was characterised by open hostility, with merger talks having failed no fewer than four times. CRS was also in even deeper financial trouble than CWS, because while the latter's performance (see Figure 2.2) was underpinned by the Co-operative Bank, the former did not have recourse to such an asset, reporting losses throughout the late 1990s, in spite of significant investment in a marketing drive to push own-brand foods. In 1999, CRS was obliged to close fifty-two of its non-food stores that traded under the names *Living* and *Homeworld*, as well as announcing that its food business would be terminated and all future purchases would be made through the Co-operative Retail Trading Group (CRTG), a body formed in 1993 by CWS and sixteen retail co-operative societies to co-ordinate buying activities. Although CRS chief executive Andy Meehan refused to accept that this was the inevitable prelude to a merger with CWS,[60] many observers felt that once both parties realised the benefits of a CRTG with buying-power of £4.5 billion, then it was inevitable that they would combine.[61] With the co-operative movement's share of the food market having fallen to just 4.4% in 2000 and competition from the large multiple retailers intensifying by the year, this merger was also vital to the future of both bodies. The Report of the Co-operative Commission, published in January 2001, was extremely critical of commercial performance across the sector, highlighting the consistent failure to generate adequate returns on capital employed.[62] By that time, following CWS's strategic review in 1998, Melmoth had persuaded CRS executives to agree to a merger, finally securing accession in October 1999. Although the merger was not fully operational until 2001, along with major structural and strategic innovations across the Manchester-based organisation this represented a significant tipping-point for the co-operative movement's commercial activities, after several decades of strife and decline. Crucially, the CRS merger changed the nature of the organisation, specifically prompting the shift in the balance from corporate to individual membership, because of the influx of the much larger CRS membership base. It also allowed Melmoth and his team to move decisively towards creating the 'family of co-operative businesses' that lay at the root of his organisational aspirations.

Of course, as consistently argued throughout this chapter, it is difficult to see these events in isolation from an evolutionary process that reflected the way in which CWS had adapted to its environment over the course of its fascinating history. Nevertheless, the robust rejection of Regan's bid, Melmoth's decisive leadership both during the early months of 1997 and after, imaginative organisational and marketing drives, and the merger with CRS all combined to build the solid foundations on which the Co-operative Group (as it became in 2001) would enact a renaissance over the next decade. One might even go so far as to say that Regan had done CWS a great favour in both highlighting its commercial weaknesses and reviving the dynamism that had been so evident in its first decades, because Melmoth was able to use these as figurative 'sticks' to beat his board into agreeing with his aim to build a 'family of co-operative businesses'. Just to reinforce the message, this was used as the sub-title to the Co-operative Commission's 2001 report, leaving nobody in any doubt that change was both essential and achievable. The achievements since then indicate clearly that this message was widely accepted and effectively implemented, providing a conducive environment for a 'renaissance' that continues to underpin the Co-operative Group's performance.

Notes

1 Research for this chapter was derived from the author's work with Tony Webster and Rachael Vorberg-Rugh on a history of the Co-operative Group for its 150th anniversary. I acknowledge the generous support of

the Co-operative Group for this project, in particular Russell Gill and Mervyn Wilson, while Gillian Lonergan and her team have been invaluable in providing abundant primary sources. Professor Jim Quinn (Trinity College, Dublin) has also provided invaluable assistance, while the editors have offered constructive advice on the chapter.

2 *Sunday Times*, 27 April 1997.

3 J. Birchall, 'The Lanica Affair: An Attempted Takeover of a Consumer Co-operative Society', *Journal of Co-operative Studies* 31:2, 15–32, and S. Yeo, *A Chapter in the Making of a Successful Co-operative Business: The Co-operative Wholesale Society, 1973–2001* (Manchester: Zeebra Publishing, 2001).

4 For an authoritative survey of these trends, see Espen Ekberg, *Consumer Co-operatives and the Transformation of Modern Food Retailing. A Comparative Study of the Norwegian and British Consumer Co-operatives, 1950–2002* (University of Oslo Press, 2008), especially chapters 7–8. See also John K. Walton, 'The Post-war Decline of the British Retail Co-operative Movement: Nature, Causes and Consequences', in L. Black and N. Robertson (eds), *Consumerism and the Co-operative Movement in Modern British History* (Manchester: Manchester University Press, 2009).

5 A. Seth and G. Randall, *The Grocers. The Rise and Rise of the Supermarket Chains* (London: Kogan Page, 1999), p. 142.

6 Ibid., p. 141.

7 Data derived from reports on Nielsen's trade data produced in *Grocer*, 1960–2000, provided by Professor Jim Quinn to the author.

8 Seth and Randall, *The Grocers*, pp. 140–143.

9 J. Bowes (ed.), *The Fair Trade Revolution* (London: Pluto Press 2011, especially Ch. 11.

10 This issue is further developed in A. Webster, J. F. Wilson, K. Friberg and R. Vorberg-Rugh, 'The Politics of Commercial Dynamics: Co-operative Adaptations to the Age of Affluence in the UK and Sweden, 1950–2010', paper given at conference on 'A Special Kind of Business', Milan, October 2010.

11 Data taken from a report published in *Manchester Evening News (Business Section)*, 21 April 1999.

12 For more detail, see D. Kynaston, *City of London, Vol. 4: Club No More, 1945–2000* (London: Pimlico, 2002). See also John F. Wilson, *British Business History, 1720–1994* (Manchester: Manchester University Press, 1995), pp. 233–241.

13 These issues are also covered in Chapter 16 by Myers, Maddocks and Beecher.

14 See Ian Pollock, 'Not such a good idea after all?', available at http://news.bbc.co.uk/1/hi/business/7641925.stm.

15 This data has been taken from the Department of Trade and Industry database.

16 Guerin was the American businessman who defrauded Ferranti of

approximately £210 million by merging his firm into the august British electronics venture. See J. F. Wilson, *Ferranti. A History. Vol. 3 Management, Mergers and Fraud, 1987–1993* (forthcoming).

17 Regan's father, Roger Regan, had been chairman of Fine Art Wallcoverings up to 1993, at which point, and largely as a result of a shareholder revolt against incumbent management, he was appointed chairman of Spring Ram, the building materials group that had recently experienced severe difficulties. *Independent*, 12 July 1993.

18 *Sunday Times*, 27 April 1997.

19 *Sunday Telegraph*, 13 Feb 1994.

20 By 1994, CWS had just fourteen food manufacturing operations, compared to over 200 in 1945, having either closed or sold many ventures, especially in the 1960s and 1970s. These operations had an output of £415 million in 1993, employing 3,250 people.

21 CWS board minute 3, 30 March 1994.

22 *Independent*, 24 April 1997.

23 *Sunday Times*, 9 Feb 1997.

24 *Express on Sunday*, 16 Feb 1997.

25 Ibid.

26 *Sunday Times*, 9 Feb 1997.

27 This section is based on an interview with Sir Graham Melmoth.

28 Owen left CWS in 1997 to pursue a career in private sector retailing.

29 CWS board minutes, 6 Nov 1996.

30 *Independent*, 5 Nov 1996.

31 *Sunday Times*, 13 April 1997.

32 *Guardian*, 26 April 1997.

33 *Guardian*, 17 May 1997.

34 Interview with Sir Graham Melmoth.

35 *Sunday Telegraph*, 27 April 1997.

36 *The Times*, 19 April 1997; *Grocer*, 26 April 1997.

37 CWS paid £70,000 for Control Risks' services. *Financial Times*, 21 April 1997.

38 *Financial Times*, 18 April 1997.

39 *Guardian*, 26 April 1997.

40 *The Times*, 24 April 1997; *Daily Mail*, 24 April 1997.

41 *Daily Telegraph*, 24 April 1997.

42 *Guardian*, 26 April 1997.

43 *Daily Express*, 22 April 1997.

44 *Independent*, 29 April 1997.

45 Three executives (Nigel Pantling, Peter Large and Andrew Salmon) were also fined for their parts in the bid. *Scotsman*, 17 Sept 1999. In December 1997, Hambros Bank was bought for £300 million by Société Générale.

46 *Financial Times*, 13 May 1997.

47 Paul Thomas, the solicitor advising on the 1995 CWS–Hobson deal, was also charged on the same day. *Independent*, 22 Sept 1997.

48 These included the NAAFI and Select Catalogues. *Independent on Sunday*, 25 May 1997.
49 *Sunday Telegraph*, 21 Nov 1999.
50 *Scotsman*, 26 April 1997.
51 See further coverage in *Independent*, *Observer*, *Daily Telegraph* and *Sunday Telegraph*, all of which on 26–27 April 1997 devoted full-page articles to Regan's demise.
52 *Daily Telegraph*, 26 April 1997.
53 *Daily Express*, 9 April 1997.
54 *Daily Telegraph*, 19 May 1997.
55 Interview with Sir Graham Melmoth.
56 *Northwest Business Insider*, May 1997.
57 Interviews with Russell Gill and Mervyn Wilson.
58 These issues are further developed in Chapter 16 by Myers, Maddocks and Beecher.
59 *Financial Times*, 2 May 1997.
60 *Supermarketing*, 30 April 1999.
61 *Sunday Business*, 11 July 1999.
62 *The Co-operative Advantage. Creating a Successful Family of Co-operative Businesses*, report of the Co-operative commission, Jan 2001.

3

Values and vocation: educating the co-operative workforce, 1918–39

Keith Vernon

Introduction

Education has long been recognised as a central pillar of co-operative values and activity. Providing for the social and cultural development of its members was an essential feature that distinguished the movement from being simply a retail organisation. Historians of co-operation note the significance of education, highlighting the importance of self-instruction and mutual instruction and improvement within the working classes.[1] In the great tradition of the autodidact, the movement would help to raise the cultural tone of working people by providing resources for their own education. This emphasis chimes with the wider view of working-class self-education, which focuses primarily on liberal studies through such means as the Workers' Educational Association (WEA).[2] Another component of co-operative education was propaganda to enlighten people to the iniquities of the prevailing system of private profit-making and the benefits of co-operation. This reminds us that the co-operative movement was a commercial organisation, requiring skilled personnel. While giving it somewhat less attention, historians do indicate that, from the late nineteenth century, there was an increasing interest in the better training of the workforce.[3]

It is this final aspect that is the focus of this chapter. Although building on earlier foundations, following the First World War there was a major initiative to enhance the technical education of employees, which enjoyed a great deal of success. A hugely ambitious, and very impressive, educational framework was established and many more employees, especially junior ones, took advantage of the opportunities provided; a great progressive impetus to the movement from the extension of education was anticipated. Setting out syllabuses and writing textbooks, however, was more straightforward than providing the means of instruction or the motivation to study and, although much was achieved, disappointment remained that more was not. This chapter considers the emergence and development of this new scheme for technical education between the wars. It will consider the foundations laid earlier in the century, but focus on the advent, nature and achievements of the post-war initiative, up to a change in policy in the early 1930s. We should note that although termed 'technical', the scheme was aimed at the retail organisation and so the education was primarily in commercial subjects. The main sources used are printed documents produced by central bodies of the movement, especially the reports of the Central Educational Committee of the Co-operative Union to Congress and the principal mouthpiece for educational matters *The Co-operative Educator*.[4] Limits of space preclude more detailed analysis of the provision of technical education at a local level but, since the main concern here is with policy, the sources are appropriate to the purpose. The first section will consider where the impetus for the initiative came from; then the nature of the programme of studies that was put in place will be examined, before an analysis of the extension and achievements, as well as the problems and limitations, of the scheme. A key question will be whether there was anything distinctively co-operative about what was provided. If the main objective was to improve the efficiency of the workforce, was there room for anything other than strictly business considerations? I shall argue that this was a great co-operative venture, although not without some tensions and contradictions, and one that appears to have been pioneering.

A new initiative in technical education

Although education was regarded as laudable in principle, several authors suggest that, through much of the nineteenth century, local societies were less than assiduous in putting the principle into practice.[5] Within a few years of its formation, the Pioneers established the precedent of committing 2.5% of trading surpluses to support a library, which was the origin of an educational fund, but this meant that activity was dependent on the trading environment. Some societies maintained the tradition of providing for education, although almost any activity that was not retailing could be regarded as educational. This included comradely social and cultural events, as well as propaganda on the benefits of co-operation. Through the late nineteenth century, state-supported elementary education became more widely available to the working classes, while the WEA catered for those with higher aspirations. Consequently, the need for mutual instruction seemed less urgent and many societies left educational matters to the local authorities or the WEA. This creeping neglect of the educational ideal seems to have prompted a campaign within the movement to press for an extension of education in co-operation and formal classes under co-operative control. Basic elementary instruction perhaps could be left to the local authorities, but members ought to be taught some of the fundamental principles, practices and history of co-operation, and there was an imperative to expand educational opportunity more generally.

From the 1880s to the outbreak of war, an infrastructure was constructed to promote education.[6] The Co-operative Union created a Central Education Department with supervising committee; regional committees were established in the sections and larger societies began to set up educational associations to organise activity. The education department drew up syllabuses and lesson plans, launched correspondence courses and set examinations, and issued an annual programme of activities. Classes for junior co-operators were started in 1895 and, the following year, Congress supported calls for a major survey of educational provision. Although the sweeping changes urged by the resulting report were not accepted, educational activity expanded with more educational associations founded, funds allocated and classes run. It remained the case that co-operative educational endeavour encompassed a wide spectrum of activities, including a great deal of social and recreational activity and general propaganda, with formal classes occupying a relatively minor place. Of these, general education took pride of place.

In the programme issued for the year 1910–11, the objects of co-operative education were defined as:

> primarily, the formation of character and opinions by teaching the history, theory, and principles of the movement ... and, secondarily ... the training of men and women to take part in industrial and social reforms and civic life generally.[7]

Most space was devoted to the classes in co-operation, which included industrial history, citizenship and economics and were aimed at members and their children. There were indications, however, of a growing concern with technical training. Outlines were given for courses in co-operative bookkeeping, organised in three parts geared towards those taking up progressively more responsible posts in the movement. There was also a correspondence course for co-operative secretaries aimed at those running local societies. It was acknowledged, however, that more needed to be done for employees working in the stores. Classes had been organised for managers, which had proved successful, but seemed to have started at too high a level and many had struggled. For the most part, even managers only had an elementary school education, usually some years previously, and there was a good deal of basic revision to be done. It was decided, therefore, to revise the training scheme into four stages: 1) The Training of Apprentices and Junior Employees; 2) The Training of Salesmen and Countermen; 3) The General Manager's Certificate; 4) An 'Honours' Stage in Management.[8]

In 1914, the educational cause was boosted by the appointment of Fred Hall as Adviser of Studies to the movement, based at Holyoake House in Manchester.[9] Hall saw his chief role as developing an academic underpinning for the movement's educational endeavours and he immediately starting campaigning for a Co-operative College, to serve as a centre of expertise. In the difficult post-war period, it proved impossible to establish anything very substantial. Undaunted, Hall made a start with lectures and classes at Holyoake House and threw himself into the revision and re-organisation of the whole educational programme.[10] An opportunity to do so came with the resolution at the Dublin Congress of 1914 for a general survey of all the movement's activities. Three interim reports were received by the Lancaster Congress of 1916: on Trade, Education and Constitution. The following year, Hall reviewed the recommendations regarding education. These were wide-ranging, envisaging a considerable expansion and administrative re-organisation. Some of the key issues were to establish a national advisory body with an additional educational executive, which would receive larger subscriptions from societies to finance a general expansion of activities, and it was recommended that educational grants be calculated according to membership rather than a percentage of surpluses, which might yield larger and more consistent funds. However, there was disappointment about the still-limited work of a great many local societies, which focused too much effort on recreational events rather than systematic classes. Hall's priority remained the co-operative subjects, including industrial and social history, economics, citizenship and new courses in sociology and education. He acknowledged that the technical subjects had not yet been addressed, but thought it better 'to develop first the changes in non-technical subjects'.[11]

Although the specifically co-operative components of the programme came first, important foundations for the organisation of technical education for employees had been put in place; the four-stage structure for management training proved a long-lasting innovation. The First World War, however, reinforced the national importance of scientific and technical training as Britain's reliance on Germany for key products was exposed, as the combatants sought innovations to break the deadlock of trench warfare and the sheer scale of the war demanded new systems that put a premium on educational capacity.[12] A whole new impetus was given to promoting technical education and expertise on a broad front. From early in the war, the government planned initiatives in scientific and technical education and research. Deficiencies in science and modern languages were investigated. Private industry was mobilised to make good the deficiencies, and began to acknowledge that a better-educated workforce was a worthwhile investment. Reconstruction also demanded that the requirements and desires of the population at large were addressed, not merely to make better workers, but to fulfil social and educational aspirations. Adult education was reviewed and, from 1917, the Minister for Education, H.A.L. Fisher, began fashioning new legislation. Hindsight tends to dismiss the 1918 Education Act as lacking in ambition and ultimately a failure as it fell victim to Geddes' Axe,[13] but for contemporary supporters of education, it was an important measure, potentially offering a valuable extension of opportunity. For our purposes, the most far-reaching provision was for day continuation schools whereby 14–16-year-olds in work could receive further education during work time.[14] Moreover, the act allowed that schools and colleges outwith the Local Education Authorities might be recognised as appropriate venues for continuing education.

These portents of educational change were noted in *The Co-operative Educator* and Fisher's Bill heartily welcomed.[15] Although it was affirmed that full secondary education should be available for those suited to it, it was acknowledged that this was a path only a few working-class children were likely to take. For the vast majority, it was important that there was some provision to allow them to continue their education after full-time schooling finished at age 14. There was apprehension when the Bill was withdrawn the following year and supporters of education were admonished to involve themselves more strenuously in the matter.[16] Ultimately, the Act was passed, requiring employers of adolescents to make provision for their continuing education, and it behoved co-operative societies as professedly committed to education to react positively.[17] Moreover, it was clear that other progressive employers were already moving in this direction; the training offered at Cadbury's Bourneville works was praised as a model for co-operators.[18] The business case was clear:

Co-operative business as a moral system of business need not be an inefficient system of business, and co-operative societies should provide
adequate educational facilities for their employees so that the co-operative
movement may be as efficient as its competitors.[19]

Equally clearly, business efficiency was not the sole criterion. From
the late nineteenth century, some within the movement had held that
technical education was probably best provided by the local authorities, but public education was geared too much towards individual
'getting on' and the pursuit of competitive enterprise.[20] Co-operators
needed to train their employees for mutual betterment and, since the
1918 Act allowed for non-public bodies to provide continuation
schools, this was urged as the way to proceed.[21] In trenchant terms,
Hall maintained that '[t]hose who were engaged in co-operative
industry should be inspired by the spirit of service, and should know
that they were employed not to produce private profits but to provide
social advantages for the community'. Similarly, it was 'the duty of
co-operators to make suitable provision for their own young people.
Co-operative employees ought to be trained in a co-operative atmosphere, and should study the needs of the co-operative movement
beneath a co-operative roof.'[22]

In the years before the outbreak of war, there had been a good deal
of effort devoted to raising the profile of education within the
movement, and much had been achieved in developing an administrative structure at a central and sectional level, and in some of the larger
societies, while curricula had been re-organised, including for the
technical training of employees. Hall's appointment gave an additional
impetus, starting with the co-operative subjects for the wider membership. Wartime experience, however, and especially the development of
the 1918 Act, highlighted the importance of employee training and
provided a legislative fillip and framework.

The organisation of technical education

Although firm foundations had in fact been laid, technical training was
recognised as relatively neglected before the war. During the 1920s,
there was much more attention to revising this whole area of
provision. The emphasis was on extending the range and scope of the
curriculum, with more careful gradation and co-ordination of subjects
and stages, to try to ensure a smoother progression through the
programme. By the end of the decade, it was felt that a fairly complete
system had been put in place, taking the employee from an often inadequate preparation in the elementary schools and offering a dual series

of stages that would take them on the one hand through shop work to managerial status, and on the other through the office-based financial and legal training required of a society secretary and auditor.

Preparatory Course
Introductory Course

Shop Assistants	Office Assistants
Apprentices' Course	Clerks' Course
Salesmen's Course	Bookkeepers' Course
General Managers' Ordinary Course	Secretarial Course (Part I)
General Managers' Honours Course	Secretarial Course (Part II)[23]

It was nothing if not ambitious, providing a complete scheme of training 'from the day of their first entry as a junior employee ... to the day when they secure the highest diploma the movement can offer them as a certified manager, secretary or auditor'.[24] Here we review the nature and extent of the programme put in place by the end of the 1920s and the recommendations that were issued to guide how the instruction should be delivered at a local level.[25]

A great deal of emphasis was placed on the early preparation of junior employees. This began at a basic level with the Preparatory Course, intended as a revision of school work, but experience showed that it was often necessary to make good the deficiencies of inadequate elementary schooling. At the beginning of the decade, the course comprised English, arithmetic and bookkeeping. In 1929, the Introductory Course was inserted to ease the transition from the preparatory work to the Apprentices' and Clerks' courses. The new course consisted of further work in arithmetic, and the geography and commodities of commerce, plus the bookkeeping component moved from the preparatory course, which in turn was replaced by a more basic section on business methods. If the junior was to follow a shop-front career route they would then take the Apprentices' Course, which covered an initial grounding in the practical topics of apprenticeship and bookkeeping stage I, but they also had to continue their study of co-operation to stage II. It was recommended that classes for apprentices be organised locally by societies and be taught by a manager, or another qualified co-operative employee. The classes should be held during work hours and organised in two ten-week sessions either side of Christmas. Correspondence tuition was available if it proved impossible to form a local class. The Central Education Department set the examinations and issued certificates to successful candidates.

The Salesmen's Course was thoroughly revised in the early 1920s to allow for greater specialisation. Classes were re-organised into three areas – grocery and foodstuffs, drapery and apparel, furnishing and hardware. For small societies, a truncated course comprising the first and a summary of the latter two areas was offered. Three new textbooks were prepared to support these more specialised syllabuses. Classes would be formed under the direct supervision of the Central Committee at agreed locations for a minimum of 15 students, and be held on the day of the usual half-holiday in the district. Each course would be of at least twenty lessons of two hours for a fee of 15s. Students were also expected to pass the examination in advanced stage co-operation. To ensure students were properly prepared, the classes were only open to those who had passed the Apprentices' Course or had attained the age of 21. For students who had successfully mastered the Salesmen's Course and aimed to qualify as general managers, the next stage was the Manager's Ordinary Course. This took the three areas of the Salesmen's Course to a more advanced level, and added topics in general and co-operative economics, commercial law and co-operative accounting. Correspondence and local classes were offered for fees of 10/6 for the two economics subjects and a guinea each for the others. Students could take as many subjects as they wanted per session and a separate certificate was issued for each one passed. Passes in all subjects were required for a manager's diploma. For the truly ambitious, the Honours Course in Co-operative Management reprised the subjects of the Ordinary Course and further demanded knowledge of co-operative law, the economics of business organisation, the organisation of industry and commerce, and co-operative statistics and statistical methods. Correspondence tuition was offered for fees of two guineas for the law component and a guinea each for the others. It was noted that the exams 'will not be so much a memory test of the contents of any text book as a test of whether a man is ready, resourceful, practical and possessed of personal initiative and force of character'.[26]

For those going down the office-based route or aiming for secretarial or auditing work, there was an equally impressive series of courses with supporting syllabuses, textbooks and regulations. Bookkeeping was re-organised during the mid-1920s, partly to cater for the introduction of a standard balance sheet for use by societies nationally. A two-stage course replaced the existing three-part one. Each half covered co-operative bookkeeping – based on the standard double-entry methods but with somewhat different application – and general co-operation. The first stage was based on the accounts of a small society with one distributive and no productive department, the second on the books of a larger and more complex society, and including more practical experience of actual accounts. No certificates would be issued unless the candidate had passed an appropriate examination in arithmetic. The Secretaries' Course required at least a further two years' study: the first part dealt with co-operative accounts, commercial law and stage III co-operation, the second with co-operative law and administration, office organisation and secretarial work, and co-operative statistics and statistical methods. This division was mainly for convenience of study rather than degree of difficulty and subjects could be taken at will. Correspondence classes in each part were arranged centrally and offered in alternate years. Advanced co-operation had 24 weekly lessons at a charge of 7/6; the other subjects had 12 fortnightly lessons for a guinea per subject. Only students who had completed two-thirds of the correspondence papers were admitted to the examinations, but if they had managed half, or been admitted and failed the examination, they were entitled to re-take the course the following session for only half fees. Success yielded the Secretaries' Diploma. Up to the mid-1920s, there was also an Auditors' Course with a more legal emphasis, but this was replaced by an arrangement with the Incorporated Society of Accountants and Auditors to admit co-operative students to their examinations.[27]

The re-organisation of the technical classes was heroic and represented a huge investment of effort, led by Hall and his colleagues in the Education Department at Holyoake House. Syllabuses were prepared, and examinations produced and marked for each of the subjects discussed, with new textbooks for several areas. Considerable attention had been given to grading the courses and implementing regulations to try to ensure that students had completed one stage before tackling the next. There was no dissembling about how tough some of the courses could be. Nevertheless, a sequence was put in place that could, in principle, take an elementary school leaver to an honours course in management that could stand comparison 'with those offered by the highest type of educational institution and those required by the best professional associations'.[28]

The expansion and limitations of employee education

It was all very well to devise impressively structured programmes of
education. To what extent, however, were classes actually run and did
employees take advantage of them? Through the inter-war period,
there was significant expansion on both fronts, classes were organised
and teachers found, junior employees particularly were encouraged to
follow classes and sit examinations, and various reward systems were
put in place for those who did. There was much enthusiasm for a great
advance in co-operative education run by and for the movement. The
formation of an educational in association conjunction with the
Co-operative Wholesale Society (CWS) brought a further impetus to
the scheme. There were always going to be limitations, however.
Education remained, largely, a voluntary activity with many societies
unable or unwilling to provide classes and the majority of employees
disinterested. How actually to provide the education was an issue,
and the local organisation of classes was varied. The failure of the
1918 Act was a blow and increasingly, albeit partly owing to success,
the movement looked to make connections with local education
authorities (LEAs).

A convenient review of co-operative education towards the
beginning of our period was published by H.J. Twigg in 1924.[29] His
inquiries revealed that under half of the retail distributive societies in
Great Britain had an independent educational committee, while just on
a half made some kind of educational grant, averaging 9.3d per
member. It was not a uniform experience: of smaller societies up to
1,000 members, barely 24% made grants while 62% of those with up
to 2,000 members did. For larger societies with over 10,000 members,
the proportion offering grants rose to almost 100%. Twigg also
detailed the variety of activities that local societies regarded as educational, which remained very diverse; for many societies, it seemed, any
money not spent on retailing was regarded as educational. Of these
activities, he calculated that propaganda consumed 28% and socially
oriented activities another 25%, while formal instruction enjoyed only
9.25% of grants for education. Few societies had dedicated space for
instruction, while some regarded education as the province of the
WEA.

While unimpressed with the general situation, Twigg noted that more
extensive work was being done with respect to technical classes. The
Manchester and Salford societies led the way by sending about 50 of
their apprentices to special classes at Holyoake House during work time
with no deductions from wages.[30] Other societies in the area followed

and it was not long before the initiative attracted wider attention. A special congress held in Leicester in 1920 considered the training of co-operative employees, while the Central Education Committee issued a circular to local management committees urging them to take immediate steps to deal with training, especially of junior employees.[31] Later the same year, the issue emerged as a key topic at the Bristol Congress.[32] Duly inspired, local societies began to take up the matter and *The Co-operative Educator* regularly reported on activities.[33] For example, the Royal Arsenal Society paid the fees of employees studying technical subjects; Ilkeston Society arranged classes during work hours for those under 18; salesmen's and managers' classes were taught at Leicester, Nottingham and Warrington; and the Newcastle-upon-Tyne Society had 178 employees attending seven evening classes organised in three districts. The Leeds educational committee issued a circular to all employees over 16 and called a meeting to explain the courses on offer and to enrol them into classes.

The numbers taking technical subjects increased noticeably.[34] In 1923/24, there were 4,235 students enrolled in 313 technical classes, which increased steadily to 13,597 in 634 classes by the end of the decade. Those entering for the examinations were somewhat fewer.[35] For the year 1920/21, there were 2,418 candidates; the following year there were 2,753. By 1925/26, the numbers had risen to 4,017 and by the end of the decade they were up to 7,426. Co-operative bookkeeping remained the single most popular course, consistently attracting about a quarter of all those taking technical examinations. Otherwise, it was the junior courses that drew most candidates, the elementary English and arithmetic proving highly popular, followed by the Preparatory and Apprentices' courses. Among the higher level courses, Salesmanship, primarily in the foodstuffs department, drew appreciable numbers of the order of a few hundred in the later 1920s. Unsurprisingly, the highest level courses had only a few tens of candidates and the Honours course only the occasional aspirant. The administration of technical classes was re-organised in 1930 following an arrangement with the CWS, which was also becoming interested in employee education.[36] A Joint Committee of the Co-operative Union and the CWS was formed to supervise the more advanced classes for salesmen and higher grade employees, while the Central Educational Committee continued its supervision of the more junior Preparatory, Introductory and Apprenticeship courses. Numbers in all technical classes were boosted to over 16,000 in the early 1930s, remaining at that level for the next several years.[37] With the re-organisation, it becomes more difficult to follow the precise numbers taking examinations, but the patterns identified for the 1920s continued.

Successful recruitment bred its own problems, however – how, and by whom, were these students to be taught? Initially, the aspiration was for the movement to provide its own training under the auspices of the 1918 Education Act, which would recognise efficient 'works schools' and Hall was firmly of the view that co-operative education should remain under its own roof: '[W]hilst it is necessary that co-operative employees should have the best training that can be given them, it is no less essential that they should receive that training in a co-operative school.'[38] Enthusiasm surrounding the 1918 Education Act was short-lived as government funding for continuation schools was axed in the post-war depression. Although lamented as an unwise and short-termist policy, it nevertheless highlighted the need for the movement to live up to its rhetoric and provide its own training from its own resources.[39] It was intended that employee training, especially of juniors, should mainly be achieved in-house and, noticeably, this was regarded as primarily the responsibility of managerial committees.[40] There were some reports of friction over this policy, but the principle seems to have been established that the general educational activities of the movement fell to the educational committees, whereas the training of employees was the responsibility of their managers.[41]

How far, though, did managers have the capacity, or desire, to undertake employee training? It might have been possible to organise basic instruction in literacy, numeracy, elementary business practice or co-operative bookkeeping in-house, but in many cases even this was quickly farmed out. As noted above, in the Manchester region, it was the Education Department itself at Holyoake House that initially supplied apprentice training for local societies. This work was, in turn, soon transferred to the Manchester Education Committee which formed a day continuation school, providing the premises and teachers for the general academic subjects, while the teachers from Holyoake House taught the more vocational classes.[42] The school thrived, growing from 250 students to over 800 in less than a decade.[43] There was a great deal of interest in the training of junior employees reported, but, since no systematic figures were collected by the Central Education Committee, they acknowledged that it was difficult to tell how many local societies actually offered it.[44] Certainly, it was felt that more could, using *The Co-operative Apprentices' Textbook* so helpfully provided by the Education Department. As in the case of Manchester, and as we shall explore further below, most examples of the training of junior employees came from liaison with LEAs.

If arranging the instruction of junior employees proved difficult to achieve in-house, higher-level training was even more problematic. For those within reach of Manchester, Holyoake House, bolstered by an expanding staff, provided a wide range of day and evening courses, including several of the courses in Salesmanship, Secretaryship and General Management.[45] The Managers' Honours Course and Part II of the Secretaries' Course were mainly dealt with through correspondence with the tutors at Holyoake House supplemented by residential courses.[46] For example, a special course for secretaries held in Manchester in 1925 lasted two weeks.[47] The first week concentrated on practical subjects led by experts from the CWS and the Co-operative Insurance Society (CIS), while the second week focused on more generic subjects and were led by Hall and colleagues. One of the reasons for developing the carefully graded courses with supporting textbooks and the availability of correspondence courses was to try to overcome the shortage of expert teachers.[48] Through the 1920s, a system of travelling teachers was established to try to meet the demand for classes for salesmen and managers. The Central Education Committee approached the United Board for funds to support the scheme for several years before it was finally sanctioned.[49] First appointed was Mr Ramsden, who was soon fully occupied with classes in Warrington, Leicester and Nottingham.[50] The example was picked up in the South West section where a Mr Ellison taught classes for adult grocery employees in Bristol, Bath and Torquay, which also included students from the Brixham, Portsmouth and Paignton societies.[51] The United Board approved support for the post, but it took a short while before the local societies raised sufficient matching funds to help sustain the appointment for several years.[52] Another joint appointment was made between the four London societies and the Education Department.[53]

Much was achieved by this mixed economy of in-house training, itinerant lecturers, specialist residential courses and correspondence, but an increasing number of societies made connections with their LEAs and began to farm out both the education of junior employees and more specialist technical classes. We have already seen the example of the day continuation school in Manchester, which operated so successfully.[54] The education committee provided the teaching staff, building and equipment and the societies allowed employees the time off work and paid for travel. A broadly based curriculum covered basic academic subjects and physical education as well as specifically co-operative subjects. In 1921, Middlesbrough decided to stop arranging its own junior classes and seek the assistance of the town's director of education.[55] A class for 24 was launched with the local authority providing a hall and teacher, while the society provided tea during the interval between sessions. In the same year, Ashington Industrial Society established a joint scheme with the county council to educate employees financed by the two bodies together with government grants.[56] The scheme thrived and ten years later there was a fully fledged Apprentices' Training Centre recruiting from nine societies for a wide range of subjects taught over two years and including visits to CWS works and practical lessons in shops by the managers.[57] In the Southern section, an arrangement had been reached with the London County Council soon after the war whereby the LCC would provide rooms, pay the salaries of teachers and not interfere with the syllabus, provided it was reasonably broad, and the Royal Arsenal Society had organised several classes on this basis.[58]

By 1930, the North West section was discussing relationships with LEAs in more general terms,[59] and the Midland section was actively developing a policy that would lead to closer relationships with their LEAs, potentially leading to a co-operative educational centre for the Midlands.[60] In 1935, the Joint Committee on Technical Education announced a new policy that pushed local societies further towards the local authorities.[61] There were two main parts to the policy. Firstly, the Joint Committee decided that it would no longer find or fund teachers for salesmanship courses. When these were launched, there were few courses and fewer teachers, so the committee had undertaken to provide teachers from its own staff, or help societies to find suitable candidates. Now that the scheme had expanded so successfully, it was no longer possible to meet the demand. Henceforth, therefore, local societies would have to find and pay such teachers themselves. It was noted that almost a thousand students had passed the relevant examinations in recent years, so finding suitable teachers should not be a problem. To assist the societies, the Joint Committee would approve the appointment of organisers of technical education to the sections. Effectively, the policy was to turn the itinerant teachers into organisers.[62] This worked fine in London, while the Midland section simply appointed an organiser rather than a teacher.[63] The policy was resisted in the South West section, which wanted to continue with a teacher rather than just an organiser, and, ultimately, this was allowed.[64] The second, undoubtedly related, element to the new policy was the recommendation that local societies forge closer connections with their LEAs. A survey indicated that of 212 societies, 123 were already organising classes in this way. Of the rest, many had not yet broached the subject, and there were only a few recorded cases where a society had actually been rebuffed by their LEA.

Arranging classes and finding suitable teachers was only half the battle. If it was left to local societies whether to offer technical classes, it was similarly up to the employees whether they would avail themselves of the opportunities. We have seen that a significant, and steadily rising, number of employees did pursue courses and sit examinations, yet disappointment remained that more did not. While pleased that in 1919 there were over 2,000 people taking technical classes, it was remarked that more than 130,000 were employed by retail societies,[65] and after a decade of considerable expansion the total number of enrolments was still less than 10% of employees.[66] Students were criticised for lack of seriousness and poor attendance; they might attend a class for a year, but few demonstrated a deep commitment to education.[67] On the other hand, inducements were sporadic. Classes were often held in work time, perhaps up to half a day, with no deductions of pay. Sometimes fees were paid or books provided; the Middlesbrough society offered tea; often prizes were awarded to successful or diligent students.[68]

Although there was plenty of encouragement, there is not much evidence of compulsion. This was a long way from the aspirations of the Central Educational Committee, which really wanted to make 'the holding of certificates a condition of appointment or promotions'.[69] Belfast Society, early in the period, announced that it was obligatory for all junior employees to attend classes at the Technical Institute, although there is no indication of any support or rewards.[70] By the 1930s, there are more indications of a systematic approach. The Whaley Bridge and Buxton Society circularised their employees to encourage attendance at classes and indicated that important positions were, henceforth, more likely to be awarded on efficiency than length of service.[71] A comprehensive scheme of linking recruitment and promotion to educational success was approved by the Tweedside Industrial Society in 1934.[72] Junior employees were expected to attend evening classes and have completed a two-year course before commencing an apprenticeship. The apprenticeship course should be completed by age 24, with regular progress reports, and the society felt no obligation to continue to employ anyone with an unsatisfactory record. At the higher levels of First Counter Hand or Branch Manager, suitable qualifications were also expected. Any existing employees under the age of 30 who had not followed the required courses within ten years would not be eligible for promotion. By way of encouragement, there was also a comprehensive system of prizes ranging from 5s for a pass for the junior evening classes up to five guineas for the Branch Manager's Diploma.

One factor that may have dampened students' enthusiasm was that the examinations were undoubtedly tough. *The Co-operative Educator* noted that the examinations for the auditing course were 'searching ones; but the standard is not too high for those who aspire to the responsible position of auditor to an industrial and provident society'.[73] For a great many candidates, however, the standards were far too high and the number of failures was quite shocking.[74] Thus, in 1921/22, out of 2,753 candidates for technical examinations, 1,020 were unsuccessful. There is not much evidence of improvement through the period; there were 2,176 failures out of 4,599 entrants in 1926/27 and 3,040 failures out of 7,426 in 1928/29. Nor did the examiners pull any punches in their annual reports: 'The unsuccessful candidates would be well-advised to take the course again, as they require a much more thorough knowledge of the subjects ... before they can be said to be qualified as a general manager.'[75] *The Co-operative Educator* was even more damning: 'The report of the examiners of the Bookkeeping papers makes for dismal reading.' Yet the blame was placed primarily on the teachers:

> The repetition, year after year, of the same errors of method, shows that a natural tendency is not sufficiently corrected by the teachers ... Whilst the object of co-operative education is not to secure facility in passing examinations, yet, so far as examinations reveal defects, it is of the utmost importance that teachers should note these defects and try to remedy them.[76]

For those few who scaled the pinnacles of co-operative education, it was perhaps true that they had acquired an education comparable with the highest found anywhere in the land. Clearly, however, it was far too demanding for those employees who struggled with piecemeal and unsystematic teaching arrangements, and uncertain rewards.

Conclusion

The co-operative movement's inter-war initiative in technical education was ambitious, and met with much success. A hugely impressive set of syllabuses and examinations completely overhauled training for employees. Recognising that most began with only a rudimentary elementary schooling, a carefully graded system was established that could take a raw recruit to 'honours' level. Alternative pathways were introduced for different kinds of work and careers, all with supporting textbooks, examinations and, frequently, correspondence courses. Clearly, a significant number, and rising proportion, of the workforce attended classes and entered for examinations, primarily at the junior stages, but going up to the highest levels. Equally clearly, only a small minority of employees took advantage of the opportunities and, although it was stated that the purpose of education was not merely to pass examinations, this was the measure of success, and many did not reach it. Nor were the examiners very sympathetic. If the ethos was self-improvement through mutual instruction, those who did not demonstrate sufficient self-improvement were told about it in no uncertain terms – there was to be no dumbing down here! There was a mismatch between the very systematic production of educational materials, and the more *ad hoc* means of delivery. Juniors might be taught in-house, and the higher levels by correspondence and residential courses, but the specialised intermediate stages were more difficult to cater for. There was also the problem of motivating employees. A number of societies offered various inducements, but few seemed to make educational qualifications the basis of recruitment or promotion. Woefully high failure rates indicate the discrepancy between aspiration and achievement.

Whatever the achievements or otherwise of the scheme, can we regard it as distinctively co-operative in nature? Does it reflect a set of co-operative values, or simply hard-headed commercial sense? There is no doubt that the movement saw education as a means of improving efficiency; other companies were investing in educational capacity and the co-operative movement could not be left behind. Yet the movement was conscious of its traditional commitment to education, and embraced the responsibility to expand it. Moreover, it is apparent that all the technical training was to be couched in a co-operative framework: Hall's somewhat pious statements nevertheless affirmed that the classes should instil proper co-operative principles into employees. More practically, courses in co-operation were foundational to the educational programme and no potential salesman or manager could scale the educational ladder without a thorough grounding in the history and principles of the movement. On the office side, the most popular course was the specifically tailored co-operative bookkeeping and the higher levels required an understanding of co-operative law, auditing and statistics. To begin with, the intention was that the movement would provide its own education in its own spaces with its own teachers. Ultimately, this proved impossible to sustain. Much was achieved under its own auspices, but many societies established connections with their LEAs from an early date and, by the mid-1930s, partly through success, it was recognised that this was the best way to proceed. Co-operation, however, remained central to the syllabuses.

What also stands out, and constitutes one of the most striking features of this episode, is the sheer scale and ambition of the programme of technical education. Historians have long argued that the provision of technical education for industry in England generally was limited, while firms were reluctant to recognise the value of formal training.[77] There was a particular lack of preparation for management, the prevailing view being that managers were born, usually within the firm's own family, rather than made. Although there are indications that, in the wake of the First World War, some firms were assessing the training of their workers, the evidence is patchy.[78] Some larger, and arguably more progressive, employers, such as Lever and Cadbury, were keen and, regionally, firms could forge close connections with local colleges. It is difficult to tell, however, the extent of this development. *The Co-operative Educator* was aware of it, although the main example given was Cadbury's. It would seem, then, that the scale and scope of what co-operators attempted and achieved was far in advance of what was taking place elsewhere. Again, the breadth is remarkable, encompassing remedial education, vocational training, and structured preparation for managerial positions. This confirms the initiative as a great co-operative venture, the product of an organisation deeply committed to education, which wanted to extend the opportunities and advantages of education to all of its employees, high and low, with equal access.

Notes

1 F. Hall and W.P. Watkins, *Co-operation. A Survey of the History, Principles, and Organisation of the Co-operative Movement in Great Britain and Ireland* (Manchester: Co-operative Union Ltd, 1937); G.D.H. Cole, *A Century of Co-operation* (Manchester: Co-operative Union Ltd, 1947); J. Bailey, *The British Co-operative Movement* (London: Hutchinson, 1955); A. Bonner, *British Co-operation. The History, Principles and Organisation of the British Co-operative Movement* (Manchester: Co-operative Union Ltd, 1961); P. Gurney, *Co-operative Culture and the Politics of Consumption in England, 1870–1930* (Manchester: Manchester University Press, 1996).

2 J.F.C. Harrison, *Learning and Living 1790–1960. A Study in the History of the English Adult Education Movement* (London: RKP, 1961); T. Kelly, *A History of Adult Education in Great Britain*, 3rd edn (Liverpool: Liverpool University Press, 1992); B. Simon, *Education and the Labour Movement 1870–1920* (London: Lawrence and Wishart, 1965); L. Goldman, *Dons and Workers. Oxford and Adult Education Since 1850* (Oxford: Clarendon Press, 1995).

3 Hall and Watkins, *Co-operation*; Bonner, *British Co-operation*; Gurney, *Co-operative Culture*.

4 These are held at the National Co-operative Archive, Holyoake House, Manchester. I should like to acknowledge here the considerable help and advice of Gillian Lonergan and her colleagues at the archive.

5 Cole, *A Century of Co-operation*; Gurney, *Co-operative Culture*.

6 Cole, *A Century of Co-operation*; Gurney, *Co-operative Culture*. 'Co-operative Education: Past and Present', *The Co-operative Educator* IV:1 (January 1920). There is a difference of interpretation here; Hall and Watkins argue that local societies, relieved by the local authorities of providing standard education, turned voluntarily to classes in co-operation. Bonner argues that it was the Co-operative Union that drove developments. The evidence here supports the latter.

7 *Co-operative Educational Programme 1910* (Manchester: Co-operative Union Limited, 1910).

8 Ibid., p. 33.

9 Hall and Watkins, *Co-operation*.

10 F. Hall, *The Extended Programme of Co-operative Education. An Address Delivered at the Educational Conference at the Swansea Congress 26th May, 1917* (Manchester: Co-operative Printing Society Limited, 1917). Some of the background to the review is given in: F. Hall, *A Review of the Education Report of the Survey Committee as Presented to the Swansea Congress of 1917* (Manchester: Co-operative Printing Society limited, 1919).

11 Hall, *The Extended Programme*, p. 11.

12 K. Vernon, 'Science and Technology', in S. Constantine, M.W. Kirby and M.B. Rose (eds), *The First World War in British History* (London: Edward Arnold, 1995), pp. 81–105.

13 L. Andrews, *The Education Act 1918* (London: RKP, 1976). D.W. Dean, 'H. A. L. Fisher, Reconstruction and the Development of the 1918 Education Act', *British Journal of Educational Studies* 18 (1970), 259–276; D.W. Thoms, 'The Emergence and Failure of the Day Continuation School Experiment', *History of Education* 4 (1976), 36–50.

14 'The 1918 Education Act', *Public General Statutes* (London: Eyre and Spottiswood, 1918).

15 'Labour and Educational Reconstruction', *The Co-operative Educator* I:1 (January 1917).

16 'A New Purpose in Education', *The Co-operative Educator* II:1 (January 1918).

17 'Co-operators and the New Education Act', *The Co-operative Educator* III:2 (April 1919).

18 'Notes of Interest', *The Co-operative Educator* II:1 (January 1918).

19 *The Co-operative Union Ltd Educational Department. Educational Programme 1926–1927* (Manchester: Holyoake House, 1926), p. 6.

20 'A New Purpose in Education', *The Co-operative Educator* II:1 (January 1918).

21 'Training for Co-operative Employees', *The Co-operative Educator* IV:4 (October 1920).

22 'Education at the Bristol Congress. Notes and Impressions', *The Co-operative Educator* IV:3 (July 1920), 67–68.

23 Diagram after that given in *The Co-operative Educator* XIII:3 (September 1929).

24 *Educational Programme 1926–1927*, p. 135.

25 Details of the courses are taken from *Educational Programme 1926–1927* and 'The Training of Co-operative Employees', *The Co-operative Educator* XIII:3 (September 1929).

26 *Educational Programme 1926–1927*, p. 153.

27 'Report of the Central Education Committee', *59th Annual Co-operative Congress* (Manchester: Co-operative Union, 1927).

28 'The Outlook', *The Co-operative Educator* XIII:2 (May 1929), 1.

29 H.J. Twigg, *The Organisation and Extent of Co-operative Education* (Manchester: The Co-operative Union Ltd, 1924).

30 'Notes of Interest', *The Co-operative Educator* IV:1 (January 1920).

31 'Notes of Interest', *The Co-operative Educator* IV:2 (April 1920).

32 'Education at the Bristol Congress', *The Co-operative Educator* IV:3 (July 1920).

33 'With the Educational Committees and Educational Associations', *The Co-operative Educator* IX:1 (February 1925); 'With the Educational Committees and Educational Associations', *The Co-operative Educator* XI: 1 (April 1927).

34 'Report of the National Educational Council', *68th Annual Congress* (Manchester: Co-operative Union, 1936), table, p. 78.

35 Figures taken from *The Co-operative Union Ltd Education Department Session 1921–22, Results of Examinations* (Manchester, 1922); *Results of Examinations 1926–27* (Manchester, 1927); *Results of Examinations 1929–30* (Manchester, 1930).

36 'Co-operative Employees and Education', *The Co-operative Educator* XIII:3 (September 1929).

37 'Report of National Educational Council' 1936.

38 'Training for Co-operative Employees', *The Co-operative Educator* IV:4 (October 1920), 91.

39 'The Educational Outlook', *The Co-operative Educator* V:1 (January 1921).

40 *Educational Programme 1926–27*.

41 'Notes of Interest', *The Co-operative Educator* IV:3 (July 1920); 'Notes of Interest', *The Co-operative Educator* XIII:1 (February 1929).

42 W.P. Rutter, *Continued Education for Junior Co-operative Employees. An account of the Classes Attended by Junior Employees in the Manchester Area* (Manchester: Co-operative Union Ltd, 1928).

43 'Report of the Central Educational Committee', *54th Annual Congress* (Manchester: Co-operative Union Ltd, 1922); 'Report of the Central Educational Committee', *62nd Annual Congress* (Manchester: Co-operative Union Ltd, 1930).

44 'Report of the Central Educational Committee', *57th Annual Congress* (Manchester: Co-operative Union Ltd, 1925).

45 'Notes of Interest', *The Co-operative Educator* XIV:1 (January 1930).

46 *Educational Programme 1926–1927.*

47 'Businessmen as Students', *The Co-operative Educator* IX:2 (June 1925).

48 'Report of the Central Educational Committee' 1925.

49 'Report of the Central Educational Committee', *56th Annual Congress* (Manchester: Co-operative Union Ltd, 1924).

50 'Report of the Central Educational Committee' 1925.

51 'With the Educational Committees and Educational Associations', *The Co-operative Educator* XIV:1 (January 1930).

52 'With the Educational Associations', *The Co-operative Educator* XIV:3 (July 1930); XV:2 (April 1931); XV:3 (July 1931).

53 'Report of the Central Educational Committee' 1930.

54 Rutter, *Continued Education for Junior Co-operative Employees.*

55 'With the Educational Committees and Educational Associations', *The Co-operative Educator* V:3 (May 1921).

56 'With the Educational Committees and Educational Associations', *The Co-operative Educator* V:2 (March 1921).

57 'With the Educational Committees and Educational Associations', *The Co-operative Educator* XIV:1 (January 1930).

58 'With the Educational Secretaries', *The Co-operative Educator* XIV:2 (April 1930).

59 'With the Educational Committees and Educational Associations', *The Co-operative Educator* XIII:1 (February 1929).

60 'With the Educational Secretaries', *The Co-operative Educator* XIV:2 (April 1930).

61 'New Policy', *The Co-operative Educator* XIX:2 (April 1935).

62 'Report of the Joint Committee on Technical Education', *67th Annual Congress* (Manchester: Co-operative Union Ltd, 1935).

63 'Important Changes for Next Session', *The Co-operative Educator* XIX:3 (July 1935).

64 'With the Educational Associations', *The Co-operative Educator* XIX:3 (July 1935); 'Report of the Joint Committee on Technical Education', *68th Annual Congress* (Manchester: Co-operative Union Ltd, 1936).

65 'Training for Co-operative Employees', *The Co-operative Educator* IV:4 (October 1920).

66 'The Training of Co-operative Employees', *The Co-operative Educator* XIII:2 (May 1929).

67 'Student's Corner', *The Co-operative Educator* VII:2 (July 1923).

68 'With the Educational Committees and Educational Associations', *The Co-operative Educator* V:3 (May 1921); 'With the Educational Committees and Educational Associations', *The Co-operative Educator* IX:1 (February 1925).

69 *Educational Programme 1926–1927*, p. 6.

70 'With the Educational Committees', *The Co-operative Educator* II:4 (October 1918).

71 'Notes of Interest', *The Co-operative Educator* XIX:1 (January 1935).

72 'Promotion Scheme', *The Co-operative Educator* XIX:2 (April 1935).

73 'Student's Corner', *The Co-operative Educator* VIII:1 (February 1924).

74 Figures taken from *Results of Examinations 1921–22*; *Results of Examinations 1926–27*; *Results of Examinations 1929–30*.

75 *Results of Examinations 1926–27*, p. 64.

76 'The Teachers' Page', *The Co-operative Educator* I:4 (October 1917), 105.

77 J.F. Wilson, *British Business History, 1720–1994* (Manchester: Manchester University Press, 1995); J. F. Wilson and A. Thompson, *The Making of Modern Management. British Management in Historical Perspective* (Oxford: Oxford University Press, 2006). I am grateful to Tony Webster and John Wilson for advice on this point.

78 K. Burgess, 'Education Policy in Relation to Employment in Britain, 1935–45: A Decade of "Missed Opportunities"?' *History of Education* 22 (1993), 363–390; D. Thoms, 'Technical Education and the Transformation of Coventry's Industrial Economy, 1900–1939', in P. Summerfield and E.J. Evans (eds), *Technical Education and the State since 1850: Historical and Contemporary Perspectives* (Manchester: Manchester University Press, 1990), pp. 37–54.

4

International perspectives on co-operative education

Linda Shaw

No form of education can be effective unless those who take part in it are clear in their minds about four things: its necessity, its purpose, its substance and its methods.[1]

The stimulus for this chapter comes from recent research into co-operative education in Africa carried out for a large scale co-operative development programme. The study revealed that six national level Co-operative Colleges provided the main vehicle for co-operative education with over 8,000 students in co-operative education programmes across eight countries in east and southern Africa: Tanzania, Uganda, Kenya, Swaziland, Lesotho, Botswana, Zambia and Ethiopia.[2] However, framing co-operative education within a wider context, either within the academic literature or in relation to internal debates within the co-operative movement, proved to be a major challenge. Though education and training is a core co-operative principle it currently receives little attention either from researchers or practitioners.

For those not familiar with the co-operative movement but interested in education and development these issues may, at first sight, seem of limited relevance. Co-operative education is widely assumed to be only a minor type of educational provision. However, this underplays the global reach of the movement. With a global membership of nearly a billion, co-operatives and their members contribute to the livelihoods of nearly half the world's population.[3] Co-operative education programmes, even if they reach only a small proportion of co-operative members, still have the potential to impact on the lives of many millions of people. Yet many questions about the broader aspects of co-operative education remain largely unanswered despite the presence of a number of other co-operative colleges in Asia, Africa and Latin America. Table 4.1 shows that all but two are located in developing countries.

Table 4.1 List of co-operative colleges in Asia, Africa and Latin America

Co-operative colleges, 2010	
Americas	
Guyana	KuruKuru Co-operative College (www.kurukuru.edu.gy/index.html)
Trinidad	Cipriani College of Co-operative and Labour Studies (www.cclcs.edu.tt/)
Africa	
Ghana	Co-operative College of Ghana, Kumasi
Nigeria	3 federal colleges
	• Ibadan
	• Kaduna (www.fcckaduna.com/index.php)
	• Oji river, Enugu State
Cameroun	National Co-operative College, Bamenda
Uganda	Co-operative College, Masindi
Tanzania	Moshi University College of Co-operative and Business Studies (www.muccobs.ac.tz)
Swaziland	Co-operative College
Kenya	Co-operative College, Nairobi (www.cooperative.ac.ke)
Lesotho	Co-operative College, Maseru
Botswana	Co-operative Education and Development Centre, Gaborone
Zambia	Katete College of Agricultural Marketing, Eastern Province Co-operative College, Lusaka
Asia	
Malaysia	Co-operative College (www.mkm.edu.my/home#)
Sri Lanka	National Institute of Co-operative Development (www.nicd.edu.lk/aboutus.php)
India	National Council for Co-operative Training, New Delhi (www.ncct.info/index.html)
	5 regional institutes of co-operative management
	14 institutes of co-operative management

The widespread presence of co-operative colleges raises broader questions about the origins and prevalence of the co-operative college model. Why are they concentrated in certain regions? Where does the college model fit within the broader contours of provision of co-operative education? What are the strengths and weaknesses of the college model? What are the specific learning needs of co-operatives and their members and how are they being met?

This chapter begins to answer some of these questions by discussing the wider context of co-operative education and proposing a broad typology of institutional providers; thereafter it reviews the history and current roles of the colleges in east Africa and suggests some areas for further research. The focus will be on educational programmes and courses for co-operatives themselves as well as related teaching and research.

Defining co-operative education

Education is frequently referred to in the histories of co-operation, but typically as part of larger studies and as one among a number of broader themes. In the case of the UK, existing historical studies of co-operatives in the nineteenth century have revealed the wide scope and shape of co-operative education and tapped into a rich seam of internal debate over its nature and direction.[4] Several studies have emphasised the variety of ways in which knowledge and learning about co-operation was transmitted as the movement grew rapidly in the nineteenth century.[5] The Rochdale Pioneers Society placed a high priority on education and believed that co-operatives should fund education themselves with a definite percentage of the profits, normally 2.5% of surplus.[6]

The nineteenth century has been characterised as a 'golden age for co-operative education'[7] with a wide range of educational provision which continued as an integral part of the work of co-operative societies until well into the twentieth century.[8] The UK College was established in 1919 to provide a 'centre for higher education … and the cultivation of the co-operative spirit'.[9] As other authors in this volume attest, one of the primary goals of co-operative education was not simply to impart knowledge and skills but also to 'make co-operators' – people committed to promoting co-operation and actively participating in the wider movement.[10]

More recently, commentators on contemporary co-operative education have tended to adopt a normative approach and addressed internal debates within the movement. Fairbairn, for example, argues that co-operative education 'needs to be an agency for holding the co-operative and its members together and on course'.[11] Nakagawa stresses the importance of co-operative education despite the present neglect of educational activities within the movement. He argues that there is a close connection with citizenship education and that this offers a starting point for a renewal of co-operative education.[12] There are scarcely any contemporary studies of co-operative education provision with the exception of the Mondragón Co-operatives in Spain. Studies of the development of these co-operatives have emphasised the centrality of education in fostering innovation and co-operative development.[13]

A global revival

Increasingly, the mounting evidence of the growth *and* renewal among co-operatives globally makes the absence of research and debate into co-operative education particularly telling. It is not just in the UK that co-operatives are undergoing a revival. A survey of the co-operative sector in Africa, for example, revealed that a much larger number of co-operatives than was commonly thought have survived the rigours of the structural adjustment programmes common across Africa during the decades of the 1980s and 1990s.[14] Revisiting the survey in 2009, Pollet found continuing growth in the co-operative sector and a growing emphasis on the entrepreneurial aspects of co-operatives.[15] In a World Bank study, Cuevas and Fischer found similar patterns of growth among financial co-operatives globally.[16] An International Labour Organization (ILO) report demonstrated how existing co-operatives were showing resilience to the financial and economic crisis of 2008–9 and how some sectors, such as worker co-operatives, were growing as workers and consumers opted for co-operative models as a response to the crisis.[17]

This process of renewal for co-operatives has also gained momentum from the growing clarity and consensus on the co-operative identity and values. Agreed in Manchester, the 1995 Statement on the Co-operative Identity is now embedded in Recommendation 193 from the ILO, providing the only internationally agreed guidelines for co-operative development. They are helping to drive legal reform at country level.[18] For many co-operatives in the developing world, these reforms are limiting government control and providing a much-needed space for market-led rather than state-led co-operative development.

So far, unfortunately, the role of education in the co-operative revival remains little explored. This is despite the growing recognition by many of the critical role of education in fostering economic as well as social development across both the developed and the developing world. Increasingly, intangible assets such as knowledge, skills and innovative potential are viewed as central to tackling global poverty and the achievement of the Millennium Development Goals (MDGs).[19]

Improving access to educational opportunities still remains a huge challenge in the rural areas where over 70% of the world's poor live. Though the focus of the MDGs is on children's education, the provision of education for adults in rural areas such as that provided by agricultural extension is extremely weak in many countries. The lack of adequate extension services has inevitably adversely impacted on rural co-operatives and the rural economy in general. The World Bank Development Report of 2009 highlighted the need for more institutional development and capacity building for rural educational providers.[20] Another World Bank paper also called for the further development of co-operative colleges, highlighting this as one possible strategy in relation to the development of financial services for the rural poor.[21] Despite this, recognition of the role of colleges as education providers for farmers and their organisations still remains absent from debates over the reshaping of extension services for farmer organisations such as co-operatives. This is hardly surprising given the lack of basic information until now about the presence of the co-operative colleges as key institutions providing education in many rural areas.

A typology of co-operative education

Colleges, of course, are not the only type of provider of co-operative education. Based on information from the co-operative movement and relevant research, as well as the international development programmes managed by the UK College, the following typology for co-operative education has been developed. It identifies four main types of providers: universities; government provision; co-operative movement provision; and co-operative colleges.

These are listed in Table 4.2, together with a summary of the main types of education-related actvities they undertake.

Most of these types of provision have a very long history and although it is not the intention here to discuss this in any depth, it is important to signal the important role played by the movement in the transmission of educational ideas and the adoption of institutional models. From the earliest years of the movement, co-operators began to visit each other's countries 'to find out what forms co-operation was taking and to take the lessons home'.[22] Histories of co-operation are replete with examples of the ways in which ideas and inspiration flowed across national boundaries. The promotion of co-operation in the colonies, for example, was never solely the prerogative of the colonial powers but also involved the influence of individual co-operators within the context of a wider movement. The adoption of the co-operative college model, which will be discussed in more detail below, provides a good example of the complexity of government and movement influences on the development of co-operative education in Africa.

Table 4.2 Co-operative education providers

Provider	Key features	Main type of provision	Other features
University	Strongest in agricultural universities Greater presence in developed world but also in Brazil, Thailand Links with social economy research and teaching	Research Teaching internal students Some extension programmes for wider movement	Development of Co-operative Studies programmes
Government	Co-operatives department staff Extension programmes Greater presence in developing world	Supervisory role Training with a focus on compliance	Lack of resources
Co-operatives	Normally provided by large co-operatives	Training for professional staff Limited focus on education for members	Informal learning likely to be important but limited evidence
Co-operative Colleges	36 in developing world 2 in Europe	Co-operative and business studies programmes up to and including degree level Extension programmes Limited research	Recent increase in student numbers in Africa Lack of global or regional networks

University provision

Universities, for example, also have a long history of working with co-operatives in terms of both providing extension programmes and in carrying out research. Historically, such provision has been strongly linked to rural co-operatives and agricultural departments, particularly in universities in the USA, Canada and the Netherlands. This has generated a substantive literature on agricultural co-operatives in North America and Europe as well as mainstream degree programmes and extension work.

Unfortunately, outside the focus on agriculture, co-operatives are scarcely mentioned in the curriculum of business schools or in university departments specialising in international development or economics. In several academic disciplines, co-operatives have disappeared. In relation to the study of economics, for example, Kalmi has charted the growing exclusion of co-operatives from mainstream economics textbooks from the 1930s onwards.[23]

This is slowly beginning to change. On the one hand, the increasing academic interest in social entrepreneurship and the social economy has helped to rekindle a wider interest in research and learning about co-operatives.[24] On the other hand, some of the researchers who did continue to work on co-operatives have begun to argue the case for developing a place within academia for co-operative studies. One of its key proponents, Ian MacPherson, has argued that a fundamental tenet of co-operative studies has been its connection to the wider movement and a commitment to 'improving, diversifying and expanding the application of the co-operative model'.[25] Both the UK and Canada have Societies for Co-operative Studies which organise conferences and publish journals that bring together scholars and practitioners with a shared agenda for supporting co-operative change and development.

The wider dissemination of their research findings to a greater audience presents a challenge for many university-based researchers. By contrast, the links forged between many co-operative studies departments and the wider movement provide some effective vehicles for dissemination and knowledge exchange. One example is the role of the Committee for Co-operative Research (ICACCR),[26] which as a constituent part of the apex body for the global movement, the International Co-operative Alliance, arranges regular research conferences alongside international co-operative assemblies and meetings. National co-operative networks offer opportunities for a range of academics, co-operative members and staff as well as young people to work together. The papers in this book, for example, were first presented at a conference, held in the Manchester headquarters of the Co-operative Group, to an audience of academics, co-operative staff and members as well as school students.

Government provision

The second main type of provider for co-operative education is government departments. This is normally in the form of the provision of agricultural extension services. In the USA, the Department of Agriculture has been mandated since 1926 to disseminate knowledge about co-operative principles and practices; it has worked closely with the co-operative sector to achieve this. This has involved co-operative training programmes, publications and educational materials typically directed at grassroots co-operatives and their boards. However, as has been noted earlier, in many developing countries the delivery of effective extension services and programmes has proved problematic.[27] To help improve reach and effectiveness many extension providers in the developing world have targeted collaboration with farmers' organisations at the village and regional levels. This, of course, involves increasingly working with primary and secondary co-operatives which can act as a conduit for education and market access services.[28]

In many developing countries, there are specialised field staff working with co-operatives. Their primary role is to ensure that co-operatives are complying with the legal requirements for registration and audit, although frequently this has a training dimension. In Ethiopia, for example, field staff from the Federal Department of Co-operatives are located throughout the country. Their tasks include registration, auditing and dispute resolution as well as training and the dissemination of information about co-operatives. However, these departments are frequently under-resourced and employ young, inexperienced staff with limited teaching skills and little understanding of co-operatives.

Provision by co-operatives

Co-operative societies themselves constitute a third type of education provider. They have provided education in several different ways. Firstly, some co-operatives run their own education and training programmes for members and staff. This inevitably tends to be the preserve of the larger and more successful co-operatives and is common in Europe, North America and Japan. Given the lack of research it is difficult to make generalisations about the nature of this kind of provision. However, it appears that the type of education delivered in-house will frequently be designed in response to the immediate business and training needs of the co-operative and frequently focused on provision for staff. At its best, such provision can be highly relevant and responsive to current learning needs; at its worst it can mean a very narrow agenda and a very short-term focus. Very few co-operatives, even in the developed world, offer well-resourced and structured education programmes for their active members, even those elected to postions of high responsibility such as board members for large-scale enterprises.

In the developing world, the capacity of individual co-operatives to resource and deliver training for members and staff understandably remains extremely limited. There are some exceptions to this. Some of the larger financial co-operatives in Kenya, for example, deliver their own education programmes, but most co-operatives in the developing world simply do not possess the resources or capacity to ensure appropriate training for their board members even though it is clearly needed.[29]

Some co-operatives (especially co-operative unions) benefit from training from other providers – often via engagement in Fair Trade supply chains. The revival of co-operatives and renewed focus on agriculture is resulting in a growth in the number of private training providers and consultancies offering education services to co-operatives. A recent study of co-operative education in Rwanda (which does not currently have a national Co-operative College) identified a growing number of private sector providers raising issues for the national Co-operatives Agency of how to co-ordinate and ensure effective quality standards. In Rwanda, as elsewhere, problems can sometimes occur when training providers lack a co-operative background and are unaware of key legal and governance requirements.[30]

The co-operative college model

Finally, the fourth type of provider of co-operative education is the co-operative colleges. This model is the one that is unique to the co-operative movement. Perhaps because of this, these institutions have not been researched, despite their long history. Colleges were first established in European countries such as Sweden, Denmark, Iceland, Germany and Switzerland in the years following the First World War. The model was adopted in North America in the 1930s with the establishment of a college in Canada.[31] A co-operative college was started in New York in 1937 with 22 students and a registrar who was a former student at the UK college. The co-operative press in the UK reported that the US college was

> a model of the Co-operative College in Manchester, and the students from the United States who have attended our British College emphasise their indebtedness to co-operative education in this country.[32]

The New York College was typical of the first wave of colleges which tended to have a close relationship to pre-existing national co-operative movements and apex bodies.

Some of these colleges, as in the case of Iceland for example, have not survived as dedicated colleges for the co-operative movement. The reasons for this merit further research but their disappearance undoubtedly reflects the fluctuating fortunes of the co-operative sector. In the case of Canada, the college was not able to survive as an independent educational body in the 1980s.This decline may also reflect the capacity of some of the larger co-operatives to run their own training provision. Crewe reports that both of these factors played a role, as did growth of a co-operative membership delinked from an understanding of core values and principles.[33]

The UK college had to radically revise its modus operandi as a residential college in the late 1990s as it struggled to both sustain its historic house and develop courses for the movement. Stanford Hall was sold in order to allow the college to move back to Manchester (its original home) and concentrate on renewing its co-operative education programmes within the UK and also internationally.

A second wave of colleges was established in the developing world following the Second World War. Little is known about the early histories of these colleges established in developing countries as they are not mentioned in contemporary literature on co-operative development.[34] Their concentration in specific regions, Africa and India, reflects their origins as a key feature of the British colonial regime. Patterns of co-operative development reflected the co-operative characteristics of the colonising country whether it was Belgium, France, Portugal or Britain. In the latter case, the British legacy has been characterised as a 'unified tradition' with a single movement and a single legal model.[35] And often, it may be added, a single national level co-operative college. Typically, government co-operative departments headed by a registrar were established in British colonies. This 'welfare and development approach' to colonial development in Africa is explored by Kelemen in relation to the influence of the Labour Party. Unfortunately the discussion of the colonial co-operative development strategies does not include a consideration of education.[36] Nonetheless, the influential Fabian Colonial Bureau argued that the registrar, 'should be regarded as the head of a department of adult education', with the proviso that control as well as education was needed for the colonial peoples, 'to whom the co-operative society is a strange and possibly a dangerous instrument'.[37]

The UK Co-operative College played an important role in shaping the colonial co-operative agenda. From 1947, the UK government funded education and training for students from the colonies provided by the college at its then home, Stanford Hall. A nine-month course, Co-operation Overseas, was delivered, which was designed for Assistant Registrars and other co-operative officials. The course also offered the opportunity to 'examine British institutions and values'. It was hardly surprising that many overseas students returned home with the dream of setting up a college.

> The last dream should be the establishment of a high grade Co-operative College in every country. Such a college will not only train high ranking officials of the co-operative organisations but also leaders of co-operative thought and opinion who will carry the movement forward on its next steps forward to its goal of social betterment. From such a college will come people not only technically equipped to face the gigantic task before us but mentally equipped and imbued with a strong faith in the movement.[38]

Co-operative colleges became an integral part of the national co-operative development strategies of the newly independent countries of Africa and Asia. Extensive and modern college campuses were built with donor support, and most colleges operated at tertiary level providing one- and two-year certificate and diploma programmes on a residential basis. Many students went on to work as civil servants in co-operative ministries. There was also a strong emphasis on professional training for co-operative managers – one which still remains today, for example, in the Indian colleges. By contrast, there was much less emphasis on outreach programmes for elected board directors and membership. The colleges in Zambia and Botswana, however, did prioritise outreach programmes for the wider movement rather than campus-based learning. All of these colleges were directly funded by the government and were an integral part of the state-centred co-operative policy.

However, the shortcomings of this largely state-controlled model of co-operative development have been well documented.[39] It was neither successful in fostering the development of vibrant co-operatives nor in promoting the development of a wider movement. Most co-operatives remained subject to government control, subordinate to party political interests and often dominated by local elites. They were part of the broader state-centred approach to economic and social development in Africa, which was swept away in the 1980s with the advent of liberalisation and structural adjustment programmes. In countries such as Uganda and Zambia state support for the co-operative sector was abruptly withdrawn and many co-operatives struggled to meet the challenges of operating in competitive markets. In many countries, co-operatives were viewed as part of the discredited state systems and were often regarded very negatively.

Many co-operatives did indeed collapse and much of the literature on them assumes that the co-operative model is one that has essentially failed.[40] More recent studies, however, have revealed just how many co-operatives did, in fact, survive and have begun to grow again. They remain one of the most common forms of farmer- and village-level organisation across Africa.[41] Similar views were held about the colleges which have also survived and, as the following case study shows, have also begun to grow again. This was the first regional survey of the work of the colleges ever to be carried out.

A contemporary case study – the role of co-operative colleges in east and southern Africa

That the colleges have survived through some turbulent times for co-operatives is a tribute to the resilience and commitment of many of the college staff and the wider movement. They are now in a position to both support and benefit from the renewal of the co-operative movement now apparent in Africa, as elsewhere. Drawing on evidence from recent research into the colleges undertaken on behalf of the CoopAfrica programme, the following section summarises some of the key findings from the study.

The aim was to map the state of co-operative education as delivered by the colleges and assess the extent to which their provision was able to meet the demands from growing co-operative movements. Evidence was gained across six key areas of college activity: relations with external stakeholders; governance and management; curriculum; resources and staffing. The methodology included deskwork and also field visits which included semi-structured interviews, focus group discussions on and off the campus and visits to co-operatives and other key stakeholders. The main findings are summarised in Table 4.3.

The survey revealed that the colleges still remained major providers of co-operative education in the region. In 2009, for example, over 8,000 students were enrolled in co-operative education programmes (including in Ethiopia). However, the survey also revealed the hetero-geneous nature of the colleges as there were considerable variations observed in size, programmes, strategic direction, governance and outreach. The largest college, for example, has almost 2,000 full-time students and nearly 5,000 enrolled in outreach programmes. One college has a residential student body numbering only 70 and with no outreach programmes.

Despite this heterogeneity, the colleges clearly fall into one of two major categories: firstly those colleges offering degree programmes and operating (or seeking to operate) in the Higher Education Sector. They comprise Moshi University College of Co-operative and Business

Table 4.3 Summary table of co-operative colleges in Africa

College	Numbers of staff and students	Programmes	Ministry
Moshi University College of Co-operative and Business Studies, Tanzania	108 academic 1,861 campus 4,810 outreach	Certificate, Diploma, Degree	Constituent College of Sokoine University, Ministry of Education
Co-operative College of Kenya	34 academic 900 students (campus)	Certificate, Diploma, Degree	Ministry of Co-operative Development and Marketing
Co-operative Education and Development Centre, Botswana	6 trainers 15 residential 200 outreach		Reports to Department of Co-operative Development, Ministry of Trade and Industry
Swaziland	8 academic 70 students (campus)	Certificate	Department of Co-operatives
Lesotho	17 academic 78 students (campus)	Diploma	Ministry of Trade and Industry, Co-operatives and Marketing
Uganda	20 academic 410 students (campus)	Certificate, Diploma	Ministry of Sports and Education
Zambia - Lusaka	18 academic 170 students (campus)	Certificate, Diploma	Ministry of Agriculture and Co-operatives
Zambia - Katete	11 academic 50 students (campus) 100 outreach	Certificate	Ministry of Agriculture and Co-operatives

Studies, Tanzania and the Co-operative College of Kenya. Secondly, there is a larger group of colleges with much closer ties to government departments and offering lower-level programmes. These include Lusaka Co-operative College and Katete College of Agricultural Marketing in Zambia; co-operative colleges in Lesotho and Swaziland; and the Co-operative Development Centre of Botswana.

In terms of governance, the models used did vary, though on the whole there were reasonably good standards of governance and management. This was especially true for colleges that had accountability to wider stakeholders built into their governance systems. This was typically via a board or advisory council. Some colleges remain under the direct control of the ministry responsible for co-operatives and report directly to that department. Broadly speaking, colleges in Kenya, Uganda and Tanzania had more autonomy vis-à-vis direct government control than those of their neighbours in Lesotho, Zambia, Botswana and Swaziland. Funding dependence on the government can often lead to a lack of motivation for programme development and also to the risk of increased vulnerability to changes at government level. Some colleges, for example, derive no benefit from extra revenue generation, and are obliged to give any additional monies raised from entrepreneurial activities, such as room rent or additional teaching courses, directly to the government.

In terms of the curriculum, all colleges operated at the tertiary level offering a range of one-, two- and three-year programmes i.e. certificate, diploma and degree level courses. Programmes covered management, business and accounting, with a strong focus on bookkeeping and accountancy functions. Programmes tended to cover the technical aspects of bookkeeping, rather than wider issues of financial control and risk management. In addition, the emphasis was on courses relevant for already established co-operatives rather than offering the knowledge and skills needed for starting up new ones. For most colleges, the delivery of their education programmes tended to be based on a traditional 'chalk and talk' approach with a limited role for skills development or the adoption of active learning methodologies.

The exception to this was in Zambia, where the college had been registered as a national training provider for vocational education. Following a major curriculum review, all college courses will become part of the new National Qualifications Framework. The Co-operative College will then become part of a transferable credit system. The new course curriculum will be both competency- and knowledge-based.

The level of curriculum content relating specifically to the co-operative model varied from institution to institution. This undoubtedly reflects the lack of sufficient academic material and teaching resources on co-operatives – a problem not just for the African Colleges but for all providers of co-operative education. Much more needed to be done to identify and meet the training needs of changing co-operative sectors. On the positive side, the 1995 Co-operative Identity Statement and Values did underpin most of the curriculum content on co-operatives with a concomitant emphasis on co-operatives as autonomous enterprises.

In terms of teaching standards, colleges generally offered good- or high-quality teaching but often faced competition from a growing number of other providers. Specialist co-operative knowledge and experience tended to be the province of the older members of staff with younger members lacking in this respect. Most colleges struggled to retain staff because of the opportunities to earn higher salaries in other sectors. The colleges in Tanzania and Kenya faced the additional challenge of building their research capacity and increasing the number of staff with postgraduate degrees as they worked to achieve full university status.

There has been considerable pressure on colleges to concentrate on the provision of education for school leavers as this has helped guarantee income when the co-operative sector was not able to finance training by the colleges. Therefore campus-based students do not necessarily come from co-operative backgrounds, nor do they necessarily go on to co-operative work destinations. As regards post-course employment, there is a diminishing capacity of co-operative ministries to provide job destinations, though this remained a key aspiration for students. Unfortunately the destinations of students were not being tracked by the colleges, so little is known about what graduates do after they leave. It is thought that many do not go on to co-operative organisations, but elect instead to work in conventional businesses. Several colleges still have Ministry staff attending their courses as well, though the numbers have diminished overall and as a proportion of the overall student body.

The challenge for colleges is to run programmes to meet popular demand for non-co-operative-based courses and survive financially, whilst not distancing themselves further from the needs of the co-operative movement.

In many colleges, there was very limited outreach education provision for the wider co-operative sector whether it was for staff or members. All stakeholders reported on greater demand for more education and training for co-operatives. This included provision for paid staff, elected directors and ordinary members as well as for the agencies that work with them, e.g. government co-operative promotion staff, NGOs, etc. A co-operative development officer in Zambia reported that the co-operative sector is 'crying out for training' and this was a common theme in all the countries. However, although many small co-operatives lack the resources to provide and fund training for their members and staff, the increase in other education providers indicates that funding and resources are available.

Some colleges did have a wider reach. The Tanzanian College, for example, operated a network of 18 regional centres delivering outreach programmes. Following an investigation with support from the Nuffield Foundation, into their role in 2007, a re-organisation and review has taken place. In 2009, the college reported that these centres had over 4,000 learners enrolled in them. In Botswana, most co-operative training and education was being delivered locally, though this balance may alter following the completion of new premises currently (in 2011) under construction in the capital, Gabarone.

With the 'rediscovery' of co-operatives, there have been initiatives in several countries in the region and beyond aimed at setting up new co-operative colleges and higher education programmes. In several cases, serious consideration is being given to establishing new colleges. In Ethiopia, several university departments of co-operatives have been set up. One of the new departments, at Ambo University, was included in the research. Like some of the longer-established colleges, this department delivered a mix of full-time degree programmes for school leavers with an expanding amount of outreach provision for co-operative department staff and increasingly for co-operative staff and members. The university plans to set up a separate co-operative and leadership training institute with close ties to the co-operative sector.

In Rwanda, government support for co-operative development has resulted in a large increase in the number of co-operatives. There has also been a concomitant increase in the amount of training provided by NGOs and training consultancies. The government is currently considering the establishment of a national level college. This is also the case in South Africa.

The co-operative college model remains a very distinctive feature of co-operative education globally and one which appears to be receiving more attention from governments and policy-makers. In Africa, their varying fortunes have reflected the chequered history of co-operatives in that region.

A second golden age?

Compared to the nineteenth century, it may be true that co-operative education today is a long way from enjoying a second 'golden age', but the number and reach of co-operative education providers is far more extensive than often thought. The challenge for co-operative educators is to try and ensure they can meet the education needs of a movement enjoying a period of global growth and renewal.

To achieve this, there needs to be much more research into both the history and contemporary role of co-operative education and its relationship to the wider movement. Several studies in this volume have begun to address this and hopefully will help to stimulate further research. At the same time, education needs to become recognised by the movement as central to the global renewal of co-operatives. Developing a robust defintion of co-operative education also remains a critical challenge and one beyond the scope of this paper. However, any analysis of the nature of co-operative education needs to engage with its history and philosophy of 'making co-operators' and an understanding of the importance of, as Fairbairn describes it, 'the formal and informal ways in which members are recruited, informed, educated and involved'.[42]

The importance of education, in this wider sense, needs greater recognition both inside and outside of the movement. A study of co-operatives, young people and education in Uganda has revealed that education, both informal and formal, is of critical benefit for young people ranking alongside any income they may generate from being a member of a co-operative.[43] If this proves to be the case elsewhere in Africa, and indeed in the UK, then there is much work to be done to put education at the heart of co-operation in the twenty-first century – as did the Rochdale Pioneers in the nineteenth century.

Notes

1 W. Watkins, *Adult Education for Co-operators* (Manchester: Co-operative Societies Joint Education Committee, nd).
2 The findings from this research are presented in fuller detail in a CoopAfrica working paper. Thanks to CoopAfrica for allowing the use of the research findings in this paper. L. Shaw, *Co-operative Education in East and Southern Africa* (Dar es Salaam: CoopAfrica Working Paper, 2011).
3 A. Bibby and L. Shaw, *Making a Difference: Co-operative Solutions to Global Poverty* (Manchester: Co-operative College, 2005).
4 J. Birchall, *Co-op: The People's Business* (Manchester: Manchester University Press, 1994).
5 P. Gurney, *Co-operative Culture and the Politics of Consumption* (Manchester: Manchester University Press, 1996); I. MacPherson, 'Encouraging Associative Intelligence', in *Co-operative College*, (Manchester: Co-operative College, Working Paper No. 1, 2002).
6 Birchall, *Co-op: The People's Business*.

7   Macpherson, 'Encouraging Associative Intelligence'.

8   N. Robertson, *The Co-operative Movement and Communities in Britain* (Farnham: Ashgate, 2010).

9   L. Shaw, *Making Connections: Education for Co-operatives* (Manchester: Co-operative College, 2009), p. 32.

10 See Chapter 12 by Molina and Walton, and Chapter 3 by Vernon.

11 B. Fairbairn, *Three Strategic Concepts for the Guidance of Co-operatives* (Saskatoon: Centre for the Study of Co-operatives, University of Sasketchewan, 2003), p. 23.

12 Y. Nakagawa, 'Co-operative Education and Citizenship' in C. Tsuzichi, N. Hijikata and A. Kurimoto, *The Emergence of Global Citizenship: Utopian Ideas, Co-operative Movements and the Third Sector* (Tokyo: Robert Owen Association of Japan, 2005).

13 W. Whyte, 'Learning from the Mondragon Cooperative Experience', *Studies in Comparative International Development* 30:2, 58–67; see Molina and Walton, Chapter 12.

14 P. Develtere, I. Pollet and F. Wanyama, *Co-operating Out of Poverty: The Renaissance of the African Co-operative Movement*, (Geneva: ILO & World Bank, 2008).

15 I. Pollet, *Co-operatives in Africa: The Age of Reconstruction* (Dar Es Salaam: CoopAfrica Working Paper No. 9, 2009).

16 C. Cuevas, and K. Fischer, *Co-operative Financial Institutions – Governance, Supervision and Regulation* (Washington: World Bank, 2007).

17 J. Birchall and L. Ketilson, *The Resilience of the Co-operative Business Model in Times of Crisis* (Geneva: ILO, 2009).

18 S. Smith, *Promoting Co-operatives: A Guide to ILO Recommendation 193* (Manchester: ILO & Co-operative College, 2004).

19 World Bank (2009) *Education and the World Bank*, available at http://web.worldbank.org/WBSITE/EXTERNAL/TOPICS /EXTEDUCATION/0, menuPK:282391 (accessed 17 June 2010).

20 World Bank, *World Development Report 2008: Agriculture for Development* (Washington: World Bank, 2007).

21 World Bank, *Providing Financial Services in Rural Areas – A Fresh Look At Financial Co-operatives* (Washington: World Bank, 2007).

22 Birchall, *Co-op: The People's Business*, p. 54.

23 P. Kalmi, 'The Disappearance of Cooperatives from Economics Textbooks', in *Cambridge Journal of Economics* 31:4 (2007) 625–647.

24 J. Monzon and R. Chaves, 'The European Social Economy: Concept and Dimensions of the Third Sector', *Annals of Public and Cooperative Economics* 79:3–4 (2008), 549–577.

25 I. MacPherson, 'Confluence, Context and Community: The Expanding Boundaries of Co-operative Studies', in I. MacPherson, and E. McLaughlin-Jenkins, *Integrating Diversities Within a Complex Heritage* (Victoria: British Colombia Institute for Co-operative Studies, 2008), p. 548.

26 For information on the work of the Research Committee, see www.ica .coop/research.

27 I. Christopolos, *Poverty, Pluralism, and Extension Practice* (London: IIED, 1996); World Bank, *Gender and Governance in Rural Services: Insights fromm India, Ghana, and Ethiopia,* (Washington: World Bank, 2010).

28 B. Wennink and W. Heemskerk, *Farmers' Organizations and Agricultural Innovation* (Amsterdam: Royal Tropical Institute, 2006).

29 Consultative Group to Assist the Poor, *Working with Savings and Credit Cooperatives,* Donor Brief No. 25 (2005), available at www.cgap.org/gm /document-1.9.5254/DonorBrief_25_Eng.pdf (accessed 15 June 2010).

30 Shaw, *Co-operative Education in East and Southern Africa.*

31 J. Crewe, *An Educational Institution of Untold Value: The Evolution of the Co-operative College of Canada, 1953–1987* (Saskatoon: Centre for the Study of Co-operatives, University of Saskatchewan, 2001).

32 *Co-operative News,* 7 May 1938.

33 Crewe, *An Educational Institution of Untold Value.*

34 H. Hedlund (ed.), *Cooperatives Revisited* (Uppsala: Scandinavian Institute of African Studies, 1998); P. Develtere, *Co-operation and Development* (Leuven: ACCO, 1994).

35 Develtere, Pollet and Wanyama, *Co-operating Out of Poverty.*

36 P. Kelemen, 'Planning for Africa: The British Labour Party's Colonial Development Policy, 1920–1964', *Journal of Agrarian Change* 7:1 (2007), 76–98.

37 Fabian Colonial Bureau, *Co-operation in the Colonies* (London: Fabian Society, 1946), p. 143.

38 This appeared in the UK College journal. See S. Huq, 'Co-operative Education in an Underdeveloped Country', *Spectrum* (1960–1), 26–27.

39 R. Simmons and J. Birchall, 'The Role of Co-operatives in Poverty Reduction: Network Perspectives', *Journal of Socio-Economics* 37:2 (2008), 131–2140; Develtere, Pollet and Wanyama, *Co-operating Out of Poverty.*

40 Wennink and Heemskerk, *Farmers' Organizations and Agricultural Innovation.*

41 Develtere, Pollet and Wanyama, *Co-operating Out of Poverty.*

42 B. Fairbairn, 'Social Movements and Co-operatives: Implications for History and Development', *Review of International Co-operation* 94:1 (2001), 24–34.

43 S. Hartley, *A New Space for a New Generation: The Rise of Co-operatives Amongst Young People in Africa* (Manchester: Co-operative College, 2011).

5

Co-operative education in Britain during the nineteenth and early twentieth centuries: context, identity and learning

Tom Woodin

Over the previous two centuries, education has been central to the development of the consumer co-operative movement in Britain. Yet it remains a paradox that, despite considerable depth and achievements, co-operative education has not received significant attention, either in studies of education or of co-operation. Education within labour and social movements remains an under-researched area and this is particularly true of co-operation.[1]

Where it has been addressed, co-operative education has been commonly viewed as contributing to the growth of adult education and mainstream compulsory education. Its distinctive features have been downplayed – not only practices and structures but also the impulses and sensibilities that marked out a co-operative educational idiom. For example, Brian Simon's four-volume history of education touched upon educational aspects of the co-operative movement which, in the long run, were presented as feeding into growing demands for common schooling. This account was valuable but tended to sweep the movement up into more general trends and paid little attention to specifically co-operative ideals and practices.[2] The unique contributions of co-operatives, along with other examples of private working-class education,[3] could easily be lost in such overviews.

The tendency to impose wider educational and social lenses upon co-operative learning has been resilient. At the time of the second reform act in 1867, the very existence of the movement testified to the 'improvement' of the working class and showed that social and educational advance was indeed possible, a belief which bolstered the case for growing state involvement in education.[4] Over half a century later in 1919, the Report of the Ministry of Reconstruction Adult Education Committee noted the co-operative movement as one of a number of nineteenth-century educational precursors; these were portrayed as the beginnings of a bigger project to be taken forward by other bodies. Preparing the field of education for cultivation by the state was indeed a persistent theme: in addressing co-operators in 1912, R.H. Tawney argued that their 'special responsibility' now lay with higher education, to act 'as pioneers in building up those parts ... which the State has left almost untouched'.[5] In the long run, however, these creative processes of state formation would serve to constrict the extension of voluntary co-operative activity.

The marginalisation of co-operative education has also resulted from the way in which 'education' has been narrowly conceived as structured and directed learning. This perception has often been replicated within the movement itself where education commonly played second fiddle to more important economic and political developments. As a result, historians of the consumer movement have tended to isolate education from other activities.[6]

To begin the process of recognising and assessing co-operative education, we must be alert to the fact that it is possible to identify a wide diversity of practices which fostered change through individual and mutual learning, from the establishment of the Co-operative College, the provision of libraries and newspapers, to the more diffuse areas of informal learning, socialisation and participation by members as well as vocational training for employees. In doing this we can draw upon recent important reappraisals which have placed co-operation within a broader cultural and social setting.[7] As a movement which incubated social transformation, co-operation nurtured particular cultural understandings for much of its history, many of which cannot easily be encapsulated as 'education'. This paper will focus upon some of the meanings, practices and tensions surrounding co-operative learning in the nineteenth and early twentieth centuries. It offers an indicative overview which blends thematic and chronological approaches. Archival records, including journals, press, reports and autobiographies, form the basis for this study.[8]

'Something tangible' – beginnings

The early nineteenth century witnessed a diverse array of experiments in working-class emancipation. Many co-operative societies grew out of a milieu in which education and learning were inextricably linked to a range of collective self-help initiatives. There were considerable continuities between the early Owenite movements, the co-operatives which briefly flourished from the late 1820s, and the later co-operative movement.[9] Dr John Watts, an Owenite, noted that the later co-operative stores and manufactories from 1844–60, 'originated amongst men who were formerly communists of the school of Robert Owen – who, undaunted by many failures, have retained their faith in the Co-operative principle, until they have achieved success'.[10] Watts accurately identified a sense of determination to develop avenues of self-help through the most available means to hand. In this way, learning from experience was inscribed into the early achievements of the movement.[11]

Mutuality rapidly became a significant working-class organisational form from the mid-nineteenth century when shared impulses and tendencies found expression in social, economic, religious and educational enterprises. Education and co-operation were at times coterminous, woven into interconnected webs of working-class activity. The Manchester and Salford Equitable Co-operative Society was established in 1858 by the Roby Brotherhood. They had been members of the Roby Sunday School who formed themselves into a mutual improvement society and essay class helped by 'the kindness and co-operation of well disposed friends'. However, they wanted 'something tangible' and followed others in subscribing pound shares to form a co-operative. The Tame Street Institute and Phonetic Sunday School followed suit by dissolving itself in 1859 and joined the store, en masse, presenting its library, tables and tea service. But members were angered by the fact that the society was unable to register its rules with the Registrar of Friendly Societies because it proposed to devote a percentage of profits to education, a provision which had been left out of the Industrial and Provident Societies Act of 1852. Following amendments to the Friendly Societies Act of 1855, co-operative education became a bone of contention with Tidd Pratt, the Registrar of Friendly Societies, who refused to accept educational aims.[12] These legal wranglings illustrate how co-operative education, from its inception, was intertwined with the regulatory role of the state.

The Manchester situation appeared to be particularly unfair as the Rochdale Pioneers, established in 1844, had successfully devoted 2.5% of their surplus to educational purposes. Ten per cent had been proposed but this had also been disallowed by the Registrar. Co-operators had to wait until the 1862 Industrial and Provident Societies Act, when provision for education once again became permissible. Despite legal obstacles, the Pioneers were tenacious in their commitment to education and, by 1875, had a library of some 11,000 volumes, a full-time librarian and eleven reading rooms and laboratories.[13] Education was closely tied into wider social aspirations; an original object of the Rochdale Pioneers was to 're-arrange the powers of production, distribution, education, and government, or in other words to establish a self-supporting home colony of united interests'.[14]

During these early years of consumer co-operation, it is possible to gain glimpses into a learnt associational identity which had developed from a shared cultural and class background. Co-operatives developed through aggregated ownership, personal sacrifice and a determination to improve economic security. The experience gave rise to a corporate feeling which rapidly became apparent to a stonemason building a co-operative store in a mining district:

> most of the miners had shares in a local Co-operative Society … they came and sat, crouched on their heels, all over the building. As they were really, though indirectly, our employers, they were tolerated, although sometimes they were sadly in the way … I have never heard politics discussed with more force and directness than among these men … Their debates, couched in the very plainest English, were interesting to follow, and differed totally from the vague generalities and hackneyed phrases heard when an MP addresses a meeting of working men. All this struck me because, in our own trade, politics, as a rule, were left to so-called 'cranks' … The new building was on the roadside, and soon became the Trafalgar Square where everything was discussed … those miners … seemed to me to have reached the high water mark of industrial prosperity; the most striking thing about them was the fact that they had gained their advantages by organisation.[15]

As an outsider, the stonemason attested to the way in which co-operative ownership extended out into a sense of entitlement, control and engagement with political forces. Co-operation not only reflected wider social formations but, in addition, represented a structured articulation and further development of work and community-based identities. George Jacob Holyoake, an Owenite, free thinker and historian of the movement, would call this the 'spirit of association' or 'social education' to 'prepare members for companionship'. He realised that it gave co-operative education a characteristic purpose; co-operators

> did not require classical, scientific, and historical knowledge in order to sell oatmeal and candles … Education is not co-operative, because it is given by co-operators to co-operators, unless it is conducive to the formation of the co-operative mind.[16]

The interconnection between ownership, learning and common identity was to be an enduring theme in the history of the movement. The very buildings which housed co-operative activity could inspire awe and pride. A Bury co-operator described his feelings on entering the Rochdale Pioneers' central newsroom, 'capacious, lofty and neat ... When in it, one feels as if he had got into the Temple of Wisdom ... what noble thoughts of the wise, the great, and the good, are collected here!'[17]

Co-operative control of physical assets represented something durable and tied the individual into the co-operative body; buildings would continue to cement corporate feelings and fuel co-operative visions. From the late nineteenth century, the opening of new premises would become grand affairs with packed crowds who celebrated the visible representations of their joint power. In the early twentieth century, Linda McCullough Thew would lovingly describe the buildings of the Ashington co-operative, a reflection of her pride and personal investment in the society.[18] By the 1930s, these impulses would also feed into co-operative film which regularly offered panoramic views across the range and scope of consumer societies.[19] The built environment of the movement offered a visual resource, 'a distinctive grammar of construction and design', that provided a continuing induction into the palpable identity and values of co-operation.[20]

Similarly, participation in co-operative institutions could spark utopian desires which embraced education. The climactic and millenarian impulses of early nineteenth-century thinkers would continue to reverberate into the twentieth century. For example, T.W. Mercer, speaking at the Lytham summer school for co-operators in 1917, stressed that co-operation

> must be a deeply religious movement and a living faith ... co-operation was a life to be lived as well as a new order to be established ... if civilisation was to endure, society must be organised, and unless co-operators were prepared to apply their principles in the great work of social reorganisation he feared that it would be reconstructed from above, and that free institutions would disappear ... The laws of God and the laws of wise economy were one, and co-operators believed that by discovering and applying those laws they would at last be able to establish the new Utopia, the splendid city of God ... co-operation ... became a splendid crusade, a high adventure, a holy religion.[21]

Mercer blended religious belief with co-operative and educational ideas which animated the bricks and mortar of co-operative expansion: the interconnection between vision and materiality was inherent in the co-operative educational project.

Growth through knowledge

Nineteenth-century co-operators were imbued with a strong sense of history and progress. This was complemented by an enlightenment faith that the simple distribution of knowledge could have quite transcendental effects. Again, 'knowledge' was viewed in both spiritual and physical terms. Books and lectures with the correct message needed simply be spread among the people in order to transform society. This demand for knowledge was met through the proliferation of co-operative libraries, journals and newspapers which appeared both locally and nationally and became established features of the co-operative landscape by the late nineteenth century.

Whilst knowledge was to be distributed like tea and flour, a typical co-operative metaphor, its effects could be far-reaching. Holyoake himself favoured 'that old propagandist feeling' to counteract 'this sordid side of materialism ... we ought to make it a condition that every member should take a periodical which his society should supply to him along with his butter and cheese'.[22] This was not merely a fanciful aspiration and there were many concrete examples of the ways in which knowledge had a direct impact. For example, Holyoake's own *Self-Help, A History of the Rochdale Pioneers* (1857) was a highly influential text, perhaps the most significant co-operative tract ever written in the UK. By charting the history of the Pioneers, it offered an accessible model which could be copied and so facilitated the establishment and growth of co-operative societies. Holyoake's book had a tremendous impact at the York Equitable Industrial Society, where Chas Ernest recorded that the text

> came amongst them as a revelation. The lamp of faith which had been glimmering for years, at once became full and bright. It was a message of inspiration. It even caused many old deserters to give themselves up ... caused ... many societies to spring into existence.[23]

Through shared readings and group learning, co-operators helped to alleviate issues of literacy. Examples from the text were given in meetings which helped to win over the doubters and thus increased a sense of corporate identity. Knowledge was shared in a social context and co-operative education helped to facilitate this communication; the Prestwich Co-operative Society held a 'discussion and essay class' where everyone 'should read and speak on his feet, and thus improve them in the art of thinking in that posture'.[24]

However, the focus upon knowledge could lead to a seriousness that excluded others. Establishing successful societies was one stage in development; broadening their appeal to a larger group of members was another. Tensions would arise that centred on class and gender which, at times, appeared to undermine the ostensible focus upon education. As societies expanded their membership and extended their range of social provision, divergent forms of learning and culture came into conflict with one another. Social occasions and performances became widespread in the 1860s and 1870s, including recitations and humorous dialogues – Edwin Waugh, the dialect poet, featured at some societies.[25] But activists feared that opportunities for improvement and learning were deteriorating into mere entertainment. From the late 1860s, complaints about frivolity escalated as wider social and cultural distinctions congealed within some societies. This often took place along gender lines: for instance, 'A True Co-operator' complained of co-operative tea meetings, where coarseness and popularisation coincided with the appearance of women:

> times have changed; for whereas the meetings used to be of a few working men, who sought for knowledge and instruction – now the meetings are large to excess, composed principally of women, babies, children and youths of both sexes, tempted to come by a richly got-up tea, and lots of ham sandwiches, tarts and spice cakes, and very little plain bread and butter ... To teach, to learn, to sympathise, and to instruct used to be the object and principle of the meeting; but now these are decidedly secondary, and the music, singing, and buffoonery are the principle attractions ... as the meetings become more popular their utility declines ... I protest against the prevalence of mere sensual indulgences, under the name of co-operative meetings.[26]

These criticisms reflected a puritan fear of sensuality and unstructured social occasions at a time when early editions of the *Co-operative News* would warn about 'comic ribaldry' replacing 'elevating music'.[27] In the process of incorporating 'women and children', distinctions between 'high' and 'low', quality and popular became more common. This was a complex picture with local societies often at variance with stated aims and congress presentations, just as respectability could be a strategy adopted at appropriate moments and dropped at others.[28] In reality, in the mid-nineteenth century, women had been central to the formation and growth of many societies although the onset of structured organisations appeared to marginalise them.[29] Even though they became less visible, their participation was nonetheless essential to the growth of the movement and reached a critical mass in 1883 with the formation of the Women's Co-operative Guild. The very process of utilising knowledge to bring about the growth of co-operation gave rise to contradictions and tensions that rumbled on in future years.

There were gentlemen

As co-operation became a significant force in nineteenth-century society, debates surrounding social class also became prominent. The movement attracted many middle-class observers who viewed it in education terms. Co-operators appeared to offer a source of learning and understanding which was in line with dominant trends in the nineteenth century in so far as it projected a harmonious image of society with those at the bottom gradually improving themselves. In 1886, Miss Sharp from Rugby, an activist in the Women's Co-operative Guild, recognised this alignment between the co-operative movement and the improvement of society:

> the moral qualities necessary to the economic success of co-operative undertakings are also those on which the growth of true civilization depends – they are patience, foresight, care, self-control, mutual forbearance, willingness to sacrifice individual claims to the good of the whole.[30]

The meaning of these words could vary considerably across class divides. For example, one liberal politician argued that co-operation taught the virtues of capital and served as 'a great preservative against strikes'.[31] By contrast, co-operators were certainly alert to the ways in which capital could be utilised for emancipation and they read their own messages into this shared script. As a result, latent but significant class differences in relation to education can be identified, which simmered within mid to late Victorian Britain.

Christian socialists were particularly active supporters of the movement and offered legal services, publicity and public support. But they stereotyped northern working class co-operators as 'materialist', a position which hardened in the later nineteenth century under the influence of idealist philosophers such as T.H. Green. This position reflected wider class tendencies: in 1874, the then university extension lecturer Edward Carpenter had urged Leeds co-operators to embrace spiritual matters and question materialism and science.[32]

Working class co-operators were more apt to perceive business development to be at the heart of educational processes; 'materialism' was in fact bound up with learning. Education was perceived as central to developing new business models, such as federations, branch structures, banking and insurance. Informing members, building on values and responding to needs was a learning process at the heart of commercial success. Education was to be a galvanising force, disseminating new ideas and practices which underpinned the proliferation of co-operation.[33] The Owenite co-operator, William Pare, recommended reading the *Co-operative News* backed up by personal visits to members as the basis on which to expand banking.[34]

As the contrasting assumptions of Christian socialists and co-operators rubbed up against one another, they produced moments of friction. Whether the consumer movement should share profits with employees proved to be a vexed issue that spilled over into educational matters. One such affair in the early 1870s was the establishment of the *Co-operative News*. Co-operators considered it to be an essential democratic means of circulating knowledge among members across the movement. The issue became fraught when the Christian socialist Lloyd Jones and lawyer, author and M.P. Thomas Hughes, attempted to exert control over the paper and publish it from London under the generic title of *The Citizen*. The Scottish co-operator, 'Mr McInnes', distrusted their motives and justified this in terms of a perceived distinction between 'practical' and 'theoretical' knowledge – it was better to have the *Co-operative News* in the hands of trusted men in Manchester who would make a success of it rather than gentlemen in London.[35] Such spatial distinctions were a further feature of these debates given that many successful societies were located in the North.

Holyoake harboured fears about materialism but realised that, for many middle-class men, the movement offered opportunities for engaging with the 'problem' of the working class. While he was supportive of Christian socialists, they represented temporary partici-pants who were only able to connect with working-class people through the conduit of the movement:

> There were gentlemen ... who could never have been interested in the welfare of the working classes in the way they had, but for the rise of Co-operation, which enlisted their sympathies, and on which they had bestowed a large amount of attention'.[36]

In time, the co-operators would afford more permanent spaces where such tensions were expressed. The widening opposition between 'materialist' and 'theoretical' tendencies were to be stoked up further by Edward Vansittart Neale, as the General Secretary of the Co-operative Union, a position he used to criticise the materialism of the movement, often represented in the figure of J.T.W. Mitchell, the head of the Co-operative Wholesale Society.[37] In the long run, with the decline of the movement from the mid-twentieth century, wariness about theoretical knowledge would inhibit the ability to respond adequately to changing circumstances.

Structure and enthusiasm

The expansion of education within the co-operative movement quickened after 1885 when the Co-operative Union established an Education Committee. Educational opportunities were offered for both members and staff. Course syllabuses were established in subjects such as economics, citizenship, industrial history and the history and principles of co-operation. Examinations, testing and qualifications infused this educational structure with prizes, certificates and scholarships on offer for different age groups. By 1900, 1,154 members were enrolled and 582 were examined on co-operation, industrial history and bookkeeping. Sectional Educational Associations were set up from 1898. This was a conscious attempt to provide a staged educational hierarchy, the apex of which was to be the Co-operative College, established in 1919.

Significant advances also took place in technical training for employees, an area in which the co-operative movement was at the forefront of developments. Education and training became necessary as the size and scope of business operations increased. Previously, personal experience had been an adequate basis for employment, but, as societies developed in scale and complexity, with multiple branches, federations, wholesaling, banking and insurance, staff required a more thorough training. Courses were developed in vocational areas such as bookkeeping, sales and managing the various departments of a co-operative store. These blended personal experience, informal on-the-job learning and formal educational provision. Correspondence courses were developed from 1890 which reflected the wide dispersal of co-operative societies across the country; by the turn of the century the number of independent societies stood at approximately 1,500.[38]

This systematic structure did not meet the needs of all and there were drawbacks to formal organisation. Throughout its history the movement had acted as a seedbed for a broad range of educational innovations, notably university extension and the Workers' Educational Association which focused upon 'liberal' rather than 'technical' education. Some co-operators found avenues for wider learning based on liberal education and personal development.[39] But the growth of institutions and structures created problems for co-operative educators who at times felt they were losing out to other more popular forms. One contributor to the *Co-operative Educator* complained that, 'Vast funds of enthusiasm, which are ours by right, are secured by other bodies', and that classes 'should not exhaust the missionary spirit'.[40] Having developed structures to deal with an increasingly sophisticated and large-scale movement, co-operatives found that they had inadvertently constrained the spirit of mutuality and self-help.

Having said this, we must place the rather stern, 'traditional' image of co-operative education, as concerned with testing and qualifications, within a broader context. A more nuanced picture emerges when we begin to appreciate the multiple meanings, purpose and pedagogy of co-operative education. Education was part of a democratic and autonomous movement that was trusted by its members. The curriculum of co-operative education increasingly drew on the movement itself, from Robert Owen and early co-operative societies to later developments in business and retailing. While it was a voluntary activity for members, high standards were expected for a democratic working-class organisation that offered considerable avenues for development and learning. Moreover, as members, employees could take advantage of multiple opportunities for learning. McCullough Thew, an assistant in the Ashington store, did not necessarily expect to pass bookkeeping exams the first time and many failed them.[41] But she persisted with 'store classes' and recalled with great excitement when she won two scholarships and, as a young woman, attended summer schools on her own.[42]

Teaching and pedagogy served to further strengthen a sense of collaboration among co-operators. In 1917, W.R. Rae, chairman of the Co-operative Union Education Committee, argued strongly in favour of an inclusive pedagogy in children's classes so that 'triers' were rewarded, not just those who did well. In this way, co-operation would serve as a force to uplift everyone together.[43] In addition, he supported teaching bookkeeping to women, which had been opposed by others in the movement, and recommended that tutors, 'Proceed along the lines that are closely parallel to their work' and develop role-playing as 'Mrs Cash Book' and 'Mrs Trade'. Yet, in outlining his case, limiting assumptions about women were incorporated – associating participative teaching with lower mental capacity to some extent. He emphasised the need to keep it simple for women: 'The average woman is not quick in arithmetic, and cannot quickly add up long columns of big figures.'[44] The urge for freedom and equality through education could be curtailed by assumptions about different ability levels. Nevertheless, Rae's account represents an early and innovative attempt to think through the detailed problems of pedagogy and classroom experience in a co-operative context.[45]

The concept of pedagogy helps us to understand not only the co-operative classroom but also the wider transformative potential of the movement as a whole. Co-operative education links to the notion of 'subjectivity' and the sense of self engendered within a specific collective context. Educational practices were articulated in terms of developing an individual and social being: 'primarily the formation of co-operative character'. Co-operation was a way of life in which individuals might be immersed from birth and subjectivity was fostered through participation in such a way that the co-operative movement 'produced' distinctive types of people. By the turn of the twentieth century co-operators who were fluent in business, accountancy and bookkeeping as well as citizenship, principles and social science, became a visible part of the social landscape. J.T.W. Mitchell reveals this complex character – running an international business as well as a Sunday School.[46]

Of course subjectivity was heavily gendered, and this was very clear in the work of the Women's Co-operative Guild which was based upon a sense of self which not only engendered fierce loyalty to the co-op, but engaged in wider citizenship and campaigning activities on behalf of women and mothers. Virginia Woolf, on visiting a Guild conference, was both impressed and troubled by the detailed knowledge of the working-class women who could not be placed in neat categories. This dissonance felt by outsiders demonstrated the way in which co-operation could serve as an educative force.[47] Learning within a democratic social and economic movement was thus connected to wider purposes and social changes. It may be viewed in terms of a broad social history of learning which revolved around the 'character' of the working class in an emerging industrial democracy.

In this context, co-operators bridged the widening dichotomy between technical and more general educational development. The strong focus on technical issues could paradoxically stimulate a concern with co-operative values. For instance, Ben Jones, author of *Co-operative Production*, referred to 'technical instruction in co-operation … careful and systematic teaching of the principles and practice of co-operation'.[48] The fact that, for Jones, the principles of co-operation were tied into business development meant that 'technical' education could not easily be dissected into a set of discrete skills. Right into the mid-twentieth century, the principal of the Co-operative College, Robert Marshall, resisted the then prevailing distinctions within adult education between liberal and vocational streams:

> The old definitions are no longer accepted, that the 'social' student is concerned with ends and the 'technical' student with means. Both are

concerned with ends and means; and 'technical' studies can be the opportunity of educating that familiar figure in educational addresses 'the
whole man'.[49]

The manifest need to 'train' co-operators encompassed wider educational aims and aspirations. Indeed, these examples of technical
education testify to the serious way in which vocational learning was
understood and practised within the movement, as an induction into a
way of life as well as gaining skills. Learning was conceived as part of
one's whole sense of self within a social context, a perspective which
resonates with continental notions of 'formation' in France,
'formazione' in Italy and 'bildung' in Germany.[50]

In the ensuing years, co-operative education would broaden out in a
number of directions. Nurturing a 'co-operative consciousness'
became a priority in the face of unfair treatment of the movement
during the First World War and the subsequent entry into politics.[51]
One result was the growth of cultural participation by co-operative
members in order to enhance loyalty and build support. A snapshot of
the 1920s and 1930s would reveal a plethora of educational and
cultural activity, including drama, choral, musical, film and dance
groups. Along with the guilds and youth groups, the Woodcraft Folk
and Comrades Circles, they provided pathways into the governance of
co-operative societies. Paradoxically, the shift into politics and the
'labour movement' would create further problems for co-operators
who tended to be subordinated beneath the 'economic wing' of trade
unions and the 'political wing' of the Labour Party which focused
attention upon the state. Co-operators had always had an ambiguous
relation to the state, extracting benefits and funding for education but
also, in the words of Joseph Reeves, the education secretary of the
Royal Arsenal Co-operative Society, attempting to claim 'full
autonomy' which needed to be 'constantly safeguarded'.[52] Rae noted
how some local authorities had taken on co-operative libraries and
classes but then 'managed them out of existence'.[53] In the twentieth
century, as state ownership emerged as a dominant means of taming
capitalism, co-operative messages became muffled. Co-operative
educational and cultural life would struggle to thrive in this rapidly
changing world.

Conclusions

Various modes of learning have been illuminated through the prism of
co-operative education: supporting a common identity, developing

skills for business development; nurturing individual co-operators; entertainment; book learning; and fostering social change and participation in wider social institutions. Education was enmeshed within virtually every aspect of the movement. The project of remaking social relations, which was central to the co-operative movement, necessarily incurred novel and widespread examples of learning. One danger of this approach is that a broad range of activity is simply collapsed into an educational eclecticism which envelops the whole movement. We must be alert to the need to tease out learning from other connected areas of activity.

A number of persistent issues have been identified in this outline. A widely shared thirst for knowledge helped to bring the co-operative movement into being and was further stimulated by the experience of collective ownership and business development. Education itself was perceived through metaphors of growth and the distribution of goods in which the movement was deeply imbricated. The moral economy of co-operation coalesced around material forms which in turn stimulated democratic and educational ideas.

Extending co-operative education to ever-wider audiences proved difficult amid restrictive expectations that permeated the movement, particularly in relation to women. From 1883, the Women's Co-operative Guild would actively challenge these limiting assumptions while also campaigning in wider society. In addition, the very success of the movement led to a tension between self-help and structure that became embedded within the co-operative educational project. The rapid growth of the co-operative movement went hand-in-hand with the institutionalisation of personal relationships resulting in structures which might both enable and inhibit further creativity. Increasing formality and organisation was necessary to handle the burgeoning activity but, in turn, could weaken common feelings and activism which had invigorated early societies. The difficulties that arose related to a further dilemma between supporting general educational advances and providing a distinctive co-operative education. Co-operators found it necessary to engage with wider political, economic and educational developments in order to avoid insularity and ensure that their message was propagated. Yet, in the process of engaging with these social institutions, where different assumptions prevailed, the co-operative message could, in the long term, become subdued.

Today, the re-configuration of wider social and economic forces has created spaces which co-operatives have begun to inhabit. In this new context, both changes and continuities with the past can be identified.

For example, the potential for influencing mainstream compulsory education through 'co-operative schools',[54] and the widening scope of the Co-operative College, will necessarily involve both an extension and a dilution of co-operative education. The challenge to maintain and extend co-operative values while fostering broader growth will be a contradictory but necessary process which builds on deep historical roots. Re-discovering the historical depth and range of co-operative education may offer resources for the potential futures inherent in these new developments.

Notes

1 For example, C. Griggs, *The Trades Union Congress and the Struggle for Education 1868–1925* (Barcombe: Falmer, 1983); C. Griggs, *The TUC and Educational Reform 1926–1970* (London: Woburn Press, 2002); D. Lawton, *Education and Labour Party Ideologies 1900–2001 and Beyond* (London: Routledge-Falmer, 2004); K. Manton, *Socialism and Education in Britain 1883–1902* (London: Woburn, 1999).

2 *Ministry of Reconstruction Adult Education Committee. Final Report* (London: HMSO, 1919); B. Simon, *The Two Nations and the Educational Structure 1780–1870* (London: Lawrence and Wishart, 1974); B. Simon, *Education and the Labour Movement* (London: Lawrence and Wishart, 1965); B. Simon, 'Can Education Change Society?', in B. Simon (ed.), *Does Education Matter?* (London: Lawrence and Wishart, 1985); T. Woodin, 'Working Class Education and Social Change in Nineteenth and Twentieth Century Britain', *History of Education* 36:4/5 (2007), 483–496.

3 See P. Gardner, *The Lost Elementary Schools of Victorian England* (London: Croom Helm, 1984).

4 L. Jones and J.M. Ludlow, *The Progress of the Working Class, 1832–1867* (Clifton: Augustus Kelley, 1973/1867); on the capacity for improvement, see C. Hall, K. McClelland and J. Rendell, *Defining the Victorian Nation* (Cambridge: Cambridge University Press, 2000).

5 R.H. Tawney, *Education and Social Progress* (Manchester: Co-operative Union, 1912).

6 For example, A. Bonner, *British Co-operation: The History, Principles and Organisation of the British Co-operative Movement* (Manchester: Co-operative Union, 1961).

7 S. Yeo (ed.), *New Views of Co-operation* (London: Routledge, 1988); P. Gurney, *Co-operative Culture and the Politics of Consumption in England 1870–1930* (Manchester: Manchester University Press, 1996); P. Gurney, 'Labour's Great Arch: Co-operation and Cultural Revolution in Britain, 1795–1926', in E. Furlough and C. Strickwerda (eds), *Consumers Against Capitalism? Consumer Competition in Europe, North America*

and Japan, 1840–1990 (Lanham: Rowan and Littlefield, 1999); I. MacPherson and S. Yeo, *Pioneers of Co-operation* (Manchester: Co-operative College, 2005); see also F. Hall and W.P. Watkins, *Co-operation* (Manchester, Co-operative Union, 1937); G.D.H. Cole, *A Century of Co-operation* (Manchester: Co-operative Union, 1944); J. Attfield, *With Light of Knowledge: a Hundred Years of Education in RACS, 1877–1977* (London: RACS/Journeyman, 1981); L. Black and N. Robertson (eds), *Consumerism and the Co-operative Movement in Modern British History* (Manchester: Manchester University Press, 2009); N. Robertson, *The Co-operative Movement and Communities in Britain, 1914–1960* (Farnham: Ashgate, 2010).

8 I would like to thank Gillian Lonergan at the National Co-operative Archive.

9 Contrary to the argument of S. Pollard, 'Nineteenth Century Co-operation: From Community Building to Shopkeeping', in A. Briggs and J. Saville (eds), *Essays in Labour History* (London: Macmillan, 1960).

10 J. Watts, *Co-operator* 8 (1861), 115.

11 Learning from experience was a theme of E.P. Thompson's classic, *Making of the English Working Class* (Harmondsworth: Penguin, 1968).

12 'JHS', 'Sketch of the Origin and Progress of the Manchester and Salford Equitable Co-operative Society', *Co-operator* 1 (June 1860), 4–5; see Cole, *Century of Co-operation*, pp. 85–86.

13 A. Greenwood, *The Educational Department of the Rochdale Equitable Pioneers' Society Limited: Its Origin and Development* (Manchester: Central Co-operative Board, 1877).

14 Reproduced in Cole, *Century of Co-operation*, p. 75 and Bonner, *British Co-operation*, p. 46.

15 'A Working Man', *Reminiscences of a Stonemason* (London: John Murray, 1908), pp. 223–225.

16 G.J. Holyoake, *The Essentials of Co-operative Education* (London: Labour Association, 1898), p. 7; I. MacPherson, 'Encouraging Associative Intelligence: Co-operatives, Shared Learning and Responsible Citizenship', in *Co-operative Learning and Responsible Citizenship in the 21st Century* (Manchester: Co-operative College, 2002), p. 14.

17 T. Slater, 'Co-operation and Education', in *Co-operative Congress 1870* (Manchester: Co-operative Union, 1870), p. 58.

18 L. McCullough Thew, *The Pit Village and the Store* (London: Pluto, 1985), p. 71.

19 A. Burton, *The British Consumer Co-operative Movement and Film, 1890s-1960s* (Manchester: Manchester University Press, 2005).

20 J.K. Walton, 'Commemorating the Co-op: Nostalgia, Identity and the Visual Traces of the Co-operative Movement in Twentieth-century Britain', *Visual Resources* 24:2 (June 2008), 159–172.

21 T.W. Mercer, 'The Co-operative Faith', *Co-operative Educator* I:1 (1917), 20.

22 *Co-operative Congress 1870*, p. 20; see also Cole, *Century of Co-operation* and S. Yeo, 'A celebration of the Modern Personality of "Co-op Original"' in MacPherson and Yeo, *Pioneers of Co-operation*.

23 *Co-operator* 10 (1861), 139; see also *Co-operator* 13 (1861), 7.

24 *Co-operative News*, 9 Dec 1871, p. 159.

25 *Co-operator*, 8 (1861), 116–117.

26 *Co-operative News*, 2 March 1872, p. 98.

27 *Co-operative News*, 2 March 1872, p. 102; see also S. Yeo, *Religion and Voluntary Organisations in Crisis* (London: Croom Helm, 1977).

28 P. Bailey, 'Will the Real Will Banks Please Stand Up? Towards a Role Analysis of Mid-Victorian Respectability', *Journal of Social History*, 12 (1979), 336–353.

29 D. Thompson, 'Women and Nineteenth-century Radical Politics: A Lost Dimension', in D. Thompson (ed.), *Outsiders: Class, Gender and Nation* (London: Verso, 1993).

30 'Miss Sharp', *Co-operative Education Congress*, 1886, p. 14.

31 *Co-operative News*, 10 February 1872, p. 63.

32 S. Rowbotham, *Edward Carpenter* (London: Verso, 2008), p. 47.

33 *Co-operative Congress 1871* (Manchester: Co-operative Union, 1871), pp. 13 and 20.

34 Ibid., p. 38.

35 *Co-operative Congress 1971*, p. 44.

36 *Co-operative Congress 1872* (Manchester: Co-operative Union, 1872), p. 59.

37 P.N. Backstrom, *Christian Socialism and Co-operation in Victorian England* (London: Croom Helm, 1974).

38 See Keith Vernon's Chapter 3 in this book for a detailed account.

39 S. Rowbotham, 'Travellers in a Strange Country', in S. Rowbotham (ed.), *Threads Through Time* (London, Penguin, 1999), pp. 260–301.

40 'The Work of an Educational Association', *Co-operative Educator* I:2 (1917), 44.

41 McCullough Thew, *Pit Village*, p. 40.

42 Ibid, ch.13.

43 W.R. Rae, 'The Art of Teaching', *Co-operative Educator* I:1 (1917), 17.

44 Ibid, 19.

45 See B. Simon, 'Why No Pedagogy in England?', in B. Simon and W. Taylor (eds), *Education in the Eighties: The Central Issues* (London: Batsford, 1981), pp. 124–45.

46 Compare S. Yeo, *Who Was J.T.W. Mitchell?* (Manchester: Co-operative Wholesale Society, 1995) with P.N. Backstrom, *Christian Socialism*.

47 See V. Woolf, 'Introductory Letter to Margaret Llewelyn Davies', in M. Llewlyn Davies, *Life as We Have Known It* (London: Virago, 1984); G. Scott, *Feminism and the Politics of Working Women* (London: UCL Press, 1998).

48 B. Jones, *Co-operative Congress 1882* (Manchester: Co-operative Union, 1882).

49 R. Marshall, 'The Co-operative College', *Adult Education* 20:3 (1948), 131.

50 On learning see G. McCulloch and T. Woodin, 'Histories of Learning in the Modern World', *Oxford Review of Education* 36:2 (2010).

51 W.H. Brown, *The Political Education of Co-operators* (Manchester: North Western Section Co-operative Educational Committees' Association, 1919).

52 J. Reeves, *Educational Organisation* (Manchester: Co-operative Union, 1921), p. 4.

53 W.R. Rae, 'How Best Can Co-operative Societies Utilise Their Educational Funds in View of the Educational Facilities Now Provided by Municipal and Local Authorities?', *Co-operative Congress 1904* (Co-operative Union: Manchester, 1904), p. 5. Also see Gurney, *Co-operative Culture*.

54 DCSF, *Co-operative Schools – Making a Difference* (London: DCSF, 2009).

6

Beyond a fair price

Samantha Lacey

Introduction

The co-operative and Fair Trade movements were both established as alternatives to inequalities and unjust market practices.[1] Both movements have endeavoured to empower and inform both producers and consumers and have often worked together to this end.[2] At the producer end of the value chain (all the activities involved in producing, processing, manufacturing, trading and marketing products), both Fair Trade and producer co-operatives work to try to empower farmers and return as much of the profit of their produce back to them as possible.[3] Co-operatives do this by distributing surplus to members in the form of dividends whereas products certified by the Fairtrade Labelling Organisation (FLO) do it by returning a premium to producers, who democratically decide how to spend it. Democratic involvement of producers in the decision regarding how to spend the surplus/premium is central to both processes and is often achieved via a vote at the Annual General Meeting. At the consumer end of the value chain, consumers or workers own retail co-operatives. They could demand that the business be run to return maximum surplus back to them. However, workers and consumers are frequently drawn towards the values of co-operatives, which include concern for community. Hence, they frequently consider ethical sourcing and co-operation among co-operatives to be important business considerations and have often been pioneers in ethical retailing.[4]

The fact that each co-operative is owned by its members helps to increase their voice within the value chain. A producer co-operative is owned by producers and therefore represents their interests in negotiations rather than those of shareholders who, in the case of a plantation company, may be in another country and whose interests may not be aligned with those of the workers.

Producer, worker and consumer co-operatives exist all over the world, including in the South, and trading relationships exist between some of them. However, unlike Fair Trade, co-operatives are not primarily motivated to create North–South trading relationships specifically to benefit Southern producers (see also the chapter by Friberg in this volume).[5] Co-operatives exist to solve a problem for their members: they are *self*-help organisations, and it is this aspect that facilitates empowerment of producers and consumers. Co-operatives are also united by their common values and principles, which include 'Co-operation among co-operatives' and many co-operatives run or support co-operative development programmes overseas.[6]

Aims

A large body of research exists which looks at the impact of Fair Trade on producers in developing countries and many of these studies use co-operatives as case studies. However, very few examine the impact that being a member-owner of a co-operative has on producers' livelihoods or the specific challenges that producer co-operatives face in trying to support their members, particularly the poorest in their communities.[7] There have also been numerous consumer surveys about awareness of the issues that producers face and how this affects shopping habits in relation to Fair Trade, but very few have looked at the role of retail co-operatives in promoting Fair Trade.[8] Develtere and Pollet reviewed the similarities and differences between Fair Trade and co-operatives as well as the advantages and challenges they have faced working together, and Jones *et al.* reviewed the role of European co-operatives in bringing Fair Trade to consumers in the UK, Sweden, Italy and Belgium.[9] Nicholls and Opal also examined the support given by the Fair Trade system to co-operatives, although only within a short section on the 'Indirect Impacts of Fair Trade on Participants'.[10] It seems that there is a need for further research into the role that co-operatives as democratic, inclusive and member-based organisations, at both ends of the value chain, have played in the Fair Trade movement and the potential for the development of this role in future.

The findings of this chapter are based upon informal research via semi-structured interviews conducted between October 2008 and May 2009 with twenty-four co-operative and Fair Trade stakeholders including producer representatives and experts in the field from the UK, Kenya and Tanzania, combined with literature searches including academic and other published material. Responses have been kept anonymous to encourage frank answers, except where the explicit permission of the interviewee was sought for a quotation. The research is explored in more detail in the Co-operative College paper of the same title.[11] It focuses primarily on the consumer and retail perspective in the UK and the views of producer co-operative representatives, non-governmental organisations (NGOs) and Fair Trade networks from Africa, although other case studies are included.

Two movements provide alternative models

Both the Fair Trade movement and the co-operative movement have their roots in producer and consumer empowerment and in balancing economic needs with social justice. Co-operatives have played a role in producer, worker and consumer empowerment in Europe and elsewhere since the late eighteenth century. Building on ideas and experiences from these early co-operatives, five different traditions were established in Europe during the nineteenth century. All of these aimed to help people to access business services, from shops to credit, in a more equitable fashion. Many of these are the same issues faced by people in developing countries today. For example, agricultural co-operatives arose because people were migrating from rural areas to the cities, creating a new group of people who needed to buy food since they no longer grew their own. Farmers found they needed new agricultural techniques, access to finance, inputs such as fertiliser and an ability to market their produce in order to compete to serve the new urban market. Many achieved this by coming together to form agricultural co-operatives.[12] Smallholder farmers in developing countries today face similar challenges when trying to supply the global market.

Co-operatives have since continued to spread and grow in countries around the globe. Many were started by immigrants in North and South America, Australasia and some parts of Africa. In Latin America, co-operatives fitted well with the traditional values of many people and with strong social movements. Agricultural and fishing marketing co-operatives grew throughout the continent.[13] In Africa, Asia and the Caribbean, although co-operative type endeavours such as savings clubs were part of traditional community life, modern co-operatives were set up by European settlers and colonial governments to facilitate the export of staple commodities, such as cocoa, bananas, coffee and cotton.[14] In Rwanda, for example, during the colonial era, co-operatives were organised around export commodities such as tea, coffee and mining. [15] This often led to a 'top-down' approach designed to meet business or government needs rather than those of the members.[16]

After independence, many ex-colonial governments also encouraged, supported and, in some cases, managed co-operatives. Co-operatives were seen as a way to achieve government objectives such as national unity and economic development, by both east- and west-leaning regimes. Government control of co-operatives was therefore intensified. Co-operatives were supported with reduced taxes and market monopolies. For example, in Uganda and Tanzania, co-operatives were granted a virtual monopoly of cotton ginning and coffee factories.[17] However, this created co-operative movements that were bureaucratic parts of government, with no ownership by co-operative members, and the advantages they enjoyed allowed them to become inefficient and in some cases corrupt.[18]

During the 1970s, organisations such as the UN Research Institute for Social Development recommended in a series of reports that a more participative approach should be encouraged and that the role of governments should be reduced.[19] However, it was not until the Structural Adjustment Programmes of the 1980s that government control and support of co-operatives was reduced or removed as part of a broader suite of economic policies developing countries had to implement in order to receive loans from the International Monetary Fund or the World Bank.[20] These included measures to liberalise their economies by reducing protectionism and privatising state-owned services and resources. Forced to suddenly compete, many co-operatives went bankrupt. However, many adapted to become competitive, member-controlled businesses serving the needs of their members rather than those of the state.[21]

The Fair Trade movement arose via a number of different initiatives in the 1950s to 1960s as a trading model through which to protect marginalised and economically disadvantaged producers. For example the Dutch organisation Fair Trade Original was founded in 1959 and Oxfam began to sell handicrafts from disadvantaged communities in 1964. By providing farmers and artisans with market access, it aimed to improve incomes, thus raising their standard of living.[22] At that time, most Fair Trade products, initially handicrafts and later coffee, were sourced from Central and Southern America where co-operatives were rooted in strong social movements. Co-operatives, as producer-owned and controlled enterprises, made natural partners for Fair Trade buyers wanting to support producers.

Fair Trade started sourcing from African producers in the 1980s when African co-operatives were struggling. During interviews for this research, Jennifer Mbuvi, the Fairtrade Liaison Officer for FLO in East Africa, argued that Fair Trade played a significant role in helping co-operatives to survive during this period:

FLO does not work with individual farmers, but with legal institutions with at least some democratic structure. The market for Fairtrade came from European consumers who wanted to ensure that the farmers and workers were properly remunerated. In order to trade with the Fairtrade system farmers needed to be organised. This is helping to support the revival of many co-operatives. However, some of these societies have old debts dating from when governments were more involved in their management and they have lost confidence so farmers have to put effort into rebuilding them democratically and getting rid of the debts.

Co-operatives have also played a significant role in the growth of Fair Trade at the consumer end of the value chain. Fair Trade products were initially sold through world shops, charitable events and churches. In the 1990s, some co-operative retailers played a key role in bringing Fair Trade products to mainstream consumers who do not frequent specialist shops.[23] For example, consumer co-operatives in the UK started stocking Fair Trade products as early as 1992 and in 1999 the UK Co-operative Group was the first UK supermarket to sell Fair Trade products throughout all of its stores, meaning it had the largest number of outlets selling Fair Trade products nationwide.[24] In converting many of its own-brand products to Fairtrade certified, the Co-operative Group has also contributed significantly to increasing Fairtrade sales, for example, converting its own-brand chocolate to Fairtrade in 2002 doubled the size of the UK Fairtrade chocolate market.[25] The Italian co-operative, Legacoop also claims to be the first Italian supermarket chain to stock Fair Trade products.[26]

A number of European labelling initiatives joined forces to establish the Fairtrade Labelling Organisation in 1997. They developed internationally agreed standards against which individual products could be audited and certified with the now well-recognised FLO Fairtrade Mark. This brand has helped to make Fairtrade recognisable and understandable to consumers. Consumer commitment to Fairtrade has been further enhanced by community-based activities. Schools, towns and even cities have been encouraged to work towards Fairtrade status. In the UK, the first Fairtrade town was established in 2000, and there are now more than 400 Fairtrade Towns, with a further 200 working towards Fairtrade status. Since 2003, the date of the first Fairtrade University, over 120 Universities and Colleges have also been granted Fairtrade status.[27]

Fairtrade groups run educational activities around Fairtrade Fortnight in February to March each year, supported by local Fair Trade retailers, often co-operatives. The Co-operative Group in the UK has also made an important contribution through its educational membership events, in-store promotions and support for the Fairtrade Foundation's work. The approach has paid off. According to interviewees, support for Fairtrade contributed to the rebranding of the Co-operative Group as an ethical retailer and its return to being a major UK food store. Other supermarkets and major food brands have since followed suit so that by the end of 2007, sales of Fairtrade certified products in the UK were at £493 million, around twenty-one times what they were only eight years before.[28] Even during 2009, despite the financial crisis, the value of Fairtrade sales increased by 12% to an estimated retail value of almost £800m.[29] If sales of non-FLO branded Fair Trade were included then total Fair Trade sales figures would be even higher. The challenge for consumer co-operatives now is how they demonstrate 'the co-operative difference' and raise the 'ethical bar' once more, now that other retailers have followed their lead. Some are looking to direct trade with and support for producer co-operatives to help demonstrate co-operative values in action.

Balancing growth and values

The Fair Trade movement has reached great prominence in recent years, primarily through the FLO's Fairtrade brand, and is struggling to balance the commercial realities of moving into the mainstream, with its pro-poor, development roots.[30] Concurrently, the global co-operative movement is emerging from a period of decline and is undergoing a global revival following a refocusing on its core values and the importance of member ownership, particularly in the UK and in Africa.[31] The biggest challenge for both movements is how to be commercially competitive to achieve the growth they need in order to benefit more members and producers, while maintaining a strong focus on the needs of those key stakeholders.

The increased demand for ethically sourced products has had both positive and negative effects. It has increased the amount of food and other produce bought under Fair Trade and other 'ethical' terms, hence returning millions of dollars to producers in developing countries and improving their access to international markets. For example, as illustrated by Nicholls and Opal, Cafédirect alone returned $5 million in additional income to its coffee suppliers in 2003, and Transfair USA estimates that over a period of five years, Fair Trade returned more than $16.8 million over what the conventional trade market would have paid to coffee farmers in developing countries.[32] However, interviewees reported that the rapid mainstreaming of Fair Trade has also increased competition at both ends of the supply chain for smaller, dedicated Fair Trade organisations and has increased the demands placed on them.[33] Smallholder farmers find themselves competing with plantations certified under the hired labour standards, and having to meet increasingly stringent quality standards and audits, particularly under the FLO system. This is in line with the findings of Reed, who concludes that the impact of corporates engaging with Fair Trade is that support for producers is focused on technical and quality issues rather than livelihoods and civic political activity.[34]

At the consumer end of the value chain, dedicated Fair Trade brands, such as Cafédirect and Divine, that go beyond the requirements of the FLO Fairtrade standards, are now competing with supermarket own brand Fairtrade products that are produced more cheaply and which may not follow broader Fair Trade principles, such as forming long-term relationships based on dialogue and respect.[35] FLO currently labels individual products rather than whole organisations. However, at present it is only producers who are audited against comprehensive standards; other key players involved in processing, manufacturing, trading, transporting and marketing products (value chain actors) are only audited to ensure they have paid the minimum price and social premium. Some interviewees argued that there should be holistic standards for other members of the value chain too.

The World Fair Trade Organisation (WFTO, formerly IFAT) takes a different approach to that of the FLO. Rather than labelling individual products, it labels entire organisations from any part of the value chain, and only works with dedicated Fair Trade organisations. However, it is only now developing auditable standards to which the Fair Trade organisations that carry its logo must adhere. Working with dedicated Fair Trade businesses arguably gives it more freedom to play a challenging, campaigning role in international discussions about trade rules because it does not have to incorporate the concerns of large corporations for whom Fair Trade is only a small element of their business. However, its smaller size may limit its influence.

Producer perspective

The findings in this section are primarily based on discussions with producer organisations such as Kagera Co-operative Union, the African Fairtrade Network, and others who have worked intimately with producer groups, such as NGOs. They reflect a summary of the accumulated views of numerous individuals, African and European, who have spent years listening to producers both inside and outside of the Fair Trade system. Most of them had experience of the FLO Fairtrade certification system and of producer co-operatives. Eight key themes emerged from discussions centring on the difficulties producers face and what they would like to see change in the Fair Trade system for it to be more effective at meeting their needs. These themes were as follows:

Trading partnerships: Despite the fact that the FLO encourages the establishment of long-term relationships based on dialogue, information gathered from producer organisations indicated that the power imbalances in value chains prevent their voices from being heard. Respondents claimed that many supermarkets just buy Fairtrade certified commodities from traders without forming a relationship with the producer, so although the community still gets the Fairtrade premium, they do not get any of the other benefits of long-term relationships or extra development support provided by some of the Fair Trade specialists. Respondents also complained of a lack of transparency within value chains, both within and outside the Fair Trade system. There was often a sense of isolation and of communication and demands being top-down and audit-led rather than two-way and pragmatic. Buyers were unwilling to consider supporting producers to maintain long-term productivity, for example by establishing long-term contracts. At present, traders can simply switch to alternative suppliers if crops fail or costs increase.

Consultation: The FLO Standards Committee includes a broad consultation phase following the requirements of the ISEAL Code of Good Practice in Standard Setting (the ISEAL Alliance works to improve social auditing processes in agriculture). Despite this, interviewees in Kenya and Tanzania felt that many 'ethical' standards were created in developed countries and were dominated by the views of Western stakeholders. Although these standards are supposed to protect producers, they felt they had limited input into ensuring the standards were realistic, achievable and effective at improving their lives.

Flexibility and commitment: In order to help small-scale producers to develop to better supply the market and to meet their own need for income, interviewees felt that producers should be supported to improve rather than simply having to comply with demands and costly audits. They felt that they often face practical problems when trying to meet international standards and that two-way communication involving the auditors and buyers listening to their difficulties and providing support for them to adapt would be much more effective at improving conditions than simply being told in an audit that they have a 'major non-compliance' and they have failed. This language is often hard for producers to understand and they may not have access to the necessary information or capital to enable them to comply. They also felt that deadlines for implementing changes should be more realistic.

Responsive support that builds capacity, not dependence: Producer representatives felt that any training and support they were given should be relevant to their needs rather than driven by the donor. It should also be more focused on giving them the skills to solve their own problems.

Level playing field: Interviewees said that the difficulties small producers face when trying to access markets and comply with international 'ethical' and quality standards put them at a dis-advantage compared to larger companies, for example plantations. Although most did not object to the FLO 'hired labour' standards, as they recognised the needs that the landless poor have, they also said that it meant that they are now competing with big companies that find it easy to comply with international standards, even within the FLO system. Some interviewees did say that the bargaining and educational power of co-operatives can help them get better prices and adapt to international demands if they're managed efficiently, but that these co-operatives need support in order to be able to fulfil that role effectively.

Standards for other value chain actors: Many of the producer respondents, and those who work with producers, argued that the current certification system is too focused on making demands of the producers and not sufficiently demanding of the rest of the value chain. They supported the view, expressed in papers such as Smith and Barrientos, that the involvement of some Multi National Corporations (MNCs) has changed the nature of the Fair Trade system, making it more demanding for producers, but has not significantly changed the approach of those MNCs to their value chains.[36] They said that the growth of Fair Trade has led to increased competition, demands and pressure within the system which needs to be balanced by creating standards of continual improvement for other stakeholders.

Further scaling up: There was a consensus among interviewees involved with FLO Fairtrade that although they appreciated the premium, competition within the system is increasing as more producers become certified. This means that certified producers will often only sell about 10% of their crop at Fairtrade prices, the rest just being sold on the open market. Also, given that there is no guarantee of selling to the Fairtrade market from one year to the next, the risk of paying for an FLO audit and then not selling enough of your crop at Fairtrade prices to cover costs is quite high.

Producers said that the market for Fairtrade needs to become bigger, maybe by expanding into selling within Southern countries as well as Northern ones. Comercio Justo Mexico has taken this approach.[37] Ruth Simba, co-ordinator of the Africa Fair Trade Network said:

> In South Africa there is a growing market for Fair Trade. All countries may be able to afford them (Fair Trade products). There are some chain stores with high prices that they could sell to. As a movement they have not been able to advocate in the south. People are willing to contribute to charity but don't know about Fair Trade at the moment. Even the government don't know about it. It needs to be incorporated into education so people know and understand it.

Recognition of and support for the role of producer co-operatives: Respondents from the co-operative movement also said that the FLO places a lot of emphasis on the benefit of the premium to producers. However, coming together into democratic groups that are well managed is a complex process that requires support, particularly in the form of training, but this is often overlooked by Fairtrade and value chain stakeholders who see the premium as key to supporting small-holders. Although democratic representation is a requirement for FLO certification, there is often little support to help producers through this process since there are no requirements for organisations further up the value chain to support the development of their suppliers. Many of the most marginalised individual smallholders are unable to join or form farmer associations and are therefore unable to achieve Fair Trade certification.

Most producer co-operatives only sell a small proportion of their crops to Fair Trade buyers, so farmers rely on their co-operative to negotiate contracts on their behalf for the rest of their produce. If the co-operative is not managed democratically and in their interests, the ability of the co-operative to empower farmers and meet their basic needs is compromised. Stakeholders in the co-operative movement in Tanzania said that co-operatives had historically operated in a top- down, state dominated manner, so needed member, board and management training to empower their members to engage with, and take ownership of, their co-operatives. They also needed training to enable the management of the co-operatives to run them more efficiently. The provision of this kind of organisational development training would help the influence of Fair Trade to extend beyond sales of Fairtrade certified products to leave a lasting legacy of strengthened, producer-owned enterprises.

Side selling was also cited as a problem for co-operatives. If the members of a producers' co-operative sell to other buyers, the co-operative's income is reduced since costs are usually covered by charging a percentage fee on all goods sold through the co-operative. However, it is impractical to stop people selling to private buyers if they offer good prices or a faster sale. Co-operatives therefore face hard choices regarding what restrictions to place on members, how to police these rules and who to offer their services to. This emphasises the need for co-operatives to receive training and support to enable them to operate efficiently in their members' interests, and for members to understand the benefits of supporting their co-operative.

Tallontire also argues that in order for Fair Trade to be more than just another consumer standard, it needs to address both value chain and institutional governance.[38] She cites examples of value chains, such as Liberation Nuts, Divine Chocolate and Cafédirect, which have enabled producer co-operatives to co-own consumer-facing brands and receive a proportion of the profits of those brands in addition to the Fairtrade premium, so have become participants in, rather than recipients of, Fair Trade.

Challenges and opportunities for co-operatives

The views of people interviewed for this paper reflect the troubled history of co-operatives in many developing countries, but also a strong belief in their capacity for economic and social empowerment of individuals and communities. Interviewees expressed an acknowledgement of the difficulties faced in achieving good governance as well as efficient management. However, they could also cite examples of the added benefits of a co-operative style of governance when it is done well. These benefits go beyond just economic stability to start to tackle much more intangible problems such as lack of confidence and community cohesion.

Benefits of co-operatives

Strength from joining forces

Respondents cited the enhanced negotiating power farmers gained through joining together in a co-operative, both for sales of crops and purchasing of inputs, to be one of their key advantages. They said this had knock-on effects in the local economy as private traders had to compete with the co-operatives to deal with the farmers. They also listed other important benefits of joining together: improved access to loans; the ability to share knowledge and skills in tackling common challenges; the inclusion of farmers in remote areas that private traders would not collect from; and community cohesion. This is in line with findings by the International Labour Organisation (ILO), which state that

> Agricultural cooperatives enhance productive capacity and give access to markets to those … who when operating individually would not be able to benefit from these opportunities due for instance to a low purchasing power, a lack of productive assets, or cultural barriers.[39]

Owning their own business

This is the defining characteristic of co-operatives. Interviewees felt that it enabled farmers to gain transferable business skills. Their co-operative could advocate the needs of the farmers and any surplus is retained in the local economy. Crucially, it also enables them to gain more control over their livelihoods, for example by owning their own scales, to help to prevent them from being exploited. Similar benefits have been reported in other studies, for example at the Nronga Women Dairy Cooperative in Tanzania, where business training conducted by the co-operative and the ILO has resulted in women becoming more knowledgeable about the market and no longer being 'scared to take risks and start new business ventures'.[40] Assurance of a fair price has been found by Gijselinckx to be one of the top three benefits of membership most cited by co-operative members.[41]

More than just a business

The values basis of co-operatives was seen by NGOs interviewed to align well with development objectives. This alignment is also noted by Spielman, who says that 'cooperatives in Ethiopia share many characteristics with nongovernmental, membership-based civil society organizations even though they also seek to generate distinctly financial benefits for their members'.[42] Co-operatives also often provide members with a range of services they may not otherwise have access to in rural areas, such as loans and health insurance.

Challenges for co-operatives and possible solutions

The Fair Trade system provides a range of benefits to producer
co-operatives, including the premium which, because it is used for
community projects, can help co-operatives to retain the loyalty of
their members. However, as has been indicated previously, FLO
Fairtrade, especially when involving MNCs, often does not provide
capacity-building beyond quality issues.[43] If co-operatives are to
achieve their potential for producer empowerment as outlined above,
this research indicates that they need much more than premiums, they
need support from organisations that understand the specific challenges they face as co-operatives.

Numerous European and North American co-operatives have established co-operative development agencies to support the role of
co-operatives in development. In some cases, this is undertaken by a
co-operative apex body as one of its many functions, for example the
Canadian Co-operative Association. In some countries, a specialised
agency has been set up to focus on co-operative development, for
example the Swedish Co-operative Centre (SCC), and in other cases,
individual co-operatives undertake their own co-operative development activities, such as Legacoop in Italy.[44] The Fair Trade movement
could join forces with or learn from these agencies, and individual
retail co-operatives, to ensure that support for producer co-operatives
is tailored to their needs.

Interviews conducted for this research highlighted active member
participation, governance and leadership as three interlinked areas
that co-operatives find particularly challenging. Despite their democratic structures, co-operatives often find it hard to engage members in
decisions, especially where literacy levels are low. Organising
members' Annual General Meetings takes time and money. Running
member education campaigns is time-consuming and costly and the
gender balance can be poor, particularly where membership requires
land ownership or where women have household duties that prevent
them from attending meetings. Low levels of education among
members, combined with a cultural tendency to elect powerful
members of a community into prominent positions, can also make
it hard for co-operatives to attain the necessary range of skills among
its board and management and can lead to corruption. These findings
are in line with the experience of the SCC, working with small co-
operatives in Kenya.[45] These factors contribute to the view held by
some interviewees that co-operatives are inefficient.

Many co-operative development agencies run programmes on

member and board training, 'train the trainer' schemes and organisational development skills for leaders. Pollet and Develtere find that when compared to NGOs, co-operative development agencies focus more on technical co-operative and business-related assistance, often drawing on their own experiences as co-operatives.[46] For example, Rabobank Foundation makes expertise on co-operative financial systems available to developing countries, drawing on its own experience as an international financial services provider.[47] The SCC is running a project to support leadership development for managers and board members of co-operatives across several countries, including through exchange studies, peer learning, mentoring, seminars and coaching.[48]

Member training aims to increase members' understanding of how to participate in the voting and decision-making processes of their co-operatives as well as why it is necessary to contribute financially. It can encourage the cultivation of the next generation of board members, helping to overcome the challenge of corrupt and entrenched leaders. It also helps leaders to improve their management and business skills and promote good governance, ensuring that decisions are taken in the best interests of the members.[49]

Co-operative development agencies are also active in promoting the adoption of supportive government policy towards co-operatives.[50] Excessive intervention and control by governments was cited by interviewees as one of the challenges faced by co-operatives, along with excessive bureaucracy. The International Labour Organisation addressed this issue in 2002 with its recommendation 193 *Promotion of Co-operatives*, followed two years later by a guidance pack aiming to help co-operatives and governments to review the co-operative legislation in their countries.[51]

Rural co-operatives often struggle to adopt new technologies, such as IT systems and modern farming equipment, in order to access information on market trends, manage their businesses efficiently and compete in global markets. This can be due to a lack of capital, since co-operatives often find it hard to obtain loans at affordable rates and in most countries are unable to raise capital through issuing shares. Shared Interest is a co-operative lending society that was established specifically to provide affordable loans to Fair Trade businesses, including co-operatives. However, a lack of knowledge and willingness to innovate among management can also hold co-operatives back. The global co-operative movement can help through the provision of affordable loans and through skills share schemes involving staff secondments or training. For example, the Canadian Co-operative

Association provides opportunities for staff from Canadian credit unions to coach or mentor developing country credit unions in a range of skills including management, governance, co-operative legislation and leadership for women.[52]

Due to their location in frequently poor, rural areas, co-operatives often also suffer from a lack of decent infrastructure such as roads and power. This can limit their ability to collect members' produce and get it to market, or to remain competitive. John Kanjagaile, Export Manager at Kagera Co-operative Union explained:

> Some areas are very difficult to reach. The co-op must try to reach the members wherever they are and to give the same price to producers in all areas even though some are harder to reach. This is how the costs and profits are shared. The private man will not go somewhere with bad roads or no bridge. He [the private man] therefore gets cheaper coffee.

The global co-operative movement has national and international apex bodies designed to share skills and experience among their member co-operatives and advocate on their behalf. However, many of these apex bodies have become weak and ineffective. Fair Trade producer networks also now exist in Africa, Latin America and Asia. Since many of their members are co-operatives, they can also play a role in advocating the interests of producer co-operatives, connecting them with relevant agencies and helping them to learn from each other's experiences.

However, if co-operatives are developed without attention to where the products will be sold, a successful development project can fall at the last hurdle. If retail co-operatives link their development work with their trading or Fair Trade activities, the approach becomes much more integrated. The Co-operative Group has taken this approach in their project with tea farmers in Kenya. Working with their tea suppliers, Finlays, and with co-funding from the Department for International Development, they are helping 8,000 smallholder tea farmers to form into five farmer-owned co-operatives. These new co-operatives will then be assisted to become Fairtrade certified and to diversify into other products to reduce their reliance on tea. The Co-operative Group will then sell their tea, and hopefully some of their other products, in its UK stores.[53]

Conclusion

This chapter has highlighted the significant overlaps between the co-operative and Fair Trade movements and how they have historically supported one another's growth and development. However, it has also revealed that there is a lot more that both movements could do to better address the specific needs of producer co-operatives.

Co-operatives need all of the factors necessary for a normal business to flourish, such as market access and good infrastructure. However, co-operatives also face some specific challenges due to their democratic principles, which only work if members are engaged in the running of their business. Furthermore, the fact that co-operatives are frequently established by poor, isolated communities in order to help them to access markets means that they often have to overcome numerous developmental challenges such as education, empowerment and finding sources of capital. Privately owned businesses can avoid these issues by not doing business in areas with such challenges, which is one reason why farmers in those areas establish co-operatives.

Often what is holding producer organisations back is not a lack of capital alone, but a lack of skills and knowledge. The co-operative movement as a whole, and especially larger co-operatives in developed countries, as well as development agencies and Fair Trade organisations, have significant potential to support communities in the formation of co-operatives and in helping existing co-operatives to access new markets and become more efficient. This can be achieved through skills exchange programmes, training, networking and long-term partnerships where the co-operative plays a dominant role in determining its own needs. The co-operative movement is founded on principles of democracy, self-help and balancing member economic and social needs and so it is particularly important that the members are supported in taking ownership of any programme of work. Tallontire argues that Fair Trade needs to be seen not as something that happens to producers (they are not 'beneficiaries'), but something which they are a part of, can shape, and own.[54]

Notes

1 J. Birchall, *Co-op: The People's Business* (Manchester: Manchester University Press, 1994); F. Saenz-Segura and G. Zuniga-Arias, 'Assessment of the Effect of Fair Trade on Smallholder Producers in Costa Rica: A Comparative Study in the Coffee Sector', in R. Ruben (ed.), *The Impact of Fair Trade* (Wageningen: Wageningen Academic Publishers, 2008).

2 P. Develtere and I. Pollet, *Co-operatives and Fair-Trade: Background Paper Commissioned by the Committee for the Promotion and Advancement of Cooperatives (COPAC) for the COPAC Open Forum on Fair Trade and Cooperatives, Berlin* (Geneva: COPAC, 2005).

3   R. Kaplinsky and M. Morris, *A Handbook for Value Chain Research* (Ottowa: IDRC, 2001).

4   L. Shaw (ed.), *Co-operation, Social Responsibility and Fair Trade in Europe* (Manchester: The Co-operative College, 2006).

5   Develtere and Pollet, *Co-operatives and Fair-Trade.*

6   I. Pollet and P. Develtere, *Development Co-operation: How Co-operatives Cope – A Survey of the Major Co-operative Development Agencies* (Leuven: Hilde Talloen, 2004).

7   V. Nelson and B. Pound, *The Last Ten Years: A Comprehensive Review of the Literature on the Impact of Fairtrade* (London: Fairtrade Foundation, 2009).

8   Fairtrade Foundation, 'Awareness of FAIRTRADE Mark leaps to 70%', Press releases and statements, available at www.fairtrade.org.uk /press_office/press_releases_and_statements/may_2008/press_office/press _releases_and_statements/april_2008/press_office/press_releases_and_sta tements/april_2008/awareness_of_fairtrade_mark_leaps_to_70.aspx; The Co-operative Group, *The Ethical Consumerism Report 2008* (Manchester: The Co-operative Group, 2008); Ethical Consumer, 'Market Research reports', available at www.ethicalconsumer.org /CommentAnalysis/marketresearch.aspx#2009.

9   Develtere and Pollet, *Co-operatives and Fair-Trade;* Jones, Shaw, Björnér, Garancini *et al.* in Shaw (ed.) *Co-operation.*

10 A. Nicholls and C. Opal, *Fair Trade: Market-driven Ethical Consumption* (London: SAGE Publications Ltd, 2005).

11 S. Lacey, *Beyond a Fair Price: The Co-operative Movement and Fair Trade* (Manchester: The Co-operative College, 2009).

12 J. Birchall, *Cooperatives and the Millennium Development Goals* (Geneva: ILO, 2004); I. MacPherson, *Co-operative Principles for the 21st Century* (Geneva: ICA, 1996).

13 MacPherson, ibid.

14 P. Develtere, I. Pollet and F.O. Wanyama, *Cooperating Out of Poverty: The Renaissance of the African Cooperative Movement* (Geneva: ILO, 2008).

15 Ibid, p. 282.

16 J. Birchall, *Rediscovering the Cooperative Advantage: Poverty Reduction Through Self-help* (Geneva: ILO, 2003); MacPherson, *Co-operative Principles for the 21st Century*, Pollet and Develtere, *Development Co-operation.*

17 Develtere, Pollet and Wanyama, *Cooperating Out of Poverty*, p. 14.

18 Pollet and Develtere, *Development Co-operation*, p. 15; R. Apthorpe, *Rural Cooperatives and Planned Change in Africa: An Analytical Overview* (Geneva: UNRISD, 1972), R. Apthorpe, *Rural Cooperatives and Planned Change in Africa: Case Materials* (Geneva: UNRISD, 1970).

20 Birchall, *Co-op: The People's Business.*

21 Pollet and Develtere, *Development Co-operation*, pp. 15–17.

22 Saenz-Segura and Zuniga-Arias, 'Assessment of the Effect of Fair Trade'.
23 S. Barrientos and S. Smith, 'Mainstreaming Fair Trade in Global Production Networks: Own Brand Fruit and Chocolate in UK Supermarkets', in L.T. Raynolds, D. Murray and J. Wilkinson (eds), *Fair Trade: The Challenges of Transforming Globalization* (Abingdon: Routledge, 2007); Nicholls and Opal, *Fair Trade*, p. 193.
24 The Co-operative Group, 'Fairtrade History 1992–2001', available at www.co-operative.coop/food/ethics/Ethical-trading/Fairtrade/Our-fairtrade-achievements/#1999.
25 Ibid.
26 Pollet and Develtere, *Development Co-operation*, p. 10; Jones, Shaw, Björnér, Garancini *et al.* in Shaw (ed.) *Co-operation;* Develtere and Pollet, *Co-operatives and Fair-Trade.*
27 Fairtrade Foundation, 'About Fair Trade Towns', available at www.fairtrade.org.uk/get_involved/campaigns/fairtrade_towns/about_fairtrade_towns.aspx.
28 Fairtrade Foundation, 'Facts and Figures on Fairtrade', available at www.fairtrade.org.uk/what_is_fairtrade/facts_and_figures.aspx.
29 Fairtrade Foundation, 'Public Loyalty to Fairtrade in 2009's Tough Economic Climate Leads to Double Digit Growth as Fairtrade Sales Reach £800m', available at www.fairtrade.org.uk/press_office/press_releases_and_statements/february_2010/public_loyalty_to_fairtrade_in_2009s_tough_economic_climate_leads_to_double_digit_growth_as_fairtrade_sales_reach_800m.aspx.
30 Birchall, *Co-op: The People's Business*; D. Reed, 'What Do Corporations Have to do With Fair Trade? Positive and Normative Analysis from a Value Chain Perspective', *Journal of Business Ethics* 86:s1 (2008), 3–26.
31 OCDC, *Cooperatives: Pathways to Economic, Democratic and Social Development in the Global Economy* (Arlington: OCDC, 2007); Develtere, Pollet and Wanyama, *Cooperating Out of Poverty,* p. 25.
32 Nicholls and Opal, *Fair Trade*, p. 27.
33 Barrientos and Smith, 'Mainstreaming Fair Trade', pp. 116–118.
34 Reed, 'What do Corporations Have to do With Fair Trade?'.
35 S. Smith and S. Barrientos, 'Fair Trade and Ethical Trade: Are There Moves Towards Convergence?' *Sustainable Development* 13:3 (2005), 190–193.
36 Ibid.
37 Lacey, *Beyond a Fair Price.*
38 A. Tallontire, 'Top Heavy? Governance Issues and Policy Decisions for the Fair Trade Movement', *Journal of International Development* 21 (2009), 1004–1014.
39 CO-OPAfrica, *Promising Practices: How Cooperatives Work for Working Women in Africa* (Dar es Salaam: CO-OPAfrica, 2008).
40 Ibid.
41 C. Gijselinckx, *Co-operative Stakeholders. Who Counts in Co-operatives, and How?* (Leuven: HIVA, 2009), pp. 1–34.

42 D.J. Spielman, *Mobilizing Rural Institutions for Sustainable Livelihoods and Equitable Development – A Case Study of Farmer Cooperatives in Ethiopia: An Overview* (Washington DC: IFPRI, 2008).
43 Reed, 'What do Corporations Have to do With Fair Trade?'.
44 Pollet and Develtere, *Development Co-operation*.
45 B. Okeyo, *Working With Co-operatives: A View From Kenya* (Manchester: Co-operatives for Development, 2010).
46 Pollet and Develtere, *Development Co-operation*, pp. 39–43.
47 Ibid.
48 Swedish Cooperative Centre (SCC), 'New Study on Leadership Development', available at www.sccportal.org/News-1.aspx?M =News&PID=56&NewsID=3960.
49 G. Warner, *Africa Co-operative Development Agencies Forum Draft Notes: November 20–21, 2008* (Nairobi: Africa Co-operative Development Agencies Forum, 2009); Pollet and Develtere, *Development Co-operation*.
50 Pollet and Develtere, Ibid.
51 International Labour Organization (ILO), *R193 Promotion of Cooperatives Recommendation* (2002), 1–10; S. Smith, *Promoting Co-operatives: A Guide to ILO Recommendation 193* (Manchester: The Co-operative College, 2004).
52 Canadian Co-operative Association (CCA), 'CCA International Programs', available at (2010) www.coopscanada.coop/en/international _dev/CCA_International_Programs.
53 Food Retail Industry Challenge Fund (FRICH), 'Finlays & The Co-operative', available at www.frich.co.uk/default.htm.
54 Tallontire, 'Top Heavy?'.

7

Negotiating consumer and producer interests – a challenge for the Co-operative Movement and Fair Trade

Katarina Friberg

Introduction

Can consumers' interests be successfully combined with workers' rights to achieve a just reward for the goods they produce? Today this question tours the world under the Fair Trade logo and it has become a North–South issue. It concerns topics such as trade or aid, the conditions and effects of free trade, consumer choice, solidarity and workers' possibilities and abilities to organise and demand their rights. However, the question about the possibilities and problems of combining consumer interest and labour rights has intricate historical roots, the exploration of which can shed light on the present. There is a substantial literature on workers' struggles for labour rights, while the study of consumption and consumer society is growing minute by minute. Largely absent from the literature are historical studies focusing on these issues and their intersection. And with a few exceptions, most literature on the role of consumption and consumers in relation to trade and labour rights focuses on the present.[1] Even more uncommon are studies from a co-operative perspective; yet this line of inquiry presents a promising venue for relating the present Fair Trade practice to its historical antecedents.

It is the unfair distribution of resources between the South and the North that activists in the Fair Trade movement generally oppose – an untenable situation established in colonial days and, according to Fair Trade activists, maintained by the unfair world trade system. Apart from trying to politically influence trade politics, Fair Trade activists in practice promote Fair Trade goods. The question of how to bridge the gap between producers in the South and consumers in the North remains central to the Fair Trade movement.[2] Gavin Fridell, scholar and Fair Trade activist, has identified different traditions and ideas of the Fair Trade movement. Summarising the tradition he calls 'Fair Trade as Decommodification', he ventures to give his own suggestion about how to bridge the gap between producers and consumers: 'The only way to truly bridge this gap would be for producers and consumers to engage in a democratic political process in which all are given equal input and equal responsibility for decisions concerning production and distribution.'[3]

But where can consumers and producers engage in such a process? Not in the open market where the only possible link between consumers and producers is a moral one, answers Fridell. Perhaps the state can initiate such a politically regulated democratic process. Fridell, who is critical of the market strategy for social justice, is clearly attracted to a model of democratically controlled state marketing boards with direct links between Northern consumers and Southern producers, resembling what Michael Barratt Brown sketched in his book *Fair Trade* (1993).[4] Neither Fridell nor Barratt Brown search for historic examples where producers and consumers actually have engaged in a democratic political process. Barratt Brown does pay homage to the co-operative movement.[5] However, he does not explore whether and how a democratic political process concerning decisions about production and distribution was established within this movement. This is, however, what we are going to address in this chapter.

The co-operative movement and Fair Trade today

One of the British retail chains selling Fair Trade products today is the Co-operative. Here, the alignment with Fair Trade has taken on special significance. The sale and promotion of Fair Trade products has become part of the Co-operative's efforts to signal a co-operative identity. They wish to show that the Co-operative is no ordinary store, and that the ethical dimension is an important element in co-operative campaigns. The following statement from the Co-operative Group can serve as an illustration: 'It matters to our members that we are an ethical business. It always has. We have been trading since 1863 when the North of England Co-operative Wholesale Industrial and Provident Society came into being – run by members for members, selling good quality products at *a fair price*. And we've carried on ever since' (italics added).[6]

What is suggested here is that the sale of Fair Trade goods today fits nicely into a co-operative practice with roots in the mid-nineteenth century. Yet taken as a historical claim, this promotional message does not stand up to scrutiny. Matthew Anderson's study 'Cost of a cup of tea' demonstrates that British co-operation, as represented by the Co-operative Wholesale Society (CWS) and its involvement in the tea trade and in tea production, could not live up to the expectations of an ethical business.[7] What Anderson describes simply was not ethical business in the sense of Fair Trade today. The search for the roots of the Fair Trade movement had better start elsewhere. In a different sense, however, the promotional message may not be wide of the mark.

In the previous quote, the Co-operative Group states that it has always been an ethical business 'selling good quality products at a fair price'. The relevant question to ask is: Fair to whom? In the context of the Fair Trade movement of today, fairness means being fair to the producer in terms of a just reward and labour rights, and being fair to the consumer in terms of information about the origin of the product. This, however, is but one way to construe the parties, their respective entitlements and the notion of fairness. And co-operators have long had to grapple with issues of fairness – with the equitable distribution of resources – in the movement's own parlance.

Throughout the movement's history, co-operators have discussed and debated the most equitable distribution of control and surplus between those who invest in a co-operative business, those who produce the goods and those who purchase them. Within the co-operative movement, the idea of what is fair, and to whom it should be fair, changes over time and varies between different organisational levels and different countries. Yet in all this flux, the recurrent preoccupation with fairness is a common element.

In the context of this chapter, both the variation and the common element are of interest. If co-operators are repeatedly involved in the practice of negotiating fairness, then their historical experiences may be studied as antecedents of the Fair Trade movement and its predicament. By studying the history of co-operation as the antecedents rather than the roots of the Fair Trade movement we can identify structurally similar problems and thereby shed light on the present. In addition, the historical change and geographical variation that we find in the negotiation of fairness within the co-operative movement is a rich source of insights about such problems.

I will argue that these changes – at least in the formative years of the co-operative movement – have depended a great deal upon the relationship between producer and consumer interests within specific co-operative organisations and within the wider movement. To explore this, we shall first examine attempts to set up an alternative market for the distribution of co-operatively produced goods in England in the 1830s. Secondly, we examine the relationship between co-operative retail societies, co-operative wholesale societies and co-operative producer societies in Britain in the second half of the nineteenth century and in Sweden in the early twentieth century.

An alternative co-operative market – experiments in 1830s England

Those engaged in co-operative ventures in the 1820s and 1830s wished to use the means of co-operation to achieve other ends, such as Owenite or non-conformist communities. This implied two things: first, that co-operation was seen as a method; second, that co-operation became closely connected with the ideas of Robert Owen, or with religious groups.[8] There were exceptions to this rule, but the ideological package that came with Owenism had a significant influence upon the development of co-operation and the co-operative movement in Britain well into the second half of the nineteenth century. Its most important, but today somewhat forgotten, legacy was the understanding of production as the essence of social relations and society making.[9]

Production was the hub of Owen's plans for a new society in which all existing social arrangements that had previously produced sectional interests would be replaced by federations of mixed agricultural and industrial villages. He wanted to replace the profit motive with the fruits of co-operation, and the vices of individualism with mutuality.[10] Owen turned to people as producers, workers as well as employers, when he presented his ideas. As long as Owen's plans were drawn up for and tested in self-sufficient communities, the focus on production and on producers/workers was not problematic. That is not to say that establishing and developing these communities was uncomplicated – far from it – but all problems that arose could and had to be dealt with by the members of the community and supportive organisations.[11] Once co-operators began to manufacture goods for sale to other co-operative societies or for the market in general, they faced legal restrictions and distribution difficulties that were challenging in a different manner. In the 1830s, co-operative societies registered under the Friendly Societies Act could only trade with members, thus limiting co-operative retail trade and making manufacturing ventures almost impossible. The federations of agricultural and industrial villages that Owen proposed could have been a solution, but only if co-operatives were prepared to work without legal protection. Co-operatives could not legally form federal trading societies until the Industrial and Provident Act was revised in 1862.[12] Thus, other solutions had to be found. At this juncture the British Association for Promoting Co-operative Knowledge introduced labour exchanges.

When the element of exchange appeared it became obvious that the Owenite conceptual framework was restricted. It was developed for co-operation in co-operative communities. Moreover, while the community idea was very much alive in the 1830s, the new co-operative practices and organisations demanded a new conceptual framework. It was not as if Owen and the members of the British Association for Promoting Co-operative Knowledge lacked visions for the labour exchanges.[13] The problem lay elsewhere and was related to the inclination of the founders of the labour exchanges to hold on to their understanding of production as the essence of social relations and society making. The grand plan was to create an alternative market based on the idea that products be exchanged according to the labour embodied in them.[14] The depositors of goods were members and they could display their goods for sale/exchange without any middlemen. With such an exchange, the enthusiasts thought that it was possible to get rid of the profit motive. This was in line both with Owen's ideas for co-operative communities and with 'the craftsman's sense of custom and a fair price'.[15] The flaw in this plan, as we shall see, was the proponents' lack of insight into the sphere of consumption: the exchange and distribution of goods and their implications for the relation between depositors (producers) and purchasers (consumers).

Equitable Labour Exchanges were founded in 1832 and 1833 in Birmingham and London.[16] The National Labour Exchange that opened in Gray's Inn Road, London, was not only a place for trade with co-operatively produced goods, it was also an Owenite branch and a multi-purpose institution for members of the movement: not unlike the world shops of the 1970s, where the exchange of goods was embedded in a social, cultural and political context. Festivals, lectures, dancing, discussions, general socialising and tea parties had the function of preparing members for a community life in friendship and brotherly love. Nevertheless, life at the Owenite institution in Gray's Inn Road was not life in a self-sufficient co-operative community, and the effects of 'the irrational system of competition and contest' became manifest when goods were priced at the Labour Exchange.[17]

Those in charge of the exchanges had ideas about what they should be like, but in reality, it was difficult to challenge or even evade the system of market competition. Since it was an exchange, the ideal situation would be if the depositors of goods found products they themselves needed at the exchange. This, however, was not always the case, and the administrators of the exchange had to set a price with a more open market in mind. Owen apparently did not think that persons coming to the exchange to buy goods had any ethical considerations, as is evident from the following reply to a displeased depositor. Owen said:

> our answer is the following explanation, which has been repeated a thousand times to the depositors who are misled by the notion of 6*d*. an hour for labour and the cost price of materials. The 6*d*. per hour is merely nominal, and is put to assist calculations ... What regulates our real valuation of articles is the lowest market price out of doors ... Every person goes to the cheapest market. Except we are as cheap as others nobody will come near us; and if nobody come near us to take goods away, it will be to no purpose for depositors to bring them.[18]

'Every person goes to the cheapest market': he stated this even though he must have known that some buyers at the labour exchange were supporters of a market where products were exchanged according to the labour embodied in them. Apparently, however, the members of the British Association for Promoting Co-operative Knowledge, and Owen in particular, did not consider the existence of a conscientious consumer. They established a market for co-operatively produced goods with little or no consideration for the practice of distribution. Accounts of the labour exchanges reveal that their experience in the field of distribution was poor. Socially and culturally, the Owenite clubs and the labour exchanges might have been successful. However, when it came to equitable distribution and the establishment of a viable alternative market they were not.

There are some similarities between the labour exchanges and the alternative market for Fair Trade goods established in the 1960s and 1970s. Both had limited experience of the distributive sector.[19] The Owenites were, and the Fair Trade activists are enthusiasts for an idea of a socially and economically more just society (world). However, they both focus on the interests of producers. One major difference though is that the founders of world shops in the 1960s and 1970s had a tremendous faith in conscientious consumers. Fair Trade activists still have. Another difference is that world shops are not exchanges and producers and consumers are separated in space, although the activists, the shops and the products are meant to bridge the gap between producers in the South and consumers in the North. And like the labour exchanges, the world shops provide a social setting for alternative ideas about the rules of the market; but they do not provide a setting for Fridell's ideal of a 'democratic political process in which all are given equal input and equal responsibility for decisions concerning production and distribution'. Let us see if the co-operative market established in mid-nineteenth-century Britain and early twentieth-century Sweden invited producers and consumers into such a democratic political process.

A co-operative market and inter-co-operative relations

Distribution of co-operative produced goods continued to be a challenge in mid-nineteenth-century Britain. However, new legislation facilitating the growth of retail societies and of the co-operative movement as a whole improved the situation. Already in 1834, legislative changes had granted co-operative societies legal protection of their funds and properties. The introduction of a frugal investment clause in the legislation for friendly societies in 1846 gave co-operative societies a legal incentive to promote their members' present social and economic situation, which they did by distributing goods, providing education, arranging social gatherings and introducing saving schemes.[20] The focus on present predicaments did not prevent them from raising funds for co-operative communities as in the Owenite days, but it certainly gave new emphasis to the interests of members as consumers. The dividend on purchase, introduced in the 1840s, was a visible sign of the equitable distribution of resources to members as consumers. This kind of reimbursement distinguished co-operative societies from other enterprises. It demonstrated that the co-operative societies did not accumulate resources for the benefit of the few, but created values in terms of services and savings for all members. The retail element of co-operative societies became popular and people joined these societies in their capacity as consumers. Co-operators did not give up on production, but legislative obstacles continued to inhibit the development of co-operative production.[21] What was new and important for the argument in this text is that co-operators in the mid-nineteenth century tried to create a business model that would incorporate both the interest of members as producers and members as consumers.

Changes in the Industrial and Provident Societies Act in 1862 granted co-operative societies limited liability, which improved the situation considerably for distribution as well as production.[22] Legal restraints on the development of a co-operative market were gone but it was up to co-operators themselves to develop one. Negotiations between consumers and producers took place in this market through the medium of retail societies and producer societies. It is important however to remember that these consumers and producers, in their capacity as members of co-operative societies, were not so much representing consumer and producer interests in general; they were – at least to start with – trying to find the best means of furthering co-operation and creating a co-operative commonwealth.

We start our exploration of the co-operative market in mid-nineteenth-century northern England. In that place and time enthusiasts for co-operation had much more experience of distribution than the promoters of the labour exchanges in the 1830s. Additionally they worked within a much more competitive environment forcing them to adapt and invent strategies of distribution and marketing.[23] By the mid-nineteenth century, leaders and members of co-operative societies had realised the potential of co-operative distribution and they sought ideas and practical solutions for how to combine co-operative production and distribution of goods. In the 1860s, three forms of co-operative production existed. Firstly, production in co-operative producer societies – where those who produced the goods owned and controlled the society. Secondly, production initiated by retail societies – often flour mills or bakeries – where the workers were employees and where members as consumers owned and controlled the enterprise. And thirdly, a hybrid: after 1862, when retail societies could invest capital in producer co-operatives, members of retail societies ended up as representatives on the committee of the producer society. This resulted in a situation where consumer and producer interests had to be balanced at committee meetings of producer co-operatives.[24] Producer societies benefited from the knowledge that the representatives from retail societies had about the local and regional market and they benefited from the custom of the retail societies.[25] Here we have a forum with 'a democratic political process ... for decisions concerning production and distribution', that is, as long as an appropriate balance between representatives from the retail societies and the producer society was maintained.

Co-operative retail societies could manage without goods produced by producer co-operatives.[26] However, for co-operators concerned with the advancement of the co-operative movement, trading within the movement was very important. Co-operators in Amble in Northumberland in the 1890s even had the ambition to keep the whole of their trade within the movement.[27] Nevertheless, in the 1890s that ambition could not have meant buying goods exclusively from producer co-operatives. The producer co-operatives, about a hundred at the time, did not produce all the different kinds of products that the members of retail societies required.[28] If the Amble Society and other societies wished to conduct the whole of their trade within the movement, they had to rely on and try to influence the activities of their own wholesale society. This federal society was formed in 1863 to gain co-operative control of yet another link in the commodity chain and to make sure co-operative capital served the interest of co-operators. From the first prospectus of the North of England Co-operative Wholesale Society, from 1872 known as the Co-operative Wholesale Society (CWS), we learn that: 'The object of the society is to bring the producer and the consumer of commodities nearer to each other, and thus secure for the working classes those profits that have hitherto enriched only the individual.'[29]

The CWS quickly proved beneficial for its retail society members. However, the wholesale society still had difficulties in getting retail societies to trade exclusively with them. Many societies held on to the contracts they had with local non-co-operative wholesalers and claimed that they received a better deal for members through those channels.[30] More retail societies eventually joined the wholesale, and their trade with this society increased when the CWS could offer a wider range of products, good quality and a low price.[31] But did the wholesale society support production in producer co-operatives? It did act as agent for several producer co-operatives in the 1860s, 1870s and 1880s and bought shares in such societies.[32] Like many of its member retail societies, the representatives of the CWS also worked for the progress of the co-operative movement, and in the 1860s and 1870s, the development of producer co-operatives was seen as part of the general progress of co-operation.[33] However, investments in production co-operatives were risky since many societies failed to repay the loans and in 1881 it was proposed at the General Quarterly Meeting of the CWS to set aside £32,000 to write off all these debts.[34] The CWS bought a wide range of products from the producer co-operatives. Societies selling hosiery, cloth and clothing or shoes received the largest orders. Towards the end of the nineteenth century, the orders from agricultural societies increased. The CWS then bought raw materials for their own factories.[35] About this time, the CWS had also started to import produce from agricultural co-operatives abroad.[36]

But how much did the CWS buy from the producer co-operative societies (agricultural societies excluded)? If we take the figure of goods purchased under payments (£24,499,200) and compare it to the total amount of goods purchased from productive societies (£54,111), we find that in 1897 these purchases made up only 0.22%. The total amount purchased from productive societies other than the CWS itself increased over the years, but it never reached 1% of CWS purchases.[37]

From the beginning of the twentieth century the CWS's own production of goods increased considerably, and for most customers in Co-operative stores co-operatively produced goods were marked with the CWS label.[38] Besides promising good value for money, the CWS label claimed to signal good working conditions, a regular wage at trade union rate, paid holiday and assurance of a sufficient pension for employees in the CWS factories in Britain.[39] Thus, from the mid 1870s onwards, customers in co-operative stores could choose between two different kinds of co-operatively produced goods: those produced by a producer co-operative and those produced by the CWS. These different products represented two different co-operative ideals of production. 'Equity', a brand of high quality boots for men produced by the Leicester Manufacturing Boot and Shoe Society, represented a self-governing co-operative producer ideal.[40] Boots manufactured in the CWS factories in Leicester represented a co-operative consumer ideal stating that consumers rather than producers should own and control the means of production. The consumer co-operative ideal of co-operative production that Percy Redfern promoted as the consumer theory of co-operation in the 1920s was a vision quite contrary to that of Robert Owen's self-sufficient communities of producers.[41] The introduction of the consumer theory of co-operation was the culmination of an intense debate about the different ideals of co-operative production.[42]

Now let us turn to our Swedish case. We do this in order to gain some comparative insight into how the organisation of local and federal co-operative societies affected the relation between consumer and producer interests within the co-operative movement. Once we have learned about the differences and similarities in how British and Swedish co-operators organised their societies and made decisions on production and distribution, we are better qualified to compare the co-operative strategies for equitable distribution of resources with different ideals/strategies for Fair Trade today.

In Sweden, proponents of producer co-operation had a difficult time. Those supporting this form of co-operation could of course refer to old Swedish traditions of co-operative enterprises like those of stonecutters and fishermen in Bohuslän.[43] But Owenism as a social (r)evolutionary force did not reach the shores of Sweden, and the teachings of Schulze-Delitzsch had no major influence on craftsmen's ambitions to organise themselves.[44] In addition, there was no influential group of supporters, only a handful of middle-class promoters of co-partnership and profit-sharing who entered the leading circles of the Swedish co-operative movement.[45] Nevertheless, British co-operative ideas and the German co-operative legal framework had a significant influence on the development of consumer co-operation in Sweden. For it was as consumer co-operation that the modern co-operative movement was introduced in Sweden in the mid-nineteenth century.[46] Later, at the beginning of the twentieth century, farmers in Sweden initiated what eventually became a successful agricultural co-operative movement, but producer co-operatives owned by craftsmen and industrial workers never fared very well, and were more or less forgotten in terms of legislation.[47] What about recognition of producer co-operatives in co-operative circles then? Representatives from all kinds of co-operative societies were invited to the inaugural meeting of Kooperativa Förbundet (KF), the Swedish co-operative union, in 1899. A couple of producer co-operatives came to this meeting and joined the union, but ten years later the retail societies outnumbered them by far. In 1909, KF had 367 retail societies, 8 workers' producer societies, 4 co-operative restaurants/cafés and 6 production co-operatives owned by retail societies as members.[48] Thus, to what extent was the interest of producers/workers considered in the Swedish co-operative context? Were there any opportunities for negotiations between consumers and producers in a democratic process?

In Britain we saw that members of retail societies and members of producer societies met to discuss the terms of production and distribution in the producer societies where retail societies had invested capital. Similar kinds of societies in Sweden are hard to find, although some societies with a mixed membership, that is, members as producers and consumers, existed. One such example is the co-operative bakery society Solidar. This society was initiated by bakers in 1907, but consumers were soon invited to become members. Issues concerning the range of products, or whether the society should rent or buy a bakery, did not divide the membership into one producer and one consumer group. However, issues concerning management did. Little by little, the balance between producer interest and consumer interest tipped over to the advantage of the latter. The employment of a combined Secretary and General Manager of the society reduced the influence of the bakery workers. Finally, in 1914, demands from the Swedish Co-operative Union forced the society to choose whether they should remain a mixed society or turn into a consumer co-operative one. They chose the latter.[49] Thus was ended a democratic political process where producers and consumers had equal input and equal responsibility for decisions concerning production and distribution.

Solidar is an example of negotiations between producers and consumers taking place within a society. But what about a Swedish co-operative market? To find out more about this we have to return to the federal level. Already at the inaugural meeting of KF in 1899, it was suggested that KF should be organised as a combined union and wholesale.[50] However, it was not until 1904 that KF's wholesale operation took off.[51] The argument for a combined union and wholesale was that such an organisation would be able to concentrate the co-operative strength, reduce the number of middlemen and safeguard co-operative resources within the co-operative movement. Did this argument reflect the interest of representatives of retail societies and producer societies? Did anyone speak for the particular interests of the latter?

Martin Sundell, Secretary of KF and editor of the co-operative paper *Kooperatören* between 1905 and 1910, was a promoter of producer co-operatives. He advocated co-operation between different kinds of co-operatives. In his proposal for a Swedish co-operative programme in 1906 Sundell included producer co-operatives in the main text. However, when he summed up co-operative business principles, they all related to co-operative retail trade.[52] An alternative proposal for a programme was put forward. This alternative proposal focused on co-operative production and producer co-operatives. One signatory, 'P-on' (identity unknown), who had signed the proposal, suggests that trade unions and all organised workers should form production co-operatives. The goods they produced would be distributed by retail societies and all parties involved would share the surplus.[53] Neither Sundell's programme nor P-on's proposal were adopted at the KF congress in 1906. It did agree a proposal that KF should, when enough capital had been raised, commence the production of goods that the retail societies demanded. Such a measure, however, would take a long time to execute, and Sundell thought it wise that KF and the retail societies in the meantime established good contacts with the existing producer co-operatives.[54] Thus, what kinds of contacts were established between KF and co-operative producer societies?

KF was both union and wholesale, and at times, it seems as if it was difficult for KF representatives to handle this situation. When dealing with producer co-operatives KF could act as their representative, that is, if the producer co-operative was a member of the union. However, KF was also a potential buyer of products from these producer co-operatives. KF's published accounts are not as detailed as those of the CWS. Nevertheless, by looking at motions from KF congresses, KF board reports and the congress delegates' responses it is possible to discern KF's trade policy and find some decisions regarding trade practice. One such instance concerns Fram ('Forward') in Gävle, a producer co-operative manufacturing cigarettes and cigars. In 1909, the board of KF decided to distribute no other cigars than those from Fram.[55] It was Sundell who prepared the ground for this decision. Since 1905, he had published articles and advertisements in Kooperatören encouraging retail societies to buy goods from Fram.[56] Thus, KF could buy goods from producer societies and assist them with marketing. Another example of marketing is KF's support for a shirt and dressmaking co-operative called Linnéa. At the KF congress in 1907, representatives from Linnéa urged the co-operative retail societies to buy only co-operatively produced goods. They guaranteed that their goods were of good quality and that no sweated labour had been involved in their production. The board of KF supported their appeal.[57] Two years later, the board of KF urged all retail societies to buy goods from Linnéa.[58]

A third role as mediator was sometimes allocated to KF. In 1908 KF acted as mediator in a conflict between Linnéa and a retail society called Thule. Members of Linnéa did not think that Thule bought enough garments from them. At a meeting of the executive committee of KF, representatives from Linnéa and representatives from Thule each presented their case. The representatives from Thule declared that it was difficult to stay true to principles and idealism in the everyday toil behind the counter. To buy more goods from Linnéa was an act of idealism according to them.[59] The members of Linnéa expected co-operators to appreciate and support their mode of production – a producer-owned and controlled mode of production. Since Linnéa had been formed as a protest against bad working conditions and low wages, they would of course not compete for trade by applying any of the practices connected with sweated labour. Thule probably appreciated Linnéa's products and mode of production, but their first priority was to attract more people to trade with them and become members. They felt obliged to have competitive prices and were apparently not prepared to market garments from Linnéa in any particular way. To put it in Fair Trade terms: Thule was not prepared to promote co-operatively produced 'Fair Trade' goods and explain why these cost more than other products. Thule and other retail societies would buy co-operatively produced goods, but in most cases, they expected these products to cost no more, and preferably less, than other equivalent products.[60] Representatives from KF could not easily solve this dilemma.

From the very start of KF it is possible to see that representatives of this organisation wished to create a co-operative market – a market where KF as the co-operative wholesale society distributed co-operatively produced goods to co-operative retail societies.[61] However, co-operatively produced goods need not be produced by producer co-operatives.[62] The KF congress in 1906 supported the proposal that KF begin production as soon as enough capital had been raised.[63] This kind of production, owned and controlled by KF, could benefit from economies of scale. The savings that large-scale production and a reliable market (the retail societies) gave, meant that KF could guarantee that workers, as employees, received a proper wage and good working conditions, while at the same time KF could offer high quality and low price goods to the retail societies. KF commenced production in 1921 when it had completed the building of a margarine factory in Norrköping.[64]

The voice of producer societies within KF was never particularly strong and in 1914 the KF congress decided that only consumer co-operative societies, i.e. retail and insurance societies, would be allowed as new members of KF.[65] Martin Sundell, the champion of producer co-operatives and co-operation between different kinds of co-operatives, died in 1910. It seems as if KF from the mid 1910s no longer had the potential to become a forum for a democratic (political) process where consumers and producers had an 'equal input and equal responsibility for decisions concerning production and distribution'. But then KF had never had any official ambition to bring producers and consumers nearer to each other. As a union, its aim was to encourage more people to join the co-operative movement and to assist its member organisations with legal advice and economic education. As a wholesaler it aimed at reducing the number of middlemen between consumers and producers. Sundell and some of his fellow co-operators had seen co-operation between producer co-operatives, retail societies and KF as a means to reach that aim. But Anders Örne, Sundell's successor as editor of Kooperatören and leading co-operative figure, as well as a majority of KF's members, believed in production owned and controlled by KF as a means of reducing the number of middlemen and building a strong co-operative economy.[66]

Past co-operative strategies and Fair Trade today

From the history explored in this chapter we learn that, like Fair Trade activists, co-operators have tried to create a market with its own set of rules. Co-operators tried different strategies in order to create a co-operative economy and to evade 'the irrational system of competition and contest' as Robert Owen put it. Individual ventures have not succeeded in the way they were intended but the underlying values have survived and travelled in space and time. Looking at the examples of co-operative strategies in the text and comparing them with Fair Trade strategies from the 1970s and onwards we find that both have difficulties in finding a balance between producer and consumer interests. The advantage for the co-operators, however, was their ambition to support a co-operative movement and not, at least not in theory, exclusively benefit consumer or producer interests. The challenge was to find practical working arrangements for this. The creation of a co-operative market in mid-nineteenth-century Britain, and early twentieth-century Sweden, and the mixed co-operative societies, are the best examples of such practical working arrangements. The main difference between the two is the fact that the process was more prolonged in Britain and that the fragmented co-operative organisational landscape in Britain implied a better opportunity for producer co-operatives and the establishment of a producer co-operative ideal. When co-operative ideas started to gain influence in Sweden in the 1880s and 1890s British co-operators with several decades of co-operative experience debated which way to go; to ride on the success of consumer co-operative control and ownership of production, to form a co-partnership between consumers and producers, or to leave production to the producer and agricultural co-operatives.[67] The success of consumer co-operation in Britain inspired many co-operators in Sweden and in particular those instrumental in the formation of a Swedish Co-operative Union. There was never any real chance for producer co-operatives to gain ground in Sweden. And the fact that KF turned into a pure consumer co-operative union in 1914 did not benefit the few producer co-operatives that were members and had trading agreements with KF.

It is of course possible for a consumer movement to act in the interests of producers. Fighting for greater access to the world of goods can, as Matthew Hilton has shown, imply a concern also for those producing the products.[68] The consumer co-operative movement is one example, although in both Britain and Sweden the strategy of KF and the CWS to start their own factories implied that negotiations with producers as members of producer co-operatives soon turned into meetings with employees and trade union representatives.[69]

So what insights can the British and Swedish co-operative experiences, together with the debate over who should control and own production, give those interested in Fair Trade today? The question of ownership and control is of course pivotal for producers engaged in the Fair Trade network today. A significant number of producer co-operatives currently produce Fair Trade goods. Their members appreciate what a co-operative economy can imply, at least from a producer perspective.[70] On the other side of the supply chain we have the consumers buying Fair Trade goods: they can be members of consumer co-operatives but their purchase of Fair Trade goods is not linked to their membership. There is a gap between producers of Fair Trade goods and consumers that is difficult but not impossible to overcome. Co-operative organisations like the Co-operative Group can take and have taken steps towards more formal links with producer co-operatives, which will entail consumer co-operative investments and involvement in producer co-operative ventures.[71] In dealing with these new constellations of co-operation it would be wise to return to the debates about mixed consumer and producer co-operative societies of the past.

Notes

1 For exceptions see: F. Trentmann, *Free Trade Nation: Commerce, Consumption, and Civil Society in Modern Britain* (Oxford: Oxford Univeristy Press, 2008); M. Daunton and M. Hilton (eds), *The Politics of Consumption: Material Culture and Citizenship in Europe and North America* (Oxford: Berg, 2001); L.R.Y. Storrs, *Civilizing Capitalism: The National Consumer League, Women's Activism and Labor Standards in the New Deal Era* (Chapel Hill: University of North Carolina Press, 2000).

2 See e.g. M. Barratt Brown, *Fair Trade: Reform and Realities in the International Trading System* (London and New Jersey: Zed Books, 1993); H. Rignell, *Rättvis handel: Rörelse i rätt riktning?* (Göteborg: Världsbutikerna för rättvis handel, 2002).

3 G. Fridell, *Fair Trade Coffee: The Prospects and Pitfalls of Market-Driven Social Justice* (Toronto: University of Toronto Press, 2007) p. 282.

4 Fridell, *Fair Trade Coffee*, pp. 42–44; Barratt Brown, *Fair Trade*.

5 Barratt Brown, *Fair Trade*, pp. 184–187.

6 *We Are Britain's Most Ethical Brand. The Co-operative Little Book of Facts* (Manchester: Co-operative Brands Ltd, 2007).

7 M. Anderson, '"Cost of a Cup of Tea": Fair Trade and the British Co-operative Movement *c.* 1960–2000', in L. Black and N. Robertson (eds), *Consumerism and the Co-operative Movement in Modern British History: Taking Stock* (Manchester: Manchester University Press, 2009).

8 S. Pollard and J. Salt (eds), *Robert Owen, Prophet of the Poor: Essays in Honour of the Two Hundredth Anniversary of his Birth* (London: Macmillan, 1971); Mick Reed, '"The Lord Does Combination Love": Religion and Co-operation Amongst a Peculiar People', in S. Yeo (ed.), *New Views on Co-operation* (London: Routledge, 1988).

9 Discussing the legacy of Owen in connection with the lives and work of artisans, E.P. Thompson emphasised the idea of production as the essence of social relations and society-making. E.P. Thompson, *The Making of the English Working Class* (London: Penguin Books, 1991/1963); see also R. Bickley and M. Scott Cato (eds), *New Views of Society: Robert Owen for the 21st century* (Biggar: Scottish Left Review Press, 2008).

10 Thompson, *The Making*, pp. 858–867; see also E. Royle, *Robert Owen and the Commencement of the Millennium: A Study of the Harmony Community* (Manchester and New York: Manchester University Press, 1998).

11 Royle, *Robert Owen*.

12 P.H.J.H. Gosden, *Self-Help: Voluntary Associations in Nineteenth-century Britain* (London: Batsford, 1973), pp. 190–194; B. Jones, *Co-operative Production* (New York: August M Kelley Publishers, 1968/1894), p. 87.

13 M. Scott Cato, 'Emancipation from Monetary Exploitation: Owen's Vision in Practice Around The World Today', in Bickley and Scott Cato, *New Views of Society*.

14 Cf. notice in Owen's paper *The Crisis*, quoted in Jones, *Co-operative Production*, p. 89.

15 Thompson, *The Making*, p. 869.

16 Jones, *Co-operative Production*, pp. 87–95.

17 E. Yeo, 'Owen and the Radical Culture', in Pollard and Salt, *Robert Owen: Prophet of the Poor*, pp.86–7.

18 Extract from the paper *The Crisis* in Jones, *Co-operative Production*, p. 92.

19 The World Shops and other alternative distribution centres of the Fair Trade network with roots in the 1940s were managed by activists. Southern producers interested in selling their products in the 'real markets' initiated the process that eventually led to the establishment of fair trade labelling. See Fridell, *Fair Trade Coffee*, pp. 39–63; For a discussion of the dispute between Fair Trade activists about the most efficient way to establish Fair Trade see D. Kleine, 'How Fair is Fair Enough? Negotiating Alterity and Compromise Within the German Fair Trade Movement', paper presented at RGS-IBG Annual Conference 2006, London.

20 For details on the 'frugal investment clause' in the Friendly Societies Act of 1846 see Gosden, *Self-Help*, p.191.

21 Societies registered under the Friendly Societies Act of 1846 could sell goods to members only. This was a severe restraint on co-operatives formed for the purpose of production and sale of co-operatively produced goods. See Jones, *Co-operative Production*, p. 87. It also imposed some limitations upon retail societies producing goods for their members. Some had difficulties selling by-products from their production such as flour. Promoters of co-operative production, co-partnerships and profit-sharing,

many of them organised as Christian Socialists, were much engaged in the introduction of a proper legal framework for co-operative societies. Their efforts led to the Industrial and Provident Societies Act of 1852 that permitted co-operative societies to carry on or exercise 'in common any labour, trade, or handicraft, or several labours, trades, or handicrafts with the exception of mining, quarrying and banking.' See Gosden, *Self-Help*, pp. 192–193.

22 Gosden, *Self-Help*, pp. 192–193.
23 D. Hodson, '"The Municipal Store": Adaption and Development in the Retail Markets of Nineteenth Century Industrial Lancashire', *Business History* 40:4 (1998), 94–114; M. Winstanley, *The Shopkeeper's World 1830–1914* (Manchester: Manchester University Press, 1983).
24 B. Lancaster, *Radicalism, Cooperation and Socialism: Leicester Working-Class politics 1860–1906* (Leicester: Leicester University Press, 1987), pp. 136–139. See also G.D.H. Cole, *A Century of Co-operation* (London: George Allen & Unwin Ltd, 1947), pp. 163–165 on the Ouseburn Iron Works and the Industrial Bank; A. Mann, 'Co-operative Production From the Labour Co-partnership Standpoint', paper read at a Conference arranged by the Co-partnership Educational Committee at Hebden Bridge, 23 September 1911. Mann gives a few examples of co-operative co-partnership enterprises that began production in the second half of the nineteenth century and where consumers and workers shared ownership and control.
25 Lancaster, *Radicalism, Cooperation*, p.138–139.
26 Martin Purvis, 'Stocking the Store: Co-operative Retailers in North East England and Systems of Wholesale Supply, circa 1860–77', in N. Alexander and G. Akehurst (eds), *The Emergence of Modern Retailing, 1750–1950* (London and Portland: Frank Cass, 1999).
27 Letter from Ed Foreman, Secretary of the Amble Co-operative Society Limited to Keighling [*sic*] Iron Workers Society, October 19th 1897, in Letter Book NRO. 361/18 21 April 1897–25 July 1906, Northumberland Record Office.
28 The producer co-operatives had a peak in the 1890s and at the turn of the nineteenth century. The statistics before 1920 are not very reliable but figures from Congress Reports, the *Co-operative Union*, *Labour Co-partnership Association* and *Co-operative Productive Federation* all indicate that a little over 100 producer co-operatives were active in Wales, England and Scotland in the mid-1890s; D.C. Jones, 'British Producer Cooperatives and the Views of the Webbs on Participation and Ability to Survive', *Annals of Public and Co-operative Economics* 46:1 (1975), 26 and 28.
29 Quoted in Jones, *Co-operative Production*, p. 218.
30 Purvis, 'Stocking the Store'.
31 P. Redfern, *The Story of the CWS 1863–1913* (Manchester: The Co-operative Wholesale Society Ltd, 1913).

32 Ibid., pp.182–183.
33 Jones, *Co-operative Production*, pp. 402–415.
34 Minutes of General Quarterly Meeting, Manchester, 18 June 1881, Minutes of General Committee of CWS, Vol. 6, pp. 143–144.
35 In the Balance Sheets of the *CWS* – available from 1897 and onwards – it is possible to see in detail what the wholesale bought from producer co-operatives up until the 1940s. The balance sheets towards the end of the 1940s change design and there is no longer a separate account of what goods are bought, or from where. This observation is based on a study of the CWS balance sheets every tenth year starting in 1897. For information on the kind of products the CWS bought see *CWS Balance Sheets* 1897 to 1937.
36 H. Kaufmann, 'The Direct Exchange of Goods between Distributive Societies, Agricultural and other Productive Societies, Also Between the Wholesale Societies in Different Countries', paper presented at the 1913 Congress of the International Co-operative Alliance, Glasgow, p. 69.
37 *CWS Balance Sheets* 1897 to 1937.
38 The total sales of the CWS for the 13 weeks ended 10 April 1937 amounted to £27,745,796. Supplies from the CWS's own factories during the same time reached the figure of £9,971,016.
39 J. Birchall, *Co-op: The People's Business* (Manchester: Manchester University Press, 1994), pp. 132–133; undoubtedly, several CWS policies promoted labour rights and in the *Wheatsheaf* and the *Co-operative News* advertisements for CWS products at times used the promotion of labour rights as a sales argument. However, these promises were not always fulfilled. In 1973 the Board of the Co-operative Tea Society (controlled by the CWS and its sister organisation the Scottish CWS) resolved to compensate the oldest pensioners who still had not received the promised amount of pension. See Minutes of Board Meeting, 9th May 1973, in *Minutes of the Co-operative Tea Society Limited*. For more on the relation between CWS and employees see N. Robertson, *The Co-operative Movement and Communities in Britain 1914–1960* (Farnham: Ashgate, 2010); J.B. Southern, *The Co-operative Movement in the North West of England, 1919–1939: Images and Realities* (PhD dissertation, Lancaster University, 1996).
40 The Leicester Manufacturing Boot and Shoe Society called Equity was formed in 1887 by a large group of former employees from the CWS boot and shoe factory in Leicester. See E. O. Greening, *A Pioneer Co-partnership: Being the History of the Leicester Co-operative Boot and Shoe Manufacturing Society Ltd* (London: Labour Co-partnership Association, 1923).
41 P. Redfern, *The Consumers' Place in Society* (Manchester: Co-operative Union Ltd, 1920), p. 39.
42 See The National Co-operative Archive, Co-operative Productive Federation, Labour Association & Labour Co-partnership Association,

and Co-operative Co-partnership Propaganda Committee Collection. This is a collection of pamphlets and books on the issue of co-operative production, which illustrates the diversity of arguments and also the division into three camps (consumer, producer and consumer-producer).

43 It was in fact on the west coast in the landscape called Bohuslän that the most successful and long-lived producer co-operatives were established. A. Thörnquist, 'Egna brott, köpeprissystemet och arbetskooperation bland svenska, danska och norska stenindustriarbetare', *Arbejder Historia* (December 2003), 81–103.

44 There were proponents in Sweden for producer co-operative societies along the lines of Schulze-Delitzsch. Professor G.K. Hamilton and C.A. Ljungberg advocated this form of co-operation as morally superior to consumer co-operation although their publications and lectures resulted in few practical attempts. See P. Aléx, *Den rationella konsumenten. KF som folkuppfostrare 1899–1939* (Stehag: Symposion, 1994), pp. 52–53.

45 The Swedish middle class supported co-operation as an educational movement, and favoured education in economics and citizenship. The liberals and conservatives who spoke highly of co-operation saw it as a means to create a cross-class movement for social and economic activities. The first Secretary of KF, G.H. von Koch, steered the movement in this direction and hindered those co-operators more attracted by the Belgian socialist ideal to set the agenda. See Aléx, *Den rationella*. Middle-class support in Britain was stronger and more interested in promoting a producer-orientated ideal of co-operation. See Peter Gurney, 'The Middle-Class Embrace: Language, Representation, and the Contest Over Co-operative Forms in Britain, c. 1860–1914', *Victorian Studies* 37:2, 253–286.

46 Aléx, *Den rationella*.

47 T. Johansson, 'Samhällets spelregler i förändring – kooperativ lagstiftning', in P. Aléx, J. Ottoson and B. Wikström (eds), *Mellan stat & marknad – ett sekel av kooperation* (Årsbok: Kooperativ, 1999), pp. 11–12.

48 O. Ruin, *Kooperativa Förbundet 1899–1929 en organisationsstudie* (Stockholm: Rabén & Sjögren, 1960), p. 21.

49 K. Friberg, *The Workings of Co-operation. A Comparative Study of Consumer Co-operative Organisaton in Britain and Sweden 1860 to 1970* (Växjö: Växjö University Press, 2005), ch. 3.

50 Berättelse över Kooperativa Förbundets första kongress 1899, in *Berättelser över Kooperativa Förbundets kongresser 1899–1906* Collection of KF Congress Reports (Stockholm, 1912), p. 17.

51 Berättelse över Kooperativa Förbundets första kongress 1900, första kongressen, in *Berättelser över Kooperativa Förbundets kongresser 1899–1906*; W. Sjölin, *Med förenade krafter. Kooperativa Förbundet 1899–1949* (Stockholm: Kooperativa Förbundet, 1949).

52 Berättelse över Kooperativa Förbundets 7:e kongress 1906, in *Berättelser*

över Kooperativa Förbundets kongresser 1899–1906, pp. 310–311; See also M. Sundell, 'Ett kooperatörernas program', *Kooperatören* Nr 6, 15 mars 1906; Ruin, *Kooperativa Förbundet*, p. 84.

53 Berättelse över Kooperativa Förbundets 7:e kongress 1906, in *Berättelser över Kooperativa Förbundets kongresser 1899–1906*, pp. 312–313; See also P-on, 'Kooperatörernas program – Ett inlägg i diskussionen', *Kooperatören* Nr 10, 15 maj 1906.

54 Ruin, *Kooperativa Förbundet*, pp. 83–84.

55 *Berättelse avgiven av Kooperativa Förbundets styrelse till Kooperativa Förbundets styrelse* 1909), p. 32.

56 'Kooperativa produktionsföretag i Sverige', *Kooperatören* Nr 9, 16 september 1905, unsigned but certainly written by the editor Martin Sundell who later in an article (Nr 4, 15 February 1906) defended his opinions and KF's position in relation to *Fram*. The same message can also be found in advertisements in several issues of *Kooperatören* from 1905.

57 Motion 'Om Kooperativa distributionsföreningars ställning till kooperativa produktionsföreningar och avståndstagande från svettade varor', in *Dagordning och Motioner vid Kooperativa Förbundets Åttonde Kongress 1907 jämte styrelsens motivering*.

58 See board's response to motion 6, *Dagordning och Motioner vid Kooperativa Förbundets Tionde Kongress 1909 jämte styrelsens motivering*.

59 Ruin, *Kooperativa Förbundet*, p. 85.

60 Ibid.

61 See board's response to motion 3, *Dagordning och Motioner vid Kooperativa Förbundets Tionde Kongress 1909 jämte styrelsens motivering*.

62 See KF board's response to motion 2, *Dagordning och Motioner vid Kooperativa Förbundets Tionde Kongress 1909 jämte styrelsens motivering*.

63 Ruin, *Kooperativa Förbundet*, p. 83.

64 Sjölin, *Med förenade krafter*, p. 111.

65 The motions presented at KF congress in 1914 were discussed in *Kooperatören*. The proposal to only admit consumer co-operative societies as members is reported in a very technical matter. No arguments for or against are presented: see *Kooperatören*, 10 oktober 1914; Ruin, *Kooperativa Förbundet*, p. 22.

66 Ruin, *Kooperativa Förbundet*; Aléx, *Den rationella*; see also the first information folder from KF reprinted in E. Giertz and B. U. Strömberg, *Samverkan till egen nytta. Boken om konsumentkooperativ idé och verklighet i Sverige* (Stockholm: Prisma, 1999), p. 47.

67 Gurney, 'The Middle-Class Embrace'.

68 M. Hilton, *Prosperity For All: Consumer Activism in an Era of Globalization* (Ithaca and London: Cornell University Press, 2009).

69 Robertson, *The Co-operative Movement and Communities*; R. Vorberg-

Rugh, 'Employers and Workers: Conflicting Identities Over Women's Wages in the Co-operative Movement, 1906–18', in Black and Robertson, *Consumerism and the Co-operative movement*.

70 K.M. Grimes and B.L. Milgram (eds), *Artisans and Cooperatives: Developing Alternative Trade for the Global Economy* (Tucson: The University of Arizona Press, 2000).

71 'The Kibagenge Project', *Co-operatives for Development Newsletter* 1:1 (April 2010). This project entails direct co-operative trade with small-scale tea farmers in Kenya.

8

'A party within a party'? The Co–operative Party-Labour Party alliance and the formation of the Social Democratic Party, 1974–81

David Stewart

The British co-operative movement's relationship with politics has been complex. Although co-operation on the Rochdale model entails the conception of an alternative socialist economic and social order, party political neutrality was enshrined in the rules of the Rochdale Pioneers, who viewed party politics as ideologically divisive and the antithesis of working-class association.[1] From its formation in 1917, however, the Co-operative Party, the only co-operative political party in the world, has aligned itself with the Labour Party. The Co-operative Party–Labour Party alliance seeks to combine the interests of working-class consumers and producers, but it has been characterised by tensions over the best means to achieve this goal. In 1927 the Co-operative Party's parent body, the Co-operative Union, signed an electoral agreement with the Labour Party that would be renewed at subsequent general elections.[2] Between 1945 and 1983 the Co-operative Party was the third largest party in the British Parliament. Although its MPs have traditionally been associated with the centre-right of the Parliamentary Labour Party (PLP),[3] the Co-operative Party is a 'broad church' incorporating centre-left opinions. In 1981, however, the defection of four Co-operative Party and two Royal Arsenal Co-operative Society-sponsored MPs to a new 'progressive centre party', the Social Democratic Party (SDP), brought into focus the perceived clash between co-operative and Labour values, and threatened the stability of the alliance.

The co-operative movement has tended to be overlooked in histories of the Labour Party and research into the Co-operative Party is limited. Tom Carbery's history of the Co-operative Party, published in 1969, is the only full-scale academic study of the party.[4] Nicole Robertson focuses on the Co-operative Party's defence of consumer interests, local society activism and Co-operative–Labour relations in the Midlands during the inter-war years.[5] Furthermore, Kevin Manton's work has highlighted tensions in the broader Co-operative–Labour alliance between 1918 and 1958, and Lawrence Black has explored the relationship of the leading Labour Party revisionist, Anthony Crosland, with the Co-operative movement.[6] However, none of these scholars have examined the period since 1970, and, with the exception of Robertson, they have devoted limited coverage to the Co-operative Party. Indeed, the Co-operative Party's role in the SDP split, a highly significant and revealing moment in twentieth-century British politics, has never been explored. This chapter seeks to fill the void by analysing the factors that precipitated the defection of Co-operative Party MPs to the SDP. It examines the reasons why the Co-operative Party remained committed to the Labour Party alliance, despite its marginal and neglected position within the Labour Party, and is under-pinned by analysis of the compatibility of Co-operative, labourist and state socialist values. The chapter begins by briefly focusing on Co-operative Party–Labour Party relations in the period 1917–74.

'Co-operative Commonwealth' and 'New Jerusalem': Co-operative Party–Labour Party relations, 1917–74

Since its inception the British co-operative movement has been committed to arranging the powers of production, distribution, education and government on a co-operative basis to create a social economy or 'Co-operative Commonwealth' that would operate in the interests of all consumers.[7] Peter Gurney interprets co-operation as a form of working-class association that 'bridged the capitalist and socialist worlds'.[8] The Rochdale Pioneers regarded co-operative association and its values of self-help, democracy, mutuality, equality and solidarity as a means of transcending the factionalism of politics, but the Co-operative Party's formation in 1917 dissolved this formal separation of party political and economic spheres.[9] During the First World War, the experience of conscription and rationing combined with co-operators' activity within the labour movement to convince the co-operative movement that it required a stronger political voice to protect its interests.[10] Hopes for a fusion of trade union, Labour, and co-operative politics proved short-lived. Unlike trade unions and the Royal Arsenal Co-operative Society, the Co-operative Party did not affiliate directly to the Labour Party, denying the party a block vote at the Labour Party conference.[11] Instead, the Co-operative Party acted as a broker between the co-operative movement and the Labour Party,[12] and at constituency level local co-operative parties affiliated to Constituency Labour Parties (CLPs). There were three reasons for this. The Co-operative Union and co-operative societies were unwilling to fund the cost of affiliation fees in addition to the cost of running the party. They also realised that they would be unable to compete with trade union block votes at the Labour Party conference. Moreover, they deemed that an autonomous Co-operative Party would be better placed to defend co-operative interests.

The party initially harboured hopes of forging a political alliance with the Labour Party as an equal partner, but due to Co-operative Congress indecision and Labour's electoral breakthrough at the 1922 General Election the opportunity did not materialise. In 1927 the party signed an electoral agreement with the Labour Party agreeing not to contest the same seats.[13] From this point onwards, the Co-operative–Labour alliance was shaped by the Co-operative Party's desire to retain autonomy and the Labour Party's desire to encourage direct affiliation to minimise this independence, bolster its finances, and project a coherent party identity. In 1937 an agreement was reached that all Co-operative Party candidates at national and local level would henceforth use the Labour/Co-operative label. From 1958 the Co-operative Party was limited to thirty candidacies per general election, including those seats already held by the party.[14] In order to discourage CLPs and trade unions from contesting the reselection of sitting Co-operative Party MPs, the party developed the convention of not opposing the reselection of sitting Labour MPs after 1958.

This partly represented a reaction to the concerns of the Labour Party National Executive Committee (NEC) that 'the extension of the Co-operative Party was giving rise to the danger of a party within a party'.[15] This perception also stemmed from the co-operative movement's scepticism towards state socialism. Co-operative and state socialist ideas of community were fiercely contested at national level.[16] Co-operators perceived state socialism as wedded to producer interests and more hierarchical and less democratic than co-operative association. However, state socialist critics argued that the poorest working-class consumers did not have sufficient money to participate in co-operative association, which meant that co-operative expansion risked reinforcing existing divisions amongst the workers. In their eyes, only the state could act as a buffer between labour and capital and meet the social and economic needs of the entire community.[17] Relations with the trade unions were equally tense. The co-operative movement's national leadership questioned the purpose of strike action, and during the inter-war years was accused by its Manchester-based ally, the National Union of Distributive and Allied Workers (NUDAW), of paying low wages in order to maximise the dividend.[18]

With labourism and state socialism dominating the Labour Party's ethos and political thought, co-operative values were excluded from mainstream strategy and policy formation.[19] The co-operative movement's experience of the Attlee governments gradually sharpened this sense of exclusion. In particular, the movement was alienated by the proposed nationalisation of the insurance sector in 1949, which jeopardised the status of the Co-operative Insurance Society (CIS).[20] Despite successfully lobbying against the measure, this episode intensified Co-operative Party criticism of the centralised, statist monopoly model of public ownership adopted by the Labour Party. Within the Labour Party and amongst the Labour left in particular, however, these criticisms were frequently interpreted as the self-interested promotion of Co-operative business interests.

The 1958 Co-operative Commission, chaired by Labour Party leader Hugh Gaitskell, rejected elements of the co-operative business model, such as localised lay management and cash trading in preference to credit, as obstacles to modernisation.[21] Gaitskell was influenced by the Commission's secretary, Tony Crosland, who had challenged the Labour Party's pursuit of state ownership in his seminal 1956 book, *The Future of Socialism*.[22] The report 'trod on [the] hallowed traditions of local autonomy and egalitarianism' by encouraging the separation of lay elected boards from professional, specialist management, but concluded that co-operative association was compatible with efficiency and skilled management. Gaitskell's recommendations, which equated the co-operative business model with state ownership in terms of its perceived lack of responsiveness to consumer demand, were strongly contested by the co-operative movement. Nevertheless, the co-operative enterprises and societies' declining financial performance and membership during the 1960s and 1970s appeared to confirm the report's critical findings.[23]

This decline coincided with an upsurge in left activism within the labour movement, which led to closer Labour Party–trade union integration and stronger advocacy of nationalisation. Meanwhile, the left's strategy of allying with other excluded groups within the Labour Party saw them seek to embrace a version of co-operative values through support for state-funded co-operatives. These developments created deep unease amongst the Co-operative Party leadership.

Sowing the seeds of discord: the parliamentary right of the Co-operative Party, 1974–79

By 1974 the Co-operative Party continued to attract MPs from all wings of the labour movement, including former Independent Labour Party activist Bob Edwards, MP for Bilston, and revisionists like Dickson Mabon, MP for Greenock and Port Glasgow, but the centre-right held the balance of power.[24] In October 1974, Mabon and Jim Wellbeloved, Royal Arsenal Co-operative Society-sponsored MP for Erith and Crayford, founded the Manifesto Group, which sought to maintain a centre-right majority in PLP Parliamentary Committee[25] elections and support the Labour government against left-wing attacks.[26] The group's membership included influential co-operators such as Ted Graham, MP for Edmonton, Ian Wrigglesworth, MP for Thornaby, John Roper, MP for Farnworth, John Cartwright, Royal Arsenal Co-operative Society-sponsored MP for Woolwich East, and Mike Thomas, MP for Newcastle East. Thomas, Wrigglesworth and Roper would become senior office bearers. The group was united by hostility towards the Alternative Economic Strategy (AES), and concern over left activism and Trotskyite entryism.

The Marxist-influenced Alternative Economic Strategy, which had been launched in 1973, envisaged an expansion of state-funded worker co-operatives in tandem with state control of the 25 largest companies in the UK, the implementation of import controls, and withdrawal from the European Economic Community (EEC).[27] The Co-operative Union was supportive of plans for the establishment of a Co-operative Development Agency. However, it was concerned that the proposed statutory right of workers in private firms to convert their enterprise to a co-operative was inconsistent with the voluntary co-operative principle, while the CIS opposed industrial democracy and state control of financial services.[28] The European issue tended to cut across left/right divisions, but the co-operative movement leadership was supportive of EEC membership due to the co-operative enterprises' advocacy of free trade and the movement's internationalist values and interaction with European co-operators through Euro-Co-op and the International Co-operative Alliance. Cartwright, Wrigglesworth, Roper, Wellbeloved and Mabon were particularly vociferous Europhiles. These co-operators came to view British membership of the EEC as a matter of principle. However, they were by no means isolated within the Co-operative Party, as Edwards embraced the European ideal with a view to building a socialist Europe.[29]

The Co-operative Party was equally concerned by the perceived threat to democracy posed by the Labour left. In 1977 Wrigglesworth and Roper established the Campaign for Labour Victory in order to organise against the left at constituency level.[30] This was a particularly pressing issue as a newly radicalised generation of left-wing labour movement activists had emerged and the Trotskyite Militant Tendency was aggressively seeking to infiltrate CLPs and local co-operative parties. Cartwright and Wellbeloved were confronted by these tactics on the Royal Arsenal Co-operative Society Political Committee.[31]

For the Co-operative Party trade union power was an inter-related issue. It argued that industrial militancy and free collective bargaining ran contrary to the consumer interest, and condemned the unions for defending state monopolies and bureaucracy. Thomas contended that trade union block votes at the Labour Party conference were undemocratic and incompatible with the Rochdale Principle of one-member-one-vote. Furthermore, Roper and Wrigglesworth raised the prospect of a Bill of Rights to prevent abuses of trade union power,[32] and Graham attributed Labour's defeat at the 1979 General Election to working-class disillusionment with 'irresponsible' trade union strike action during the 'winter of discontent'.[33] The Co-operative Party Midlands Section's 1978 Annual Report encapsulated these sentiments, emphasising that 'co-operative ideals were better than free collective bargaining or nationalisation of the 200 major companies'.[34]

By 1979, therefore, several Co-operative Party and Royal Arsenal Co-operative Society-sponsored MPs diverged sharply from the rising and most assertive currents of thought within the Labour Party. Their opposition to state ownership, trade union militancy and union 'restrictive practices' fed into the wider critique of post-war democratic socialism being advanced by liberal revisionists within the Labour Party, who interpreted the expansion of the state, progressive taxation and corporatism as a threat to the market-based economy and individual liberties.[35] This vocal Co-operative Party dissent failed to provoke alarm as it was perceived as an outgrowth of the historic tensions between producer and consumer interests within the Co-operative Party–Labour Party alliance, and because the MPs concerned were associated with an organised centre-right faction informally recognised by the Labour Party leader, Jim Callaghan.

Democracy and disharmony: Labour Party constitutional reform and Co-operative Party factionalism

This friction between the parties reflected wider Co-operative Party concern over the labour movement's perceived ignorance of

Co-operative identity and values, and the Labour Party's growing insularity.[36] At the 1979 Co-operative Congress and that year's Co-operative Party conference, the Secretary of the Co-operative Party, David Wise, bemoaned the Labour Party's preoccupation with producer interests and the extent to which Co-operative councillors were detached from the Parliamentary Group and insufficiently aware of Co-operative Party policies.[37] Developments at local society level exacerbated this problem.

The Northampton, Lincoln, Manchester and Liverpool Wavertree parties were experiencing severe factional in-fighting that reflected wider left/right conflict within the Labour Party.[38] At the 1979 Congress the London Co-operative Society (LCS) Political Committee sought to enable local societies to affiliate directly to the Labour Party.[39] The LCS contended that this would bolster the co-operative voice and vote at the Labour Party conference. In reality, the LCS Political Committee, which was dominated by the left, viewed this measure as a means of advancing the left's programme.[40] Although Wise emphasised that there was no disagreement over the Co-operative Party's alliance with the Labour Party, he warned that the proposal risked weakening the ability of Congress and the Co-operative Party to represent co-operative interests. Nevertheless, the LCS affiliated to the Labour Party that year, and subsequently generated friction with the Royal Arsenal co-operative Society over the co-operative candidacy for the Socialist Societies seat on the Labour Party NEC.[41]

The left had controlled the NEC by virtue of a tactical alliance with Broad Left and newly radicalised public service unions and CLPs since 1975.[42] In the process of wresting control from the centre-right, the Royal Arsenal Co-operative Society candidate, Cartwright, was pitted against Les Huckfield, the left-wing National Union of Labour and Socialist Clubs' candidate.[43] In 1979, LCS support for Huckfield led Cartwright to lose his seat on the NEC. These developments reflected a wider move to the left in the Labour Party. The left's foremost spokesperson, Tony Benn, MP for Bristol South East, argued that the 1979 General Election defeat was a direct consequence of the Labour government's failure to deliver socialist policies endorsed by the NEC and party conference.[44] The left demanded internal constitutional changes, such as mandatory reselection of MPs and the establishment of an electoral college to elect the party leader in order to transform the Labour Party into a populist vehicle for radical economic and social change.[45] In common with a majority of the PLP, the National Executive of the Co-operative Party opposed all of the left's proposed constitutional reforms, which it deemed to conflict with the co-operative commitment to one-member-one-vote.[46] Indeed, the co-operative movement's misgivings about the left were particularly acute as the Co-operative Bank was helping to sustain the Labour Party's finances, which had deteriorated sharply under the left's stewardship of the NEC. Between 1979 and 1982 the Labour Party's annual deficit rose from £65,893 to £292,000, largely due to the higher than anticipated cost of moving to new headquarters at Walworth Road in London.[47] The Labour Party only avoided bankruptcy through a combination of generous Co-operative Bank overdrafts, trade union loans, and adherence to business plans drawn up by the bank.[48]

The 1979 Labour Party Conference's approval of the mandatory reselection of MPs deepened Co-operative Party unease.[49] Mandatory reselection undermined the party's electoral agreement with the Labour Party, and made MPs on the centre-right of the Co-operative Party more vulnerable to challenges from the left.[50] The Co-operative Party responded to the reselection issue by adopting the practice of convening local Co-operative Party meetings to confirm the re-nomination of sitting Co-operative Party MPs.[51] Thomas drafted the PLP's submission to the 1980 Labour Party Commission of Enquiry, which described mandatory reselection as a 'recipe for creating factionalism and disunity in constituency parties where none exists'.[52] He also used this opportunity to promote a version of one-member-one-vote in which 'all party members could be directly involved in the selection of their parliamentary candidate and in the reselection of Labour MPs'. Meanwhile, the Co-operative Party North East Section bemoaned the factional divisions generated within the labour movement by discussion of one-member-one-vote, arguing that one-member-one-vote most closely reflected co-operative values.[53] However, the deep fissures caused by the debate over internal Labour Party democracy led liberal revisionist and social democratic groupings within the Labour Party to consider a breach with Labour.

Severing ties: the Co-operative Party and the formation of the SDP

The Jenkinsites, a small group of pro-EEC middle-class intellectuals, who congregated around the former Chancellor and Home Secretary, Roy Jenkins, adopted the highest profile. They were disillusioned with class-based two-party politics and were attracted by the prospect of an electoral alliance with the Liberal Party.[54] Mabon and Wrigglesworth were the only Co-operative Party MPs closely associated with this group. After Jenkins used the annual televised Dimbleby Lecture in November 1979 to call for 'a strengthening of the radical centre', rumours began to circulate of plans for a new 'centre party'. Jenkins' vision of a centre party drawing support from across the political spectrum competed with conceptions of a social democratic alternative to Labour. Shortly after Jenkins' lecture, Bill Rodgers, the former Transport Secretary and MP for Stockton, argued that if the left were to betray Labour's social democratic principles, these values 'would survive because there would be men and women prepared to carry on the fight'.[55]

Following the hostile treatment of centre-right MPs at the May 1980 Wembley Conference and the approval of a programme based upon the AES and nuclear disarmament, David Owen, the former Foreign Secretary, and Shirley Williams, the former Education Secretary, formed a loose alliance with Rodgers.[56] They sought to detach the language of community, democracy and freedom from class-based politics, and Williams wrote in admiration of Robert Owen's community building. The media branded them as the 'Gang of Three' and encouraged talk of a schism. During 1980 the North West, Midlands and North East Sections of the Co-operative Party openly acknowledged the prospect of a split and emphasised that any defectors to a new 'centre party' would have to leave the Co-operative Party.[57] Meanwhile, Alf Morris, MP for Manchester Wythenshawe, condemned the 'eminent defectors' as unrepresentative of working people and accused them of giving comfort to the 'most reactionary and vindictive Conservative Government in living memory'.[58]

Owen, who shared the co-operative commitment to one-member-one-vote and represented a Plymouth constituency with a thriving co-operative society, had the closest connections with the co-operative movement. During the early months of 1980, Owen collaborated with the Co-operative Union and the Industrial Common Ownership Movement to produce a pamphlet entitled *Co-operative Ownership*.[59] The pamphlet promoted a tripartite economy encompassing 'private industry, balanced by co-operatives and a state sector expanding only where it was necessary and suitable'.[60] Owen argued that this would create 'a genuine third way between the polarised debate about workers and owners', and produce 'realistic market socialism ... with an emphasis on efficiency and competition'. The Annual Report of the Co-operative Party Midlands Section reinforced this sentiment by criticising over-manning as anti-socialist and condemning the trade unions for defending these practices.[61] The trade unions responded by expressing concern that workers' co-operatives would undermine national wage bargaining agreements in the public sector and lead to lower wages and reduced trade union membership in these enterprises.[62] By challenging central tenets of labourism and post-war democratic socialism in relation to state ownership, trade unionism and market-based competition, the Co-operative Union was endorsing Owen's alternative centrist programme, which conflicted with co-operative social economy and risked heightening existing divisions within the Labour Party.

In September 1980 Thomas, Cartwright, Wrigglesworth, Roper and eight other Manifesto Group MPs published a letter in *The Times* attacking trade union influence in the party and raising the prospect of a new Centre Party contesting Labour-held seats at the next general election.[63] At meetings of the Manifesto Group these issues were openly discussed, although opinion was deeply divided. Wrigglesworth was amongst those MPs most enthusiastic about 'going it alone' to secure greater freedom to act against the left, while Cartwright favoured building an anti-left alliance within the Labour Party.[64] Events at the 1980 Labour Party Conference proved a turning point. The adoption of an electoral college to elect the Labour Party leadership sent shockwaves throughout the centre-right as this enhanced the prospect of a left-wing leadership being elected.[65] The formula of the electoral college was to be agreed at a special conference in January 1981. Jim Callaghan resigned as Labour Party leader in October 1980, and Michael Foot, the left-wing MP for Ebbw Vale, unexpectedly replaced him that November. In the intervening months, Graham called upon Foot to be stronger with those on the left who 'sought to wreck' the movement.[66]

Most of the centre-right set itself against an electoral college formula that allocated the PLP less than 50% of the vote, while the left demanded a 33:33:33 split.[67] Co-operative Party MPs and liberal revisionists, who supported Owen's motion in favour of one-member-one-vote, were intent on preventing the trade unions from dominating the electoral college. Ironically, all of these formulas were rejected and the Union of Shop, Distributive and Allied Workers delivered a compromise 40:30:30 formula weighted in favour of the unions to placate its left-wing sponsored MP, Audrey Wise. As Dianne Hayter explains, the 'result could not have been better for the potential defectors. Instead of having to launch their party on the unpopular cause of Europe, they had their ready-made and popular cause – that the leader of the Labour Party was henceforth to be elected with the votes of distrusted unions.'[68]

On 26 January 1981, the 'Gang of Four', Jenkins, Owen, Williams and Rodgers, issued the Limehouse Declaration, and announced the establishment of the Council for Social Democracy.[69] Graham accepted the formation of a Social Democratic Party as inevitable and identified trade union block votes as a major factor in the split.[70] The North East and North West Sections of the Co-operative Party blamed the left for the breakaway, and demanded that the Labour Party reject doctrinal ideology in order to demonstrate its commitment to the values of democracy.[71] Dick Douglas, MP for Dunfermline, contended that the Co-operative Party was 'a broad church' capable of 'representing all wings of the labour movement committed to parliamentary democracy', while Mabon disingenuously urged co-operators to support 'the Leader of the Party in his attempts to keep the Labour Movement together'.[72] In contrast, Thomas contended that the fight against the left had been lost, while Wrigglesworth reasoned that he was not prepared to restrict moderate and centre-left voters to a choice between the extremes of Thatcherism and the Labour left.[73]

The salience of these arguments within the co-operative movement was demonstrated by the *Co-op News*, which struck an equivocal tone calling for a 'wider discussion in the movement'.[74] The Co-operative Party National Executive recognised the right of co-operators to join the Council and expressed sympathy with their position, blaming the left and the trade unions for the split.[75] However, it emphasised that the formal agreement between the Co-operative Union and the Labour Party 'remained the most appropriate and advantageous constitutional basis for political action by the British Co-operative Movement'.

A question of values? Understanding the impact of the SDP split on the Co-operative Party–Labour Party alliance

According to Ivor Crewe and Anthony King, the 'European question', union membership and local government experience were key factors determining which Labour MPs defected to the SDP.[76] However, defections from the Co-operative Party were also influenced by the party's exclusion within the Labour Party, and the acute sense of marginalisation felt by the centre-right of the party following Labour's leftwards shift. In the period between January and July 1981, Thomas, Cartwright, Roper, Wrigglesworth and Wellbeloved defected to the SDP, and they were joined by Lord Taylor of Gryfe, a former president of the Scottish Co-operative Wholesale Society. Wise unsuccessfully sought to dissuade Roper from defecting while Foot was equally unsuccessful with Cartwright.[77] Mabon's departure in October proved particularly acrimonious as he was suspected of acting as an SDP mole, while the Royal Arsenal Co-operative Society Political Secretary, Paul Rossi, caused great embarrassment by resigning at the 1981 Labour Party conference.[78] The SDP established a Co-operative Group in Parliament and a Co-operative Association in the country and wrote to co-operative societies urging them to question the movement's political association with the Labour Party.[79]

The Co-operative Party suffered particularly heavy losses in the South East, which resulted in the Islington Co-operative Retail Services (CRS) branch being suspended, the Wessex CRS branch falling under the control of the 'hard left', and South Suburban CRS branch becoming polarised between the 'hard left [and] pro-SDP elements seeking to close the party down'.[80] Defections in the Midlands also led to the Northampton and Lincoln co-operative parties folding.[81] Indeed, Wellbeloved continued to sit on the Royal Arsenal Co-operative Society Political Committee until 1984 and Cartwright retained his position until 1992.[82] *Tribune* reported that 'throughout the movement, especially among managers, a view appears to be developing that party politics should be taken out of Co-operative affairs' and speculated about possible defections from the Co-operative Union Central Executive.[83]

Defectors were frustrated by the Co-operative Party's ongoing accommodation with labourism and state socialism, the Labour Party leadership's hostility towards the EEC, and the perceived advance of the left's quasi-Marxist policies and constitutional reforms. On the surface, it appeared to them that co-operative values could be sustained within the new 'progressive centre party'. However, the SDP directed its appeal to the 'new middle classes', who defined themselves according to individual consumption and local community rather than work or class.[84] This vision sought to use the language of community to undermine working-class political consciousness and harmonise social relations without disturbing inequalities, which conflicted with the co-operative commitment to working-class association and represented the antithesis of co-operative social economy.[85] Moreover, the SDP's efforts to divorce welfare and equality from social class were deemed implausible in the co-operative movement's predominantly working-class heartlands.

Wise used his positions on the boards of the Co-operative Wholesale Society (CWS), CIS and Invicta Co-op Society to defend the Co-operative–Labour alliance and reassure the co-operative movement that the Labour left could be defeated.[86] His reasoning was credible as the defections did not reflect policy differences within the Co-operative Parliamentary Group, but developments within the wider labour movement. Despite being concerned by the left's advances, both the General Secretary and Deputy General Secretary of the Co-operative Union and the Chief Executive and Secretary of the CWS were Labour Party members, who remained committed to the Co-operative–Labour alliance.[87] Given that the Co-operative Union was the parent body of the Co-operative Party and the CWS was the party's largest donor, this provided a strong leadership core opposed to collaboration with the SDP. Non-parliamentary members of the Co-operative Party National Executive, such as Jessie Carnegie and Brian Hellowell, were also solidly Labour. Furthermore, no national or regional organisers defected to the SDP, ensuring that Co-operative Party organisation in the country was hostile to approaches from the Social Democrats.

The Co-operative Party Scottish and South West Sections, which included the labour movement heartlands of West Central Scotland and South Wales, suffered minimal defections and provided solid support for the Co-operative–Labour alliance.[88] These Co-operative Party sections had a more labourist ethos than elsewhere in Britain, operated in political climates in which the labour movement represented the establishment,[89] and did not share the acute sense of exclusion felt elsewhere in the UK. They emphasised the importance of using the National Council of Labour to settle policy disputes and were less hostile towards the AES and the trade unions than the national leadership. Graham, who had been employed by the co-operative movement all of his working life, played a pivotal role in galvanising the depleted Co-operative Parliamentary Group. Graham recognised that the defectors had underestimated the bonds of solidarity generated by involvement in the co-operative and labour movements, and emphasised the importance of staying and fighting the left.[90]

Despite some senior co-operators' misgivings about developments within the Labour Party, a combination of loyalty to the Co-operative movement and unwillingness to jeopardise the movement's interests or their own prospects ensured that the Co-operative–Labour alliance would continue. The alliance was underpinned by both parties' commitment to equality and working-class association. The co-operators who remained within the party shared the sentiments of the vast majority of Co-operative Party activists who sought to restore Labour's electability and party unity. At the 1981 Co-operative Party conference, the Party Chairman, Tom Turvey, encapsulated the mood of the Parliamentary Group by asserting that the SDP had 'declared war' on the movement and by calling for the 'cliques and caucuses ... running a calculated campaign to take over the Labour Party' to be driven from office.[91] This defiant, combative rhetoric reflected a wider shift against the left within the labour movement that would break the left's grip on the Labour Party NEC in 1981 and generate a concerted campaign to marginalise the left, under Neil Kinnock's leadership. These developments combined with more regular contact between the party leaderships and greater policy convergence in relation to state ownership, trade union reform and one-member-one-vote to lessen the Co-operative Party's sense of exclusion within the Labour Party, and eventually precipitate the removal of the limit on Co-operative Party parliamentary candidates in 1996.[92] The crisis stemming from the SDP split, therefore, strengthened the Co-operative Party–Labour Party alliance by acting as a catalyst for the expansion of co-operative political representation.[93] Ironically, this coincided with the gradual emergence of New Labour after 1987 and its embrace of free market economics and the 'classless society', which rendered the achievement of the 'Co-operative Commonwealth' a distant prospect.

Indeed, the SDP split provides insights into broader themes that have shaped the Co-operative Party–Labour Party alliance. The voluntarist, democratic consumer culture of the Co-operative Party and the wider co-operative movement has conflicted with the Labour Party's statist, producer-orientated, trade union-dominated ethos. This clash of internal cultures manifested itself in divisions over one-member-one-vote, internal Labour Party democracy and the AES during the 1970s and 1980s, all of which contributed towards the SDP split. Long-held Co-operative Party concerns regarding the movement's junior status in the 'Trinity of Labour' also sharpened the sense of exclusion felt by defectors to the SDP.[94] The AES encapsulated the conflict between the evolutionary vision of co-operative social economy and Labour's desire to achieve a more rapid social and economic transformation through centrally planned, universal state socialism. Labour Party revisionists who opposed state socialism, and with whom Co-operative Party defectors to the SDP most closely associated, also tended to dismiss the movement's traditions as 'puritanical' and 'paternalist'.[95] On the surface, this clash of internal cultures appears to vindicate Carbery's argument that Co-operative–Labour relations have been characterised by 'calculated vagueness, uncertainty and instability', and it has led Manton to conclude that the alliance was shaped by the absence of shared values.[96] However, as Robertson's research and this chapter demonstrate, Manton's work neglects the ties of class, locality and labour movement activism which underpinned the Co-operative Party–Labour Party alliance.[97] These ties may have been eroded by 1981, but they generated sufficient loyalty to sustain the alliance at national and local level. The Co-operative Party and Labour

Party's shared values of equality and working-class association, which provided stability during the SDP split, continue to form the bedrock of their durable and contentious alliance.

Notes

1 Stephen Yeo, 'Towards Co-operative Politics: Using Early to Generate Late Socialism', *Journal of Co-operative Studies* 42:3 (December 2009), 23–26; in 1880 the Co-operative movement established a Parliamentary Committee to scrutinise Parliamentary legislation affecting the movement and lobby parliament. The Parliamentary Committee's membership was drawn from all sections of the movement and it remained in operation after 1917.
2 The Co-operative Union was the parent body of the Co-operative Party until the formation of Co-operatives UK in 2002. It was responsible for the Co-operative Party Fund, and between Congresses and Party Conferences the party's decisions on policy were subject to ratification by the Co-operative Union Central Executive.
3 The Parliamentary Labour Party was formed in 1906 and comprises all Labour MPs sitting in parliament.
4 Thomas F. Carbery, *Consumers in Politics: A History and General Review of the Co-operative Party* (Manchester: Manchester University Press, 1969).
5 Nicole Robertson, '"A Union of Forces Marching in the Same Direction?" The Relationship Between the Co-operative and Labour Parties, 1918–39', in Matthew Worley (ed.), *The Foundations of the British Labour Party: Identities, Cultures and Perspectives, 1900–39* (Aldershot: Ashgate, 2009); Nicole Robertson, 'The Political Dividend: Co-operative Parties in the Midlands, 1917–39', in Matthew Worley (ed.), *Labour's Grass Roots: Essays on the Activities of Local Labour Parties and Members, 1918–1945* (Aldershot: Ashgate, 2005).
6 Kevin Manton, 'The Labour Party and the Co-op, 1918–1958', *Historical Research* 82:218 (November 2009); Lawrence Black, *Redefining British Politics: Culture, Consumerism and Participation, 1954–1970* (Basingstoke: Palgrave, 2010).
7 Stephen Yeo, 'Rival Clusters of Potential: Ways of Seeing Cooperation', in Stephen Yeo (ed.), *New Views of Co-operation* (London: Routledge, 1988), pp. 3–5.
8 Peter Gurney, 'Labour's Great Arch: Cooperation and Cultural Revolution in Britain, 1795–1926', in Ellen Furlough and Carl Strikwerda (eds), *Consumers Aainst Capitalism? Consumer Cooperation in Europe, North America and Japan, 1840–1990* (Oxford: Rowman and Littlefield, 1999); Peter Gurney, *Co-operative Culture and the Politics of Consumption in England, 1870–1930* (Manchester: Manchester University Press, 1996).
9 Yeo, 'Towards Co-operative Politics', 5–9; Gurney, 'Labour's Great Arch', p. 158.

10 Sidney Pollard, 'The Foundation of the Co-operative Party', in Asa Briggs and John Saville (eds), *Essays in Labour History, 1886–1923* (London: Macmillan, 1971); Tony Adams, 'The Formation of the Co-operative Party Re-considered', *International Review of Social History* 32:1 (April 1987), 48–68.

11 Carbery, *Consumers in Politics*, pp. 28–34; Rita Rhodes, *An Arsenal for Labour: The Royal Arsenal Co-operative Society and Politics 1896–1996* (Manchester: Holyoake, 1998), pp. 39–54.

12 The National Council of Labour and the National Joint Committee of the Labour Party and the Co-operative Party (1928–39) have been the main forums for dialogue between the party leaderships.

13 Greg Rosen, *Serving the People: Co-operative Party History from Fred Perry to Gordon Brown* (London: Co-operative Party, 2007), p. 9.

14 Carbery, *Consumers in Politics*, pp. 115–120.

15 Labour History Archive and Study Centre, Manchester (hereafter LHASC), Labour Party Archive, Uncatalogued box on relations with the Co-operative Party, Report of Labour Party-Co-operative movement meeting on 29 March 1957.

16 Manton, 'Labour Party and the Co-op', 764–766; Robertson, 'A Union of Forces', pp. 225–227.

17 Eileen and Stephen Yeo, 'On the Uses of "Community": From Owenism to the Present', in Yeo, *New Views of Cooperation*, pp. 248–251.

18 Large numbers of Co-operative employees were members of the NUDAW, which had been established in 1920 through the merger of the Amalgamated Union of Co-operative Employees and the National Warehouse and General Workers' Union. In 1947 the NUDAW merged with the National Amalgamated Union of Shop Assistants, Warehousemen and Clerks to form the Union of Shop, Distributive and Allied Workers (USDAW). The Co-operative Party often operated in close alliance with USDAW representatives at Constituency Labour Party selection meetings.

19 This aspect of my research has been influenced by Keith Gildart's insightful paper, 'Constructing a British Road to Socialism: Re-thinking Political Identities in the Inter-War Labour Party', delivered at the 2010 British Scholars Conference, which examined excluded groups within the Labour Party.

20 Carbery, *Consumers in Politics*, pp. 162–169.

21 Lawrence Black, '"Trying to Sell a Parcel of Politics With a Parcel of Groceries": The Co-operative Independent Commission (CIC) and Consumerism in Post-war Britain', in Lawrence Black and Nicole Robertson (eds), *Consumerism and the Co-operative Movement in Modern British History: Taking Stock* (Manchester: Manchester University Press, 2009), pp. 34–38.

22 Anthony Crosland, *The Future of Socialism* (London: Constable, 2006), p. 9 and pp. 13–15.

23 John K. Walton, 'The Post-War Decline of the British Retail Co-operative Movement: Nature, Causes and Consequences', in Black and Robertson, *Consumerism and the Co-operative movement*, pp. 22–26.

24 At the October 1974 General Election fourteen Co-operative Party MPs and two Royal Arsenal Co-operative Society-sponsored MPs were elected.

25 The PLP Parliamentary Committee comprises members of the Labour Party's Front Bench in Parliament.

26 Dianne Hayter, *Fightback! Labour's Traditional Right in the 1970s and 1980s* (Manchester: Manchester University Press, 2005), pp. 50–52.

27 Mark Wickham-Jones, *Economic Strategy and the Labour Party: Politics and Policy-making, 1970–83* (London: Macmillan, 1996), pp. 55–79.

28 LHASC, Labour Party Archive, National Council of Labour Correspondence 1946–83, Comments by the Co-operative Movement on the Statement to the 1982 Labour Party Conference by the Labour Party's National Executive Committee; Labour's Programme 1982 – comments submitted by the Co-operative Union.

29 LHASC, *Labour and the Common Market: Report of a Special Conference of the Labour Party, 17 July 1971* (London: Labour Party, 1971), pp. 30–31.

30 Hayter, *Fightback!*, p. 56.

31 Rhodes, *Arsenal for Labour*, pp. 229–232.

32 LHASC, Dianne Hayter Papers, Box 2, David Marquand, B. Magee, John P. Mackintosh, John Roper, John Horam, Giles Radice and Ian Wrigglesworth, *What We Must Do* (London: Manifesto Group, 1977), pp. 15–16 and 33–34; Stephen Meredith, *Labours Old and New: The Parliamentary Right of the British Labour Party 1970–79 and the Roots of New Labour* (Manchester: Manchester University Press, 2008), pp. 123–125.

33 National Co-operative Archive, Manchester (hereafter NCA), Co-operative Party Archive (hereafter CPA), *Annual Report and Accounts of 1979 Co-operative Congress* (Manchester: Co-operative, 1979), p. 98; At the 1979 General Election the Co-operative Party increased its number of seats to seventeen.

34 NCA, CPA, *Co-operative Party Midland Section Annual Report 1978* (Manchester: Co-operative Union, 1979), p. 15.

35 Meredith, *Labours Old and New*, pp. 14–19.

36 NCA, CPA, Co-operative Party National Executive Minutes, 13 December 1979.

37 NCA, CPA, *Report of 1979 Co-operative Party Conference* (Manchester: Co-operative Union, 1979), p. 23.

38 NCA, CPA, *Co-operative Party Midland Section Annual Report 1979* (Manchester: Co-operative Union, 1980), p. 10; *Co-operative Party North East and North West Sections Annual Reports 1979* (Manchester: Co-operative Union, 1980), p. 8.

39 NCA, *Annual Report and Accounts of 1979 Co-operative Congress*, pp. 129–134.

40 Rhodes, *Arsenal for Labour*, pp. 233–234.

41 At this time the Labour Party NEC was responsible for policy formation, party organisation and finance. It was elected on an annual basis by the Labour Party conference.

42 David Stewart, 'Preserving the "Contentious Alliance"? The Labour Party, the Trade Unions and the Political Fund Ballots of 1985/86', *Labour History Review* 76:1 (2011) 51–69.

43 Huckfield was MP for Nuneaton and had played an influential role in the establishment of the Meriden Motorcycle Co-operative in 1977; John Golding, *Hammer of the Left: Defeating Tony Benn, Eric Heffer and Militant in the Battle for the Labour Party* (London: Politico's, 2003), pp. 178–184.

44 Leo Panitch and Colin Leys, *The End of Parliamentary Socialism* (London: Verso, 2001), pp. 168–176.

45 Since the establishment of the PLP in 1906, the Labour Party leader had been elected by the PLP.

46 The Co-operative Party National Executive administers the organisational and financial affairs of the party and contributes towards the formulation of party policy.

47 LHASC, Labour Party Archive, Labour Party NEC Minutes, Finance and General Purposes Committee Minutes, 26 March 1979; Finance and General Purposes Committee Minutes, 22 February 1982.

48 LHASC, Labour Party Archive, Labour Party NEC Minutes, Finance and General Purposes Committee Minutes, 18 May 1981; Finance and General Purposes Committee Minutes, 18 April 1983; Finance and General Purposes Committee Minutes, 14 March 1984.

49 LHASC, *Report of the Seventy-eighth Annual Conference of the Labour Party, 1979* (London: Labour Party, 1979), pp. 262–272.

50 NCA, CPA, Co-operative Party National Executive Minutes, 20 November 1980.

51 NCA, CPA, Co-operative Party National Executive Minutes, 12 February 1981.

52 LHASC, Manifesto Group Papers, LP/MANIF/17, Draft PLP Statement to the Commission of Enquiry, p. 3.

53 NCA, CPA, *Outlook – Newsletter of the North Eastern Society Co-operative Party, January 1980*.

54 Ivor Crewe and Anthony King, *SDP: The Birth, Life and Death of the Social Democratic Party* (Oxford: Oxford University Press, 1995), pp. 52–60.

55 LHASC, Manifesto Group Papers, LP/MANIF/17, Press Release by William Rodgers on 30 November 1979.

56 Crewe and King, *SDP*, pp. 39–44.

57 NCA, CPA, *Outlook – Newsletter of the North Eastern Society Co-operative Party, August 1980*; *Co-operative Party Midland Section Annual Report 1980* (Manchester: Co-operative Union, 1981), p. 6; *Co-operative*

Party North Eastern Section Annual Report 1980 (Manchester: Co-operative Union, 1981), p. 1; *Co-operative Party North Western Section Annual Report 1980* (Manchester: Co-operative Union, 1981), p. 10.

58 NCA, CPA, CPY/9/4/3/13/1, *Wythenshawe Constituency Labour Party Annual Report 1980* (Manchester: Co-operative Union, 1981), pp. 4–5.

59 The Industrial Common Ownership Movement was founded in 1971 as the central membership organisation for a new generation of worker co-operatives.

60 NCA, CPA, David Owen, *Co-operative Ownership* (Manchester: Co-operative Union, 1980), pp. 26–27; Co-operative Party National Executive Minutes, 10 July 1980.

61 NCA, CPA, *Co-operative Party Midland Section Annual Report 1979* (Manchester: Co-operative Union, 1980), pp. 1–2.

62 NCA, CPA, Party Notes on Worker Co-operatives, December 1980, No. 120, p. 16.

63 *Times*, 22 September 1980.

64 LHASC, Manifesto Group Papers, LP/MANIF/3, Manifesto Group Minutes 1980.

65 LHASC, *Report of the Annual Conference and Special Conference of the Labour Party, 1980* (London: Labour Party, 1980), pp. 148–155 and pp. 184–196.

66 LHASC, Manifesto Group Papers, LP/MANIF/3, Manifesto Group Minutes 1981.

67 Tony Benn, *The End of An Era: Diaries 1980–90* (London: Arrow, 1994), pp. 68–70.

68 Hayter, *Fightback!*, p. 14.

69 LHASC, Michael Foot Papers, MF/L27/13, The Declaration for Social Democracy.

70 LHASC, Manifesto Group Papers, LP/MANIF/3, Manifesto Group Minutes, 14 January 1981.

71 NCA, CPA, *Co-operative Party North Eastern Section Annual Report 1981* (Manchester: Co-operative Union, 1982), p. 2; *Co-operative Party North Western Section Annual Report 1981* (Manchester: Co-operative Union, 1982), p. 1.

72 LHASC, *Labour Weekly*, 17 April 1981; NCA, *Co-op News*, 11 February 1981.

73 LHASC, LP/MANIF/3, Manifesto Group Minutes, 14 January 1981.

74 NCA, *Co-op News*, 11 February 1981; *Co-op News*, 18 February 1981.

75 NCA, CPA, Co-operative Party National Executive Minutes, 12 February 1981.

76 Crewe and King, *SDP*, pp. 106–114.

77 NCA, CPA, *Co-operative Party North Western Section Annual Report 1981* (Manchester: Co-operative Union, 1982), p. 4.

78 NCA, *Co-op News*, 14 October 1981; Rhodes, *Arsenal for Labour*, pp. 227–228.

79 NCA, CPA, Co-operative Party National Executive Minutes, 17 March 1982.
80 NCA, CPA, *Co-operative Party Southern Section Annual Report 1982* (Manchester: Co-operative Union, 1983), p. 13 and p. 18.
81 NCA, CPA, *Co-operative Party Midland Section Annual Report 1981* (Manchester: Co-operative Union, 1982), p. 5.
82 Rhodes, *Arsenal for Labour*, p. 223.
83 LHASC, *Tribune*, 2 April 1982.
84 Michael Young and Peter Hall (eds), *The Middle of the Night: Suggestions Towards the Election Manifesto* (London: Tawney Society, 1982), pp. 4–5.
85 Yeo and Yeo, 'On the Uses of Community', pp. 235–238.
86 NCA, *Co-op News*, 4 February 1981.
87 NCA, *Annual Report of 1980 Co-operative Congress* (Manchester: Co-operative Union, 1980), p. 71.
88 NCA, CPA, *Co-operative Party Scottish Section Annual Report 1981* (Manchester: Co-operative Union, 1982), pp. 3–7; *Co-operative Party South Western Section Annual Report 1982* (Manchester: Co-operative Union, 1983), p. 1.
89 Although support for the labour movement was less widespread in the south-west of England, Bristol, Exeter and Plymouth formed strong bases of labour movement activism.
90 NCA, *Co-op News*, 14 January 1981.
91 NCA, CPA, *Report of 1981 Co-operative Party Conference* (Manchester: Co-operative Union, 1981), p. 1.
92 At the 1997 General Election a record number of twenty-eight Co-operative Party MPs were elected.
93 Tony Blair and New Labour 'modernisers' were enthusiastic advocates of CWS restructuring, and Blair established the Co-operative Commission in 2000 at the request of the co-operative movement, which led to the formation of Co-operatives UK.
94 This term is used to describe the three wings of the labour movement: the Labour Party; trade unions; and co-operative movement.
95 Black, *Redefining British Politics*, pp. 67–72.
96 Carbery, *Consumers in Politics*, p.119; Manton, 'Labour Party and the Co-op', 763–765.
97 Robertson, 'A Union of Forces', pp. 28–30.

9

The creation of new entities: stakeholders and shareholders in nineteenth-century Italian co-operatives

Patrizia Battilani

As a result of strong links with the most important socio-cultural issues of the nineteenth century, both the definition and promotion of co-operatives are interwoven with the development of the socio-political movements of that period. For this reason discussion of such issues was never confined to purely academic circles and a great deal has been written about the relationship between co-operation and ideologies or cultural and political stances. In Europe the focus has been on the influence that the various forms of Christianity have had on the co-operative movement[1] and on the impact of socialist ideology on the setting up of worker and consumer co-operatives.[2] In the United States scholars have analysed the role played by the Grange (or Patrons of Husbandry) and the Farmers' Alliance in the promotion of insurance and farmers' co-operatives.[3] The growth of co-operatives has been the subject of theoretical analyses by famous economists such as Walras and Mill, and has enjoyed support from a growing school of thought embodied in the creation of socialist-inspired institutions (ranging from the Trades Councils to the Resistance Leagues[4]), and from a section of the Catholic world (parish priests and parish associations) that associated this new form of enterprise with a more ethical approach to society and the economy.

The numerous studies made of the persistence of the co-operative movement during the course of the twentieth century have often distinguished between economic efficiency and the ethical values (or ideologies) in question,[5] as if the two were separate phenomena moving in parallel directions. However, over the past fifteen years at least two different approaches have been adopted by economists investigating this question. This has led to an interweaving of the cultural aspects of co-operation with the question of economic efficiency. The first of the two approaches is that of Putnam's concept of social capital, while the second is that of property rights, based on the work of Henry Hansmann.[6]

In particular, the idea of social capital, understood as sustained group-level co-operative behaviour,[7] has been utilised to explain the non-homogeneous territorial distribution of co-operatives in Italy. This is true of two interesting studies, one by Galassi and the other by A. Hearn.[8] Both papers conclude by pointing out how the inefficiency of the southern co-operatives, and the impossibility of their remaining in the market, were the result of purely economic factors which, nevertheless, were deeply rooted in the cultural heritage and traditions of the Italian South. In associating myself with this approach, where efficiency is linked with 'culture', I wish to examine the cultural components of the Italian co-operative movement which emerged from three different socio-cultural traditions: liberalism, catholicism and socialism. Despite their differences, all three seem to share what we refer to here as the 'ideal of community happiness', that is the ideal of a collaboration among citizens for the improvement of the standard of living of the whole community. In this paper we will measure the popularity of this culture in the various Italian regions by per capita welfare expenditure in 1880 and 1900. As we will explain later, at that time everything spent for helping people in need was given by friendly societies, Catholic charities and local councils and nothing came from the central state. Therefore only the spreading of non-profit societies and a proactive attitude by local councils could generate high per capita welfare expenditure. Indeed, such indicators would seem to be closely linked to co-operative expansion during the second half of the nineteenth century, and would thus appear to provide an explanation for the non-homogeneous geographical distribution of co-operatives.

We still need to identify what it is that links efficiency with the presence of the 'community happiness' ideal. At this point, it would seem a good idea to refer to Hansmann's analysis, according to which ownership (and therefore the form of the enterprise – co-operative or investor owned) should be assigned so that total transaction costs for all patrons (stakeholders)[9] are minimised. In particular the transaction costs can be distinguished into two general categories: the costs of contracting for patrons who establish a contractual relationship with the firm, and the costs of ownership for patrons who own property rights in the firm. This last category can conveniently be subdivided into three other types: monitoring costs, collective decision-making costs, and risk-bearing costs. When ownership of a firm is shared among a class of patrons, a method of collective decision-making (generally speaking a voting mechanism) must be introduced. In many co-operatives this is a one-member-one-vote scheme. Of course such a mechanism will involve some kind of cost in comparison with the contracting solution, above all if patrons are heterogeneous and therefore have different interests. Subgroups of patrons could form coalitions so as to shift benefits to their advantage, and consequently substantial effort may be required to form and break such coalitions, increasing in this way the costs of ownership.[10] Besides, a majority voting mechanism may yield decisions that are inferior to those that would be reached with a contracting mechanism – if the preferences of the median voter are not those of the mean. Therefore if we take into consideration the process of collective decision-making we can see that it involves high costs of ownership when heterogeneous interests are present.[11] In such cases the setting up of co-operatives could be less efficient than the creation of investor-owned enterprises that deal with workers, consumers or providers through market contracting.

Our point is that the link between cultural/political movements and the co-operative movement not only increased the level of inter-personal trust through a series of membership mechanisms, but it also meant that the interests of members were less heterogeneous than they had previously been: as a result, the costs normally associated with collective decision-making were reduced. Summing up then, the ideological-cultural component proved to be a vital factor in the development of co-operatives, not only because it spread knowledge of such undertakings, but also because it contributed towards their economic efficiency.

The slow construction of a new type of enterprise: the emergence of co-operatives in economic and juridical debate in Italy

In terms of the history of business enterprise, the nineteenth century saw the emergence of alternatives to individual proprietorship: innovative forms of enterprise were being created in order to provide support to long-term investments and to share risk-bearing costs.[12] This was the century in which the industrialised nations' commercial codes made it increasingly simpler to create limited liability companies.[13] As the French jurist, Ripert, wrote, these were the years in which capitalism created its laws.[14] However, nineteeth-century institutional innovations were not all designed to strengthen investor-owned business corporations, but also included the introduction of an entrepreneurial undertaking in which ownership was assigned to stakeholders who were not investors – the co-operative in other words.

The importance of this novel form of economic enterprise is empha-sised by the fact that the greatest economists of that age – including Walras, Mill and Pareto – felt the need to write about that form of undertaking which we now call the co-operative, but which at that time was known under a variety of names: *sociétés à capitale variables*; *associations populaires;* equitable pioneers; industrial and provident societies.

John Stuart Mill defined the co-operative as an association of workers with equal rights, each being a joint owner of capital stock, working under a management which the workers themselves choose and which the same workers possess the power to dismiss.[15] Walras defined the *associations populaires* as companies whose capital stock was not created by an immediate, definitive underwriting, as occurs in the case of ordinary commercial and manufacturing companies, but through a gradual process consisting of the regular payment of membership shares by the co-operative's members. The French economist defined co-operatives in terms of two basic characteristics: their purpose, that is, the creation of capital (a sales outlet, a factory or a bank) that belongs jointly to all members, and may be used in their interest; and the means that are available to them, which basically consist in the regular, systematic withdrawal of a portion of wages and of company profits, that is, of the members' overall income, for the purpose of increasing capital stock.[16]

Italy was involved in this debate from the very beginning, when a group of intellectuals, including the economists Ugo Rabbeno and Ulisse Gobbi, proposed their own definition of the co-operative enterprise as follows:

> We can safely say that the defining characteristic of any cooperative undertaking is the joint running of the undertaking in order to produce that function needed by, and exclusively for the benefit of, its members.[17]

Debate among nineteenth-century economists, both in Italy and throughout the rest of Europe, focused exclusively on technical questions, such as the type of company liability (limited or unlimited), the nature of invested capital (variable or fixed) and members' aims (to obtain ownership of capital through work; to improve living standards by having access to cheaper goods, etc.), albeit within clearly defined cultural boundaries.

The development of the co-operative movement was set against a background of pauperism and the 'social question'; indeed, the problem of pauperism was so great that Walras, the creator of the concept of general economic equilibrium, declared that 'either society destroys pauperism or pauperism will destroy society'. The above-mentioned economists saw the co-operative movement as something that would enable the poor (that is, those who were capital-less) to enter the world of production, through the creation of shops, banks and factories, and thus as something that would help increase national wealth.

The Italian case is of particular interest because the co-operative movement was created as, and remained, an amalgamation of diverse cultural areas that was to generate a wealth of debate and theoretical writings. Co-operative ideals were first promoted in Italy by a cosmo-politan group of intellectuals from various fields: liberal-minded, lay thinkers such as Viganò, Rabbeno, Luzzatti and Wollemborg. They all perceived the co-operatives as enterprises that reconciled capital with labour, and as such, capable of guaranteeing the greater commitment of their workers. Rabbeno and Wollemborg's writings clearly reveal their belief in the potential of the co-operative to create the conditions for social peace and the moral improvement of the individual, as the following extended quotations indicate.

> Smith's school of thought is based on the totally mistaken idea that labour is a commodity just like any other ... The truth is, however, very different: the 'labour commodity' is incorporated in the person of its seller, the worker; in other agreements, the seller may adapt supply to demand and thus influence price, whereas the worker cannot do this, because he cannot reduce himself; thus only the buyer establishes the sale price and terms ... However, the conflict [between capital and labour] can never be completely eliminated, unless enterprises are modified in such a way that there is no longer any separation between the functions of entrepreneur and worker. Well, the manufacturing cooperative sets itself this 'aim' ... to eliminate the said conflict ... so that there is no longer any such division between entrepreneurs and wage-earners, and so that labour is not seen as a mere 'commodity', as it is now, but is once again granted economic independence, and is paid for in just measure, thus re-establishing the balance in production which has been missing until now.[18]

This entails a re-awakening of popular morality and self-belief, with the knowledge that each individual, provided he is honest and capable of doing a useful job, may aspire to membership and to the benefits of credit. The following facts, among others, support this claim. Twenty-eight of the present members of the association learnt to write their names at the very least, so that they could sign the shareholders' register. Several made a solemn pledge to change their depraved ways, and in fact managed to keep their promise. Finally, there were those who, having been rejected on the basis of their belonging to the local charity's list of paupers, re-submitted their application after having applied to the religious charitable institute to be removed from its lists due to the fact that they no longer required charity, and were subsequently admitted to the association.[19]

Numerous co-operatives were the result of the work of men like Wollemborg and Viganò, especially in the banking and retail sectors. Generally speaking, the memberships of such co-operatives included a substantial share of middle-class individuals, but failed to include very many from the poorer classes, as can be seen from the histories of the large nineteenth-century consumers' cooperatives and from the social background of the co-operative banks' membership.

From the 1880s onwards, the worsening of the economic crisis, and the increasingly difficult process of industrialisation, were accompanied by a flourishing of Catholic and socialist associations. It is widely acknowledged that the greater social and economic involvement of the Catholics can be put down to the publication, in 1891, of the Encyclical *Rerum Novarum*, written by Pope Leo XIII, which was to shape the Catholic Church's social doctrine. At the same time, there was a growth in socialist-inspired associations, with the creation of the Trades Councils and the Leghe di Resistenza (Resistance Leagues). Here we see the emergence of two important new theoretical and practical approaches to the creation of co-operative undertakings.

As far as concerns the founding fathers of the Catholic co-operative movement, mention must be made of Chiri, Sturzo, Guetti, Portaluppi and Rezzara, all of whom contributed towards the expansion of co-operatives, and in particular of the co-operative banks, throughout Italy's rural areas. They defined the co-operatives' principal tasks as the improvement of the living standards of the poorer classes, and above all the creation of an economic order capable of overcoming the distinction between wage earners and capitalists.

> Cooperation, regardless of its form, has to date managed to fulfil its initial purpose … that of subtracting the poor and the weak from the unfair or excessive actions of the capitalist classes … This task is of fundamental importance, but from now onwards … cooperation has to raise the rural or industrial proletariat to the capitalist level, and to support small-scale enterprises in the face of competition from large companies … The underlying aim is not so much that of raising the wages of rural or industrial workers by a penny or two, but of reducing the number of wage-earners by creating a strong, constantly expanding core of small and medium-sized businesses in which the workers themselves own the means of production.[20]

The founding fathers of the socialist co-operatives, on the other hand, included the likes of Costa, Baldini, Vergnanini and Prampolini, for whom the co-operative undertaking represented the first step towards the complete transformation of the economy and society; in other words, they saw the co-operative as a form of enterprise that re-established the dignity of labour and helped to create a fairer, more egalitarian society.

> Cooperation, in the face of pure resistance, represents the passage from a unilateral phase of opposition to a positive phase of reconstruction. In fact, several of Italy's cooperatives emerged at a time when the workers' struggle proved impotent or insufficient, and when the workers found themselves faced with the task of fighting something more terrible than capitalist oppression, something hidden in the shadows: the lack of work … Thanks to the creation of worker, producer and consumer cooperatives, the working classes moved up into the middle-classes' territory, that of the harsh world of business. They attacked capitalism on its own patch, utilising the same devices and means it employed to nourish itself, creating new centres of commercial and industrial life, around which there was a gradual convergence of part of those forces constituting the clientele of private speculation. Labour, organised in a cooperative manner, had declared war on private speculation; not only in order to reduce its dependency, but also to undertake practical, direct action aimed at challenging private capital's economic monopoly of society.[21]

The earliest co-operatives appeared in various different sectors of the Italian economy during the 1850s. In keeping with standard practice, at this point we would like to provide a few significant figures for this initial period of co-operative development: the year 1854 saw the foundation of Italy's first ever consumer co-operative, Turin's *Magazzino di Previdenza della Società Generale degli Operai* (the Workers' General Society outlet); in 1856, a group of former glaziers from the town of Altare (in the province of Savona) set up the first workers' co-operative; then in 1864, the first Italian Banca Popolare (credit co-op, based on the Schulze-Delitzsch model) was set up in the town of Lodi; in 1883, at Loreggia (near Padua), the first Cassa rurale (rural co-operative bank based on the Raiffeisen model) was founded; and in 1884, Nullo Baldini, together with a group of farm labourers, set up Italy's first agricultural co-operative in Ravenna. Thus in the thirty-year period stretching from 1854 to 1884, virtually all the various forms of co-operative enterprise that had been tried out in other European countries during the previous decades made their appearance in Italy, as we see in Table 9.1 and Table 9.2.

Table 9.1 Regional breakdown of co-ops in 1893 and 1910

Region	Consumer co-ops 1893	Credit co-ops (Schulze-Delitzsch model) 1893	Rural co-operative banks (Raiffeisen model) 1894	Agricultural and worker co-ops 1894	Total co-ops 1893–94*	Consumer co-ops 1910	Credit co-ops (Schulze-Delitzsch model) 1908	Rural co-operative banks (Raiffeisen model) 1905	Total co-ops 1910
Piedmont	393	42	14	21	470	188	32	139	470
Liguria	42	6		6	54	68	6	2	245
Lombardy	195	60	50	76	381	484	77	192	1017
Veneto	58	58	149	87	352	143	75	450	431
Emilia Romagna	32	62	6	185	285	157	71	246	990
Tuscany	169	40	2	44	255	267	48	19	514
Marche	20	49		8	77	105	62	46	179
Umbria	5	16		6	27	38	17	4	61
Lazio	14	24	1	42	81	16	29	38	317
Abruzzi and Molise	1	50		1	52	32	45	19	53
Campania	11	127	1	22	161	35	104	9	163
Apulia	17	71		7	95	30	46	16	163
Basilicata	1	32		7	40	2	15	3	21
Calabria	24	25		6	55	28	29	5	58
Sicily	29	63		11	103	53	72	145	245
Sardinia	2	5	1	2	10	6	8	1	33
Italy	1013	730	224	531	2498	1652	736	1334	4960

Table 9.2 Co-operation and credit, 1870-1915

Year	Banche popolari – credit co-operatives (Schulze-Delitzsch model)				Rural co-operative bank (Raiffeisen model)			
	Number	Market share*	Loans/ liabilities	% overdue bills	Number	Market share*	Loans/ liabilities	% overdue bills
1870	50				0			
1880	140		0.61	0.28	0			
1882	206		0.62	0.27	0			
1883	250	12.3			1			
1885	407			0.22	14			
1886	516		0.67	0.23	24			
1887	608	13.0			35			
1889	672				42	0.02	2.61	
1890	694				44			
1893	730	11.1	0.62	1.55	129			
1894	720	18.8			224			
1895	714	18.8		4.5	370			
1896	710				628		2.22	
1898	696		0.66	3.04	895			
1902	736				1099			
1905					1386		1.22	0.28
1908	736	17.0	0.78	0.99	1.00			
1910					1763			
1915					2594		0.68	

*Market shares have been measured as a percentage of deposits gathered by all types of bank.

Co-operatives and the maximisation of members' satisfaction

We begin this section with the words of Maffei, pronounced in 1907, advocating the creation of an Inspectorate with the power to supervise and control the cooperatives, obviously managed by the co-operative movement itself:

> If you, dear Sirs, were in my position, as Secretary of the National League of Cooperatives, and were to receive each day letters from the poor factory workers and farm labourers – letters full of mistakes, devoid of all syntax and grammar – but letters that document the incredible efforts and self-denial of the masses of poor folk, you would be moved by the miracles that cooperation manages to perform: our three thousand cooperatives are three thousand schools, three thousand humble colleges that instruct the most poorly educated workers to administer the interests of others; schools that prepare the masses to manage public affairs, and train them to take responsibility for public works.[22]

This passage, which in just a few lines describes the epic aspect of the emergence of co-operation, clearly illustrates what is meant by the economic and cultural promotion of co-op members. In fact, one of the characteristics common to all three cultural routes taken by Italian co-operation is the idea that this is the only form of enterprise capable of associating monetary remuneration with the human and cultural growth of workers, of consumers and of co-op members in general. For example, the initial lines of the articles of association of all agricultural credit institutions indicated the purpose of co-operation as being 'the improvement of the moral and material conditions of members, providing them with money'[23]. The same principle is cited in the majority of the agricultural co-operatives' articles of association, such as the statute of the *Società anonima cooperativa di migliora-mento fra lavoratori della terra di Fabbrico*, drawn up in 1901, which was to provide the inspiration for many others thereafter:

> The purpose [of the cooperative] is the gradual improvement of the economic and moral conditions of the rural working classes, by providing them with work and encouraging them to be prudent. In order to achieve this purpose, the cooperative intends: to manage rural land, the cultivation of which shall be performed collectively by the members of the cooperative and their families; to sell those agricultural products needed by farmers (fertilisers, sulphur, sulphates, tools, machinery, etc.); to run public works enterprises that are in some way related to the improvement of the land (land reclamation, river and canal banks, embankments, tilling the soil, etc.); to provide members with an

education in farming practices; to set up a welfare fund for co-op members for when they fall ill or are in absolute poverty.[24]

Another example is given by the sector of the manufacturing co-operatives, such as the Construction Co-operative set up in Milan in 1887. This co-operative of bricklayers was founded following a strike, and it aimed to prove that it was possible to compete in the market while paying workers a proper rate of pay and ensuring they worked no more than ten hours a day. This co-operative pursued the well-being of its members through a variety of measures: it set up a pension fund for retired workers and for those no longer able to work and in 1888 it opened a technical school in the municipal buildings (jointly financed by numerous public bodies, banks and the King of Italy himself).[25] Likewise, the famous Altare glassmakers' co-operative – the very first workers' co-operative in Italy – was also committed to workers' welfare, as shown by its setting up of a pension fund and a mutual aid society.

Consumers' co-operatives also tried to distinguish themselves from private companies in their better 'material' and 'ethical' treatment of their workers. For example, the Milan Co-operative Union, headed by Buffoli – the largest consumers' co-operative in the whole of Italy and the most innovative business undertaking in Italy's retailing sector – implemented a series of measures for the benefit of its workers. In fact, it set up a pension fund (financed by 11% of its profits), introduced a day of rest for its workers and set up a library offering workers free book loans; it also offered prizes to those workers who successfully attended evening and holiday classes, and in 1906 it set up its very own school (initially for 80 young workers) offering free courses to personnel during working hours.[26] Generally speaking, consumers' co-operatives, both large and small, often provided a further service in addition to their normal sales activities, namely the running of recreational clubs designed to promote the socialisation and education of members. In Lombardy, there were frequent cases of 'conglomerated' consumers' co-operatives, consisting of a number of different co-ops and associations that were capable of meeting the various needs of their members. These included social insurance, consumption, the provision of recreational facilities and even housing.

Overall, the co-operatives utilised three main channels in their attempts to look after their members' well-being: the price mechanism (higher wages paid by manufacturing co-ops, or lower interest rates to borrowers applied by the co-op banks); the introduction of some form of social security (in the case of accidents, illnesses or old age) designed to fill the gap left by the absence of state benefits; and the promotion of activities designed to increase human capital (the creation of libraries or recreational clubs, where members could read, among other things, the local newspapers, and the organisation of professional training courses). The development of such additional services, aimed at promoting the cultural interests of co-op members, was in perfect keeping with the mutual aid associations which lay at the roots of an important part of the co-operative movement, as we have already seen. The founding fathers shared the belief that such additional activities, designed to improve the education and culture of co-op members, should not be mistaken for charity. Indeed, these activities were designed to create the prerequisites for what we today would call 'social mobility'.

The idea of community happiness underlying entrepreneurial success: the reasons for the territorial concentration of the co-operatives

As we have already mentioned, the co-operatives' expansion and market penetration was largely confined to central and northern Italy, and in particular to the regions of Piedmont, Liguria, Lombardy, Emilia-Romagna, Veneto and Tuscany. These regions were where the theoretical models of co-operatives were formulated, and were also the focal points for the experimentation and expansion of the earliest co-operative enterprises. It proved much more difficult, on the other hand, for co-operatives to gain a foothold in southern Italy, with the exception of certain successful banche popolari and communal leaseholds in Sicily, thanks to the commitment of Don Sturzo, and of a number of banche popolari and white-collar consumers' co-ops in the Lazio region. This 'map' of the early development of the co-operative movement in Italy does not, however, mirror the economic development of these regions compared with that of others: in fact, the regions with the greatest penetration of co-operative enterprises include both the country's wealthiest regions (Piedmont, Lombardy and Liguria) and others where the level of economic development was comparable with that of the south (namely Emilia-Romagna and the Veneto).

A great many explanations have been proffered for this non-homogeneous distribution of co-operatives in Italy. Some scholars have tried to explain the phenomenon in terms of the presence of communal traditions related to woodland management (e.g. in Trentino or the Veneto)[27] or to the management of waterways (in Emilia-Romagna);[28] others have focused on the presence of socialist or Catholic associations which aided the growth and promotion of the co-operatives;[29] some have argued that it was the advent of industrialisation and the disruption to the existing economic equilibrium that triggered the creation of new forms of enterprise such as the co-operatives.[30] Personally, we believe that an explanation may be found in the relationship between cultural factors and economic efficiency, as we now argue.

Our starting point is the idea that in order for co-operation to prosper, it needs a strong social fabric which it, in turn, helps to reinforce. In fact, the expansion of an enterprise based on the principles of solidarity and the promotion of the well-being of its members, required a cultural framework in which solidarity was a recognised value, and in which the principle of community happiness countered the mere pursuit of individual gain or utility. In order to lend some weight to this hypothesis, we suggest that per capita welfare expenditure in the various Italian regions in the first fifty years after Unification (in 1861) be taken as an indicator of the extent of an institutional fabric and of a deep-rooted culture of community happiness. We take the years 1880 and 1900 as our benchmarks for the welfare expenditure and 1893 and 1910 for the number of co-operatives, as they are the years for which a considerable amount of data is available. Welfare expenditure is deemed to be everything that is spent in the form of subsidies and other measures, by the mutual aid societies, by charities and by local authorities (in particular by borough councils), in response to situations of need (illness, unemployment, old age, etc.). The reasons why this variable represents a good indicator of a culture of community happiness, and why we have included local government expenditure as part thereof, are as follows. Firstly, the historical period in question was one in which citizens' rights did not include welfare measures for the less well-off sections of the population: the state did not provide this kind of safety net, and any welfare provisions there were can be put down to the work of mutual aid societies or charitable institutions; as such, they depended on the organisational capacities and energies of individuals. As regards the social policies of local councils and provincial administrations, it should be said that during this period, local authorities received no funds at all from central government, but were forced to tax residents in order to finance their own spending. In a situation in which the right to vote was strictly linked to wealth, the decision to increase welfare expenditure could only be explained in cultural terms. As Figures 9.1 and 9.2 show, there is a direct relationship between the presence of a strong institutional fabric based upon the idea of community happiness, and the expansion of co-operative enterprises.

The co-operative movement developed in those regional contexts with a stronger institutional fabric which, through non-profit-making associations and local council policies, spread the concept of community happiness and encouraged the adoption of a co-operative to remedy situations of need. This confirms what historians have traditionally affirmed, that charities and self-help associations played an important part in the initial development of the co-operative movement in Italy. In fact, it is no coincidence that in those cases where the penetration of such societies proved difficult, encountering insurmountable economic problems, co-operation came up against a great many other obstacles.[31]

The interrelationship between institutional fabric, local culture and the growth of the co-operatives also helps us to understand the reasons for the evident regional differences, which we shall now briefly describe, taking into consideration three different regions. Our obvious starting point is the Emilia-Romagna region, which in the twentieth century was to become the capital of the co-operative movement. During the decades prior to the First World War, this Italian region saw the co-operative ideals embodied above all in farm labourers' co-operatives (there were already 185 such co-ops in 1894), and in workers' co-operatives, although co-operative credit also had a role to play, with the foundation of several co-op banks and agricultural credit institutions. Despite backwardness, which was only slightly alleviated by the existence of a dense network of small and medium-sized towns, the region still managed to function as the theoretical powerhouse of the co-operative movement. The strong institutional fabric created by the emergent socialist movement, which at times flanked, and at others ran counter to, the existing Catholic movement (marked by the significant presence of religious charitable institutions), proved particularly well suited not only to the creation of co-operative enterprises, but also to the gradual introduction of a managerial culture within the co-operatives.

The other region that owes its growth to the expansion of co-operation is the Veneto. This northern Italian region has been rightly called the land of casse rurali, as a result of their considerable presence in the countryside, and of the role they played in aiding rural co-operation. Here it was the Catholic associations that mainly helped create that institutional fabric within which the co-operatives were created and gradually transformed.

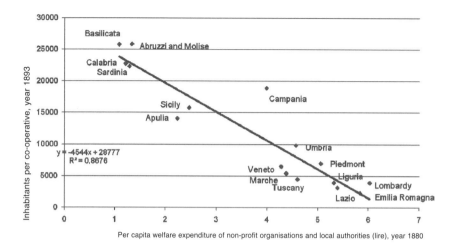

Figure 9.1 Relationship between institutional fabric and the expansion of the co-operatives, 1880–93

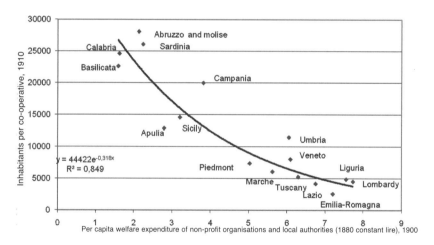

Figure 9.2 Relationship between institutional fabric and the expansion of the co-operatives, 1900–10

However, Lombardy remained the leading Italian region in terms of co-operation right up until the First World War. This region not only boasted numerous consumers' co-ops, building co-ops and banche popolari, but was also a step ahead of the others in terms of the size of its co-operatives: in fact, the co-operatives with the highest turnover and with the greatest interest in technological and organisational innovation were nearly all situated in Lombardy, thus confirming the region's economic leadership and the greater presence of an entrepreneurial attitude. Furthermore, it was also the most important 'think tank' for the elaboration of theoretical models of co-operation: a meeting place for academics, liberal politicians and the founding fathers of the co-operative movement. While the Milan area was characterised by the strong presence of liberal/lay co-operatives, supported in the main by the urban middle classes, the region's other provinces were soon to witness the establishment of Catholic co-operation as well.

Conclusion

The nineteenth century witnessed the setting up of co-operative enterprises in many European countries, in connection with the emergence of a crucial debate on pauperism and economic development. Italy was not an exception. However, from the very beginning the Italian co-operative movement differed in certain important respects from that of other countries. First of all it was never organised as a neutral, apolitical, non-religious movement so that the construction and diffusion of co-operative values became part of a wider cultural and political working out. Secondly it was never dominated by a unique ideology and it was supported by a plurality of cultural and political approaches, so far as separate umbrella organisations emerged. Despite this plurality of inspirations, the strong identification with some specific regions links all kinds of co-operative cultures. As a consequence the co-operative movement was closely tied to the local institutional fabric. This is why, although co-operatives took root across the whole of Italy, co-operation became stronger in certain regions than in others. In particular the regions with a stronger network of non-profit and charity association (Trades Councils and Resistance Leagues included) and therefore with a deep-rooted culture of 'community happiness' were those where co-operative enterprises emerged more rapidly and became more viable.

In conclusion, in contrast with what happened in other countries, Italian co-operatives can be considered the spin-off of long-lasting civic traditions going back to at least the fourteenth century, when theses on the social uses of wealth and a general revaluation of human relationships, from family to city, emerged for the first time. Over the nineteenth century idealistic and inspirational co-operative undertakings picked up and in turn reinforced that tradition of collaboration among citizens for the achievement of common goals – and the egalitarian attitude connected to this. For the same reason the different history of Italian regions explains the non-homogeneous distribution of co-operatives across the countries. Indeed, each region found its own transmission channel: in Emilia-Romagna the legacy coming from the middle ages was picked up by the socialist movement, while in Veneto by the Catholic culture.

What about the consequences of the link between co-operatives and social, religious and political movements? According to some scholars, ideological claims restricted the economic choices available to individual co-operatives in the long run and limited the spread of an entrepreneurial culture, above all in the later stages of industrialisation.[32] In contrast with that interpretation we maintain in this essay that in the early stages the link with the political and cultural movements was crucial not only for the emergence but above all for the viability of co-operative enterprises by reducing the costs associated with collective decision-making. Besides, over the nineteenth century, in regions like Trentino and Emilia-Romagna the co-operative movement itself played a crucial role in the articulation of an industrial culture. But that is another story.

Notes

1   See, for example, the many books about the Italian Catholic co-operatives; Sergio Zaninelli, *Mezzo secolo di ricerca storica sulla cooperazione Bianca: risultati e prospettive* (Verona: Società cattolica di cooperazione, 1996) and Andrea Leonardi, *Il credito cooperativo in una regione marginale. L'esperienza della Vallarsa* (Milano: FrancoAngeli, 2010). The history of the Dutch Rabobank is also very interesting because this network of credit unions dates back to 1972 when both Catholic- and Protestant-inspired banks merged.

2   See, for example, the studies that have been published of Belgian, English, Italian and Scandinavian consumer co-operation in the book edited by Ellen Furlough and Carl Strikwerda, *Consumers Against Capitalism* (Lanham: Rowman and Littlefield, 1999).

3   Marc Schneiberg and Marissa King, 'Social Movements and Organizational Form: Cooperative Alternatives to Corporations in the American Insurance, Dairy, and Grain Industry', *American Sociological Review* 73 (2008), 635–667.

4   The first Italian trade unions took the form of mutual aid societies and advocated class collaboration. By 1860 these self-help organisations numbered over 150. In the eighties socialist-inspired trade unions started to emerge with the name of Leagues of Resistance. They organised the landless peasants of the Po Valley and launched many strikes in order to end exploitation in the agricultural sector. The urban proletariat began to organise itself only in the 1890s with the setting up of the Trade Councils first in Milan then in other cities.

5 If, for example, we limit our analysis of the history of co-operation to the Italian case, we note that up until the 1970s, studies were predominantly of the political variety and focus on ideological issues; in the 1980s and 1990s, this type of study was gradually replaced by business histories, where the emphasis was on the competitive aspects of the co-operative enterprise. P. Battilani, G. Bertagnoni and S. Vignini, *Un'impresa di cooperatori, artigiani, camionisti. La Cta e il trasporto merci in Italia* (Bologna: Il Mulino, 2008); P. Battilani and G. Bertagnoni, *Cooperation, Network, Service. Innovation in Outsourcing* (Lancaster: Crucible Books–Carnegie Book Production, 2010); P. Battilani, A. Casali and V. Zamagni, *La cooperazione di consumo in Italia* (Bologna: Il Mulino, 2004).

6 Henry Hansman, *The Ownership of Enterprise* (Cambridge, MA: Harvard University Press, 1996); Robert Putnam, *Making Democracy Work: Civic Tradition in Modern Italy* (Princeton: Princeton University Press, 1993).

7 J.S. Coleman, 'Social Capital in the Creation of Human Capital', *American Journal of Sociology*, 94 (1988), 95–120; J.S. Coleman, *Foundations of Social Theory* (Cambridge, MA: Belknap Press of Harvard University, 1990); P. Dasgupta, 'Trust as a commodity', in D. Gambetta (ed.), *Trust: Making and Breaking Cooperative Relations* (Oxford: Basil Blackwell, 1988); P. Dasgupta, 'Economic Progress and the Idea of Social Capital', in P. Dasgupta and I. Serageldin (eds), *Social Capital: A Multifaceted Perspective* (World Bank, Washington, DC: 2000); R.D. Putnam, R. Leonardi and R.Y. Nanetti, *Making Democracy Work: Civic Traditions in Modern Italy* (Princeton, NJ: Princeton University Press, 1993); R.D. Putnam, *Bowling Alone: The Collapse and Revival of American Community* (New York: Simon & Schuster, 2000).

8 Brian A'Hearn, 'Could Southern Italians Cooperate? Banche Popolari in the Mezzogiorno', *Journal of Economic History* 60 (2000), 67–93; Francesco Galassi, 'Measuring Social Capital: Culture as an Explanation of Italy's Dualism', *European Review of Economic History* 5 (2001), 29–59.

9 By definition patrons are all the persons who transact with a firm: investors of capital, customers, workers or whoever.

10 When patrons deal with the firm through market contracting, they can only use the threat of withdrawing, in contrast with a collective decision-making mechanism where subgroups of patrons can achieve great influence.

11 Henry Hansmann, 'Cooperative Firms in Theory and Practice', *Liiketaloudellinen Aikakauskirja (The Finnish Journal of Business Economics)* 4 (1999), 387–403.

12 This process dates back to the twelfth century with the shaping of the first kind of for-profit enterprises, the commenda and the compagnia di negozio.

13 In France, the government authorisation for the incorporation of limited

liability companies was abolished by the 1867 Code, which also saw the introduction of the *sociètès à capitale variable*, a format including the cooperatives. In England the Joint-Stock Companies Act (1844) made incorporation possible merely by registration, and between 1844 and 1862 the full joint-stock company with limited liability for all shareholders became widespread. 1862 saw the passing of the Industrial and Provident Societies Acts (I&P Act), which for the first time gave cooperatives corporate status, with the provision of a proper legal framework for cooperatives. In Italy, cooperatives were legally recognised with the publication of the new commercial code in 1882, which at the same time abolished the need for governmental authorisation when creating a corporation.

14 George Ripert, *Aspects juridiques du capitalisme moderne* (Paris: L.G.D.J., (1951).

15 John Stuart Mill, *Principles of Political Economy: With Some of Their Applications to Social Philosophy* (London: Parker, 1852, vol. II, third edition).

16 Leon Walras, *Les Associations populaires de consommation, de production et de crédit. Leçons publique faites a Paris en 1865* (Paris: Dentu, 1865).

17 Ugo Rabbeno, *Le società cooperative di produzione* (Milan: tipografia F.lli Dumolard, 1889).

18 Ibid., pp. 424–463.

19 Leone Wollemborg, *L'ordinamento delle Casse di Prestiti*, Lecture held on 24th November 1884 at the Associazione Agraria Friulana, in Renato Marconato, *La figura e l'opera di Leone Wollemborg. Il fondatore delle casse rurali nella realtà dell'Ottocento e Novecento* (Treviso: La vita del popolo, 1984), pp. 251–258.

20 Giuseppe Toniolo, *L'avvenire della cooperazione cristiana* (Closing speech held at the International Congress of Cooperative Banks, Paris, 1900), in Giuseppe Toniolo, *Opera omnia*, section 4, *Iniziative sociali*, vol. 3, *Iniziative culturali e di azione cattolica* (Città del Vaticano: Tipografia Poliglotta Vaticana, 1951), pp. 510–524.

21 Antonio Vergnanini, *Cooperazione integrale* (Report presented at the 7th ICA International Congress held in Cremona on 23–25 September) (Reggio Emilia: Cooperativa Lavoratori Tipografi, 1907).

22 Quote taken from A. Basevi, *La legge sulla cooperazione e la sua applicazione (D.L.C.P.S. 14 settembre 1947, n. 1577)* (Roma: la Rivista della Cooperazione, 1954, second edition).

23 Lia Gheza Fabbri, *Solidarismo in Italia fra XIX e XX secolo* (Turin: Giappichelli, 2000).

24 Giuseppe Raineri, 'LE affittanze collettive in Italia. Inchiesta' (Piacenza: Federazione italiana dei consorzi agrari, 1906).

25 Renato Zangheri, Giuseppe Galasso and Valerio Castronovo, *Storia del movimento cooperativo in Italia. La Lega Nazionale delle Cooperative e Mutue, 1886–1986*, (Turin: Einaudi, 1987), pp. 60–62.

26 Luigi Buffoli, L'*organizzazione delle società cooperative di consumo* (Milano: società editrice Sonzogno, 1895).

27 Marco Casari, 'Emergence of Endogenous Legal Institutions: Property Rights and Community Governance in the Italian Alps', *Journal of Economic History* 67:1 (2007), 191–226; A. Leonardi, *Per una storia della cooperazione trentina, vol.I. La Federazione dei consorzi cooperativi dalle origini alla prima guerra mondiale (1815–1914)*, (Milan: FrancoAngeli, 1982).

28 Franco Cazzola, 'Le bonifiche nella valle padana. Un profilo', *Rivista di storia dell'agricoltura*, 27 (1987), 37–66; Franco Cazzola, *Equilibri idraulici, governo del territorio e società rurale in Valpadana, secoli XV-XIX*, in Giorgio Bigatti (ed.), *Uomini e acque*, (Milan: Giona, 1997).

29 Zangheri, Galasso and Castronovo, *Storia*; Vera Zamagni and Massimo Fornasari, *Il movimento cooperativo in Italia, un profilo storico-economico (1854–1992)* (Firenze: Vallecchi, 1997).

30 Andrea Leonardi, *Cultura dello sviluppo e cooperazione* (Trento: Federation of cooperatives Trento, 1996).

31 See the numerous essays on the failure of the mutual aid societies to establish themselves in the South of Italy. Ennio de Simone and Vittoria Ferrandino, *Assistenza, previdenza e mutualità nel Mezzogiorno moderno e contemporaneo* (Milano: FrancoAngeli, 2006) Gheza Fabbri, *Solidarismo*; Rosa Marucco, *Mutualismo e sistema politico. Il caso italiano (1862–1904)* (Turin: FrancoAngeli, 1981).

32 Zangheri, Galasso and Castronovo, *Storia*; Marco Granata, *La Lombardia cooperativa. La lega nazionale cooperative e mutue nel secondo dopoguerra* (Milano: FrancoAngeli, 2002); Tito Menzani, *La cooperazione in Emilia-Romagna. Dalla Resistenza alla svolta degli anni settanta* (Bologna: Il Mulino, 2007).

10

Co-operatives and nation-building in post-apartheid South Africa: contradictions and challenges

Vishwas Satgar and Michelle Williams

After nearly a century of struggling for a non-racial, democratic South Africa, in 1994 the African National Congress (ANC) became the first democratically elected government with the overwhelming majority of votes cast in its favour. The ANC-led government very quickly proclaimed a commitment to co-operative development through its *Reconstruction and Development Programme* (RDP). Since then the 'co-operative' idea and the 'role of a co-operative movement' in post-apartheid development have been articulated in numerous presidential State of the Nation addresses and mid-term reports to parliament. In 2005 a new Co-operatives Act was passed, having gone through five years of refinement with input from various actors such as government, the co-operative movement and independent support organisations. While the Act is an important step in post-apartheid co-operative development, co-operative policy has often been highly influenced by the neo-liberal macro-economic policy framework and discourse that the state has simultaneously pursued. More specifically, a neo-liberalised Broad Based Black Economic Empowerment (BBBEE) policy framework and discourse, with a strong emphasis on market-led development, has appropriated the role of co-operatives in development and underpinned the ANC's nation building emphasis.[1]

The emphasis on co-operatives within BBBEE discourse has been buttressed by significant policy and legislative developments since 1994.[2] In addition, both President Mbeki's and President Zuma's governments have asserted the BBBEE emphasis in their support for co-operatives. In 2007 President Mbeki kept alive the co-operative thrust within the policy agenda with interventions to address the 'second economy'.[3] Mbeki's government outlined crucial areas of policy intervention that had direct bearing on co-operative development and implementation.[4] The emphasis on co-operatives has continued in President Zuma's administration with the development of a national co-operatives strategy and planned amendments to the 2005 Co-operatives Act, as well as a financing instrument for women involved in co-operatives and Small and Medium Enterprises (SMEs) through the Isivande Women's Fund.[5] Thus, co-operatives have clearly found significant political support in the post-apartheid development landscape.

Yet at the same time, the ANC's neo-liberal macro-economic strategies placed co-operatives in a contradictory location in which there was significant legislative support for co-operative development, affirming international values and principles, but very little enabling state support that appreciated the specificities of the co-operative model and contextual challenges of developing co-operatives. Co-operatives were meant to compete almost immediately in very harsh market conditions with little or no state support (e.g. in the form of preferential tenders, tax incentives, preferential access to markets). Thus, state support for co-operatives, in the name of promoting BBBEE, treated co-operatives like any other business form, particularly SMEs, and provided legal standards and requirements. 'Black entrepreneurship' and 'enrichment', which are central values of BBBEE, were meant to be the crucial ingredients for co-operative success. This raises questions as to the actual impact of this political policy, and legal support for co-operatives. Has a BBBEE approach translated into the development of independent, viable co-operatives on the ground?

Based on three years of research, in this chapter we discuss co-operative development in post-apartheid South Africa through four themes.[6] First, we bring into focus the quantitative features of co-operative development, specifically looking at the dualistic experience of co-operative development and the push for Black Economic Empowerment (BEE). Second, we provide an overview of the policy and evolving regulatory framework buttressing the nation-building role of co-operatives. Third, we highlight the contradictions operating within a BBBEE approach to co-operatives and nation building. Finally, we unpack key challenges facing the development of co-operatives in post-apartheid South Africa.

Co-operative development trends in post-apartheid South Africa

While some date the first co-operative in South Africa to the 1860s in the Cape, from our research we found that the first *formally* registered co-operative in South Africa was the Pietermaritzburg Consumers Co-operative which formed in 1892. At this stage there was no legal framework dedicated to co-operatives. After the Anglo-Boer war co-operatives were promoted in agriculture, followed by the establishment of the National Co-operatives Dairies Limited in the early 1900s in the Natal region.[7] Co-operatives also took root in black communities during this time. For example, Gandhi and many church leaders were pivotal in promoting co-operatives in black communities at the beginning of the twentieth century.[8] In the mid-twentieth century ANC and South African Communist Party (SACP) leaders such as Govan Mbeki and Dora Tamana also played an important role in promoting co-operatives.[9] By the late 1980s co-operatives had become the backbone institutions for the agricultural sector, providing marketing channels, purchasing inputs and managing irrigation systems. Trade unions also began experimenting with co-operatives as part of defensive battles against retrenchments.[10]

However, this general history of co-operative development in South Africa was also marked by the impact of apartheid on co-operative development. With the advent of apartheid in 1948 co-operative development was explicitly racialised with 'whites only' co-operatives involved in finance, services and agriculture becoming central to the apartheid economy alongside the enormous conglomerates that dominated the racialised and exploitative 'commanding heights' of the economy. In other words, Afrikaner empowerment in the twentieth century did not just happen through the logic of capital accumulation, but coexisted with a logic that met human needs through co-operative forms of organising production and consumption, albeit underpinned by perverse and racialised relations of productions. Afrikaner nationalism positioned the apartheid state as a vehicle of racial exclusion and exploitation of the majority in order to secure resources, social mobility and development for a minority. The white co-operative movement was a key pillar of this racist nation-building project and it received tremendous policy, regulatory and financial support. In white agriculture, for example, large primary and secondary co-operatives were developed with high turnover and assets. Indeed, white co-operatives were the foundation of agricultural production in South Africa.

The numbers illustrate the story. In the early 1990s, 250 white agricultural co-operatives had approximately 142,000 members, total assets of R12.7 billion, turnover of R22.5 billion and annual pre-tax profits of more than R500 million.[11] In addition, agricultural co-operatives handled all exports of citrus and deciduous fruit, processed the entire wool clip, and marketed 90% of dried fruit. On the input side, they provided and/or financed 90% of fertiliser, 85% of fuel, 65% of chemicals, and a significant proportion of the machinery and implements used by white farmers. They also provided 25% of credit used by white farmers.[12] At the heart of this white-owned agricultural complex were eleven summer grain co-operatives. The two largest summer grain co-operatives, OTK and SWK, had annual turnovers of R2.374 billion and R2.22 billion respectively, which compares favourably with South Africa's largest food corporations such as Imperial Cold Storage with an annual turnover of R2.4 billion and Rainbow Chickens with a turnover of R1.5 billion in 1993.[13]

The white Afrikaner nationalist co-operative movement grew up as part of a racialised capitalist economy which ensured its economic success. These co-operatives were structurally implicated in reproducing white privilege. This in itself disqualified these co-operatives from being values-based and consistent with international principles. Moreover, the economic power of these co-operatives also propelled them into becoming typical capitalist businesses that were management-centred, conformed to market standards and were not member-driven, which further added to the loss of co-operative identity and practice. Unsurprisingly, many of these large white agricultural co-operatives have converted into companies since 1994.[14]

Most of the white co-operatives that have remained registered as co-operatives are only co-operatives in a formal sense, but do not conform to the principles of the International Co-operative Alliance (1996) and the new South African Co-operatives Act.[15] At the same time these co-operatives continue to hold immense economic power. By 2005 just 78 white farming and agricultural processing co-operatives (i.e. fruit and vegetables, livestock, grain and oil seeds, meat, timber, tobacco and wine) were responsible for producing a turnover of R6.7 billion, had assets valued at R5.4 billion and membership of 203,207.[16] In short, post-apartheid South Africa has seen a continued duality in terms of co-operative development: large and profitable white co-operative businesses and emergent black co-operatives. The emerging black co-operatives have grown dramatically in quantitative terms. See Figure 10.1 for an overview of co-operative growth by province.

There has been significant growth of mainly black co-operatives in the first decade of the twenty-first century. In 2007 there were 4,061 co-operatives in the country with most co-operatives registering as worker and multipurpose co-operatives followed by agricultural co-operatives.[17] This represents a massive increase from the 1,300 co-operatives that existed in 1994. The growth and concentration of co-operatives are mainly in two provinces where there is a high

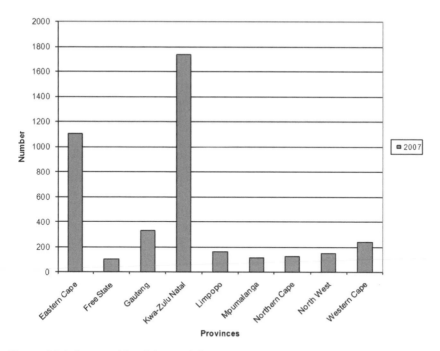

Figure 10.1 Provincial breakdown of Co-operatives

concentration of poor rural populations: Kwazulu-Natal and Eastern Cape. While these quantitative figures point to an important and significant trend, the figures are not very reliable and have numerous problems.[18]

By March 2010 there was a massive jump to 31,898 formally registered co-operatives[19] of which 54 are potential co-operative banks (i.e. 34 active Savings and Credit Co-operatives linked to the South African Savings and Credit Co-operative League (SACCOL) and 20 Financial Services Co-operatives linked to the South African Microfinance Apex (SAMAF)).[20] This rapid growth of mainly black co-operatives since 1994 can only be explained by understanding the state's role in terms of co-operatives' development policy (financial and non-financial) and regulatory reform, which are part of Broad Based Black Economic Empowerment and nation-building.

Black Economic Empowerment is the policy of the ANC government to deracialise capital and redistribute wealth. It has come under fierce criticism as it has largely benefited a handful of politically connected individuals. As an alternative to BEE the left within the ANC has called for BEE policy implementation to have a broad-based dimension, particularly through co-operatives and stakeholder equity models involving historically disadvantaged groups on the stock exchange. As a result BEE has morphed into BBBEE. For our purposes we use BEE interchangeably with BBBEE in this chapter.

Post-apartheid co-operative legal reform and policy

Co-operatives can exist under various guises in South Africa. They are often referred to as 'projects', 'self-help groups', 'mutual societies', 'village banks', 'credit unions' or 'consumer stores', and sometimes even the word 'association' is used to describe co-operatives. Despite the many names, the authenticity of a co-operative is determined by its internal characteristics. All genuine co-operatives are member-owned and democratically controlled institutions where power relations are not based on the number of shares owned, but on the universal principle of one member, one vote. While co-operatives make profits, the profits are subjected to the logic of member needs and guided by the ethical values and principles of the co-operative. The scale at which co-operatives operate can vary. For example, farming co-operatives can operate as small subsistence farmers in an urban space or can be high tech, high productivity yielding farming entities producing for established markets. The scale of a co-operative is driven by member needs and not by the dictates of a state bureaucracy or the logic of the market. Due to these institutional features co-operatives have a distinct identity separate from joint stock companies owned by share-holders, public enterprises owned and controlled by the state, or phil-anthropic organisations that provide for a target group. Co-operatives are user- and member-centred. In terms of the Co-operatives Act in South Africa co-operatives must be legally registered and cannot exist as informal institutions. In short, a co-operative cannot be an extension for government bureaucracy or a 'front' for individual 'entrepreneurs'.

The post-apartheid challenge of reconstruction and develop-ment coincided with an attempt to reclaim the authentic identity of co-operatives in the midst of the neo-liberalisation of the global political economy. The legal reform of the 1981 Co-operatives Act began through a review initiated in 2000. It attempted to take on board the lessons of co-operative development during apartheid and was informed by international standards and universal principles defining co-operatives.[21] In this regard, the new Co-operatives Act of 2005 breaks with the one-sidedness of the 1981 Act, which mainly supported the development of agricultural co-operatives. At the same time, it affirms the international principles and values of co-operatives as defined in the International Co-operative Alliance Statement of Identity and the International Labour Organization's (ILO) Recommendation 193.[22]

The Co-operative Development Policy for South Africa (2003), the Co-operatives Act (2005) and the Co-operatives Bank Act (2007) are crucial pillars for the development of a co-operative sector. The Co-operative Development Policy provides a framework for the Co-operatives Act. It sets out a vision, makes a case for the role of co-operatives in development, affirms the international identity of co-operatives, defines the policy approach of government and most importantly defines roles and responsibilities of government. Complementing the policy is the Co-operatives Act 14 of 2005 which contains 13 chapters and 2 schedules.[23] The Co-operative Banks Act 40 of 2007 contains 12 chapters and provides for a regulatory and developmental framework to support the creation of co-operative banks. Both the policy and legislative thrusts are crucial to ensure co-operatives in the post-apartheid context are not just ameliorative, but are capable of leading structural change and transformation.[24]

While the new Co-operatives Development policy and Act tilts toward reclaiming the authentic identity of co-operatives, this did not fall into place automatically. For example, the initial drafts of the new Co-operatives Act did not have a policy framework guiding it, but rather provided for a hybrid model of co-operatives and companies, was not clear about a financing mechanism for co-operatives, and maintained co-operative conversion provisions to other legal entities within the legal framework. Many of these provisions reflected the influence of white farming and agricultural co-operatives. A significant number of the agricultural co-operatives converted to companies in the 1990s, but still maintained a semblance of operating as co-operatives. Hence, they wanted a hybrid model of a company and co-operative entrenched in the law. The draft bill also contained the idea of external investor shares, which coincided with the BBBEE discourse. This notion of external investor shares would have undermined the model and principles of what a co-operative is and hence was rejected by the co-operative movement.[25] These were not the only problems with the initial co-operative draft bills. Many voices in the co-operative sector were arguing for a conceptual and policy separation between co-operatives and Small, Medium and Micro Enterprises and for a Ministry of Co-operatives to be established.[26] Many of the demands were lost (e.g. co-operatives fall within the Department of Trade and Industry (DTI) rather than a separate co-operatives ministry), but the policy process reveals the extent to which contestation from below was required to win the generally progressive Co-operatives Development Policy and Act.

The Co-operative Banks Act was also placed on the national agenda due to various factors.[27] Within government, particularly the finance department, there was general concern about the lack of regulation and support for the development of a diversified financial system. The collapse of many village co-operative banks also exposed the need for proper co-operative bank regulation and development support. This resonated with campaigns in civil society for South Africa's banks to respond to the 'unbanked', concerns by burial societies about the role of regulation and demands by the credit union movement for greater regulatory support. In response to these demands, in 2007, the Co-operative Banks Act was passed.

Informing the Co-operatives Development Policy, the new Co-operatives Act and the Co-operative Banks Act is the Broad Based Black Economic Act of (2003). This Act provides the underlying policy rationale for the development of post-apartheid co-operatives and prescribes a role for co-operatives to be part of socio-economic strategies to empower black people (defined as Africans, Coloureds and Indians).[28] One of the effects of this has been the instrumentalisation and politicisation of co-operatives with serious implications for the role of co-operatives in nation-building. For example, co-operatives have become mechanisms for local government officials to curry favour with local residents as well as co-operatives becoming entwined in party-political battles over resources.[29] Moreover, it implicates co-operatives in a process of reverse discrimination and exclusion, which is contrary to international ICA norms for co-operatives. For example, co-operatives have been used to pursue BBBEE, which exclusively targets black co-operatives, rather than promoting inclusive non-racial co-operative development. However, the BBBEE approach to co-operatives is quite complex in how it works to deracialise South African capitalism. This is explored below.

Vertical and horizontal operations of Co-operatives Development Policy

The Department of Trade and Industry is at the heart of the incipient co-operatives support system in government. Through its Co-operatives Development Unit, the DTI is responsible for the Co-operatives Development Policy and promotes horizontal and vertical support relationships for co-operatives. In addition, the Unit

has been responsible for developing the government support programmes, instruments and institutional capacities to implement the
national Co-operatives Development Policy. In this regard the Co-
operatives Development Unit has overseen the following activities: the
completion of legal drafting and legislation of the new Co-operatives
Act, the development of a new Co-operatives Development Policy, the
provision of funding to the national co-operative movement, the development of training materials, influencing regulatory standards relevant
to co-operatives and piloting of a funding incentive programme (e.g.
start-up grants); in addition it has managed key partnerships relevant to
its ambit of work. Recently the Unit has delegated many of its support
programmes and policy interventions (particularly its co-operative
capacitation role) to the Small Enterprise Development Agency. The
co-operative incentive programme has been located under one roof with
all other DTI incentive programmes.[30]

Through the Registrar of Co-operatives' role in administering the
Co-operatives Act and the national Minister's legal powers to make
regulations that buttress the operations of the Act, the DTI's role at the
centre of the co-operative support system in government is being
further re-enforced.[31] In addition, the national Co-operative Development Policy provides for other departments to co-ordinate their
co-operative promotion and development thrusts with DTI. Thus far
the Departments of Agriculture, National Treasury and Social
Development have focused on co-operative development and stream-
ing co-operative development into their various policy programmes
and interventions.[32] With the passing of the Co-operatives Banks Act
in 2007 the National Treasury has assisted the implementation of the
Act by supporting the creation of the Co-operative Banks Development
Agency as a statutory mechanism empowered to regulate and support
the development of co-operative banks. In the national Department of
Agriculture, for example, there is dedicated co-operative development
capacity through the Farmer Organisation Support Unit (FOSU). This
unit has a window of products and support services for co-operative
development which includes pre-registration support, training on
administration, linking co-operatives to governmental and non-
governmental support programmes, assisting primary co-operatives to
develop commodity production capacity, mobilising co-operatives into
co-operative support structures and finally developing a database of
agricultural co-operatives.[33] Such support capacity is also being built
vertically in provincial departments.[34]

Alongside the DTI and various other government departments with
co-operative development thrusts (e.g. the Departments of Agriculture

and Treasury) are a host of government linked institutions with mandates to support the development of co-operatives. For example, the Umsombomvu Youth Fund, the National Development Agency (NDA), the Micro Agricultural Finance Scheme of South Africa (MAFISA) and the South African Micro-finance Apex Fund (SAMAF) all support co-operative development, though a number of them are still in a programme pilot stage and are attempting to clarify their support roles and functions. Beyond these national level institutions, co-operative development and support systems are evolving in a very dynamic way in provinces. The institutional environment is diverse and is grounded in the national policy and legislative framework established by the DTI. The provinces work within the national policy framework, but have a great deal of license in the actual implementation, funding and character of support provided. Table 10.1 provides an overview of provincial structures in Gauteng and Kwazulu Natal, which contain some of the highest concentrations of co-operatives.

Table 10.1 Overview of co-operative support systems in Gauteng and Kwazulu Natal

	Policy custodian	Main implementing vehicle	Main horizontal thrusts	Local government co-operative policy programmes
Gauteng	Department of Economic Development	Gauteng Enterprise Propeller (GEP) linked with further education and training colleges and service providers	Department of Social Development	Most Councils – Ekurhuleni Metro leading
Kwazulu Natal	Department of Economic Development	Ithala Development Finance Cooperation linked to further education and training colleges (e.g. incubation centres) KZN Treasury manages procurement policy for co-operatives	Departments: Agriculture, Health, Public Works, Transport & Tourism	Most councils – Durban Metro leading

From 2005 the Kwazulu Natal (KZN) provincial government adopted an aggressive strategy to propel the development of co-operatives. Not surprisingly, Kwazulu Natal has the highest concentration of co-operatives in the country. The provincial government has injected over R300 million and has geared various institutional and departmental thrusts to support its co-operatives development push. Its general approach is to utilise co-operative development as a poverty alleviation intervention as part of its provincial development strategy.[35] In this environment, co-operatives are understood as a 'stepping-stone' to becoming medium-sized business enterprises. The KZN government is trying to fast-track the incubation of co-operatives so that they can be streamed into the 'first economy'. There has also been an emphasis on growing the numbers rather than ensuring proper co-operatives are set up. For example, in 2008 researchers from the Committee for the Promotion and Advancement of Cooperates (COPAC) met with a rural agricultural co-operative in the province of Kwazulu Natal; the co-operative had won an award from the national government as the most successful agricultural co-operative. After a site visit and interviews with the co-operative members, it was clear that none of the co-operative members knew what a co-operative was. They explained that they registered as a co-operative because the government officials instructed them to do so. In contrast, the emerging emphasis in Gauteng's Co-operative Development Policy focuses on providing non-financial technical support to emerging co-operatives.[36]

Thus, the myriad national, provincial, local government and government-linked institutions have been at the forefront of promoting co-operative development in South Africa, which helps explain the rapid growth of co-operatives in the recent period. Through its Broad Based Black Economic Empowerment policy and legislation the state has privileged co-operative development, which in turn further entrenched a BBBEE approach to co-operatives and placed them at the centre of nation-building. This BBBEE approach to co-operatives is evolving toward strengthening state intervention around co-operative development.[37] The current strategy and Co-operative Act amendments envisaged propose the introduction of a Co-operatives Development Agency (for financial and non-financial support), a Co-operative Training Academy (or 'co-operative college'), a Co-operative Tribunal (for adjudicating disputes, enforcement of the act and investigation), a Co-operative Advisory Council, a grant- and loans-based financing model and a new tax regime for co-operative promotion.

Assumptions of co-operative legislation and policy

The content of the co-operatives policy and Acts ensures three crucial assumptions underpinning the current policy and legal frameworks are institutionalised. The first assumption relates to an enabling role for the state by delineating its role in creating the conditions for co-operatives to emerge and be autonomous, self-sustaining entities. Both the Co-operatives Development Policy and the Acts envisage the state providing a carefully regulated environment for co-operatives which stops short of encroaching on the control and ownership thrusts of these institutions.[38] In addition, both the policy and legislative frameworks attempt to create the conditions for the establishment of a pathway for co-operatives to emerge, supported by panoply of institutions with mandates, resources and policy support capacity to address the structural imbalances that undermine the emergence of co-operative social relations of production and consumption. In short, co-operative based policy and legal reform is not blind to the systemic obstacles that could hinder co-operative development in post-apartheid South Africa. However, in practice the line between enabling support and autonomously developed co-operatives is often blurred and needs to be constantly monitored by co-operatives so that the bureaucracy does not capture these institutions. At the same time, there is a need to ensure that co-operatives do not become dependent on state support. This is explored further below in terms of the contradictions engendered through a BBBEE approach.

The second assumption underpinning the Co-operatives Development Policy and Acts recognises the distinct institutional identity of co-operatives. This modern co-operative identity developed over 150 years ago from utopian attempts in Europe to construct alternatives to the brutal, socially polarising, violent and uneven logic of capitalist development. It is worth reiterating that the international co-operative movement today is reclaiming the authentic people-centred identity of co-operatives, which is also reflected in the South African government's Co-operatives Development Policy and new Co-operative Acts. These are strong policy thrusts organising co-operatives around the principle of human solidarity and, therefore, not as a means to foster capital accumulation. In other words, co-operatives are about meeting human needs and hence the social logic of these institutions should not be conflated with capitalist businesses. In short, co-operatives are not another capitalist form of enterprise in which 'social capital' is the missing link for capitalist development. Genuine values-based and member-driven co-operatives are distinctive institutional forms to organise production, consumption and finance. How this distinct identity has been expressed in South Africa and impacted on through state discourse and practices is assessed below.

The third assumption inscribed in the policy and regulatory framework for co-operatives acknowledges that while it is necessary to bring in enabling state support, it is not a sufficient condition to ensure genuine, independent and self-sustaining co-operatives. In other words, co-operative development in post-apartheid South Africa is anchored in the assumption of building a dynamic co-operative movement that is self-sufficient and not controlled by the state. Both the policy and legislation for co-operative development ensures that different types of co-operatives (e.g. farming, housing and financial) can emerge and that these institutions are able to organise themselves from a primary level, to secondary and/or sectoral level and ultimately into a national apex body.[39] The assumption of building a co-operative movement that is capable of providing a voice for its members in participatory development processes is necessary to ensure the state or the market does not distort the identity of co-operatives. The symbolic and material capacities of a national co-operative movement are the key defining aspects of a co-operative approach to the politics of 'empowerment' in post-apartheid South Africa. However, the challenges of building such a movement, despite the residues of a vibrant civil society, are proving to be difficult and will be elaborated on below.

Contradictions of a BBBEE approach to Co-operatives and nation-building

Similar to other African countries, co-operative development in post-apartheid South Africa requires a role for the state given the centuries of oppression, marginalisation and deprivation endured by the majority of the population.[40] Thus, as we have shown, South Africa is developing a co-operative policy and regulatory framework to ensure the state supports co-operative development through creating an enabling environment, respects the internationally recognised ICA norms and values that provide co-operatives with a distinct institutional identity and ensures that a member-driven co-operative movement emerges from below.

However, state practices and discourses also contradict this progressive co-operative paradigm embodied in policy and legislation. These contradictions emerge from and are a direct consequence of the politicisation of co-operatives engendered by BBBEE. The first contradiction relates to the shift from revolutionary nationalism of the ANC (which understood apartheid as functional to the development of capitalism and hence apartheid capitalism had to be transformed in its totality) to 'Afro-neoliberalism'.[41] The promise of fundamental transformation of post-apartheid South Africa was envisaged in the programmatic cornerstone of revolutionary nationalism, adopted in 1955, known as the *Freedom Charter*. Instead, in 1996 the ANC government adopted a macro-economic framework supporting all the main prescriptions of neo-liberal ideology but with an African voice.

The indigenisation of an economic growth path that globalised the South African economy was directly linked to the articulation of BBBEE as a reform to placate the aspirations of the majority. Its articulation and ideological efficacy within ANC nationalism worked through the 'two economies' discourse articulated by President Thabo Mbeki.[42] The discourse envisaged a deracialisation of existing economic structures in the 'first economy' (understood as white monopoly capital and business) rather than the transformation of first economy accumulation patterns and structures that engendered underdevelopment in the so called 'second economy'. The two economies discourse also envisioned pathways, through BBBEE, from the second economy (understood as the underdeveloped rural and township reality) to the first economy. Co-operatives were the key ingredient.

The neo-liberalisation of BBBEE and its marriage to co-operative development has ensured that co-operative development is not about a co-operative sector with its own structural logic buttressed by enabling and strategic state support. Instead co-operatives were evoked as just another business form and have been treated more as Small and Medium Enterprise in state policy practice despite the existence of co-operatives development policy and legislation.[43] Thus, BBBEE was a concession to popular voices, but it has not promoted real transformation among the majority of South Africans. Rather 'empowerment' has been confined to enriching a few politically connected individuals through 'empowerment deals'. Sadly, co-operatives were politicised in this process and pushed as an avenue to enrichment. Moreover, co-operatives have often been reduced to black versions of historically white business. ANC nationalism was no longer about fundamental transformation.

The neo-liberalised BBBEE and its get-rich-quick logic of class formation, placed the profit motive at the centre of co-operative development rather than values-based practices to meet member needs. This is the second contradiction of a BBBEE approach, which is seen in the province of Kwazulu Natal.[44] For example, co-operatives have been 'hot housed' for six months in incubator processes, then resourced through finance from the KZN Ithala Bank or through procurement opportunities from the state. At the end of this process co-operatives were meant to be on their way into the first economy. The outcome has been an overwhelming failure. According to the baseline study conducted by the Department of Trade and Industry in 2008–9, despite the high rate of co-operative formation in Kwazulu Natal, it also exhibited the highest number of failed co-operatives. The study shows that out of 8,697 registered co-operatives in the province only 1,044 were surviving.[45] Moreover, while in 2009 the Registrar's office officially had 22,030 active co-operatives on its list, the baseline study shows that only 2,644 were operational, confirming a survival rate of 12% for the country.[46] These experiences have not affirmed the distinctive co-operative identity and advantages envisioned in co-operative policy and legislation, but instead have served to discredit co-operatives.

A third contradiction of a BBBEE approach to co-operative development is that it politicises co-operative development in favour of the ruling ANC, rather than affirming an autonomous bottom-up movement-building approach. Co-operatives started through BBBEE are understood as products of ANC policy.[47] What often happens is political patronage mediates the provisioning of grants and procurement opportunities in exchange for political loyalties. Thus, self-organising impulses are kept in check from above and dependencies are fostered as a means to reproduce ANC power. For example, in Bopholong Township south of Johannesburg, the local ANC council provided support for the development of an industrial hive co-operative. However, the council refused to give up control of the co-operative's finances, ensuring the co-operative remained dependent on the local council. In the end the co-operative collapsed. The market-led approach of BBBEE ironically brings in the state to drive co-operatives into the market. The accompanying squeeze of market competition and pressure further entrenches dependence on ANC state support and patronage. In most instances this pushes co-operatives back into poverty.[48] This is a form of state-centric practice linked to supporting a market-led approach to co-operative development.[49]

Finally, and flowing from the previous point, the ANC state has displayed a politics of control with regard to the existence of an independent and member-driven co-operative movement. Such a movement has a crucial role to play in nation-building in post-apartheid South Africa, not just to build solidarity to overcome the deprivations of apartheid and its inhumane consequences but to also deal with the social polarisation and eroding social cohesion of a neo-liberalised South Africa. Instead of allowing an autonomous and values-based co-operative movement to emerge to play a part in addressing these realities, the ANC state has undermined it. While the co-operative movement went through two important movement building phases since 1995, with the formation of the National Co-operative Association of South Africa (NCASA) in 1997, it stumbled on both occasions.

The first phase was approximately from 1995 to 2000, in which the Canadian co-operative movement had a great deal of influence. In this phase a founding meeting was held in 1995 for the South African National Association made up of about 30 co-operatives and a few co-operative associations. An interim committee was formed and provinces were encouraged to establish co-operative forums. On 26 August 1997 several sectoral bodies came together to launch the National Co-operative Association of South Africa, which evolved into the second phase around 2000.[50] The second phase was marked by the strong relationship between NCASA and the state, while the Canadian influence waned.[51] In 2002 NCASA secured a partnership with the DTI and received approximately R6 million over two years to advance its co-operative development strategy. The main content of this partnership was:

- Promotion of co-operative trade;
- Development of Co-operative Development Centres (CDCs);
- Co-operative development education and training;
- Establishment of a pilot project to focus on co-operative development (e.g. manufacturing co-operatives).

NCASA's record is unimpressive despite the generous funding from the state. For example, its efforts to build sectoral bodies floundered as it lacked serious organisational competencies[52] and, despite the funding, none of the envisaged interventions were realised. Its failure to deliver on the partnership agreement soured relations with government, the state was no longer willing to fund NCASA and the organisation collapsed. After a number of highly publicised scandals and years of mismanagement, by 2006 NCASA shut down.[53] Its national leadership structure disintegrated, the provincial structures were non-existent and the offices closed due to non-payment of rental. A crucial explanation for its failure is the top-down relation the state had with NCASA through the financing relationship operating between the Department of Trade and Industry and NCASA. The state envisioned an ambitious role for the co-operative movement and wanted to utilise finance as an instrument to achieve these ends.[54]

Ironically, NCASA'S failure further entrenched a state-centered but market-led approach to co-operatives found in BBBEE, which marked the beginning of a third phase to co-operative development in the country. By 2010 co-operative movement-building was co-ordinated by the state through local government forums. The new amendments to the Co-operatives Act and the new co-operative development strategy further strengthen the state-driven BBBEE approach rather than a bottom-up approach to movement building. In many ways, the state has substituted for the co-operative movement and has ensured co-operatives are just another market actor but dependent on it.

Challenges facing co-operative development

While the state-controlled NCASA died, co-operatives continued to emerge in the regulatory environment even before a new Co-operative Act was passed in 2005. The recent but sudden growth in co-operative numbers is due to the expectations created through the links with black economic empowerment. Many of these co-operatives have been reorganised by the state into local government co-operative forums and the state is trying to revive NCASA. A third phase of co-operative movement-building is emerging which poses crucial policy, movement-building and co-operative institutional development challenges. We discuss each of these challenges below.

Policy challenges

The South African government has three important policy challenges in the current context. First, it lacks a synergistic and co-ordinated intra-governmental support system for co-operative development. In practice since the early twenty-first century the state has adopted a top- down black economic empowerment approach without consolidating co-operative development support that exists horizontally across government departments and government linked institutions, as well as vertically between spheres of government. In short, government has a fragmented institutional support system for co-operative development, which must be integrated and co-ordinated through an internal government co-ordinating structure. The Co-operatives Act of 2005 provided for a national Co-operative Advisory Board to make recommendations on policy, strategic development challenges and other important issues related to co-operative development.[55] By 2010 the structure had not been set up. If and when it is set up, it is imperative that it is constituted to reflect representation from across government departments, government linked institutions promoting co-operatives, and existing co-operative movement structures. The DTI's new Co-operative Advisory Council envisaged in Amendments to the Co-operative Act is a step in this direction, even if it is a rather belated commitment.

A second policy challenge is for the state to develop a strategic and focused practice with regard to enabling co-operative development support. The big push approach ensures quantitative growth in co-operatives, but does not engender sustainable and member-driven co-operative development.[56] In this regard rethinking regulations and support for pre-co-operative registration are crucial to ensure potential co-operators receive thorough education on the co-operative concept, engage in a feasibility study and undertake proper co-operative business planning. Moreover, government has to shed its movement-building role and rethink its relationship with co-operatives. For example, the role of social science, particularly co-operative research and reliable statistics on co-operative trends and impacts, is one way in which government could assist co-operatives in understanding their challenges without intervening directly.[57]

The role of government in regulating co-operatives can also be strengthened with greater capacity in government to ensure dispute resolution, inspection and financial reporting in co-operatives. Finally, the role of financing models for co-operative development needs to be rethought. The current financing models incentivise corruption and perverse rent-seeking behaviour and do not meet the needs of co-operatives at different stages of development. Many emerging co-operatives require start-up capital and the state has been crucial in this regard. However, there is little support beyond start-up. The state could develop a financing methodology that assists co-operatives to plan, track and build capacities over the medium to long term. In addition, working capital financial streams have to be developed together with appropriate institution-building methodologies.

A third important policy challenge facing co-operative development is to rethink the BBBEE approach. As we have argued in this chapter, this policy framework has led to some perverse outcomes and has undermined the implicit co-operative empowerment paradigm embodied in existing co-operative development policy and legislation. Moreover, at the policy level it is crucial for government to deracialise co-operative development in general as part of nation-building. High levels of unemployment, deepening inequality and poverty affect all race groups. The co-operative option needs to be an option for all South Africans and BBBEE merely stands in the way of achieving this.

Movement-building challenges

Co-operative movement-building faces an important challenge in the ideational realm. Co-operatives and co-operators have to renew their own vision and practice of movement-building from below. With the state dominating the mainstream co-operative movement and attempts to tie co-operatives into a patronage system, South Africa requires an alternative approach to movement-building. Such an approach to bottom-up movement-building has to reject a black economic empowerment approach if it is to find its autonomous impulse for movement-building within ICA values and principles. Co-operatives are capable of promoting structural change from below and in a developing country like South Africa with a long tradition of grassroots movement-building the challenge lies among progressive social movements including the unemployed people's movements, trade unions and community-based co-operative movements to find this autonomous vision. Currently, such a vision is emerging among rural farmers' networks, the unemployed people's movement in Gauteng, the Workers' College in Durban, informal settlement committees, co-operative support NGOs and local grassroots co-operative movements for a Solidarity Economy Movement.

The emerging Solidarity Economy Movement in South Africa embraces and innovates on the ICA co-operative principles by affirming co-operatives as an ethical and structural alternative grounded in the idea of self and collective empowerment; it is an empowerment tradition of learning from experience and practice.[58] In concrete and practical ways it affirms the basics of movement-building to ensure member accountability, payment of membership fees, member economic contribution and linking horizontally between co-operatives. Moreover, such an incipient solidarity economy movement is promoting structural change in terms of promoting local food sovereignty, championing the need for evolving the national regulatory framework for co-operatives to ensure worker co-operative legislation, organising the unemployed to embrace a new strategic transformative practice, innovating on community development approaches and attempting to influence trade unions to rethink the role of co-operatives in trade union strategy. The emerging Solidarity Economy Movement in South Africa has not developed a structured institutional presence. It remains an activist grouping facing many challenges, but is potentially the best way to affirm co-operatives as a member-driven alternative in South Africa.

Co-operative institutional development challenges

The main institutional development challenge facing co-operatives has to do with developing a better understanding of the co-operative concept and how to utilise its advantages. Many co-operatives set up in South Africa through the government's black economic empowerment push do not understand what co-operatives are and lack knowledge about different types of co-operatives. The example above of the 'successful' KZN agricultural co-operative exemplifies this challenge. Worker co-operatives also illustrate the lack of understanding of how to institutionalise co-operative principles. Currently, none of South Africa's worker co-operatives draws on the worker owner advantages of internal share-based capitalisation linked to member-based capital accounts. [59] A crucial part of overcoming this challenge is through education on the co-operative concept, skills development, and ensuring co-operatives build a culture of education and learning. Marrying social science, particularly co-operative studies, to this challenge is crucial.

Conclusion

Post-apartheid nation-building has promoted a central role for co-operative development. As a result a big push has come to the fore through co-operative support policy, regulation and financing mechanisms. However, this paradigm of co-operative development is trapped in a paradox. On the one hand, the legal standards and general policy support provided for co-operatives harmonises with international principles and values provided for by the ICA. At the same time, this co-operative paradigm has been politicised and instrumentalised by the post-apartheid state in the context of nation-building. The marrying of co-operative development to a black economic empowerment discourse, within nation-building, has had perverse consequences for co-operative development. First, the state has come to the fore to promote the quantitative growth of co-operatives through a market-led approach that fosters dependencies and widespread institutional failure. The state is not providing strategic enabling support to co-operatives based on learning from actual practices. Second, co-operatives have been locked into a patronage system rather than being supported to form a member-driven and autonomous co-operative movement. Finally, co-operatives have been imbued with values of instant wealth creation, greed and profit-driven entrepreneurship that are central to black economic empowerment. This has simply served to corrupt many co-operatives and undermine the implicit empowerment paradigm within genuine co-operatives.

Co-operatives are not a panacea for the development challenges facing South Africa. At most co-operatives can contribute, together with other policy interventions, to the structural transformation of the racialised production, consumption and financing structures that dominate South Africa's post-apartheid political economy. In this process co-operatives can contribute to employment creation, asset formation, income distribution and market reach. However, for this to happen both the state and co-operatives have to redefine their roles through an appreciation of the inherent empowerment philosophy contained in the principles and values that define the true identity of co-operatives, and which are endorsed in the new co-operative policy and legislation in South Africa. This ethical philosophy of empowerment within co-operatives has to be the main compass for deepening co-operative development. This hidden alternative needs to be asserted more strongly from below for co-operatives to contribute to post-apartheid nation-building on their own terms.

Notes

1 On June 25, 1999 President Mbeki's mid-term parliamentary address made a clear statement on government's policy commitment to co-operatives: 'The Government will also place more emphasis on the development of a co-operative movement to combine the financial, labour and other resources among the masses of the people, rebuild our communities and engage the people in their own development through sustainable economic activity.'
2 For example, the Broad Based Black Economic Empowerment Act (No. 53 of 2003), the Co-operative Development Policy for South Africa (2003), the Co-operatives Act (No. 14 of 2005) and the Co-operatives Bank Act (No. 40 of 2007) are crucial policy pillars for developing a co-operative sector.
3 See *State of the Nation Address*, February 9, 2007, 10–11.
4 For example, there were four key areas relevant to the Co-operative Development Policy and legislative framework: (i) practical action around micro-finance including widening the reach of the Apex Fund and Agricultural Micro-credit Fund (MAFISA); (ii) ensuring the proper functioning of the Small Enterprise Development Agency (which is the main policy implementation vehicle for co-operatives at a national level); (iii) a youth co-operatives programme; and (iv) supporting the implementation of the Communal Land Rights Act through various measures including co-operative development. Thabo Mbeki, *State of the Nation Address*, February 9, 2007.
5 At the time of writing the new co-operatives strategy and amendments to the national co-operatives Act were on the cabinet agenda for approval.

Interview conducted with Geoff Ndumo, 22/08/2010, Head of Department and Trade Industry (hereafter DTI) National Co-operatives Unit.

6 Between 2007 and 2010, we conducted interviews and focus groups with practitioners, government officials and co-operators. In addition, we have also done document analysis and drawn on secondary research.

7 See Dr J.A.S. Van Niekerk, *Cooperative Theory and Practice* (SAAU: Pretoria, 1998).

8 See Judy Malqueeny, *History of Cooperatives in South Africa* (unpublished).

9 Ibid.

10 See Kate Philips, *Producer Cooperatives in South Africa: Their Economic Potential and Political Limits* (Johannesburg: Sociology of Work Project (SWOP), 1987).

11 N. Amin and H. Bernstein, *The Role of Agricultural Cooperatives in Agriculture and Rural Development* (LAPC Policy Paper 32, 1995).

12 Ibid.

13 Ibid.

14 Interview Rector Rapoo, 21/10/2010, Registrar of Co-operatives, DTI.

15 Many of these co-operatives have not deracialised or are moving extremely slowly in this direction. Interview Geoff Ndumo, 22/08/2010, Head of DTI, National Co-operatives Unit.

16 Registrar of Co-operatives and Statistics of Co-operatives in South Africa, 2002–2005 Volume No. XVI.

17 The classifications we have used are based on COPAC's interpretation of the registrar's list.

18 The registrar does not classify types of co-operatives in terms of the new Co-operatives Act (e.g. housing, transport, worker co-operatives and financial services), but maintains the 1981 Act's classification of farming, agricultural or general trading co-operatives. Moreover, the data does not specify forms of co-operatives (i.e. primary, secondary, etc.) and does not provide financial performance and member density data nor proper contact information to verify the existence of these co-operatives.

19 DTI Co-operatives Unit, Patience Gidongo, 21 October 2010.

20 These numbers are the estimates of the Co-operative Banks Development Agency. Contained in draft report on the *Status of FSCs and SACCOs*, March 2010.

21 In 2001 during the review COPAC, South African and the National Co-operative Association hosted an international conference to discuss reform of the 1981 Co-operative Act. This conference also produced a civil society agenda on co-operative legal reform.

22 ICA, *Cooperative Principles for the 21st Century* (ICA Communications Department: Geneva, 1996,), 1; International Labour Organisation Recommendation 193 (adopted in 2002); United Nations, *Guidelines on Cooperatives* (2001). Also see Preamble of Co-operatives Act (2005) and

Co-operatives Development Policy for an explicit statement of adherence to the principles and values.

23 The Act deals with definitions, scope, registration, membership issues, general meetings, management, capital structure, audits, restructuring, winding up, judicial management and administration, and provides for a co-operative advisory board, miscellaneous matters, transitional arrangements and special provisions for housing co-operatives, worker co-operatives, financial services co-operatives and agricultural co-operatives.

24 However, the role of the new democratic state in promoting an enabling a co-operative environment for different kinds of co-operatives, including worker co-operatives, is not understood. See K. Phillip, 'A Reality Check – Worker Coops in South Africa', *Labour Bulletin* 31: 1 (March/April 2007). Phillips attacks the worker co-operative model as being inherently unviable by making reference to a historical experience of trade union-linked worker co-operatives in the 1980s without appreciating the new opportunities and context for co-operative development in contemporary South Africa.

25 See COPAC, *Cooperative Movement Conference Report* (COPAC: Johannesburg, 2001).

26 Ibid.

27 These insights were gained through Vishwas Satgar's participation on the Co-operative Banks Development Agency Board since its formation in 2008. The board is a result of the Co-operative Banks Act and provides regulatory supervision and development support to emerging co-operative banks.

28 See section 1 and 1 (b) dealing with definitions and section 2 (b) regarding objectives of the Broad Based Black Economic Act, 2003, which defines a role for co-operatives.

29 COPAC has documented many failures of co-operatives in post-apartheid South Africa in which these factors loom large. The demise of the apex body in South Africa also expressed perverse state-co-operative relations.

30 Interview, Nomvula Masango-Makgotlho, Director: Co-operatives Development, DTI, 6/03/2007. By 2007 only about twenty co-operatives had been supported through the grant programme.

31 Pre-1990 co-operative development was located within the Department of Agriculture.

32 Interview, Nomvula Masango-Makgotlho, Director: Co-operatives Development, DTI, 6/03/2007.

33 Interview, Mmemogolo Malomane, Provincial Coordinator Co-operative Development: Directorate Agricultural Development Finance, 28/02/2007. The situation in the agricultural department has not changed since 2007.

34 Focus Group, Officials and Extension Offices Agricultural Unit: Department of Agriculture Kwazulu Natal, Cedara College, 12/03/2007.

35 Focus Group, Officials and Extension Offices Agricultural Unit:

Department of Agriculture Kwazulu Natal, Cedara College, 12/03/2007. Also focus group interviews with farming co-operatives in Cato Manor 13/03/2007. Interview with Judy Malqueeny, Co-operative Development Facilitator and Historian, KZN, 13/03/2007.

36 See Gauteng Government, Draft Co-operatives Development Policy and Strategy, August 2006.

37 Interview Geoff Ndumo, Head of DTI Co-operatives Unit, 23/08/2010.

38 The new Co-operatives Development Policy and Acts affirm the international principles and values that define a genuine co-operative identity and the international definition of a co-operative (i.e. 'an autonomous association of persons united voluntarily to meet their common economic and social needs and aspirations through a jointly owned and democratically controlled enterprise organised and operated on co-operative principles'). In the Co-operatives Act of 2005 'co-operative principles' are defined as 'the internationally accepted principles of co-operation', exemplified by the principles adopted by the International Co-operative Alliance, (contained in Chapter 1).

39 See Chapter 1 section 1(1) and Schedule 1 of the Co-operatives Act (2005).

40 The various traditions and state-co-operative movement relations that took root in Africa are dealt with in Patrick Develtere, Ignace Pollet and Fredrick Wanyama (eds), *Cooperating Out of Poverty: The Renaissance of the African Cooperative Movement* (Geneva: ILO, World Bank, 2007).

41 V. Satgar, 'Neoliberalised South Africa: Labour and the Roots of Passive Revolution', *Labour, Capital, and Society* 41:2 (2008), 39-69.

42 See *State of the Nation Address*, February 9, 2007, pp. 10–11.

43 Even before providing for Co-operative Development Policy and legislation the state put into place various Small and Medium Enterprise (SME) Policies and institutions like Khula Enterprise Agency, Ntsika, and the SME Council. Co-operative support continues through the Small Enterprise Development Agency. The treatment of co-operatives as any other enterprise is consistent with the neo-liberal shift expressed through ILO recommendation 193. See V. Satgar, 'Cooperative Development and Labour Solidarity: A Neo-Gramscian Perspective on the Global Struggle Against Neoliberalisation', *Labour, Capital and Society* 40:1&2 (2007).

44 Also see COPAC, *Cooperating for Transformation: Cooperative Case Studies from Amathole District, Eastern Cape*, Research Report (2010) on co-operatives in the Eastern Cape in which most of the co-operatives researched were given large financial grants by the state but were either marginal or self-developing. Only one out of the twenty-five co-operatives researched was commercially viable and operating with co-operative values and principles.

45 See DTI, *Baseline Study of Cooperatives in South Africa*, Research Report (2009), 35, available at www.dti.gove.za/. This study forms the basis of the new DTI strategy and is cited extensively in the strategy document

according to Geoff Ndumo, head of the DTI Co-operatives Unit, interviewed 22/08/2010.

46 DTI, *Baseline Study*, 37.

47 COPAC, *Cooperatives in Gauteng (a Quantitative Study): Broad Based BEE or Push Back into Poverty?*, Research Report (2005) and COPAC, *Cooperative Support Institutions in the Gauteng Cooperative Sector: Enabling Support or Dependent Development?*, Research Report (2006).

48 See COPAC's 2006 study on co-operatives in Gauteng and its 2010 study on co-operatives in the Eastern Cape.

49 This is different than the post-colonial experience in the rest of Africa which saw state support entrench bureaucracy. The outcome, however, was similar as it too reinforced political patronage. There is a contemporary literature that speaks to the state-centric control of co-operatives in Africa. See Develtere *et al.*, *Co-operating Out of Poverty* and ICA, *Cooperative Principles for the 21st Century* (Geneva: ICA Communications Department, 1996).

50 The sectors included the Agricultural Co-operative Business Chamber (ACB), the National Community Co-operative Union (NCCU), the South African Co-operative Network (SACNET) and the Savings and Credit Co-operative League (SACCOL).

51 The role of the Canadian Co-operative movement was informed by good intentions but was also not problem-free with a strong top-down tendency.

52 However, it did succeed in launching the South African Housing Co-operative Association (SAHCA), the sectoral body for housing co-operatives, but this body has not been adequately capacitated and resourced.

53 Although some individuals are still attempting to hold on to the moribund organisation for personal reasons, which further discredits co-operatives in South Africa.

54 There were also compounding factors such as personality conflicts, the destructive vanguardism of the South African Communist Party and internal corruption.

55 Chapter 12 of the 2005 Act.

56 The DTI's 2009 baseline study confirms this.

57 The DTI's 2009 baseline study was the first attempt to utilise research by the state to understand co-operative development trends and impacts and develop a new national co-operative development strategy. This study is a step in the right direction for state policy practice.

58 It is this empowerment-based ethics that clashes with the logic of capitalist business principles of short-term profit-maximising horizons, competition and survival of the strongest in the market place. Co-operatives make profits and engage competitively, but this is contingent on context-specific factors including the objectives of the co-operative. A small-scale subsistence worker co-operative engaged in garden farming works with a different logic to meet

member needs than a large, capital-intensive manufacturing worker co-operative, for example. But regardless if they are operating parallel to the market or articulating with the market, they should be grounded in the ethical and member-driven practices of a co-operative. See COPAC, *Building a Solidarity Economy Movement: A Guide for Grassroots Activism*, Activist Training Guide (2010).

59 Moreover, this lack of co-operative education was confirmed in the DTI's 2009 baseline study and in COPAC's 2010 study of twenty co-operatives in the Eastern Cape. See COPAC, *Cooperating for Transformation*.

11

Community, individuality and co-operation: the centrality of values

Ian MacPherson

They are questions that appear relentlessly throughout human history. What rights and obligations do individuals have? What are the rights and roles that accrue to the communities to which they belong? Judging from the millennia of debates and the multitude of answers that have been given, it seems clear that there are no absolute and final answers; only inescapable, necessary, and frequently acrimonious, discourse. The questions invite constant searching for appropriate responses, whether one considers them in regards to the distribution of wealth gained individually or through joint effort, the economic and social relationships within family and communities, the roles of mosques, churches and synagogues, discussions on the relative merits of charity and self-help, or the proper functioning of the organisations that people create. The bodies of thought one might consider in exploring them stretch across all ideologies and religions as well as several academic disciplines; they are undercurrents in virtually all political debates – often they are central.

The co-operative movement, what was once widely called 'co-operation', is important partly because it represents an institutional response to the tensions created by the differing and often competing appeals of individual and community rights, roles, and obligations. In fact, one could argue that it is one of the most important and distinctive characteristics of the movement – both for how it attacks excessive and exploitive individualism and how it seeks to find ways to accommodate both dimensions of the human experience.

Understanding the relationships between co-operation, community and individuality is not simple, however, because the world of co-operation is not simple, whether one tries to understand it institutionally, historically, geographically or intellectually. This can be demonstrated by considering when and why co-operatives emerged. Origins, too, are important because they create the original

frameworks within which movements and organisations are understood, even generations and many changes later. Something like a
Hartzian fragment,[1] they create the original notions of the co-
operative connections to community and individuality.

Institutionally and historically, it is widely customary to date the
beginnings of co-operative organisations back to the formation of the
Rochdale Society of Equitable Pioneers in Rochdale in 1844. It is older,
especially if one accepts the claims of some Scottish co-operators, who
would date the movement's beginnings with the creation of the
Fenwick Weavers' Society formed in 1761.[2] And those are only the
British versions of origins.

Although many national movements acknowledge the Rochdale
Pioneers as the founders of the international movement, all national
movements have their own co-operative 'creation stories', most of
which primarily emphasise the roles of their own 'pioneers'. American
co-operators, for example, trace their movement back to the work of
Benjamin Franklin in the eighteenth century, the intentional
community, worker and agrarian movements of the nineteenth
century, and the New Deal enthusiasms of the twentieth century.[3] The
French emphasise the democratic inheritance of the French
Revolution, and the solidarity, associationist movements of the nineteenth century, particularly during the Revolution of 1848 and the
Paris Commune.[4] The Italians look back to the social and economic
restructuring of the Renaissance, the communal entrepreneurship of
the Early Modern period, and particularly the struggles to create a
modern nation and economy from the late nineteenth century
onwards. It is a movement deeply embedded in Italy's social, economic
and political history, which has developed its own distinctive
co-operative forms and energy.[5] The Germans emphasise the work of
Raiffeisen and Schulze-Delitzsch and their struggles to provide
community-based credit services for specific groups and classes during
the 1850s and 1860s.[6] The financial co-operatives they created played
vital roles in the modernisation of the German countryside and in the
economic development of the bourgeoisie.

National movements in other countries stress their own co-operative
traditions, many of them, as in the case of Japan and Korea, pointing
to the ritualised collaboration of their rural ancestors during periods
of planting and harvesting.[7] African and Latin American co-operators
recall the kin group and community traditions of their indigenous
peoples, the co-operative developments associated with European
settlers, some of the imperial interventions into colonial life, and (in
some countries) associations with early trades unionism.[8] Many of the

countries of the global South experienced their first great experimentation with formal co-operative development during their independence periods, when it was linked to nation-building and their founding political leaders, though the results of those experiments, as in the case of most imperial efforts, were mixed.

The origins issue can be seen as being even older, much older, if one relates it to the general roles of co-operative tendencies in human history and development, a perspective obviously gaining greater acceptance in our times. After generations of emphasis on the centrality of competition in human development, more researchers are reassessing how collaboration, reciprocity and mutuality have contributed to human development.[9]

In short, when thought of historically, institutionally, geographically and intellectually, the meanings of 'community' and 'individuality' within co-operation are time and place specific. They emerge out of the contexts within which movements develop. They are shaped by culture and experience. They do not fit easily into the neat categories that have been so prized in the Western intellectual traditions of the past two hundred years. Co-operators at different times in different parts of the world have always attempted – will always attempt – to harmonise the concerns of individuality and community in different ways – and that is a strength, not a weakness, of the international movement. It is inevitable that co-operators in Japan, Ghana, Colombia, the United States and the Czech Republic will find different ways to harmonise the claims of communities and individuality.

One must approach the themes of community and individuality (like so much else within the field of Co-operative Studies) with humility and sensitivity. One must avoid the tendency to want to generalise too quickly, to assume too much based on whatever our own experiences might have been.

Co-operation and co-operative organisations relate to communities ambivalently. On the one hand, it is customary and substantially accurate to stress the communitarian dimensions of co-operativism. If there is a 'standard' explanation in the North Atlantic countries for how co-operative approaches have developed over the last two centuries, it is to place them within the context of geographic community, group and class responses to the ravages of the Great Transformation, as Polyani called the development of the market economy and the emergence of the modern state.[10] The list of problems they addressed is long, including the disruption of what were typically recalled as more stable rural and preindustrial relationships; the mistreatment of children, women, and men in factories; the rapid and often cruel transformations of rural societies; the emergence of impoverished ghettoes in the grimy cities of industrialism; the intolerably unfair distribution of wealth; and the scarcity of reliable, reasonably priced food. Many co-operative movements emerged as reactions to such problems, though in some instances they were also efforts to capitalise on the opportunities such changes could offer to well-organised, effective group action.

It is particularly easy in the United Kingdom to associate the rise of consumer co-operatives with class, group and community reactions to the challenges of the Great Transformation. The connection between the development of co-operatives and the culture, even the politics (or the anti-politics), of the working classes, can easily be drawn, largely because so many powerful communicators have made the case for it.[11] The most common British version of co-operative individuality is rooted in the experiences of the industrial working class to the point that it is difficult to conceive of it in any other way,[12] perhaps unfortunately.

According to this view, the communitarian emphasis begins with the work and thought of Robert Owen, a principal founder of the trade union and co-operative movements, intentional community traditions and British socialism. It continues through the work of a series of writers and activists, ending with the argument made by Sidney and Beatrice Webb (early Fabian socialist historians of welfare, the state and British working-class institutions) and adopted by others – that the salvation of the working class, if not civilisation itself, could be found in collaboration between trade unions, the Labour party, and the co-operatives, especially consumer co-operatives. It is a well-established view that approaches orthodoxy.

One can make a similar case for the importance of community-based activism within marketing and other forms of rural co-ops around the world. They succeeded, it can be easily argued, because rural people, though in many instances slowly and shallowly, came to see the benefits of collaborating in the purchase of supplies and the sale of what they produced. Such perspectives can readily be found in the co-ops that emerged in the widespread agrarian outbursts of the late nineteenth and early twentieth centuries in, for example, Ireland, the United States and Canada.[13]

One can also easily see the importance of community values within the co-operative banking traditions. One reason why consumer, agricultural and fishing organisations formed banking subsidiaries was to reinforce directly and indirectly the community interests of member organisations. More recently, it can be seen in the Co-operative Bank's support for community and ethical initiatives.[14]

In the community-based kinds of co-operative banking organisations, most notably credit unions, the 'commitment to community' is particularly engrained. Along with democratic process, it is arguably their most distinguishing characteristic.[15] One can also argue that, historically at least, the Raiffeisen movement was deeply concerned with rural communities,[16] though through strong emphases on self-help, self-governance and self-responsibility. The emphasis on 'self' is obviously important, but there was – and arguably in some areas still are – underlying concerns for rural communal life within the Raiffeisen tradition.

One can also readily identify community issues within movements beyond the North Atlantic. It was evident in many of the co-operative efforts associated with independence movements in the global South, from the stated co-operative goals of Nehru, the development of African socialism as envisioned by Nkrumah, the ujamaa programme of Nyerere, and the encouragement of co-operatives by Latin American revolutionaries/reformers influenced by Liberation theology and/or revolutionary ambitions.[17] It has been readily evident within Japanese co-operatives, some Indian co-ops, the thrift and credit co-operatives of Sri Lanka, and the emerging co-ops of recent years in Latin America.[18]

Similarly, the concern for community is readily apparent within emerging co-operatives and the changing priorities of most well-established co-operatives. In one sense, the deepening concern can be easily explained. As the twentieth century came to an end, much of the world became caught up in deepening commitments to competitive views of human history and to the idea that competition was the only sure way of ensuring 'progress'. The decline of centrally planned economies, correctly or not, was viewed by many, especially in positions of economic and political power in the West, as a climactic defeat of collective approaches; the victory of the 'market' as a triumph for indulgent and guilt-free individualism. Invariably, and as the consequences of unregulated and unrestrained markets have become evident, some of the 'lessons' that should have been indelibly learned in the wake of the economic and social history of the nineteenth and early twentieth centuries have had to be relearned. Co-operatives benefit from that reassessment; their social concerns – which had tended to be dismissed as the market 'victory' seemed to occur – once more became appreciated.

In recent years, too, alternative understandings of how healthy economies and societies can function have asserted (in some instances, reasserted) themselves. Generally, these alternative visions have been based on communitarian or issued-based sources – ethnic associations, community loyalties, class bonds, concern over environmental degradation, a desire to correct gender inequalities and a widespread search for alternative ways to deliver social services, to name only a few. New or revived forms of economic thought – the New Institutionalism, Social Economics, Feminist Economics, Environmental Economics – have challenged neoliberal views of the 'dismal science'. Economists search in games theory and business practice to find ways to reform the existing economic system so it will be more equitable and responsible. And, in many countries, the idea of 'social entrepreneurship' is increasingly gaining widespread support – and while it seems often to be largely dependent on traditional entrepreneurship and heroic management, it can embrace community needs and engagement in useful ways. It can even lead to the formation of co-operatives in name or in practice.

At the same time, as capital and economic growth flee to the most financially rewarding places, the communities left behind are weakened and are forced to consider more seriously the possibilities inherent in community-based activism, including the development of co-operatives. In fact, aroused communities often find in co-ops the most practical ways in which to expand their capacity to be 'masters of their own destinies', to use words popular in many co-operative circles a half century ago.

There are challenges, however, within these close associations. Co-operatives can readily become economic engines for people aroused by specific issues or mobilising other movements: thus advocates of organic and 'slow' food find the co-operative structure amenable; advocates of Fair Trade find co-ops useful for the assembling, processing and selling of their produce or products; and people concerned about gender inequality are attracted to the democratic structures, the possibilities of 'sweat equity', and the multiple purposes of co-operatives as they search for greater gender equality. Still others, interested in energy issues, can utilise co-operative, community-based institutional forms in developing wind power, transportation alternatives and ethanol co-ops. People wishing to develop companies with alternative employment practices can form worker co-ops. Communities facing serious social issues can organise health and other forms of social co-ops.

This absorption of the co-operative model by other movements, of course, is not new. One can even argue that the movement largely emerged historically as an associate or offshoot of other movements. The ties between the agitations of the working classes and the consumer movement were crucially important in many industrialising countries over the last 150 years, from the United Kingdom to Argentina to Singapore. The emergence of worker co-operatives was (and is) often tied to the search by workers for reliable employment through fair and equitable workplace practice. In the countryside, agrarian movements embraced a wide range of co-operatives for the economic and social improvement of rural life. One can make a case, perhaps less easily, for the intermingling of women's movements and co-operatives: for example, in Japan and India, and with the work of the co-operative women's guilds in several other countries.

This capacity of co-operatives and their movement to serve as the economic engines of other movements should not be undervalued: it was – and it is – an important contribution, a testimony to the flexibility of the co-operative model and an indication of the breadth of co-operative thought. It can mean, however, that a given co-operative is absorbed by people or organisations with little interest in co-operatives *per se*. In those situations, the co-operative dimension fades into the background, overwhelmed by the other causes the co-operative serves. It becomes difficult to distinguish which is dog, which the tail.

Establishing that distinction is not an idle or 'academic' question: the overlap perpetually raises issues invariably present in organisations with conflicting loyalties; the pressing needs of the host movement or cause may preclude association with other co-ops or undermine the democratic process of the co-op.

Co-operatives responding to deeply felt community needs benefit from the commitments of aroused citizens; they can easily suffer from their single-mindedness.

The connections between co-operation and communities are typically fruitful and important – they can often also be ambiguous.

At the same time, the co-operative movement also possesses powerful notions of the possibilities of individuality, notions that can raise other kinds of questions.[19] Partly, this is because, when the organised movement emerged in the nineteenth century, there were widespread discussions about the roles of individuals in society. For example, according to one perhaps simplistic interpretation, Alexis de Tocqueville is credited with giving the term individualism its 'still cogent'[20] meaning. In his book *Democracy in America*, published in 1835, he wrote:

Individualism is a novel expression, to which a novel idea has given birth.
Individualism is a mature and calm feeling, which disposes each member
of the community to sever himself from the mass of his fellow-creatures,
and to draw apart with his family and friends.[21]

This did not mean that de Tocqueville championed a socially uncon-
cerned or amoral individualism; in fact, when he embarked on his
American tour, he was searching for a moral compass that the new
individualism could follow. The withdrawal from community, even
family, referred to in the above definition was partly to allow individuals to select carefully the contributions they could make – like
Thomas Jefferson's farmer-citizen – to the common good. His ideal
was detached engagement, not selfish isolation.

De Tocqueville was important not because he differed from others in
his time but because he probed one of their fundamental concerns.
Understanding the legitimate claims of individuals was being widely
debated, including in co-operative movements, many of which
emerged in their institutional forms at that time. One might even say
that the co-operative views of individuality reflected many of the
moral concerns that preoccupied de Tocqueville. They added the
understanding that fiercely independent, 'splendid' individualism was
what might be called a genuine form of 'false consciousness', an
illusion for human beings, who must exist and derive much of their
identity from social contexts – perhaps even if they are hermits.

The appeal of co-operatives and co-operativism to individual
well-being is so obvious that it is rarely discussed. They offered,
for example, empowerment for ordinary people through their
commitment to democratic process. One of democracy's great appeals
is its heady promise that individuals can make a difference – even
help shape the world around them – through political democracy.
Co-operators sought to expand that promise into the realm of
economic activities, itself a transformative idea. They rewarded
individual effort in a concrete way through dividends based on use – a
kind of involvement available to all co-op members. They encouraged
extensive educational activity, not only so people could be better
members and directors of their co-operatives, but also so they could
fulfil better their own potential and could better understand the
world around them. Their concern for groups that were widely
marginalised – such as women, immigrants and the poor – though
hardly perfect was nevertheless admirable and was based largely
on individual development. Their capacity to empower specific individuals was remarkable: consider the men who sat on the board of the

Co-operative Wholesale Society by 1900 or the women who served the International Co-operative Women's Guild at the same time. Where else could they have achieved such recognition and influence? Think about the lads from the slums who became employees in local co-ops and went on to remunerative, respected managerial careers 'in the co-op'.

Parallels can be found in all co-operative movements. Co-operatives around the world have consistently provided people with a vehicle for individual upward economic and social mobility.[22] It may be, in fact, that they have often played that role too well – to the costs of their communitarian goals. It is always easy for successful leaders to believe that they were responsible for creating the wealth 'their' co-ops distributed. As in the case with relationships to communities, the relationships with individuality were – and are – not clear-cut; they were – and are – matters of choice and reflection, of institutional cultures and internal organisational dynamics.

Where then are the guides for how co-operation strengthens communities and enhances individuality for harmonising their competing demands? Bearing in mind that blanket answers are impossible, given the complex diversities of co-operation internationally, the best understandings emanate from co-operative thought, most obviously in the generally accepted principles of the international movement and the statement of values that support them.

The co-operative world started its search for a reliable and widely accepted international articulation of its principles as early as the 1860s. The task has challenged the movement ever since because there are so many different kinds of co-operatives existing within so many different cultures and operating under so many different political regimes. Moreover, because co-operatives emerge out of specific contexts to meet specific needs, they have always tended to be preoccupied with the practical and the 'real'; they seldom engage in serious introspective debates or with 'covering laws' that their leaders can apply to the situations they confront. Rather, they typically gain appreciation for their principles in the wake of practice and in association with other co-operatives. There are no universal, widely consulted tomes or sustained enquiries coming out of the academy. In fact, with very few exceptions, universities have totally ignored the issues and possibilities of co-operatives and co-operative thought, though universally they construct impressive buildings each housing scores of scholars for the benefits of conventional business.

Originally, the movement's chief intellectual source was widely called co-operative philosophy, the core thought of co-operation. It was (and it is) a complex body of thought, drawn from different co-operative types (consumer, worker, agricultural, banking, etc.) and, as suggested above, reflecting several national traditions. Moreover, it has been – and it is – constantly deprecated by other ideological systems, which have typically deprecated co-operativism (because of its alleged imprecision and tendencies to disseminate rather than concentrate power), even when they exploit co-ops for their economic effectiveness and capacities to mobilise community resources.

While co-operative thought was an important force in the ideological firmament of the late nineteenth and early twentieth centuries, it did not fare well in the war of ideas between 1914 and 1991, what Eric Hobsbawm has called the Age of Extremes,[23] a period in which the voice of co-operativism struggled to be heard.[24] It was essentially a gentle, pacifist and gradualist voice lost amid the loud and often violent clamour of more aggressive intellectual competitors.

Such diverse antecedents and uncertain location in the political economy has meant that the International Co-operative Alliance went through a long birth process as it sought to fashion unity and common purpose from national and sectoral movements. Finally, in 1936, amid the Great Depression and several complex international issues, notably the roles of co-operatives in the Union of Soviet Socialist Republics, the ICA prepared its first statement of principles. Thirty years later, it adopted another variation, to be followed by yet one more, again after the passage of some thirty years, this one adopted in the ICA Manchester Congress of 1995, and entitled *The Co-operative Identity Statement*.[25] (See Appendix A, below, pp. 220–221.)

Most people looking at the *Statement* probably concentrate upon the third section, which lists the current version of the international co-operative principles. They essentially refer to the rules that should govern co-operative organisations; a kind of checklist that people seeking to establish a co-operative or to evaluate an existing one can consult for guidance. They are the rules that govern how a co-operative should function as an entity, particularly through open membership, the practice of democracy, the emphasis on education, the distribution of surpluses to members based on their use of the co-operative's services, collaboration with other co-operatives, a commitment to independent action and caring for communities.

According to the 1995 *Statement*, the principles should be seen more as guidelines than as a checklist, guidelines mandating that co-operatives continually seek to enhance their democratic practice, their engagement of members, their commitments to education, their deepening involvement with other co-operatives, and their involvement with the communities they serve. There can be no expectation of perfection in these matters, only a regular and earnest effort to improve performance steadily.

The principles, which take on added significance when thought of as an entity rather than a number of discrete statements, can be seen as balancing the claims of community and individuality. On the one hand, they establish powerful roles for individuals (for example, they were carefully phrased to emphasise the importance of members); on the other, they are about the proper functioning of the organisations in keeping with the values on which co-operatives are based (the second part of the *Statement*).

The preparation for the *Statement* began with a three-year enquiry into the values generally accepted throughout the international movement. Led by Sven Akë Böök of Sweden and others, it undertook a literature review, followed by a series of consultations with numerous co-operative leaders and members around the world – what Böök called an 'action and dialogue' approach.[26] The consultations involved thousands of people in international meetings and its wisdom came more from practice and dialogue than philosophical systems. It generated a book, *Co-operative Values in a Changing World*, which wrestled with the resultant complexity but also demonstrated the movement's rich intellectual traditions.

Though one can argue that the process was conducted from the context of European and especially Swedish co-operative perspectives, it genuinely welcomed views from other parts of the world. It stepped beyond the usual approach whereby co-operatives 'overseas' tended to be seen as kinds of colonial gifts from established North Atlantic movements. It challenged co-operators everywhere to hear voices from other lands and from co-operative traditions different from their own. The movement's need for international consensus, aspired to since the nineteenth century but never achieved, was acknowledged and, within the resources available at the time, undertaken.

In the following three years, from 1992 to 1995, another committee fostered international dialogues examining what Böök and his committee had found, a prelude to the development of the *Co-operative Identity Statement*. The values that were adopted for the *Statement*'s second section were organised into two groups: those shaping the operations and associations within co-operatives and those that should inspire co-operators. The statement reads:

Co-operatives are based on values of self-help, self-responsibility, democracy, equality, equity, and solidarity. In the tradition of their founders, co-operative members believe in the ethical values of honesty, openness, social responsibility and caring for others.[27]

Each of these values can be placed on a scale of individuality/ communitarian spectrum, some belonging closer to one end than the other, but none completely at either extreme. For example, *self-help* appears to be directed at individuals, but in a co-operative context it means people helping themselves by working with others for recipro-cal and mutual benefit. Similarly, *self-responsibility* means taking charge of key aspects of one's life but again within a group context. Both values imply personal growth, economic and social, but they recognise that it is best accomplished within the communities of interest that co-operatives provide.

In its essence, *democracy* usually means seeking agreement if not harmony through public negotiations by individuals and groups within the political process. Co-operators seek to extend that approach to workplace relations, the production and distribution of foods, the building of neighbourhoods, and the deployment of financial resources. It is still a radical idea commonly resisted.

The co-operative commitment to *equality* defines how members relate to each other formally within the collectivity – on the basis of persons not investments – and it determines many of the ways in which co-operatives function. It is a value that can be most obviously positioned on the individualist side of the continuum, but it profoundly determines how collective power is ultimately distributed within co-operatives.

Co-operatives apply the value of *equity* primarily through rewarding participation not investment, though they may pay a reasonable return on investments beyond those required for membership. In doing so, they are rewarding contributions individuals make through engage-ment, in the process creating organisational dynamics significantly different from those of investor-driven firms.

Solidarity belongs on the communitarian side of the ledger. It prizes the benefits that flow from collaboration by both individuals and co-operative organisations. On an immediately practical level, this value creates significant economies of scale.[28] More deeply, it is central to co-operative forms of entrepreneurship, in fact, usually essential for the undertaking of significant new initiatives. Solidarity also enjoins individuals and organisations to co-operate with people and organisations sharing similar goals and visions. It is the exact antithesis of what many forms of individualism articulate.

The ethical values that are the common beliefs of co-operative members – honesty, openness, social responsibility and caring for others – have varied implications for the individuality/community continuum. Often enough, people take *honesty* for granted. They should not. It is not just honesty in the transactions that occur between a co-operative and its members and customers: for example, truth in advertising, transparent dealings, provision of accurate information – though all of these are important. It also includes honesty in relationships among members, between members and boards, boards and managers, managers and staff, co-operatives and communities – in short, it is central to the trust that makes co-operatives successful. Honesty is not a hollow or limited word.

Similarly, *openness* slips easily off the tongue, but its practice constantly challenges. It means being open to people with different views and customs, possibly even challenging one's most dearly held views. It requires that co-operatives welcome all those they can serve 'without gender, social, racial, political or religious discrimination'.[29] It too is not a hollow or limited word.

Social responsibility and *caring for others* obviously refer to how co-operatives relate to communities. In today's world, aspects of them are frequently expressed in terms of triple or even quadruple bottom lines, forms of public service and accountability in which many co-operative organisations excel. They encourage many new forms of co-operative activism, the expansion of the movement. They have been evident since the movement's beginnings, though perhaps not always as honoured as they should have been.

In short, the values are not just pleasant words to be displayed on office walls or given lip service at co-operative gatherings. They are the basis for the principles under which co-operatives function at any given time; they are the contemporary moral basis for co-operative individuality.

The distinct way in which co-operatives seek to harmonise individuality and community concerns contrasts strongly with some of the more prominent forms of individualism that have emerged, particularly within the North Atlantic world, during the last 150 years.

From the mid-nineteenth century onwards, many national movements demonised the industrialists and big tycoons of the Industrial Revolution: the 'robber barons' as they were widely known in North America. Co-operators attacked them, perhaps indiscriminately, for exploiting workers, operating dehumanising 'company towns', pursuing profits despite social consequences, and living with indecent ostentation – creating what Thorstein Veblen called a predatory culture characterised by the conspicuous consumption of

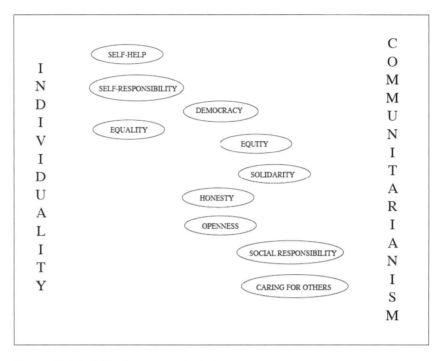

Figure 11.1 Individuality–communitarianism

valuable goods.[30] They were examples of individualism gone amuck.

In the early twentieth century, notions of co-operative individuality contrasted strongly with the individualisms of modernism: the tendencies to denigrate the past, to glorify war, to emphasise subjectivity, to destroy social norms, to celebrate irrationality, and to approve social disruption.[31] Similarly, they did not mingle easily with the extensions of modernism, the kinds of hedonistic individualism that became common in the 1920s: understandable but socially irresponsible reactions to the trauma of the First World War.

The relationships with existentialism, that rich and diverse body of thought that became so influential by the middle of the twentieth century, were more complex. To the extent that existentialism emphasised the futility of seeking to change an absurd and meaningless world and questioned the range of associations that could be meaningful, it differed from the optimism and openness (some would say the naiveté) of co-operativism.[32] At the same time, the intense demands for individuals to confront honestly and thoughtfully their own essence and purposes, the quests that underlie much existentialist thought, are not inimical to co-operative views of individuality.

During the 1930s, the totalitarian regimes that emerged in Europe and elsewhere emphasised the submergence of the individual within mass cultures, sparking great debates in co-operative circles – intense and oppositional in the case of fascism, divided and uncertain in the case of the Soviet Union.

Starting in the 1950s, the individualism associated with rights discourse and community/political activism resonated well within many co-operative circles, helping spark the expansion of housing and worker co-operatives, co-operative development in the global South, the organic food movement, and community-based co-operative banking. This synergy though was more incidental than fundamental: for those concerned about human rights issues, the Vietnam war, freedom struggles and workplace inequities, those issues were over-powering motivation – the support for co-operatives was typically inci-dental.

More recently, the most prominent individualisms have tended to be associated with neo-liberal notions of individualism, perhaps most cogently put by Margaret Thatcher when she said, echoing Ayn Rand, 'there is no such thing as society. There are only individual men and women. There are families.'[33] In North America it can be tied to the policies of Ronald Reagan and the 'common sense revolution' – the Contract with America – of Newt Gingrich. It is commonly found on Fox News and CNN as well as nearly all American radio talk shows. In Canada, it has found political strength in some provinces and within the current federal government.

Most recently, psychologists and sociologists have become alarmed by the growing tendencies within North Atlantic societies towards narcissism, finding that, in extreme cases, it amounts to a personality disorder.[34] Arguably starting with discussions and beliefs of the 'Me generation' during the 1970s, narcissistic behaviour is today expanding at a faster rate than obesity in the American population.[35] Manifestations include people who have a compulsive and deluded view of their own importance, poor listening skills, difficulties in working with others, and indulgent preoccupations with status, image and personal beauty. It is a syndrome that fits poorly within a co-operative context, though perhaps it is not unknown among those engaged within and studying co-operatives.

Finally, one other kind of individualism of great importance to our times should be mentioned: the individualisms readily associated with globalisation, the focus of the work of Anthony Eliott and Charles Lemert in their stimulating book *The New Individuality: the Emotional Costs of Globalisation*. It is a book that explores individualism from its origins down to the global ambitions and perspectives emerging in the individualisms of our own times. It finds very significant differences between Europe and North America, a perspective that might be fruitfully explored in understanding further the varieties of co-operative individuality. The book, however, ends up with (arguably) a kind of romantic fascination for individuals who swim defiantly against parochial streams, a viewpoint particularly attractive for many North Americans. It is doubtful that this kind of individualistic emphasis fits well into co-operative traditions. In fact, like all the individualisms briefly discussed above, though sometimes moderated by recognition of the rewards of reciprocal relationships and the impact of personal religious/philosophical beliefs, the typical global individualisms of today are arguably fundamentally different from co-operative ideas of individuality.

The picture becomes further complicated as one moves beyond the North Atlantic frameworks to examine co-operative understandings of individuality in other lands, understandings influenced by different religious traditions, (for example, the varieties of Buddhism and Islam), the inheritances of indigenous peoples, the nature of kinship associations, the traditions of preindustrial relationships, and the associations of industrialising communities. Those understandings obviously contrast strikingly with various forms of inherited individualism, such as machismo (in both its feminine and masculine versions) in Latin America, the arrogance associated with the upper castes of South Asia, the preening of many government leaders (however similar that might appear to be to Northern counterparts), and the arrogance of some elders in Aboriginal communities. The issues are complex and numerous; they require considerable research, understanding and reflection.

This chapter is a call for further discussion. It has argued that forms of co-operative individuality do exist and, while variously influenced by culture and experience, they can flourish when they act in symbiosis with the movement's communitarian traditions. They can be best understood in terms of the movement's underlying values, which enjoin co-operators within different cultures and traditions minimally to:

- accept responsibility for themselves and encourage others to do the same;
- believe in the power of mutual self-help;
- trust democracy and seek its wider application;

- seek genuine equality in relationships with other co-operators and within co-operatives;
- seek equity in what they do individually and collectively;
- collaborate with like-minded people and organisations and encourage their co-operatives to do the same;
- recognise the multi-faceted challenges entailed in being honest;
- strive for openness in relating with others and in operating co-operatives;
- encourage their co-operatives to build more sustainable, socially responsible, and caring communities.

These words, which many might dismiss as banal, carry easily over-looked tensions and challenges. They create a burden of commitment, limits on what is acceptable and stimulants for what is possible. Collectively, they contribute to the harmonisation of individual and collective interests. They suggest the power of the old co-operative logo 'Each for all and all for each', a symbolic way in which co-operators in less gender-respectful days tried to capture their value-based commitment to resolving the tensions inherent in the individual/communitarian continuum.

Figure 11.2 'Each for all' logo

Appendix A[36]

Statement on the Co-operative Identity
Definition
A co-operative is an autonomous association of persons united voluntarily to meet their common economic, social, and cultural needs and aspirations through a jointly-owned and democratically-controlled enterprise.

Values
Co-operatives are based on the values of self-help, self-responsibility, democracy, equality, equity and solidarity. In the tradition of their founders, co-operative members believe in the ethical values of honesty, openness, social responsibility and caring for others.

Principles
The co-operative principles are guidelines by which co-operatives put their values into practice.

1st Principle: Voluntary and Open Membership

Co-operatives are voluntary organisations, open to all persons able to use their services and willing to accept the responsibilities of membership, without gender, social, racial, political or religious discrimination.

2nd Principle: Democratic Member Control

Co-operatives are democratic organisations controlled by their members, who actively participate in setting their policies and making decisions. Men and women serving as elected representatives are accountable to the membership. In primary co-operatives members have equal voting rights (one member, one vote) and co-operatives at other levels are also organised in a democratic manner.

3rd Principle: Member Economic Participation

Members contribute equitably to, and democratically control, the capital of their co-operative. At least part of that capital is usually the common property of the co-operative. Members usually receive limited compensation, if any, on capital subscribed as a condition of membership. Members allocate surpluses for any or all of the following purposes: developing their co-operative, possibly by setting up reserves, part of which at least would be indivisible; benefiting members in proportion to their transactions with the co-operative; and supporting other activities approved by the membership.

4th Principle: Autonomy and Independence

Co-operatives are autonomous, self-help organisations controlled by their members. If they enter to agreements with other organisations, including governments, or raise capital from external sources, they do so on terms that ensure democratic control by their members and maintain their co-operative autonomy.

5th Principle: Education, Training and Information

Co-operatives provide education and training for their members, elected representatives, managers, and employees so they can contribute effectively to the development of their co-operatives. They inform the general public – particularly young people and opinion leaders – about the nature and benefits of co-operation.

6th Principle: Co-operation among Co-operatives

Co-operatives serve their members most effectively and strengthen the co-operative movement by working together through local, national, regional and international structures.

7th Principle: Concern for Community

Co-operatives work for the sustainable development of their communities through policies approved by their members.

Notes

1 Louis Hartz, an American political scientist, advanced the idea that American exceptionalism – and that of Québec, English-Canada, Canada and Australia as well – could be explained by understanding the settler societies that shaped their formative years. As a theory, it arguably sought to explain too much from a relatively simple premise, but the idea that the attitudes and assumptions of the 'formative periods' long influence what happens subsequently is an interesting insight, one that has resonance in Co-operative Studies, given the important ways in which the formative

period is stressed within so many co-ops. Almost always, the longest chapters in co-op histories are the first few; very often, the conclusions revert to discussions of the long-standing implications of the original conceptions. For Hartzian theory, see Louis Hartz, *The Liberal Tradition in America: An Interpretation of American Political Thought since the Revolution* (Chicago: Harcourt, Brace, 1955) and *The Founding of New Societies: Studies in the History of the United States, Latin America, South Africa, Canada, and Australia* (Chicago: Harcourt, Brace & World, 1964).

2 See *Co-operative Development Scotland*, available at www.cdscotland .co.uk/cds-history and, particularly, John Smith and John McFadzean, *A History of Fenwick Weavers*.

3 See Kimberly A. Zeuli and Roberet Cropp, *Cooperatves: Principles and Practices in the 21st Century* (Madison: University of Wisconsin, undated); John Curl, *For All The People: Uncovering the Hidden History of Cooperation, Cooperative Movements, and Communalism in America* (Oakland: PM Press, 2009); Steve Leiken, *The Practical Utopians: American Workers and the Cooperative Movement in the Gilded Age* (Detroit: Wayne State University Press, 2005).

4 See Jean-François Draperi, 'The Ethical Foundations and Epiatological Position of Co-operative Research', in Ian MacPherson and Erin McLaughlin Jenkins, *Integrating Diversities within a Complex Heritage* (Victoria: British Columbia Institute for Co-operative Studies, 2008), pp. 323–344; J.E.S. Hayward, 'The Official Social Philosophy of the French Third Republic: Léon Bourgeois and Solidarism', *International Review of Social History* 6 (1961), 19–48.

5 See Vera Zamagni, *Italy's Cooperatives from Marginality to Success*, available at www.helsinki.fi/iehc2006/papers2/Zamagni.pdf.

6 See Jan-Otmar Hesse, 'Co-operatives in Germany in the 20th Century, an Overview and Some Hypotheses', *Enterprises et Histoire* 56, 49–61; DGRV, available at www.dgrv.de/en/cooperatives/historyofcoopera-tives.html; Michael Prinz 'German Rural Cooperatives: Friedrich-Wilhelm Raiffeisen and the Organization of Trust, 1850–1914', available at eh.net/XIIICongress/Papers/Prinz.pdf.

7 See Madhav Madane, 'Co-operatives and Community Culture', *Review of Internaional Co-operation* 99:1 (2006); Larry L. Burmeister, 'State, Industrialization and Agricultural Policy in Korea', *Development and Change* 21 (October 2008), 197–223.

8 See F.O. Wanayama, P. Develtere and I. Pollet, 'Encountering the Evidence: Co-operatives and Poverty Reduction in Africa', *Working Papers on Social and Co-operative Entrepreneurship* (Leuven: Katolieke Universiteit Leuven, 2008); Patrick Develtere, 'Cooperative Movements in the Developing Countries', *Annals of Public and Cooperative Economics* 64: 2, 179–208; Patrick Develtere, 'Co-operatives and Development: Towards a Social Movement Perspective', *Occasional*

Papers, Centre for the Study of Co-operatives, University of Saskatchewan, 1992.

9   For example, see Peter Hammerstein, *Genetic and Cultural Evolution of Cooperation* (Cambridge: MIT Press, 2003).

10 See Karl Polyani, *The Great Transformation* (New York: Rinehart & Company, 1944).

11 See Stephen Yeo, 'Towards Co-operative Politics: Using Early to Generate Late Socialism', *Journal of Co-operative Studies* 42 (2009), 22–35; G. Claeys, *Citizens and Saints: Politics and Anti-Politics in Early British Socialism* (Cambridge: Cambridge University Press, 1989); Peter Gurney, *Co-operative Culture and the Politics of Consumption in England, 1870–1930* (Manchester: Manchester University Press, 1996); Johnston Birchall, *Co-op: The People's Business* (Manchester: University of Manchester, 1994).

12 Other lands typically have other versions of co-operative individuality: e.g., for many years, the co-operative farming class of the North American Plains/Prairies, the Sri Lanka hill farmer, the peasants of Latin America, the credit union activist in many lands, and the new economy co-operator of the present day.

13 See Patrick Bolger, *The Irish Co-Operative Movement, Its History and Development* (Dublin: Institute of Public Administration 1977); Lawrence Goodwyn, *The Populist Moment: A Short History of the Agrarian Revolt in America* (Oxford: Oxford University Press, 1978) and Ian MacPherson, *Each for All: A History of the English–Canadian Co-operative Movement, 1900–1945* (Toronto: Macmillan, 1979).

14 See the Co-operative Bank's web page on investments, available at www.co-operativeinvestments.co.uk/servlet/Satellite/1204616032483 ,CFSweb/Page/Investments-UnitTrustsAndISAs?WT.svl=footer.

15 See Ian MacPherson, *Hands Around the Globe: A History of the International Credit Union Movement and the Role and Development of World Council of Credit Unions, Inc.* (Victoria: Horsdal & Schubert, 1999).

16 See G. Aschoff and E. Hennington, *The German Co-operative System* (Frankfurt am Main: Fritz Knapp Verlag, 1986).

17 See Johnston Birchall, *The International Co-operative Movement* (Manchester: Manchester University Press, 1997).

18 Ibid., and Ian MacPherson, *Co-operative Principles for the 21st Century* (Geneva, International Co-operative Alliance, 1995)

19 The original version of this paper, entitled 'The Burdens and the Limitations, the Possibilities of History: The Values – and the Value – of Co-operation' was presented at the 2009 conference of the UK Society for Co-operative Studies in July 2009. In it I used the term 'co-operative individualism'. Stephen Yeo rightly pointed out the longstanding opposition in co-operative circles to 'individualism' as an end in itself. The point is that, within co-operative thought, co-operative forms of individuality

have life only within the context of movement bonds. The reverse is also true. Thus in this draft, the term 'understanding of individuality' is used, even though that might seem strange to modern eyes. I am grateful to Professor Yeo for his comments and reminder. The present was too much with me.

20 Anthony Eliott and Charles Lemert, *The New Individualism: The Emotional Costs of Globalisation* (Abingdon: Routledge, 2009), p. 159.

21 Ibid.

22 This theme is discussed briefly in Ian MacPherson, 'Some Fortune and a Little Fame: Co-operatives as Ladders for Upward Mobility in the Canadian West', *Journal of the West* Spring 2004, 64–76, reprinted in Ian MacPherson, *One Path to Co-operative Studies: A Selection of Papers and Presentations* (Victoria: British Columbia Institute for Co-operative Studies, 2001) pp. 123–136.

23 There are many ways in which to come to terms with the complexities of the ideological turmoil of the twentieth century. One of the most interesting is to follow the tortuous intellectual odyssey of Eric Hobsbawm, though his vantage point is not that of the conventional co-operator. See particularly his *Age of Extremes: the Short Twentieth Century, 1914–1991* (New York: Vintage Books, 1994).

24 Ibid., and MacPherson, *Co-operative Principles*.

25 See International Co-operative Alliance website, available at www.ica .coop/coop/principles.html.

26 Sven Akë Böök, *Co-operative Values in a Changing World* (edited by Margaret Pickett and Mary Tracey) (Geneva: International Co-operative Alliance, 1992), p. 6.

27 ICA website.

28 During the discussions by the committee over which word – 'solidarity'or 'mutuality' – should be used, it was decided that 'solidarity' should be employed, perhaps because it was embedded so deeply in the discourse of some European movements. In retrospect, 'mutuality' might have been a better choice because it suggests more adequately the projects co-operators and co-operatives undertake in their common interest. 'Solidarity' suggests more the way in which they support each other, important enough but arguably not as significant as working together for mutual benefit.

29 This phrase is taken from the ICA definition of a co-operative (see ICA website).

30 Thorstein Veblen, *The Theory of the Leisure Class: An Economic Study of Institutions* (New York: Macmillan, 1902), p. 69.

31 For useful introductions to this vast and complicated movement, see W.R. Everdell, *The First Moderns: Profiles in the Origins of the Twentieth Century Thought* (Chicago: the University of Chicago Press, 1997) and Peter Childs, *Modernism* (Abingdon and New York: Routledge, 2000).

32 See R.C. Solomon, *Existentialism*, 2nd edn (New York: Oxford University Press, 2005).

33 See *Everything* website, available at http://everything2.com/title/there+is+no+such+thing+as+society, for the full original quotation.
34 One study found, for example, that it affected one out of every four university students (out of some 37,000) surveyed in the United States in 2006. Jean M. Twenge and W. Keith Campbell, *Living in an Age of Entitlement: The Narcissism Epidemic* (New York: Free Press, 2009), p. 2.
35 Ibid.
36 From the ICA website.

12

An alternative co-operative tradition: the Basque co-operatives of Mondragón[1]

Fernando Molina and John K. Walton

If the co-operative movement constitutes a 'hidden alternative' to ruling economic orthodoxies, some of the traditions that contribute to its distinctive profile remain even less visible to the external gaze, especially co-operative enterprises that fall outside the dominant orthodoxy of the 'Rochdale tradition'. The economically successful complex of co-operative activities based on the small Basque town of Mondragón, in northern Spain, is an example. From humble origins in 1955, the Mondragón enterprises have extended from manufacturing and education into banking, credit, finance and retailing. In 2009 they employed over 100,000 members, accounting for 8.1% of industrial employment in the Basque Country, while running their own university and allocating considerable funding to various community schemes. 80% of the group's industrial workers on its home territory are members of their co-operative under the umbrella of the group, although if recent geographical expansion is taken into account the percentage falls sharply to 45%. It is criticised for not extending its worker-membership policies to new countries, or to its retail operations, and for allegedly behaving like just another multinational beyond its Basque heartland. Mondragón now has factories in eighteen other countries (and a presence in over 40), on five continents.[2]

Debate will continue on the extent to which Mondragón's encounter with globalisation is compromising its founding principles; but it remains difficult to find, or investigate, for those who are not plugged into Mondragón's distinctive history, culture, ethos and ways of working. Discussion of its activities remains confined to niche areas of sociology and anthropology, unorthodox economics, the international politics of the left, and co-operative studies. Within the latter framework, Mondragón remains outside the most visible genealogies of co-operation, those identified with Robert Owen and the Rochdale Pioneers, and with Fourier. Mondragón's philosophy was originally rooted in European Catholic social thought, as befitted the cultural formation of its founder, the Basque Catholic priest José María Arizmendiarrieta.[3] One illustration of the marginal status of Mondragón within the international co-operative movement is that the ambitious international collection edited by Furlough and Strikwerda did not mention Mondragón, or indeed Spain.[4]

Not that Mondragón is invisible within the broader co-operative literature. Johnston Birchall devoted several pages to the model and its virtues in his *The International Co-operative Movement*, musing on how other co-operators might learn from this successful venture.[5] This was a mainstream intervention within co-operation, and Mondragón has been influential elsewhere within the movement. At St Mary's University, Halifax, Nova Scotia, students on the Master of Management – Co-operatives and Credit Unions enjoyed an extended study visit to Mondragón in 2005, and participants were eloquent about the value of the lessons learned. Comments included: 'Standard business theory would state that the Mondragon worker co-operative system is not possible because the economic incentive to maximise return on capital is missing. Clearly this is patent nonsense as the standard theory debases the human spirit which looks to enhance society as a whole.' From such perspectives Mondragón looks like a beacon, offering a concrete real-world example of co-operative economic success.[6] The recent collaborative agreement between Mondragón and United Steelworkers, a major and innovative North American trade union, has attracted attention in the co-operative world as well as among a variety of commentators on the left, where the Mondragón model has been under discussion for over thirty years. Mondragón's efforts to enter United States markets by working with United Steelworkers to convert struggling rustbelt steel firms into worker co-operatives – and 'competitive renewal laboratories' – are still proceeding, with their US spokesman emphasising that Mondragón is in no sense 'socialistic', a word that must be avoided, indeed repudiated, in this political setting.[7]

Nor has the Basque co-operative group been prominent in the literature of conventional management trainers and business schools, although David Herrera has presented it as an alternative to monocultural assumptions about what constitutes a business enterprise, while emphasising its distinctive Catholic roots and character.[8] Peter Davis has encouraged interest in Mondragón from a Catholic perspective, as 'perhaps the most self-consciously developed alternative co-operative business model that has drawn its inspiration from Catholic Social Doctrine'.[9] Mondragón's distinctive Catholic roots were central to its philosophy and identity, although we shall see that this has been changing rapidly since the 1980s; but this distances it from the secular Anglophone Owenite and Rochdale Pioneers traditions. It is curious that several recent publications have asserted that Arizmendiarrieta was influenced by Robert Owen and Rochdale,[10] although Owen's sceptical rationalism and hostility to organised religion would have conflicted directly with the priest's core beliefs, and his association with socialism would have made him a dangerous influence to acknowledge under Franco.[11] There is, indeed, no evidence that Arizmendiarreta was directly influenced either by Owen or by the Rochdale Pioneers. The absence of an appropriate intellectual genealogy, together with the impenetrability of the Basque culture in which Mondragón is embedded, helps to explain its limited visibility to the wider co-operative movement.

The extent to which Mondragón is *sui generis* has been underlined by the differences between its declared co-operative principles and the *Co-operative Identity Statement* of the International Co-operative Alliance, as set out in 1995 and discussed elsewhere in this volume. Corcoran and Wilson have compared the two declarations. As they remark, the Mondragón principles actually expand on those of the ICA, especially as regards the role of the workers, whose role in co-operative governance is emphasised in four of the ten principles, including commitments to participatory management, wage solidarity and the subordination of capital to labour. Principles 8 and 9 endorse universality and social transformation in ways that are not matched by the ICA, and educational provision is extended to the teaching of technical issues in the running of co-operative businesses.[12]

Most academic publications on Mondragón, mainly in sociology and anthropology, are positive in tone, despite critical comments about alleged failures to live up to high ideals in practice, especially as the societies modernise, expand their activities beyond manufacturing and credit unions, and extend geographically beyond their core culture and heartland. The analysis that follows is critical of aspects of recent trends.[13] The most acerbic criticisms, suggesting that industrial democracy was a façade and that many workers in Mondragón itself felt excluded and alienated, have come from an American anthropologist who 'went native' in the radical nationalist community, although for that very reason they are unconvincing.[14] The salience of such issues underlines the ways in which Mondragón was a different and distinctive co-operative experience, and helps to explain the difficulty of assimilating it to historical and contemporary understandings of the movement as a whole.

In this chapter we explore the strange path which has led Mondragón to abandon practically all of its cultural foundations, which have been reduced to a soft focus, conventionalised memory. We begin by presenting the cultural bases of this social movement and the role of Catholicism in its identity, to the point of establishing an impossible business model aiming at the Christianisation of industrial labour. The following section will examine the cultural changes which began before the death of the movement's founder, generated by the crisis of religious identity in a region historically dominated by traditionalist Catholicism. This process gathered momentum during the 1980s and 1990s, when the managerial team which Arizmendiarrieta had placed in charge of the co-operatives was replaced by a new generation of 'lay' managers. This managerial renewal was accompanied by a transformation of Mondragón's culture, promoted by a rising generation of intellectuals based in the movement's own business university. This entailed the introduction of perspectives from the ethno-nationalist left which in some respects (nationalism apart) brought the Mondragón experience into closer compatibility with the classic Rochdale assumptions.

The foundations of Mondragón

José María Arizmendiarrieta was a priest from Vizcaya province, born in 1915 and educated in the Vitoria seminary by an intellectually brilliant cohort of professors, steeped in the Catholic social doctrine of Popes Leo XIII, Pius XI and Pius XII. Arizmendiarrieta was educated to be a 'social priest', following an ideal of the committed priesthood which had been articulated by important intellectual proponents of Catholic social doctrine. The Catholic sociologist Joaquín Azpiazu, whose texts were used in the seminary when Arizmendiarrieta was a student, saw such priests as instruments of the Church in trade union and other workplace settings. Their role was to inform and guide social life in accordance with the papal encyclicals on working practices.

Arizmendiarrieta combined this ideal of the social priesthood with participation in the Movimiento de Espiritualidad Sacerdotal (Movement of Priestly Spirituality) of Vitoria, led by Rufino Aldabalde, which sought a demanding reconstruction of the profile of the parish priest, entailing engagement with local social circumstances, active involvement in problems of poverty and lack of resources in local communities and intervention to meet popular needs in education, leisure, work and health. To make such engagement effective, Aldabalde – who was Arizmendiarrieta's real mentor – insisted that the priest avoid political and ideological struggles, following an exacting and self-abnegating ministry. He had to set aside all personal characteristics, healing the social wounds of his community, submitting himself to a demanding ethic of daily life founded on humility, extreme poverty and sacrifice, and always pursuing his role as spiritual healer.[15]

When Arizmendiarrieta was sent in 1941 to the industrial settlement of Mondragón, which had suffered severely from the ideological and political tensions which culminated in the Spanish Civil War (1936–39), he intended to adopt the double role of parish priest and social worker which Aldabalde had helped him to define. The technical college ('Escuela Profesional') that he established in 1943 with the backing of local companies, aiming to give young workers access to levels of education and technical training hitherto closed to them, and the local branch of Acción Católica, an international organisation providing social activities for lay Catholics, became privileged spaces for his ideas about social Catholicism during the second half of the 1940s. The young workers who took part in these meetings became the perfect audience for his complex expositions about property, labour and capital, social justice and the latest theories of social Catholicism.

But Arizmendiarrieta, following his mentor Aldabalde, did not confine himself to propagating social Catholic ideas, but sought to reformulate them according to local needs, drawing ideas from an eclectic array of sources. Influences on his thinking during the late 1940s included post-war social democracy in Europe, and especially the nationalisation policies of the British Labour Party, with its promotion of state intervention and the role of trade unionists in the workplace. We also find the policy proposals of the most reformist Spanish bishops, who espoused the 'redemption of the world of the workers', alongside the ideas of the revisionist Catholic intellectuals of contemporary Spain, and of Catholic philosophers such as Maritain, Leclerq and Mounier. All this helped him to develop his conception of man as a communal being who found in co-operative work and education a way of salvaging the dignity he had lost through industrialisation and secularisation.[16]

Thus inspired, Arizmendiarrieta developed a string of corporatist social initiatives during these years, based on classic strategies of Catholic social doctrine, through which he encouraged workers and employers to work together in joint organisations aimed at finding solutions to local social problems, such as housing, vocational education, health and hygiene, and sickness insurance. At the same time he formed, through his teaching in the 'Escuela Profesional' and Acción Católica, an elite of young workers who had internalised his ideas about personal renewal through the world of work. He ensured that these young men could obtain a university education and trusted them with his most cherished goal: the creation of a new Catholic enterprise to promote a social movement which subordinated capital to labour, founded in an egalitarian Christian ethic of community, and aiming to transform local society through co-operation.

During the early 1950s the leadership of this visionary priest enabled the development of a new co-operative enterprise. A group of activists from the Young Workers' groups of Acción Católica included four people who decided to go into business: José María Ormaechea, Jesús Larrañaga, Alfonso Gorroñogoitia and Luis Usatorre. These specific individuals cannot be abstracted from their social environment. Arizmendiarrieta's activities during the 1940s and 1950s, aimed at the creation of educational and cultural instititions, at aiding the poorest, at promoting the construction of workers' housing and health centres, had always had a communitarian dimension. When this found expression in a new co-operative, Christian company it could count on the backing of the local community. Everyone in Mondragón knew about their priest's project for a new enterprise based on equal shares of work and income, and supported it with personal contributions. In September 1955 the first company was founded, making stoves and heaters, and named Ulgor, from the initials of the five founders: Usatorre, Larrañaga, Gorroñogoitia, Ortubay and Ormaechea. These were members of the elite of Catholic youth whom Arizmendiarrieta had educated over the last fifteen years, and whom he invited to leave their posts in existing local firms, including the powerful Unión Cerrajera in which three of them were employed, and set out on the new project for a Christian company. Their trade mark was Fagor, and the firm was known by this name, which was formally attached to it during the 1970s.[17]

The business model of Fagor was followed by many other enterprises stimulated or suggested by Arizmendiarrieta and founded by young workers from Mondragón and nearby settlements, influenced by the talks the priest gave in the local centres of Acción Católica: Talleres Arrasate, in 1957, manufacturing machine tools; Urssa, for industrial and urban construction, Ulma, manufacturing scaffolding, and Lana, for the manufacture and marketing of agricultural products, all in 1961; Copreci, in 1962, constructing the machinery required by Fagor to put together heaters and washing machines; and Comet (soon renamed Ederlan), in 1963, for metals. Over a score of agricultural and consumer co-operatives also emerged during the 1960s and 1970s.

These co-operatives were supported financially by the credit co-operative Caja Laboral, founded by the directors of Fagor in 1959. Arizmendiarrieta was aware that these companies would face many problems in sustaining technological innovations, creating employment and developing social policies even as the home market was opening out to the rest of Europe. He also knew about the experience of the socialist co-operative Alfa, in nearby Eibar, which fell into crisis in the 1930s for want of financial assistance from the big banks, which boycotted it because of its Marxist roots. He did not want this to happen to his own social experiments. Caja Laboral was created as a co-operative bank to provide financial and managerial backing to the new companies. Its management team was drawn mainly from the founders of the first industrial co-operative, Fagor: José María Ormaechea, Alfonso Gorrogoitia and Luis Usatorre. They took charge of setting up a 'business division' which gave birth to several of the co-operatives mentioned above (Copreci, Lana, Ederlan), and subsequently to several dozen others over the next two decades.[18]

Working in parallel, Arizmendiarrieta set up the renewal of Escuela Profesional as a polytechnic, with the aim of educating the teams of technicians the companies were going to need. When in May 1964 this Escuela Politécnica opened, the three institutional pillars of Mondragón were in place: labour, represented by Fagor; finance capital, covered by Caja Laboral; and education, or human capital, by the Escuela Politécnica. Finally, when in 1969 the retail co-operative Comerco (soon renamed Eroski) was founded, the Mondragón experiment achieved all the versatility it has maintained until today, with an industrial sector, in which several diverse industrial groups are articulated around the most important co-operative, Fagor; a banking sector, with Caja Laboral and the insurance co-operative Lagun-Aro; and a distribution sector, Eroski.[19]

The leadership of Arizmendiarrieta over the four pioneers who had founded the first enterprise was passed on among themselves and the worker-members who joined it and the subsequent companies, following the explicit model envisaged by the priest, in which the young workers would assume an 'apostolic' leadership role, as described by a research project on the Mondragón co-operatives in 1974: 'The managers, authentic leaders, guided their colleagues, who were accustomed to the spontaneous acceptance of their decisions.' The pioneer managers chose the members of the new enterprises according to a profile drawn up by their mentor, who prioritised the potential member's potential for participating in co-operative culture, values and attitudes to work.[20]

The co-operatives of Mondragón

The Mondragón companies secured legal recognition as co-operatives in 1959. When on 3 April 1959 Fagor's statutes were approved by the Ministry of Labour, they provided templates for the other co-operatives that were emerging. Mondragón's founders embraced the co-operative model in their search for a Christian reconciliation between capital and labour, which gave substance to Arizmendiarrieta's ideal that a business was a social more than a judicial or economic reality. As one of his disciples, a co-founder of the movement, recalled: 'We considered that the business had to be a human community of activities and interests, based on property and private enterprise ... to provide society with a necessary or useful product, for which it received an economic recompense ... which was fairly distributed among its members.'[21]

As conceived by the pioneers of Mondragón, the company should define itself through solidarity, a value understood as innate in humanity and deeply spiritual. This was where Christian morality intervened, stimulating co-operation between workers. Mondragón co-operation was obsessed with the moral dimension. In the General Assembly of Fagor in 1959, Alfonso Gorroñogoitia advised the members: 'many things will have to change between us: our expectation of immediate gain ... our limited capacity for saving, our lack of austerity, which issues forth in this endless desire to appear better than we are and get and spend more than we can'.[22]

The business identity of the 'Mondragón co-operatives' started from the idea of 'community of labour', which confirmed the pre-eminence of labour over capital in the enterprise. Each worker was entitled to participate in the company as a member, with the right to vote in the general assembly and to a share in the profits, which were distributed monthly on the basis of their contribution to the co-operative as workers.[23] The working community was conceived as evolving, as were the individual members: one of the best-loved sayings of Arizmendiarrieta was 'our co-operation is an organic process of experience', which presupposed an expectation of permanent adaptation to social change. Another of his maxims was: 'The definition of vitality is not endurance, but rebirth and adaptation.'[24]

This 'experience' was regulated by the Social Statutes and the Regulations of Internal Governance. The Statutes acted as a 'co-operative constitution' to which the Regulations inserted 'amendments' in response to social change. According to both documents, the Mondragón workforce supplied both the labour and the capital of the business and brought them together through a co-operative contract.[25] This synthesis was represented through four principles: equality, solidarity, responsibility and democracy.

'Equality' was expressed in a set of binding conventions which compressed wage and salary differences between different strata of members, from top management to assembly-line workers. The member who worked as a manager could only receive three times the pay of the worst-paid labourer, which was unthinkable in other contemporary companies, and which only began to change in the 1970s. 'Solidarity' implied renunciation of the love of personal wealth. Opting for the solidarity principle implied the 'responsibility' of the worker not to neglect such duties as austerity, thrift and sacrifice. As Arizmendiarrieta emphasised: 'We must replace the ideal of personal riches ... by the ideal of the humane life ... helping one another and all bringing our loyal and generous collaboration to the common struggle.' Finally, the worker must contribute to the management of the firm, by accepting and participating in the co-operative 'demo-cracy' of the annual general assemblies. This version of democracy was constructed from egalitarian but not levelling perspectives: Arizmendiarrieta sustained an idealist perception of co-operative governance, which was to be based on 'the best' of the members, who were required to carry out their mandate rigorously and ensure effective management. To this end, Arizmendiarrieta had introduced rules which favoured meritocracy, sometimes more symbolically than practically, as shown by the directors having more votes than ordinary members in the General Assembly. He took great care that the co-operatives should be led, through their governing committees, by a 'co-operative aristocracy' composed of the elite among his followers, those who had most thoroughly understood his Christian co-operative work ethic and applied it to personal life and business activity.

A basic aspect of underlying co-operative expectations related to social security for the members. This was provided through the Caja Laboral, which in 1966 established a mutual insurance society called Lagun-Aro. The cover it provided extended from sickness to old age benefits and crisis loans. All the members had to pay a monthly subscription to this organisation, reinforcing expectations of community solidarity. The number of members of each 'workplace community' was 'unlimited', following the principle of 'free associa-tion' contained in the statutes of every co-operative, which entailed the absence of discrimination on grounds of gender, ethnicity, religion or ideology. Nevertheless, to join a co-operative entailed meeting certain formal requirements: age, access to sufficient capital to invest, and passing a selection test. Thus, already in the first years of the co-operatives, a flow of savings by members and their families became available to support the future capital requirements payable by their children, grandchildren or relatives by marriage when they wished to join the firm.

This regime of social austerity brought creative tension between communitarian ideals and business practice, between morality and the market. The frame of mind of the first Fagor co-operators can be seen in the regulations about surpluses on production. The more was allocated to the social support and reserve funds, the more they would enhance the resources of the local community, because the first fund was dedicated to solving social problems and the second to financing additional employment. From the beginning, the pioneers of Fagor considered that, once the human factor was satisfied by prestige among the local working class, the key necessity was the generation of capital in the service of the co-operative. Hence the concern for savings, an obsession in Arizmendiarreta's social thought, and therefore prominent in the workings of his co-operative enterprise. The tendency towards the reinvestment of all the profits in social capital would mean that the co-operative was not just supporting its members, but promoting new jobs and enterprises.[26]

Underlying all this was a strongly religious social commitment. The formula of distributing profits through wages, to be recycled into capital, aimed at achieving the social justice demanded by papal doctrine, echoing the insistence on promoting the compatibility of labour and capital in encyclicals such as Leo XIII's *Rerum Novarum* and Pius XI's *Quadragessimo Anno* and *Casti Connubii*. In the co-operative philosophy of Arizmendiarrieta it was not morally admissible to prefer individual consumption to communal investment, which created a further confrontation with prevailing assumptions about economic development through the encouragement of personal consumption: 'For us, work will never be a punishment from heaven, nor leisure a blessing, nor riches the path to our personal human paradise. For us work is the human contribution to the divine plan to transform and improve a world which may not become an earthly Paradise, but must at least aspire to become more comfortable and above all more fraternal, more equal and more bearable than is currently the case.' Self-managed work and community solidarity as instruments for worker emancipation and the construction of a more equitable Christian society were the two basic principles of the Mondragón business model.[27] This presented the paradox of a business producing items of mass consumption placing narrow restrictions on its workers' capacity for purchasing these and related goods.[28]

The Mondragón co-operative community

In November 1961, Arizmendiarrieta, whose only official role in Ulgor was that of spiritual director to its members, announced that 'co-operators' were necessary to the formation of co-operatives. He therefore founded a review which, under two successive mastheads (first *Cooperación*, then TU, signifying *Trabajo y Unión*, or 'Labour and Unity'), would serve to communicate with and educate the members. Through his monthly editorials he promoted the active spread of co-operative principles and commented on the governing documents of Ulgor. In this 'apostolic' task he was accompanied by his disciples, the leaders of the business, presenting talks, seminars and short courses to establish the new co-operative culture. In his report on the activities of Fagor in 1961, the chairman of the Management Committee, Alfonso Gorroñogoitia, wrote: 'The main concern has been perfecting our co-operative convictions and condition.' The most important co-operative, Fagor, saw regular visits from Arizmendiarrieta and from priests with social missions for whom he had intellectual respect and affinity.[29]

Education had been one of Arizmendiarrieta's obsessions, and he took care that the Escuela Profesional, a few years after becoming a Politécnica, became a nursery of co-operative values for young local workers. Education was combined with 'virtue', combining responsibility and self-discipline, values which he had espoused as a young priest. His co-operative teaching featured in the co-operatives' monthly review for internal consumption. Here he dealt systematically with everything from the practical working of co-operatives to the Catholic moral philosophy which gave them life. The editorial in the first number of *Cooperación* pulled together this reflection: 'People are born as men or women, not as woodworkers, seamstresses, doctors or engineers. To become a good craftsman or technician requires many hours of practical work and study. Equally, no-one is born a co-operator, because to be a co-operator requires social maturity and a mastery of the art of living in society ... Ultimately it is education and virtuous living that make a man into a co-operator and a solidaristic worker.'[30]

Another pedagogic outlet was Arizmendiarrieta's talks to the co-operatives. In one of these, in 1960, he emphasised ideas about the strength of co-operation under the title, with real 'management guru' overtones, of 'The kind of man who desires success'. He defined the Mondragón co-operative worker as a link in a chain of interdependence and duties. In May 1961 he insisted, 'The idea and concern that dominated the origin and development of Ulgor ... has been that of co-operation ... it is as if all my discourses on social problems led me to this goal of co-operation.'[31]

Every aspirant member received a copy of the co-operative rule book and was examined to ensure a basic understanding of the ruling principles of the business. The examination was adapted to an appropriate cultural level for the job in question, but no new worker in these years could remain unaware of the rudiments of 'co-operation'. In the central co-operative, Fagor, there were regular 'short courses for new members' which expounded the philosophy of the business, and were 'obligatory for those who wished to be admitted as members', as Arizmendiarrieta emphasised in a memorandum of 1966. These courses were complemented by others, throughout the year, aimed at the whole workforce.[32]

The central premise of this co-operative culture was the overriding sense of solidarity in work. Co-operation was inseparable from spirituality, and the route to it led through deep Christian self-examination. The review *Cooperación* was saturated with Catholic spirituality. In February 1962 a column appeared, 'God's opinion', which began by announcing the religious meaning of co-operative doctrine: 'Every genuine co-operator who is fully engaged with this movement must necessarily be guided and pushed onwards by an elevated ideal ... if, moreover, this co-operator is Christian and this means something in his life, he must try to see and apprehend what God's opinion is, if it really exists, on the regular work of daily life on earth.' Christianity was conducive to co-operation, even if the thoughtful and committed humanism which this business formula required did not have to be mediated through Jesus Christ. In August 1963 Arizmendiarrieta remarked on God's presence in the factory and in the daily tasks of the co-operator: 'A badly turned product ... tells us in itself that the man who brought them into being is simply a bungling incompetent. A perfectly turned crankshaft, a masterwork of engineering, speaks eulogistically of its manufacturer ... the work completed, in itself, glorifies the intelligence, skill and sensitivity of its creators, or we might also say, of the Creation.' These texts reflect the Christian culture on which Arizmendiarrieta and his disciples built their co-operative doctrine, which was insistently apparent in their editorials.[33]

This co-operative doctrine counted on a powerful if unexpected collaborator: the Vatican. The social teaching of John XXIII, set out in the encyclicals *Mater et Magistra* (1960) and *Pacem in terris* (1963), constituted an unprecedented reinforcement of the social ideal of Mondragón. Arizmendiarrieta, and the first generation of Mondragón business leaders which grew up around him, campaigned actively to disseminate the new papal doctrine, finding support in it for their whole business movement. Arizmendiarrieta said in October 1961, 'It is not difficult to see that the prefatory words of John XXIII in his encyclical *Mater et Magistra* bring into question the capitalist as well as the collectivist system, while containing clear support for co-operative principles.' In *Mater et Magistra*, under the general heading 'The requirements of justice regarding structures of production', the Vatican had supported the co-operative way of working as the bearer of the most genuine human values, as a harmonious society for the common good. Such papal directives underpinned the announcement of the first National Assembly of Co-operatives in Spain. Mondragón was five years ahead in the development of the Catholic co-operative project envisaged by John XXIII's encyclical.[34]

Between 1960 and 1963 Arizmendiarrieta referred insistently to the social doctrine of the papacy and its perfect adaptability to co-operative ideas, not only in the editorials of *Cooperación* but also in the multitude of talks, formal lectures and discourses which marked his immense labour as apostle of co-operation. In his evaluation of John XXIII's brief and revolutionary papacy, the creator of Mondragón underlined the intense absorption of his doctrine into its co-operative culture and stressed once more that Christian humanism was the root of its business plan: 'We try to build a new society, a new order, which may make men aware of his true position in the design of Creation ... According to the Christian vision of life and society, every believer has to be a redeemer, that is, the Christian, beginning by concerning himself more for his neighbour than himself, "must live with the hunger and thirst for justice, with the tears and cross of Christ" ... working for the mysteries of a new humane and just social order, to establish the kingdom of peace in the world.'[35]

Mondragón after Arizmendiarrieta

José María Arizmendiarrieta died in November 1976, a decade before his project began to develop an identity crisis. It was difficult to sustain a Catholic business vision when the Basque Country was experiencing the most intense secularisation process in its history. This process, one of the essential components of the social changes which shook the region – much more than the rest of Spain – between the late 1950s and early 1970s, affected the Mondragón co-operatives seriously.[36] Revolutionary Marxism gained ground among the young members while religious practice declined. The current interpretations of anthropologists and sociologists of religion indicate that Marxism and Basque nationalism became the two political cultures that filled the gap left by secularisation among the new generations, especially the most radicalised among them.[37]

From the late 1960s the Mondragón project had begun to attract members, whether locals or migrants who were arriving from other parts of Spain during these years, who lacked religious concerns applicable to the world of labour, but demonstrated contrasting political ideologies which were scarcely present in the first generation of Mondragón co-operators. The insertion of co-operation into the local traditions of Mondragón and the surrounding industrial villages, and its extraordinary economic success, made the co-operatives attractive not only for the youngest family members of the first co-operators, and for other workers in local industries, but also for the thousands of immigrants who were arriving and using the co-operatives as a channel of integration and participation in the receiving society.[38]

A former member of ETA during the Franco regime, who became one of the most well-known and respected Basque politicians after the dictatorship, articulated in his memoirs the vivid impression that the Mondragón co-operatives made on the most radical Basque youth of the late 1960s, as businesses with a 'communist' orientation which enjoyed great prestige among the ideologues of the radical left. This is a good illustration of the speed with which the transcendental conception of work which Arizmendiarrieta and his managing elite had introduced into Mondragón was now changing.[39] This continuing process explains why, in 1974, the co-operatives had to confront a serious conflict, the general strike which took place in two of them, led by young members with ideas drawn from the far left, who saw Arizmendiarrieta's 'co-operative aristocracy' as a capitalist 'oligarchy', an enemy of the working class and an ally of the dictatorship.[40]

Arizmendiarrieta's response, as he endured a painful degenerative illness, was an appeal to the austere and demanding morality which should hold sway in the ideal co-operative. He appealed to the idea of work as 'the right and duty of everyone, moral and physical', and identified this with 'solidarity', 'liberty' and 'securing communal respect and discipline'. The latter was imposed by his disciples, specifically the chairman of the Ruling Council of Fagor, Alfonso

Gorroñogoitia, who proposed that the General Assembly should expel the strike's leaders. The ruling class of the co-operative backed its mentor, who insisted on the ascetic pragmatism he had introduced into his co-operative ideal, which entailed the abandonment of all political ideologies in the workplace: 'Between divisive ideas and the way of life that leads us to unity and coexistence, we cleave to the second alternative, and therefore repudiate ideology as much as utopia ... What is interesting and vital is not the co-operatives but the co-operators, in the same way as democrats rather than democracy: it is not about ideas as much as learning from lived experience.'[41]

This pragmatism enabled new generations of co-operators to continue to feel united in a common culture in spite of the accelerating decline of its central emblem of identity, which was transcendental and religious. After Arizmendiarrieta's death, the co-operative businesses continued under the direction of two of the founding directors, Alfonso Gorroñogoitia and José María Ormaechea, who occupied key management positions in the two most powerful co-operatives, Fagor and Caja Laboral. Both reiterated (and put into practice) the necessity for this social movement to remain outside political and ideological debate, which was very intense during these years of transition to democracy in Spain. But the political geography had changed enormously and the Mondragón co-operatives found themselves in a major centre of the new left-leaning Basque nationalism, which was drawn to the sectarian violence represented by ETA. In the late 1970s Mondragón and its surrounding villages became a bastion of Basque nationalism with a substantial radical component. The cultural universe of religiosity secularised in nationalist bosses, and of extreme left-wing ideology, in which an important part of the new generation of Mondragón co-operators was formed, is well expressed in the (otherwise flawed) anthropological study by Kasmir.[42]

For the most militant and radicalised sector of the new generation of co-operative workers, which entered the workplace between the late 1960s and mid-1970s, co-operation was a work culture which installed a new God in the enterprise, no longer that of the Catholic church, but that of Basque nationalism. The second generation of co-operators, like those that followed, also saw co-operation as an emblem of collective identity, which pulled together familial memory, workplace traditions and the local environment, deeply transformed by the co-operatives in relation to leisure, sport and education as well as work. At the end of the 1970s co-operation constituted an essential element of newly hegemonic Basque nationalism, whose militants saw it as a distinctively Basque form of economic organisation which had translated imagined traditions of ethnic 'egalitarianism' from agriculture and fishing into industrial modernity. Thus Basque nationalist discourse converted industrial co-operation into an expression of the timeless and enduring qualities of the 'Basque people'. This ethnoromantic representation was swallowed whole, uncritically, in much of the British and North American literature about Mondragón.[43]

So important was co-operation, especially in its successful Mondragón version, to a Basque nationalism that was increasingly dominant in culture and politics, that one of the first laws to be debated and approved by the Basque regional parliament after its establishment in 1979 (under the first Basque government, headed by the PNV or Basque Nationalist party) was the 'Law of Basque Co-operatives'. The directors of Mondragón intervened in the debate, reinforcing the mythic value that the new Basque nationalism, both moderate and radical, conferred on co-operation, and showing amnesia about its Catholic origins, as it was reformulated on secular nationalist foundations. In 1982, while this law was being promulgated, the Basque Government held the First Symposium on Basque Co-operatives, which became an annual public event. On this occasion a member of the PNV executive, focusing on the 'informing principles' of the new law, argued that co-operation was not something 'alien to the Basque people', which had developed 'diverse economic activities throughout its history on a co-operative system', which defined itself through 'institutions such as the fishermen's guilds or the organised management of common land'. The industrial consumer and manufacturing co-operatives before the Civil War could be assimilated to this tradition, as could the post-war social phenomenon of Mondragón: an 'element of transcendental importance' in 'the economic and social reality of Euskadi'.[44]

Both the right-wing democratic nationalism of the PNV and the totalitarian ultra-leftist nationalism of the Herri Batasuna (HB) coalition, which sympathised with the terrorist violence of ETA, saw co-operation as an essential component of the 'cultural heritage' of the Basque nation. The argument of the anthropologist Sharryn Kasmir, mentioned above, is that the PNV found in co-operation a strategy for reviving the ancient egalitarian tradition which it saw as a distinguishing characteristic of the Basques as a 'people'. Consequently, she misrepresents the Mondragón co-operatives as a business project created by a group of crypto-nationalists directed by Arizmendiarrieta. This was the established position of the radical nationalists, whose critique of the PNV sometimes caught the Mondragón phenomenon in its sights.[45] But neither Arizmendiarrieta nor his managerial elite ever espoused any political position. On the contrary, it was the moderate Basque nationalism which came to power in the years after his death that adopted co-operation as an emblem of national identity in its political discourse, and consequently converted Mondragón into a 'national myth'. The ultra-leftist wing of radical nationalism did the same. The strategy was simple and shared by both tendencies: to 'forget' the religious origins of Mondragón and relocate it within the symbolic universe of ethno-nationalism.

From the late 1970s onwards the importance of the Mondragón cultural tradition would no longer lie in its original development by Christians committed to social intervention. Despite the time-lag of barely a decade between the generations, there remained no cultural sensitivity among the new political class (nor among the new rank-and-file co-operators) towards the motives underlying the establishment of the co-operatives by Arizmendiarreta and his disciples. The collective memory that became fixed within the co-operatives from the 1980s onwards combined amnesia and idealisation. Arizmendiarrieta and his followers were idealised for reviving a dormant 'national tradition', with Arizmendiarrieta repositioned as an iconic presence in all the public spaces of the movement (avenues, statues, names of buildings and co-operatives). It is no surprise that the first study of Arizmendiarrieta produced by a Basque intellectual, financed by Caja Laboral and intending to examine his co-operative thought from a philosophical perspective, said little about his Catholic spirituality. It presented a nearly 'secularised' Arizmendiarrieta, strikingly close to the ideological positions of the 1968 left with which the author – in fact, a Franciscan friar recently secularised – identified.[46]

In the late 1980s and early 1990s the generation of managers nurtured by Arizmendiarrieta or in the shadows of his immediate disciples was giving way to a new generation, under whose leadership the secularisation of the Mondragón co-operative ideal was completed. At the blessing in 1999 of Arizmendiarreta's new tomb in the Mondragón cemetery, one of his most renowned disciples (Jesús Larrañaga) noted the absence of the leading management from the ceremony: 'At this meeting of minor homage to the memory of this great man, almost all the "nomenclatura" or top management, those called to be his disciples, were absent.' Another co-founder of the movement, José María Ormaechea, had calculated that only 15% of invited members of leading management had attended, even though individual invitations had been sent out well in advance. Larrañaga lamented that Arizmendiarrieta had been abandoned by his 'supposed disciples'.[47] Despite the efforts of recent publications with academic pretensions to define the existence of a unified, intergenerational business culture in the Mondragón movement, as discussed below, the discontinuity generated by the secularisation and politicisation of the co-operative culture clearly created a sharp division between the first and subsequent generations of Mondragón co-operators. It is no coincidence that the success of the 'new co-operation' created by the consultant Koldo Saratxaga in the Irizar co-operative flowed precisely from its departure from the Mondragón group at the start of the new century.[48]

In the debates within the co-operatives to mark the fiftieth anniversary of the movement, the distance between the current Mondragón culture and that of the first generation was clear. These debates were set up by Lanki, a co-operative research institute in the University of Mondragón, which had emerged in the 1990s from Arizmendiarreta's Escuela Politécnica. Lanki brought together sociologists and business theorists, mainly academics in the university, publishing their research on Mondragón co-operation. Lanki has become the most influential 'think-tank' of the Mondragón co-operatives, capturing all the projects related to business histories, sociological studies or teaching innovations. The debates took place during 2005, involving working meetings with the social committees and management of all the co-operatives, focusing on three key axes which had been identified in the co-operative conferences as the cornerstones of Mondragón culture: co-operative education; participation and co-operation within and between co-operatives; and social transformation. The outcomes confirmed the progressive emptying out of the old Mondragón culture since the 1980s. The three main points of reference were finally recognised as 'very important' and 'necessary to protect', but the strategies for this, and the ideological framework in which to achieve these goals, were reserved for future debates in the movement's annual congresses.

In fact, the intellectual work of Lanki is the clearest reflection of the laicist transformation of the co-operative culture, and how the legacy of Arizmendiarrieta and the first generation of co-operators has been reinvented according to new ideological and cultural needs and horizons. According to one of its principal exponents, Joseba Azkarraga, the main challenge of the 'new co-operation' of Mondragón lies in how it can confront the threat of globalisation as expressed through the new neo-liberal capitalism. For this 'we need not to revive the old co-operative ideas, but to look for a new expression of their universal values under the new historical conditions'.[49]

This sociologist saw the challenges for Mondragón co-operation as global (ecology, third world, industrial democracy) and local (housing, high quality employment, Basque language issues, gender, social marginalisation), and recognised the process of 'secularisation' of co-operative thought which necessitated the definition of a 'new identity'.[50] The new identity of Mondragón co-operation drew on the two new cultures with greatest current influence: the new left of the later twentieth century, with its concerns about ecology, the 'third world' and globalisation; and Basque nationalism, with the obsessive insistence on the use of the Basque language in the co-operatives (including research and university teaching), and the assimilation of Mondragón co-operation into an imagined thousand-year-old collectivity: the Basque people. The publications of Lanki express all these concerns.[51] Their reflections on co-operation are inserted into a Mondragón tradition which has been reinterpreted in terms of 'business values' ('valores empresariales'). Arizmendiarrieta and his pioneers are redefined by the new 'Mondragón thinkers' as the creators of those secular 'values' that are used to underpin today's 'co-operative experience'.[52]

In Lanki's most complete interpretation of the Mondragón experience past and present, we find an insistent recourse to categories drawn from late twentieth-century business psychology, with the goal of linking a culturally and emotionally remote past – which, at root, the authors do not understand – with Mondragón's present, drawing on 'values' and 'co-operative principles' abstracted from their original moral foundations.[53] The cultural tradition of Mondragón's new co-operation is no longer connected to Christian Socialism, still less to Catholicism. It is a new business tradition nourished by Basque nationalist culture, especially its most leftist orientations. This is how the origins of Mondragón can be identified with the imagined characteristics of a Basque people supposedly existing in remote times, while there is no mention of the social teachings of the Catholic Church or the social Christian philosophies that inspired Arizmendiarrieta and his disciples.[54] With the loss of this tradition, the co-operative culture was reinvented following another tradition which had always been alien, that of Rochdale, whose 'universal' dimension was conflated with that of Mondragón in another publication from the same stable.[55] Recourse to a new category from business psychology, 'value', allows the spiritual content of the original movement to be secularised and abstracted, colonising the past with the 'new age' present in which Mondragón co-operation now circulates.[56]

Conclusion: reducing the distance from Rochdale

We have attempted to present a deeper and detailed historical and cultural interpretation of the Mondragón co-operatives. This alternative co-operative tradition has experienced a strange deviation in its business culture since the death of its founder in 1976. From constituting a unique example of Catholic industrial and financial co-operation Mondragón began, from the 1970s onwards, to lose the religious foundation which had nourished its business culture. This 'co-operative secularisation' ran parallel with the general secularisation of Basque society during these years. The vacuum left by religion, all-pervading in the 'national Catholic' society of the Franco regime, was filled by other cultural influences, especially the new radical Basque nationalism of the left, as symbolised by the paramilitary organisation ETA, and the more moderate version of nationalism which emerged in the 1970s as the dominant political culture and identity of the Basque Country. Since the 1990s this nationalist culture has absorbed influences from the European left, especially from the intellectual opposition to globalisation, as well as modern management theories based on ethical values, 'self-help' and corporate social responsibility. All this has created a confused 'new age' cultural system which has brought this peculiar co-operative phenomenon closer to a business tradition which had been completely alien, the broadly socialistic and secular self-management associated with Rochdale. This has coincided with a crisis of the co-operative ideal, with a fundamental conventionalisation of the once-powerful 'Mondragón culture', now converted into a superficial label papering over a deeply stratified and hierarchical business model which has displaced the former ruling philosophy of co-operative equality and solidarity.

Perhaps the best illustration of the change undergone by Mondragón's business culture can be found in the periodical which, through fifty years, has served as organ of communication and expression for this co-operative community. Here, the section devoted to reflections on co-operative culture – currently headed 'Co-operative classroom' ('Aula cooperativa') – has been given over to 'self-help', with the adjective 'co-operative' merely providing a way of conferring orthodoxy on stories which fall into this genre, bearing no relation to co-operative business culture as such. Meanwhile, the other section with potential intellectual content is entitled 'Myths and legends of the Basque Country' and is dedicated to Basque mythology and amazing stories related to the Basques, from the Holy Grail to witches. Self-help and patriotic folklore with a touch of 'kitsch' are surprising emotional and ideological points of reference for Mondragón co-operation in times of globalisation.[57]

Notes

1 Mondragón, with the accent, is the name of the town; Mondragon, without the accent, is now the name of the co-operative group. We have chosen to standardise on the former version in the text, but readers need to be aware of the distinction.

2 www.mondragon-corporation.com (accessed 30 December 2010); C. Clamp, 'Mondragon and the US Steelworkers Partnership: An Update', *GEO Newsletter* Vol. II, Issue 6, available at www.geo/coop/node/584 (accessed 3 February 2011). Exact statistics vary in different sources according to the assumptions used.

3 Fernando Molina, *José María Arizmendiarrieta, 1915–1976* (Mondragón: Caja Laboral, 2005).

4 E. Furlough and C. Strikwerda (eds), *Consumers Against Capitalism? Consumer Cooperation in Europe, North America and Japan, 1840–1990* (Lanham: Rowman and Littlefield, 1999).

5 Johnston Birchall, *The International Co-operative Movement* (Manchester: Manchester University Press, 1997), pp. 98–103, 227.

6 www.smu.ca/academic/sobey/mm/documents/mmccu-news-volume01–spring2007.pdf (accessed 29 December 2010).

7 www.co-op.ac.uk/events/article-mondragon-co-operative-united-steelworkers-deal-internationalist/ (accessed 29 December 2010); Clamp, 'Mondragon and the US Steelworkers Partnership'.

8 D. Herrera, 'Mondragon: A For-profit Organization that Embodies Catholic Social Thought', *Entrepreneur*, Winter 2004, available at www.entrepreneur.com/tradejournals/article/116926710.html (acessed 17 June 2011).

9 Peter Davis, 'The Co-operative, Catholic Social Thought and the Good Company: the Importance of Pluralism in the Market', available at www.le.ac.uk/ulsm/research/umbo/catholic/pdf (accessed 29 December 2010).

10 Examples include D. Thompson, 'Mondragon's Eroski as a Mass Retailer', *Cooperative Grocer* 97 (Nov–Dec. 2001); J.K. Gibson-Graham, 'Enabling Ethical Economies: Cooperativism and Class', *Critical Sociology* Summer 2003; R. Ridley-Duff, 'Communitarian Governance in Social Enterprises', *Social Enterprise Journal* 6 (2010), 125–145; Hazel Corcoran and David Wilson, 'The Worker Co-operative Movements in Italy, Mondragon and France: Context, Success Factors, and Lessons', available at www.coopzone.coop/files/CWCF_Research_Paper_International_16-6-2010_fml%5B1%5D.pdf (accessed 29 December 2010), 22.

11 J.F.C. Harrison, *Robert Owen and the Owenites in Britain and America* (London: Routledge and Kegan Paul, 1969).

12 Corcoran and Wilson, 'The Worker Co-operative Movements in Italy, Mondragon and France', 18.

13 Andrew Hindmoor, 'Free Riding Off Capitalism: Entrepreneurship and the Mondragon Experiment', *British Journal of Political Science* 29 (1999), 217, provides an extensive list of supportive writings.

14 S. Kasmir, *The Myth of Mondragón* (New York: SUNY Press, 1996).

15 Molina, *José María Arizmendiarrieta*, pp. 120–126, 175–186.

16 Fernando Molina and Antonio Miguez, 'The Origins of Mondragon: Catholic Co-operativism and Social Movement in a Basque Valley (1941–59)', *Social History* 33 (2008), 292–294.

17 Fernando Molina, *José María Arizmendiarrieta*, pp. 340–346, 350–352; Fernando Molina, *Fagor Electrodomésticos, 1956–2006. Historia de una experiencia cooperativa* (Mondragón: Fagor Electrodomésticos S. Coop, 2006), pp. 35–40

18 Molina, *José María Arizmendiarrieta*, pp. 375–384.

19 Molina, *Fagor Electrodomésticos*, pp. 81–82.

20 Joseba Gorroño: *Gestión empresarial y cooperativas industriales: Análisis de una experiencia de grupo*, Memoria de Licenciatura, Facultad de Ciencias Económicas y Empresariales de la Universidad Autónoma de Bilbao, October 1974, pp. 45–46; Molina, *Fagor Electrodomésticos*, pp. 42–43.

21 José María Ormaechea, *Orígenes y claves del cooperativismo de Mondragón* (Aretxabaleta: Otalora, 1998), p. 67.

22 Fernando Molina, 'The Spirituality of Economics: Historical Roots of Mondragon, 1940–1974', in E. Bakaikoa and E. Albizu (eds), *Basque Cooperativism* (Reno: Center for Basque Studies, 2011).

23 José María Ormaechea, 'José María Arizmendiarrieta Madariaga (1915–1976)', in E. Torres (ed.), *Los 100 empresarios españoles del siglo XX* (Madrid: Lid editorial, 2000), pp. 469–470.

24 Molina, *José María Arizmendiarrieta*, pp. 371, 428.

25 'Estatutos sociales y Reglamento de Régimen Interior', *T.U.*, n. 68, 1966.

26 These paragraphs are based on Molina, *Fagor Electrodomésticos*, pp. 55–67.

27 Ormaechea, 'Jose María Arizmendiarrieta Madariaga', pp. 469–470.

28 Molina, 'The Spirituality of Economics'.

29 Molina, *Fagor Electrodomésticos*, pp. 82–83.

30 *Cooperación*, n. 1, September 1960.

31 José María Arizmendiarrieta's Archive in the Otalora Center for Co-operative Education (JMAA), Aretxabaleta (Spain), Folder n. 59, 'Proyección Laboral y Social. Manuscript of talk given to the representatives of Ulgor, 24 November 1960: 'La cooperación'; 'Reunión con representantes de Ulgor. 2 de mayo de 1961' (all citations from this archive refer to the archive catalogue of August 2004).

32 JMAA, Folder n. 59, 'Promoción social', memorandum dated 2 June, 1966.

33 'Dios opina ...', *Cooperación*, n. 18, February 1962; 'El gran ausente', n. 36, August 1963; editorial of n. 1, September 1960; 'Datos que hacen pensar', n. 11, July 1961.

34 'La Producción Social', *Cooperación*, n. 14, October 1961.

35 'Nuestro recuerdo y homenaje a Juan XXIII', *Cooperación*, n. 34, June 1963.

36 Alfonso Pérez Agote, *Los lugares sociales de la religión. La secularización de la vida en el País Vasco* (Madrid: CIS, 1990); 'Religión, política y sociedad en el País Vasco', in R. Díez and S. Giner (eds), *Religión y Sociedad en España* (Madrid: CIS, 1993), pp. 243–281.

37 Joseba Zulaika, *Basque Violence. Metaphor and Sacrament* (Reno: University of Nevada Press, 1988); Izaskun Saez de la Fuente, *El Movimiento Vasco de Liberación Nacional, una religión de sustitución* (Bilbao: DDB, 2002).

38 Martín Calvo, *Cooperativismo y cohesión social en Mondragón. Relación entre la integración social de la inmigración de origen estatal y el hecho cooperativo en el Alto Deba* (Mondragón: Ayuntamiento de Mondragón, 2004).

39 Mario Onaindía, *El precio de la libertad Memorias, 1941–1977* (Madrid: Espasa, 2001), pp. 196–197.

40 Molina, *Fagor Electrodomésticos*, pp. 115–119.

41 Molina, *José María Arizmendiarrieta*, pp. 523–527.

42 Kasmir, *The Myth of Mondragón*.

43 See, for example, the otherwise useful article by C. Clamp, 'The Internationalization of Mondragón', *Annals of Public and Co-operative Economics* 71 (2000), 1–22. For a critique of this academic seduction see Molina and Miguez, 'The Origins of Mondragon', 285. This theme recurs in the neo-romantic nationalist historiography, which uses anachronistic terms like 'the Basque people' or 'Euskal Herria' (the current Basque rendering of 'the Basque nation') in studies of the Middle Ages or Early Modern period. A recent book represents 'Basque' whaling in the sixteenth century as a demonstration of the same 'co-operative spirit' that became famous through Mondragón (José Antonio Azpiazu, *La empresa vasca en Terranova* (San Sebastián: Txartalo, 2008), pp. 109 and 115.

44 Fernando Molina, *Historia del Consejo Superior de Cooperativas de Euskadi, 1983–2009* (Vitoria: CSCE, 2009), pp. 15–26. For the large number of co-operatives in the Basque Country before the Civil War, which have also remained largely invisible outside Spain, see L. Arrieta, M. Barandiaran, A. Mujika and J.A. Rodríguez Ranz, *El Movimiento Cooperativo en Euskadi, 1884–1936* (Bilbao: Fundación Sabino Arana, 1998).

45 Molina and Miguez, 'The Origins of Mondragon', 285, note 3. The phobia of radical nationalism towards the PNV, which it accused of being 'regionalist' and a 'traitor' to the cause of Basque independence, has led it to sacrifice its own myth of Mondragón, with publications aimed at

linking Arizmendiarrieta with the Franco regime or the Catholic right. One of these was sponsored by a former Mondragón co-operator who had been expelled for dubious economic activities, as explained in Ormaechea, *Orígenes y claves del cooperativismo de Mondragón*, pp. 479–480.

46 The collective memory of Arizmendiarrieta which the Mondragón co-operatives constructed from the 1980s, in José María Ormaechea, 'Último decenio. Informe a D. José María', in *Semblanzas de D. José María Arizmendiarrieta* (Bilbao: Elkar, 1991), pp. 27–29, and in Ormaechea's prologues to the *Obras Seleccionadas* (Selected Works) of Arizmendiarrieta, published by the Mondragón group in 2001. The book on Arizmendiarrieta's philosophy is Joxe Azurmendi, *El Hombre Cooperativo. Pensamiento de Arizmendiarrieta* (Aretxabaleta: Centro de Estudios Cooperativos de Otalora, 1984).

47 Jesús Larrañaga, 'Ausencias significativas', *T.U.* n. 439 (1999), 38. Another senior disciple wrote a nostalgic assessment of the difference between the original co-operators and those of the end of the century: Alfonso Gorroñogoitia: 'Recuerdos y nostalgia', *T.U.* n. 397 (1995), 17–19.

48 Iñazio Irizar and Greg McLeod, *32 claves empresariales de Mondragón* (Mondragón: Polo Garaia, 2010). The fullest treatment of the 'Irizar phenomenon' is Luxio Ugarte, *¿Sinfonía o jazz? Koldo Saratxaga y el modelo de Irízar. Un modelo basado en las personas* (Barcelona: Granica, 2004). In this book of conversations between the consultant and an anthropologist, Saratxaga recognises his debt to Arizmendiarrieta's philosophy but claims to be the inventor of a new co-operation as a 'man of 1968', completely secular and critical of the religiosity he had encountered in childhood, which had given life to the ideas of Arizmendiarrieta and his disciples.

49 Joséba Azkarraga, 'Debate cooperativo ante el cambio de época', *T.U.* n. 503 (2005), 22; 'Los cooperativistas de Mondragón ante el cambio de época', *Geu Erkide* n. 28 (2006), 2.

50 Joseba Azkarraga, 'Cooperativism and Globalization. The Basque Mondragon Cooperatives in the Face of Changing Times', *IAFEP 2006 Conference*, available at www.eteo.mondragon.edu/IAFEP /PapersIAFEP2006.pdf.

51 www.lanki.coop/argitalpenak (accessed 5 January 2011).

52 'Valores', *T.U.*, marzo de 2002; Nerea Agirre, Joseba Azkarraga, Eunate Elio, Oihana García, Jon Sarasua, Ainara Udaondo (colectivo Lanki), *Lankidetza. Arizmendiarrietaren eraldaketa proiektua* (Eskoriatza: Lanki, 2000). In José María Ormaechea, *Medio siglo de la experiencia cooperativa de Mondragón* (Aretxabaleta: Otalora, 2005), one of the last books by the greatest exponent of the original Mondragón movement, we find a completely different language from that of the new co-operation, without a single reference to 'valores'.

53 Larraitz Altuna (ed.), *La experiencia cooperativa de Mondragón. Una síntesis general* (Eskoriatza: Lanki, 2008), pp. 175–182.

54 Ibid., pp. 85–107.

55 José Ramón Fernández, *La experiencia cooperativa de Mondragón cumple 50 años* (Mondragón: MCC, 2006), pp. 164–166. The 'new age' ideologues are unaware that one of the most important scholars of international co-operation, the sociologist Henri Desroche, pointed out how easy it was to connect the Rochdale movement with the humanism implicit in the Mondragon project: Henri Desroche, 'Preface. Mondragon, ensemble intercoopératif non conventionnel', in Quintin García, *Les cooperatives industrielles de Mondragón* (París: Les éditions ouvrieres, 1970), pp. 7–21.

56 The attractions of the 'timeless values' of Mondragon has stimulated monographs like that of George Cheney, *Values at work. Employee Participation Meets Market Pressure at Mondragon* (Ithaca: Cornell University Press, 2002).

57 It will be difficult for this form of co-operation to face up to its problems of globalisation and 'multinationalisation', as reflected in the bitter documentary work of Anne Argouse and Hugues Peyret, *Les Fagor et les Brandt* (2007). Here they recount the business problems encountered when Spanish Basque co-operators become the collective employers of several thousand French workers in businesses which they have purchased, turning the French employees into an inferior caste.

13

'A co-operative of intellectuals': the encounter between co-operative values and urban planning. An Italian case-study

Marzia Maccaferri

Caire-Co-operative of Architects and Engineers in Reggio Emilia is a highly original co-operative institution – unique in its kind in Italy and we believe abroad as well; it may be said to have been born in the classrooms of the Milan Polytechnic. Some of its students after graduation came together in a co-operative for the study of urban planning, development plans, road works, etc.; in a short time it was able to establish its presence and reputation thanks to its fruitful activity in the field of social housing.[1]

This is how Alberto Basevi,[2] one of the protagonists of the history of Italian co-operative movement, presented the 'anomaly' of the *Caire-Co-operative of Architects and Engineers in Reggio Emilia* in his pamphlet written in 1952 dedicated to what he believed was *the* Italian cooperative province *par excellence*: Reggio Emilia, a province in the north of Italy, in the middle of one of the most co-operative Italian regions: Emilia-Romagna.

Some preliminary points

If as early as 1901 Bolton King and Thomas Okey were able to observe that the co-operative movement in Italy was relatively undeveloped but optimistic,[3] by the second half of the twentieth century the situation had changed profoundly. Italy had experienced impressive economic development within which co-operatives had played a significant role. One of the regions leading this 'co-operative miracle'[4] was Emilia-Romagna. Here, organisational and quantitative co-operative development had a strong ideological basis, a feature which was reinforced by national developments and political radicalisation linked to the Cold War. On the one hand co-operation, in Italy as in the rest of Europe, was the expression of two related aspirations: a general improvement in living standards and the inclusion of impoverished and marginalised social groups. On the other, in the feverish transition from fascism to republican democracy, the co-operative movement acted as a mouthpiece for the progressive message by taking an anti-fascist stance as a central component of its own 'modern' identity. This ideological combination of inclusive social improvement and rejection of Italy's fascist past was an important reason for Italian co-operation's lasting post-war success. But beneath this facade of co-operative unity lay a serious internal contradiction within the movement: between those co-operatives linked to the Communist and Socialist Parties, and those tied to the Christian Democrats, the Catholic Party that had won the first free elections. This gave rise to two different models of co-operation, which were frequently antago-nistic: a 'red' version, aspiring to a vision of co-operation which had the potential to replace the market economy; and a 'white' version, drawing inspiration from the social doctrine of the Catholic Church, which postulated a co-operative model which could operate success-fully within, and compatibly with, the capitalist system.[5] However, in spite of these wider ideological differences within Italian co-operation, during post-war reconstruction, the movement in Emilia-Romagna was characterised by a pragmatic emphasis upon developing co-oper-atives which met local needs, preferences, aspirations and identities, in which these larger ideological issues and divisions were downplayed. The result has been seen as a case of virtuous 'path dependence', producing co-operative organisations shaped by the historical contexts which engendered them, and rooted in local loyalties and identities.[6]

This was the local context which gave rise to a unique co-operative. *Caire* was a co-operative of young graduates from various disciplines (architects, engineers, economists, urban planners), ex-school mates or university companions (from Milan Polytechnic) but all originally from Reggio Emilia. They were exploring new ways of working together, of combining their multifarious skills to develop new ways of organising the local human environment. They believed that co-operative principles could be applied to meet the social and economic challenges of post-war reconstruction; and in co-operation they also saw a space in which they could express the new role to which the intellectual – a category to which they felt they belonged – was being summoned.

Focusing attention on the 'highly original' character of this co-operative, as Basevi put it, is fascinating not so much because *Caire* was unique in Italy and Europe in the early post-war period. It was also an important exemplar of a more general phenomenon: the so-called 'Emilia model'. Building upon paradigms introduced by Sebastiano Brusco and Robert Putman, the term 'Emilia model' evokes an expression of *civicness* which originated in early twentieth-century socialist municipalism, and became well established in Emilia-Romagna between the mid 1940s and the late 1970s.[7] In this, one of the 'reddest' regions of Italy, emerged a form of social market economy in which different, frequently antagonistic interests successfully interacted and collaborated.[8] This was all the more remarkable in the context of the difficult years of the great Italian post-war transformation. It cross-fertilised Marxist dialectic materialism with the ideas of Togliatti, the 'nuovo corso' theorised by the Italian leader of the Italian Communist Party (Partito Communista Italiano – PCI), producing a hybrid model of co-operative enterprise and endeavour, which, though replete with contradictions and often torn by internal conflicts, was capable of uniting and orienting society.[9] Within this perspective, Emilia became a local-territorial system, that is a physical, economic, cultural and political space which, notwithstanding all of its contradictions, was both 'shared and divided'. It was a place where the wishes of the single actors moved according to a common rationale and were crystallised in a strongly recognisable form of self-representation. In this historical process the co-operative movement played a leading role.

In considering this emerging model, two elements stand out. Firstly, the notion that territory and space can be managed was central to *Caire*, especially in its commitment to urban planning. Secondly, *Caire* passionately believed in co-operative principles as the basis for taking such planning forward. There thus emerged a distinctive approach to tackling the problems of reconstruction which combined urban planning, notions of the importance of the intellectual as a shaper of modern society and the Emilia model of co-operation. Analysis of its evolution during the period in question throws new light upon the development of co-operation and its role in post-war Italian economic and political history.

It is important to define what is meant here by the role and function of intellectuals, for this has been the subject of some debate. Gramsci described the post-Second World War intellectuals, or *literati*, as having abandoned their own ivory towers (*turris eburnean*), to take on an 'organicist' function in order to mobilise working-class and constructing hegemony, the leadership of a collective body for social improvement and human liberation. In opposition to the Gramscian type, the intellectual was described elsewhere as a 'treacherous altar boy', who had failed to fulfil his ethical responsibilities.[10] The definition of intellectual used here is based on the ideas of the historian Stefan Collini. According to these, the intellectual is a person who possesses a specific and recognisable expertise in a particular field of study, who has the capacity to publicise her/his ideas and actions. The intellectual is committed to addressing questions of a general interest, and aspires to and manages to establish a reputation for this.[11] These characteristics make the intellectual an actor in the political arena frequently contributing to the formation of public opinion and shaping political decision-making through her/his command of technical expertise. As a custodian of specialist knowledge and skills, intellectuals (especially in the new social sciences) became more influential in the post-war Italian context. In the specific case of *Caire's* intellectuals, it was their expertise in territorial science, the new geography and emerging, ecological ideas which secured for them a position of influence and leadership.

Caire's intellectuals saw themselves, and succeeded in imposing themselves, as interlocutors 'on an equal standing' with the political classes. By virtue of this they contributed to the construction of a specific mental *habitus* and a *modus operandi*, especially through the reshaping of public space in Emilia-Romagna. Whilst presenting themselves at times as disinterested technical experts, they did not, however, shy away from the ideological debate. Rather they made use of their expertise to secure leverage for their beliefs and ideas. While they defined themselves as experts and technicians they were quite willing to 'get their hands dirty' in the political arena. Specifically, they harnessed the analytical potential of the social, geographical and ecological sciences to intervene in and shape the urban environment. Central to their approach was the notion that co-operative principles were essential to achieve their aims as urban planners. This reflected the fact that co-operative ideas played a significant role in the debates about what modernity meant for post-war Italy.

The first Italian co-operatives of intellectuals

The Civil Design Studio was founded in Reggio Emilia on 28 November 1947, and adopted a co-operative form on 4, January 1952, together with its title '*Caire*'.[12] During this period a group of friends chose the co-operative as a set-up for their professional business. The partners were: Osvaldo Piacentini, Ennio Barbieri, Silvano Gasparini, Aldo Ligabue, Antonio Pastorini, Pasquale Pataccini, Athos Porta,

Antonio Rossi, Eugenio Salvarani and Franco Valli. During 1950s, 1960s and 1970s *Caire* drafted the urban development plans for the principal Emilian cities (i.e. Modena, Bologna and Parma, amongst others). They also drafted the local and regional urban plans for areas such as Emilia-Romagna and Piedmont, and led the *Progetto Appennino* (a territorial plan for environmental management in the Italian Apennine area). *Caire* also developed the territorial projections of the so-called *Progetto '80* (the planning policies of the 1960s Italian centre-left governments that appeared to have a modern environmentalist sensibility).[13] Their methodological approach extended *Caire's* influence to the level of the European Community.[14]

In their regional and local projects, *Caire* focused much of their efforts on both planning, and the development of planning methodology. Thus, in both specific urban and town planning projects, and in the wider development of the field, *Caire* established an eminent reputation. Their approach was interdisciplinary, combining the use of geological and geographical data with sociological and economic analysis, but also drawing upon the ecological sciences. They were 'intellectuals of the territory', who, in the feverish and bustling phase of the 'Italian way' to modernisation, tried to hybridise the analytical potential of the new social sciences with urban intervention. In addition, they were committed to articulating the concept of the 'environment' in urban and territorial planning, and to embedding notions of 'environmental protection' in urban policies. In short, they conceptualised urban planning as a two-way interaction between human intervention and the counter-response of the landscape and the environment.

In post-war Italy, and above all in Emilia-Romagna and central Italy where *Caire* worked, the 'vibrant eagerness to recover', to use the words of the Italian urban planner Giovanni Astengo,[15] was fuelled by the climate of renewal and hope in the promise of modernisation. Two elements were of critical importance in this context. Firstly there was the urgent need to respond to primary needs, such as housing, water, electricity and basic infrastructure, in as short a time as possible. Secondly there were the activities of private building speculators, who saw in reconstruction and modernisation irresistible commercial temptation. 'House and work' became the bywords of urban development, and in the dialectics between management of the urgent post-war need for reconstruction and support for private initiatives, house-building emerged as the main priority, to the detriment of coherent urban planning, an imbalance which caused many problems.[16] In an effort to remedy these, post-war Italian urban planning sought to pursue the collective good. In keeping with Western ideas about state intervention during this period, its *animus* was to simultaneously build houses and increase worker employment. In this, it was an integral part of the search for an 'Italian way' to reformist welfare politics.[17]

As part of this wider trend, *Caire's* intellectuals became involved in popular housing, designing in 1952 the Saint Gobain neighbourhood of Pisa; and in 1953 the neighbourhoods of Sant'Agnese in Modena, San Donato in Bologna, and the Barene di San Giuliano in Mestre. From the outset, *Caire's* guiding principles were to meet communal needs for open spaces, and much effort went into the design of common green areas.

There were two main strands in *Caire's* 'urban planning ideology'. Firstly, there was a strong emphasis upon 'social fairness', following the notion that progress should be collective and not confined to privileged individuals or groups. Although reassigning the heroic task of Italy's ethical-moral post-war emancipation to architecture and urban planning, *Caire* also recognised the need for a 'holistic' approach to territorial planning which addressed the needs of rural and agrarian hinterlands as well as urban centres. This linked with the second strand of *Caire's* urban planning philosophy: the need to care for the environment. In an emerging context of economic abundance (the so-called 'affluent society'), in which primary needs seemed to be satisfied for a growing portion of the population, *Caire* turned its attention to the long-term problem of finite environmental resources. Although mindful of the need to satisfy the aspirations of an urban culture obsessed with the new demands of the property market, *Caire's* intellectuals looked for those solutions which would be least traumatic to the urban landscape and rural hinterland. This attention to the environment occasionally brought *Caire* into conflict with the contemporary demands for more housing development; but their emphasis was upon a balance between pressing human needs for housing and urban amenities and the more long-term environmental imperative. For example, this awareness of an ineluctable relationship between social and economic development and environmental transformation was at the heart of the *Relazione programmatica per la formazione del Piano di sviluppo della Provincia di Reggio Emilia* (Planning report for the Formation of the Development Plan for the Province of Reggio Emilia) presented in 1971.[18] In it the urban planners embraced the methodological thinking of the ecologist Eugene P. Odum.[19] But, if this ecological discourse was 'the continuous control of how man modifies the territory', their objectives were however that of not modifying it 'too rapidly'.[20] Not, therefore, a sort of religion of nature as an

alternative to anthropocentrism; not a mere freezing or a mummifica-
tion of the environment as an end unto itself, but rather an organic,
planned co-evolution.

In short, *Caire* and its architects were at the forefront of the
reformist urban planning movement in post-war Italy.[21] But *Caire* was
unique in its collective organisation as a co-operative.

Co-operative values and intellectual discourse

In attempting to explain the emergence of *Caire*, as a unique form of
co-operative within the Italian context, a simple question needs to be
addressed: how, and why, did a group of friends and university
companions on their way to becoming freelance professionals as
architects or engineers, decide to create a co-operative?

A co-operative of intellectuals in 1952 was an oddity, and indeed
of questionable legality. At the time, Mussolini's 1939 law, which
severely restricted the organisation of professional partnerships and
co-operatives (aimed at preventing Jewish professionals from continuing to practise by forming anonymous partnerships with other
non-Jews) was still in force. This affected co-operatives of partners
especially severely. But in spite of this, the city tribunal of Reggio
Emilia, like many others in Italy during the post-war period of legislative uncertainty, chose to ignore this law and unreservedly accepted
Caire's legality.

But the fact that *Caire's* founders were prepared to take such risks
with the law is significant. It shows just how strongly the partners were
committed to the co-operative option, since this was not the easiest
way to start up a business: a point made by the partners to one of their
critics.[22] On the one hand, they wanted to be part of the co-operative
movement because they were looking for a form of work organisation
based on reciprocal discussion and which could develop greater
potential. On the other hand, the intellectual impetus of being able to
overcome 'traditional capitalist form' was seen as a tool to construct a
real and sound democracy.

In addition to the desire to be a co-operative were the influences of
the external context which also moulded this organisational choice.
First among these was the strength of the cultural and political
influence of the Italian co-operative tradition. In Reggio Emilia the
co-operative movement embodied the aspirations of some of the
founding fathers of the post-war republic such as Meuccio Ruini and
Alberto Simonini.[23] It also boasted a longstanding and significant
presence in the Italian political and cultural fabric. 'Only in Reggio,'

one of *Caire's* intellectuals indeed recalled, could *Caire* have been 'founded and become consolidated'.[24] Although fascism had made deep changes to the structure and the administration of the co-operative consortia, such as the centralisation of control over all co-operatives by 'Ente Nazionale per la Cooperazione' (the National Co-operation Board) and the creation of 'Opera nazionale dopola-voro' (the National Workers' Social and Recreation Club) which provided pensions and health benefits,[25] the 'fascistisation' of the co-operative movement in the Reggio Emilia area was unable to dig up roots firmly embedded in early twentieth-century socialist reformism and the experience of Socialist municipalism.

Naturally, the fact that Reggio was a small town, in which everybody knew everybody else, had fostered the network of friend-ships which made the co-operative possible.[26] These were friendships that, born in the school desks or in the Sunday Schools, grew stronger during university years in Milan; even that special condition of 'exile,' to a young man coming from the furthest province during his under-graduate studies in a big city, played a significant role in the birth of *Caire*, nurturing close and intense relationships and loyalties. This emerging solidarity between peers was strengthened by the emergence of strong and influential leaders who helped shape the ideas and aspirations of this cohort of young architects and engineers. One such individual was the Right Honourable Ivano Curti, member of the National Liberation Council, among the founders of the Socialist Party in Reggio and Member of Parliament from 1953. Appointed in the early post-war years as Commissioner of the Consortium of Co-operatives, he opened the minds of the group to the possibilities offered by co-operation in the fertile climate of the reconstruction.[27]

In addition, in the immediate post-war, period, Milan, where *Caire's* founders had studied, was a city infused with an energetic desire to rebuild and reconstruct the city itself and the national economy as well. While reconstruction inevitably addressed material concerns concerned with the legacy of damage left by war, it was also a social, political and cultural project designed to eliminate the last vestiges of fascism. Many of the most committed to the reconstruction process had been active in the Resistance to both Mussolini and the Nazi occu-pation, and this desire to create a new social and political order certainly played a considerable role in the co-operative form chosen by *Caire*. Co-operation was seen as a way to create in microcosm the essence of a new fledgling society and in some respects even a new kind of human being. 'The idea of searching for synergies by means of intel-lectual collaboration,' one of the leading players of that experience recalled, 'was absolutely revolutionary.'[28]

Another major influence on the co-operative choice was Professor Franco Marescotti, important architect and member of the Italian Communist Party, with whom some of the future partners of *Caire* collaborated during their university years, in a study on the housing problem in Reggio. This was presented in 1947 to the Milan *Triennale*.[29] Marescotti, as other Italian architects such as Franco Albini or Irenio Diotallevi, was strongly interested in Italian reconstruction.[30] He was especially committed to citizens enjoying the right to a home, and to this end he became interested in new ways of addressing the housing question. He delivered lectures, attended debates and produced reports in many cities at the *Case della Cultura* and in the *Case del Popolo* (part of the cultural network of the Italian Communist Party). Marescotti introduced the co-operative system, particularly as it existed in Lombardy and Milan, to the architects and engineers who were to form *Caire*. At the time, co-operatives were better established and more mature in these locations than in Reggio Emilia. A particularly important model was the Co-operative Union of Milan, a white-collar co-operative set up under the influence of Luigi Buffoli in late 1886.[31] Buffoli was also the co-operator who financed the first Italian garden-city, Milanino, in Lombardy. Founded to satisfy the housing needs of the middle-class clerical workers, and influenced by the urban development theories of Ebenezer Howard and Lewis Mumford,[32] Milanino was endowed with leisure and cultural services, thus displaying a desire to engineer and shape the urban fabric of the city. It also exerted its role in this wider cultural and social aspect of urban planning to ensure a sustainable market for its services. From the outset point *Caire's* work on the New Towns during the 1950s and 1960s was imbued with these ideas, especially creating environments in neighbourhoods which were congenial to community spirit and preservation of the environment.[33]

If the years in Milan at the Politecnico University were undoubtedly formative from the educational standpoint, key *Caire* partners such as Osvaldo Piacentini, Franco Valli, Athos Porta and Antonio Pastorini were influenced by more immediate practical social needs. While in the Milan faculty there prevailed a polemical, sterile, self-referential and purely empirical form of experimentation, the belief that all the problems linked to the architectural design needed to have an ethical significance, a primarily social objective, persuaded the young architects that architectural projects needed to address the question of the position of human beings within the community and the need for collective organisation. Their objective was to pass from the 'grammar' learnt in the academy to the architectural discipline of 'doing urban planning'.

This group of young professionals saw in the co-operative model a way of working conducted on principles of egalitarian debate, mutuality and solidarity rather than through hierarchical capitalist forms. In this way, the co-operative formula strengthened awareness of the potential of a non-hierarchical and collaborative organisation, structure and ethos. It particularly offered an alternative view of the role of the architect in society and the commercial organisation, which was different from the sometimes detached and abstract figure who imposed upon passive recipients and communities the products of his imagination.[34]

Different political and cultural traditions were in combined in the co-operative option as well. As shown, the context of Reggio Emilia played an important role. The socialist orientation of the reformist tradition, drawing inspiration from Camillo Prampolini, was the most representative inside *Caire's* experiment (Ligabue, Pastorini and Porta, founders of *Caire*, were very close to the Socialist Party);[35] followed by the liberal democrat tradition linked to the professional bourgeoisie (Valli and Salvarani, founders of *Caire*, declared themselves as liberal democrats). In addition, the social Catholic tradition was reinvigorated after the fascist years and inside *Caire* important figures in this were Gasparini, Rossi and Piacentini; the latter linked by a very solid friendship to Giuseppe Dossetti. Dossetti was one of the most fascinating, problematic and debated figures of the post-Second World War Italian political scene, one of the fathers of the Italian Constitution and the Christian Democrat Party, a man with an absolute intellectual charisma and yet a restless, tormented personality.[36] The non-hierarchical and open culture of *Caire* allowed these differing traditions to be assimilated within both its personnel and its approaches to organisation and work. Given this openness to different co-operative traditions, the decision by *Caire* to join *Lega Nazionale delle Cooperative e Mutue* (the National Co-operative League), the home of the 'red' Italian co-operatives, requires some comment. Following the congress held in Reggio Emilia in 1947 the Italian Communist Party emerged as the dominant political force within that organisation.[37] Recent research suggests that the tendency to interpret the history of the co-operative movement within the context of histories of the working class and the European left generally oversimplifies the re-establishment of post-war European co-operation as a story of a clash between Reformism and Communism. The case of *Caire* suggests that regardless of its allegiance to the communist-dominated *Lega Nazionale*, it remained a site of civil growth and modernisation and a place of intellectual debate.

But above all, in the co-operative structure, the young architects and engineers found a space for democratic acculturation and the construction of their own 'workshop' for democracy. As they declared in 1963:

> The propensity for group work that began from the school desks clarified increasingly in each one of us the extent of our own limits and the chance to overcome them with a close-knit compensatory collaboration.

> The co-operative structure ... offered the most ample and most tested possibilities: broad collaboration, specialisation, integration and organisation of work, joint participation of all the collective responsibilities of society, conception of work as a collective produce and not as an individual work.[38]

It was on the deontological aspects that co-operative added-value became welded to the urban planning question. *Caire* was able as a consequence to make an important contribution to Italy's post-war reconstruction and rehabilitation following the defeat of fascism. It achieved this through its unique and original contributions to the planning of the urban dimension of post-fascist Italian life and its material reconstruction. For *Caire*, this activity was about reaching out for a new, modern Italy based on the principles of community and co-operation. It was seen by *Caire's* partners as an opportunity to 'shape history'. Consequently, while the *technicalities* learnt during university education were undoubtedly critical elements in the organisation, it was in its commitment to addressing social needs that the uniqueness of its contribution lay; and crucial to this wider social mission was its adoption of co-operative values and co-operative methods of working. *Caire's* intellectuals were to state:

> The analysis that we have carried out in Reggio on the building problem convinced us that a single problem cannot be dealt with in a fragmented way, but that it is necessary to study a whole new life of the society where each manifestation is inserted within an interconnected body of functions.[39]

Caire's history appears to be doubly significant: on the one hand, because it helps us to understand the seminal dynamics and the enduring fecundity of a form of mutualism and co-operation that developed in a sector – that is, intellectual work and the analysis of planning – traditionally extraneous to the co-operative movement. On the other, precisely because of this 'anomaly', it offers material for a study of the legacy, identity and function of the co-operative movement that today has to face up to sweeping changes.

Notes

1   A. Basevi, *La provincia cooperativa* (Rome: Biblioteca de 'La Rivista della Cooperazione', 1952).

2   Alberto Basevi is one of the pillars of the Italian co-operative ideology; his name is linked to the law passed on 14 December 1947, still known as the *Legge Basevi*, which represented, notwithstanding all of its contradictions, the main instrument for the expansion of the co-operative movement in the post-war period. Cf. V. Castronovo, 'Dal dopoguerra a oggi', in R. Zangheri, G. Galasso and V. Castronovo, *Storia del movimento cooperative in Italia, 1886–1986* (Turin: Einaudi, 1987), pp. 538–549.

3   B. King and T. Okey, *Italy Today* (London: J. Nisbet, 1901), pp. 193–214.

4   M. Bianchini, M. Cattini and M. Mussini, *Dal solidarismo al mercato, 1945–1962* (Reggio Emilia: Acm, 1987), p. 19.

5   For an introduction see T. Menzani, *La cooperazione in Emilia-Romagna* (Bologna: Mulino, 2007).

6   V. Zamagni, P. Battilani and A. Casali, *La cooperazione di consumo in Italia* (Bologna: Il Mulino, 2004).

7   S. Brusco, 'The Emilian Model: Productive Decentralisation and Social Integration', *Cambridge Journal of Economics* 6 (1982), 167–184; R.D. Putmann, *La tradizione civica nelle regioni italiane* (Milan: A. Mondadori, 1993).

8   R. Balzani, 'Le tradizioni amministrative locali', in R. Finzi (ed.), *Storia d'Italia. Le regioni dall'unità a oggi. L'Emilia-Romagna* (Turin: Einaudi, 1997).

9   See D. Sassoon, *Togliatti e la via italiana al socialismo* (Turin: Einaudi, 1980).

10 See B. Bongiovanni, 'Gli intellettuali, la cultura e i miti del dopoguerra', in G. Sabbatucci and V. Vidotto (eds), *Storia d'Italia. 5. La Repubblica* (Rome: Laterza, 1997).

11 S. Collini, *Absent Minds. Intellectuals in Britain* (Oxford: Oxford University Press, 2006).

12 The main source for the reconstruction of the history of *Caire-Cooperative of Architects and Engineers in Reggio Emilia* is the *Fondo Civile* of the Osvaldo Piacentini papers stored at the Osvaldo Piacentini Archive in Reggio Emilia. The register of the works drafted by the *Caire* intellectuals along with the material relating to the preliminary studies are also stored at the same archive.

13 See A. Zavodnik Lamovšek, 'Settlement Patterns in Europe: Elements and Comparative Typology', in P. Getimis and G. Kafkalas (eds), *Overcoming Fragmentation in Southeast Europe* (Aldershot: Ashgate, 2007), pp. 254–255.

14 The reference is to the Centro Piani, directed by the architect Franco Archibugi, with whom Osvaldo Piacentini and *Caire* collaborated within the scope of the *Progetto '80*. The Centro Piani was called upon to draft

a plan at the European level within the scope of the Regional Policy of the European Community. See L. Grazi, *L'Europa e la città. La questione urbana nel processo di integrazione europea, 1957–1999* (Bologna: Il Mulino, 2006).

15 On the great Italian architect see F. Indovina (ed.), *La ragione del piano, Giovanni Astengo e l'urbanistica italiana* (Milan: F. Angeli, 1991).

16 G. Longhi, 'Alcune contraddizioni del secondo dopoguerra italiano', *Storia urbana* 73 (1995), 179–212.

17 G. De Rosa (ed.), *Fanfani e la casa. Gli anni Cinquanta e il modello italiano di welfare state. Il piano Ina-casa* (Soveria Mannelli: Rubbettino, 2002).

18 Published in G. Lupatelli and F. Sacchetti (eds), 'Osvaldo Piacentini. Un architetto del territorio', *Quaderni di Urbanistica-Urbanistica Informazioni* 107 (1989).

19 American biologist and son of the sociologist Howard W. Odum, Eugene, starting from the *Fundamentals of Ecology* (1953) and *Ecology* (1963), based his own thinking on the Man-Nature relationship around the concept of the ecosystem. Man is part of a complex environment that must be studied, treated and modified as a whole, and not with isolated approaches and projects. See E.P. Odum, 'The Strategy of Ecosystem Development', *Science* 164 (1969), 262–270.

20 O. Piacentini, 'Registrazione dell'intervento al Convegno Indirizzo per lo sviluppo economico e sociale della Vallata del Marecchia, March 1973', in Lupatelli and Sacchetti, 'Osvaldo Piacentini', 117.

21 An introduction to the history of Italian 'reformist urban planning' in G. Campos Venuti, *La terza generazione dell'urbanistica* (Milan: F. Angeli, 1994).

22 This is remembered by the *Caire* partners in *La Cooperativa Architetti e Ingegneri di Reggio Emilia: quindici anni di attività* (Reggio Emilia, 1963).

23 Meuccio Bartolomeo Ruini and Alberto Simonini were both members of the 'Costituente', the Constituent Assembly which ruled Italy from 1946 to 1948 with the task of writing the Constitution of the new Republic of Italy. For Ruini, see S. Campanozzi, *Il pensiero giuridico e politico di Meuccio Ruini* (Milan: Giuffrè, 2002); for the co-operative's contribution to Italian democracy, see V. Feretti, *Riformisti di Lenin. La cooperazione reggiana nel secondo dopoguerra* (Reggio Emilia: Tecnostampa, 1982) and *Sette giornate di Cooperazione. Come crescere senza perdere l'anima* (Correggio: Area Stampa, 2007).

24 F. Valli, 'La Cooperativa e la città', *RS-Ricerche Storiche* 90 (2001), 53–57.

25 See M. Degl'Innocenti, *Il movimento cooperativo in Italia. Storia e problemi* (Turin: Einaudi, 1981).

26 Franco Valli was the high-school companion of Osvaldo Piacentini's brother; the latter was in turn the schoolmate of Antonio Pastorini, Aldo Ligabue and Athos Porta.

27 See Valli, 'La Cooperativa e la città'.

28 Ibid.

29 The *Triennale* was founded in Monza in 1923 on the occasion of the *Prima Biennale delle Arti Decorative dell'Istituto Superiore di Industrie Artistiche*. Transferred to Milan in 1933, it set itself the aim of interacting between industry, the productive world and applied arts, an ambitious and innovative role for the Italian culture and economy testified to by the presence in its exhibition halls of artists such as Giorgio De Chirico, Mario Sironi and Carlo Carrà (they took part in 1933). Suspended during the Second World War years, the *Triennale* restarted its activity in 1947, turning its attention to the frenetic work of post-war reconstruction, during which it took on a pre-eminent role in the realisation of the QT8 quarter of Milan. Precisely from that experience the interest of the *Triennale* in urban planning was born and became the fundamental theme of the exhibitions during the 1950s and 1960s and, although its exhibitions were more discontinuous, also in the 1970s. The 1947 exhibition was entitled *The Home: International Exhibition of the Modern Decorative and Industrial Arts and Modern Architecture* held in Milan from 31 May to 14 November, and was dominated by the rationalist architect Piero Bottoni. For an introduction to the urban planning debate in the years following the Second World War, see D. Calabi, *Storia dell'urbanistica europea* (Milan: B. Mondadori, 2004).

30 Multidisciplinary architect, Franco Albini, over a career lasting nearly fifty years merged the dimensions of design, architecture and urban planning according to the humanist orientation of the Modern Movement. A committed intellectual, Irenio Diotallevi's central themes were those of the reconstruction of the country, the right to a home and the new methods of intervention in the housing question. See P. Di Biagi (ed.), *Il Piano Ina-casa e l'Italia degli anni Cinquanta* (Rome: Donzelli, 2001).

31 Luigi Buffoli (Milan, 1850–1914) was an important pioneer of the Italian co-operative movement. Among the founders of consumer co-operation in Lombardy, he was also the promoter of the Società Cooperativa that built the Popular Hotel, a structure dedicated to housing workers and disadvantaged people. Inaugurated in 1901 and situated in the centre of Milan and active until the Second World War, the Popular Hotel could accommodate over 500 people at the same time and represented an island of solidarity for the Milanese working classes in the hard years of the industrial boom. See M. Degl'Innocenti, *Le imprese cooperative in Europa* (Pisa: Nistri-Lischi, 1986)

32 Ebenezer Howard and Lewis Mumford are among the many intellectuals (economists, sociologists and philosophers) who mostly influenced twentieth-century urban development. Theorist of the garden-city, the former dominated the English and European debate up to the 1930s with his ideas for the creation of new suburban towns of limited size, planned

in advance, and surrounded by a permanent belt of agricultural land. Mumford, of the generation after Howard, was an eclectic character. A historian and sociologist, with his *The Cultures of Cities* (1938) he would introduce, in urban planning theory, the importance of keeping intact the historico-cultural groundwork of the city plan just as it had come to be created over the centuries, and he would come to personify the main warning against the elephantine expansion of the metropolises and the suburbs. For an introduction, see P. Di Biagi (ed.), *I Classici del pensiero urbanistico moderno* (Rome: Donzelli, 2009).

33 See my 'I prodromi dell'approccio ecologico alla pianificazione territoriale. Alle origini della cultura ambientale di Osvaldo Piacentini', *I Frutti di Demetra* 19 (2009), 27–44.

34 A. Porta, *Premio Provincia di Reggio Emilia, medaglia d'oro per l'architettura*, in *La Cooperativa Architetti e Ingegneri di Reggio Emilia*.

35 D. Sassoon, *One Hundred Years of Socialism: The West European Left in the Twentieth Century* (London: Tauris, 1996).

36 Giuseppe Dossetti, a life-time close friend to Osvaldo Piacentini, was one of the most influential Catholic Italian personalities. A member of the Resistance movement in Reggio Emilia, after the war Dossetti was a Christian Democratic (Italian Catholic party) leader. He abandoned politics in the 1950s to become a priest. Among the copious literature concerning Dossetti see A. Melloni (ed.), *Giuseppe Dossetti. Studies on an Italian Catholic Reformer* (Münster: Lit, 2008).

37 Castronovo, 'Dal dopoguerra a oggi', pp. 522–531.

38 *La Cooperativa Architetti e Ingegneri di Reggio Emilia.*

39 Osvaldo Piacentini Archive, F2, envelope 'Primo studio urbanistico'.

14

Government to governance: the challenge of co-operative revival in India

L.K. Vaswani

Government control gives rise to fraud, suppression of truth, intensification of the black market and artificial scarcity. Above all, it unmans the people and deprives them of initiative; it undoes the teaching of self-help.

Mahatma Gandhi

Introduction

The Indian co-operative movement was initiated by the government and it was thanks to government support that it became the world's largest and most diverse co-operative movement. As a result the co-operative sector came to occupy an extremely important place in the Indian economy. However, the government control which was pursued in the early years of independence was neither required nor desirable after economic reforms were initiated in 1991. The government-controlled co-operatives, in credit and non-credit sectors, have not been able to perform to their desired level and capabilities.

It is time to recognise the contemporary issues facing co-operatives in the emerging economic, political and social realities of the twenty-first century and to offer adequate solutions to some of these problems, in order to successfully facilitate paradigm change. These emerging issues need to be addressed along with the traditional issues of capital formation and enabling legislation for co-operatives in developing countries.

This chapter sets out a case for improvements in the quality of governance and other corrective measures for co-operatives through the establishment of greater autonomy and stronger channels of accountability. There is a real need to bring about a radical paradigm shift i.e. from government to governance. The chapter also identifies areas in which critical intervention is needed, including competition, leadership, member commitment, structure and operations, which will be necessary for an effective change from the current paradigm of government to that of governance.

Emergence of co-operatives

The co-operative movement in India started in 1904 and has expanded into all sectors of the economy. To describe the emergence of this vast network, where co-operatives functioning in different sectors face diverse problems, proved a difficult task. In order to simplify it, representative typologies of the co-operative sector have been developed, based on available literature, along with a description for each typology identified. As a result, three typologies have been identified and characterised, namely government-controlled, government-supported and member-controlled co-operatives.

The 'government-controlled' co-operatives were promoted as part of state policy on recommendations of the All India Rural Credit Survey Committee (1951–54) which led to state partnership both in the share capital of co-operatives and in their management. The Committee on Co-operative Law (1955) appointed by the Government of India suggested the concept of the state partnership and accordingly various State Co-operative Societies' Acts were amended which, in effect, also strengthened the government control over co-operative institutions.

The 'government-supported co-operatives' model is based on the situation of the sugar co-operatives in Maharashtra state in India, where the state provides support to both the sugarcane crop and to the sugar co-operatives. Here co-operatives have been able to shape policy decisions in their favour, especially those relating to irrigation, as well as 'capture' the regulation of the market price; to have the government as a shareholder in sugar factories and acting as default guarantor; to benefit from cheap credit, storage facilities and export incentives in years of surplus production – all in the name of providing a 'fair price' to the producer. Price controls initiated in the 1950s to maintain price stability have been used by the powerful sugar lobby to suit their vested interests.

The 'member-controlled' model is typified by the Anand Dairy Co-operatives, popularly known as Amul, which operates on a three-tier structure with each level owned and controlled by milk producers though elected boards. The Village Dairy Co-operative Society (VS), the primary tier, is comprised of milk producers. The second tier is the District Co-operative Society (DCS) processor, which collects milk from primary processes and markets the milk. All of Gujarat's district unions came together to form the apex marketing federation, the Gujarat Co-operative Milk Marketing Federation (GCMMF). The third tier was established as a marketing and distribution network for dairy products across India abroad under the single brand name of Amul.

Government-controlled co-operatives – victims of bureaucratisation and politicisation

The foundation for government-controlled co-operatives was formalised in legislation enacted in the 1904 Co-operative Credit Societies Act. The Act set out to address the twin issues of farmers' indebtedness and poverty. This initiative of the government continued for the next five decades, and was supported by further legislation, including the Co-operative Societies Act of 1912, which provided for the formation of non-credit societies and federal co-operative organisations. With the emergence of co-operatives with a multi-state membership, the Multi-Unit Co-operative Societies Act was passed in 1942, delegating the power of the Central Registrar of Co-operatives to the State Registrars for all practical purposes.

Following independence, government control of co-operatives continued. In the early 1960s, new co-operative legislation emerged as a result of the findings of the All India Rural Credit Survey Committee (1951–54). The Committee recommended that the state should play an active role in the spread of the co-operative movement and many state governments amended their Acts to give additional powers to the government and place government nominees on the boards of co-operatives. These powers included the power of veto of board decisions, issue of directives to co-operatives by the Government/ Registrar and appointment of personnel in co-operatives. These provisions led to further erosion of the autonomy of co-operatives. The politicians came to dominate the boards of a majority of co-operatives and used their position as a stepping stone for their political ambitions.[1] A separate comprehensive central legislative act, the Multi State Co-operative Societies Act of 1984, was enacted to facilitate the functioning of genuine multi-state societies.

The government focus until 1990 remained on the implementation of co-operative development schemes through share capital contributions, loans, subsidies and financial guarantees. This resulted in an increase in the number of co-operatives in various sectors of the Indian economy, making it one of the largest movements of its kind in the world.

During a century of its existence, this sector has built a network consisting of more than 545 million individual co-operative organisations and over 236 million members with a working capital base of 3,400,555 million rupees. However, their performance in qualitative terms has not been up to the desired level. The economic sectors in which government-controlled co-operatives became prominent included credit, agricultural produce marketing, consumer goods, spinning, agro-processing, fisheries, handloom textiles, transport, handicrafts, housing, irrigation and electricity generation.

Today, however, the co-operative sector, as it exists in most of the states, is weak and inactive. Co-operatives look towards government patronage both for business and capital requirement as illustrated by the status of the two largest sub-sectors, namely credit and agricultural marketing.

As we have seen, the co-operative movement in India originated as a co-operative credit movement. The Short Term Co-operative Credit Structure (STCCS), organised in a three-tier structure, mostly provides crop and other working capital loans primarily for a short period to farmers and rural artisans. The first tier of the Primary Agricultural Credit Societies (PACS), however, has fared poorly in its management of the deployed funds. While loans advanced per borrowing member have increased 42 times between 1960–61 and 2005–6, during the same period overdue payments increased by 69 times per borrowing member. In 2005–6, while 44,321 PACS were making profits, another 53,026 were incurring losses. Further, the aggregate losses of the PACS, at 19,200 million rupees, outweighed the profits of 71,930 million rupees. The other important sub-sector of marketing co-operatives is by and large two-tier, with Primary Co-operative Marketing Societies (PCMS) at rural regulated market level, and marketing federations at state level. There is an existing network of 28 State-level Federations, 171 District Marketing Societies, and 3,632 PCMS. Additionally, 29 Commodity Federations and 3,920 PCMSs are engaged in handling single commodities. After the 1980s, the PCMS showed a two-fold increase to 10,807 but sharply declined to 6,836 by 2000–1, mainly due to their inefficient functioning. During this period membership declined from 7.3 to 4.2 million with a corresponding decline in profit of 32%.[2]

The sickness in co-operatives is fairly widespread and growing. Considering the gravity of the situation, a High Powered Committee on Co-operatives was constituted by the Government of India in 2005. The Terms of Reference for the Committee were to review the achievements of the co-operatives during the last hundred years; to identify the challenges and to suggest measures to address them; to suggest an appropriate policy and legislative framework; and to identify the

changes required in the co-operative legislation to ensure the democratic, autonomous and professional functioning of co-operatives. The
Committee submitted its report in May 2009. The observations and
recommendations of this committee have been included where
relevant.

Government-supported sugar co-operatives – sweet dream turned sour
Sugar co-operatives in Maharashtra provide a good case study of the
negative impact of government support. In Maharashtra, the Pravara
Co-operative Sugar Factory, set up in 1950–51, proved highly successful and similar co-operative factories were set up all over Maharashtra.
They performed well initially but today are in serious trouble, with
nearly 40% of the mills losing money and facing closure despite having
received state support for over five decades.

The government buys a percentage of the sugar produced at a
subsidised price to be sold via the Public Distribution System (PDS) at
prices lower than the market price in India. During periods of good
availability the government, via the mechanism of monthly release, has
assisted the sugar industry with cheap credit and storage facilities and
export incentives in the name of providing a 'fair price' to the
producer. During periods of low availability, the government increased
free sale releases or deregulated the industry only to re-introduce regulation at the behest of the industry as soon as prices began to fall.

Much of the cost of sugar factories is borne by the state government.
In addition, during the 1980s, 50–70% of the incremental volume of
irrigation water alone was diverted to the sugarcane crop, at the
expense of other crops.[3] Furthermore, the sugarcane farmers also
receive loans from the government.

The links between the sugar co-operatives with politics in general,
and the Congress Party in particular, is made in a study by Khekale.[4]
He finds that 21 chairmen of sugar co-operatives held important
positions in the Congress Party between 1952 and 1972. During this
period he found that 74% of the chairs of sugar co-operatives were
elected as legislators and MPs. The status and power that a chair and
directors command makes them highly sought after by political
parties, who offer them tickets to contest state and local-level
elections.

Being politically important, the western Maharashtra sugar co-operatives have been able to use the political power to 'capture' the cane
price regulation. Cane price appears to have been used as an instrument to disburse patronage and garner votes. On the other hand, sugar
price controls were used by the powerful sugar lobby to suit their

vested interests. The government has acted as 'cartel manager on behalf of the sugar industry'.[5]

The 'special' status and assured government support, irrespective of performance, took away from the sector any incentive to perform well leading to poor performance, both in technical and in financial terms.[6] Today things have come to such an impasse that even the political leadership is telling the industry that it should not expect more financial help from the state government and that the co-operatives need to improve their performance to take on challenges in fast-changing Indian markets.

Member-controlled co-operatives: Amul – success amid failures

Originating in 1946 in the village of Anand in Gujarat, the member-driven model popularly known as the 'Amul model' or Anand pattern of milk co-operatives has been the silver lining where 'government-controlled' and 'government-supported' co-operatives have achieved limited success. The Amul model has been successfully emulated all over the country. In its basic form, the Anand pattern consists of a three-tier organisational structure that comprised village co-operative societies, district-level dairy unions and state-level federations. The success of the Gujarat Cooperative Milk Marketing Federation (GCMMF) and its Amul model, with its products marketed under the Amul brand name, is widely recognised inside and outside India.

The GCMMF co-operatives operate as a true representative of farmers and are run by professionally qualified managers.[7] However, this has not been an easy task. Building an organisational network and ensuring representation of farmers at different levels of decision-making throughout the network – the board of directors of societies, unions and the federation – was a very complicated task. However, their example presents a successful model for developing world economies characterised by either large under-developed suppliers and/or markets with high potential.[8]

Today, in Gujarat alone, GCMMF co-operatives have a membership of 2.9 million milk producers spread over 15,322 Village Societies and 13 District Unions, with a daily milk collection of 9.1 million litres. The model has been widely adopted in India though not with the same degree of success (see below for further discussion). The Anand Pattern Co-operative Model now includes 177 District Co-operative Unions and 22 State Dairy Federations throughout India covering 346 districts, and 140,227 village-level societies. They are owned by around 14 million farmer members of which four million are women.[9]

India's Dairy Development Programme is officially recognised as promoting both economic and participatory development, by linking dairy farmers to urban markets and providing them with a fair price for high-quality milk, as well as enabling the formation of collective spaces for social and political interaction through its co-operatives.[10] In the case of Amul, we find that the co-operative was able to drop the trappings of the caste system and cultivate the queue system at the milk collection centres where people stood in line without paying attention to whether the person next to them was an untouchable.[11]

In most other states, the dairy co-operatives are managed by civil servants, function more as government bodies and are weak representatives of farmers. Of the 14 major state dairy co-operatives (out of 22) in the country, 10 have state government equity, of which 6 have government equity in excess of 51%. Twelve have government officers as managing directors who are appointed by the state government. Because of such governance, these dairy co-operatives are mere parastatals. This governance structure influences the functioning of the entire chain, from the state federation to the village societies and thus significantly impacts farmers' involvement in the chain.[12]

Understanding co-operative success and failures

There is a need for stronger conceptual frameworks which can be used by managers to better understand the underlying causes of success and failure. At the same time studying successes without looking at failures also tends to create a misleading, if not entirely wrong picture of what it takes to succeed. This analysis is constrained by the fact that the literature on co-operatives in India is predominantly narrative. This section re-visits empirical and narrative work to understand the reasons for the success and failure of co-operatives, with particular reference to the three typologies described earlier, to discover some pointers for developing successful co-operatives.

Design and management issues: empirical findings
The empirical work done so far has brought to the surface some of the basic issues that remain contentious in understanding co-operatives. This section draws on B. S. Misra's study on PACS for the period 1988–2005 which identified some broad determinants of their performance at the macro level.[13] Misra found that, in conformity with popular perception, the government's contribution to the share capital was detrimental to the improvement in the performance of the PACS. A government contribution to share capital not only gives it a hand to meddle with the affairs of the PACS; it also provides the comfort of a

government bailout in case of difficulty. In addition, the Vaidyanthan Committee observed that STCCS has never realised the enormous potential of its vast outreach, owing mainly to a 'deep impairment of governance'. The state governments have become the dominant share-holders, managers, regulators, supervisors and auditors. In view of the adverse consequences of a government contribution to share capital, Misra suggested that the recommendation of the Vaidyanthan Committee, that the government can retain 25% of equity capital in PACS, needs to be reconsidered. He argues the need for either completely dislodging government equity in the PACS or reframing the PACS as quasi-government ventures for which the parameters of performance need to be revisited.

Secondly, as membership size grows in the PACS, it is detrimental to recovery.[14] As the membership size of PACS has grown over the years from 42 members per society in 1950–51 to 1,176 in 2005–6, this has impeded their recovery by weakening peer pressure. There is a need to revisit the issue of optimal member size of PACS in relation to their viability.

Baviskar and Attwood's comparative study of co-operatives in Maharashtra, Gujarat, West Bengal, Tamil Nadu, Uttar Pradesh and Kerala utilises a political economy perspective.[15] Their main contention is that the broad characteristics of the regional political economy (a non-interfering state), the social structure (some homo-geneity in class and caste composition) and the internal design of a co-operative are essential factors in co-operative success. Conversely, the absence of these conditions produces co-operative failure.

We have seen how large-scale state intervention proved a source of problems for sugarcane co-operatives. Their 'special' status and assured government support, irrespective of performance, diminished competitive pressure for the sector to perform. This situation builds a fairly strong case for the rolling back of the state from its role both as a stakeholder and a regulator in the sugar sector.

Banerjeee et al. propose a theory of rent-seeking within sugar co-operatives leading to lump-sum transfers from poorer members and disproportionate control rights wielded by wealthier members.[16] Transfers of rents to the latter are achieved by depressing prices of sugarcane supplied by members and diverting the resulting retained earnings. The increased heterogeneity of landholdings in the local area causes increased inefficiency by inducing a lower input price and a lower level of installed crushing capacity. These effects are confirmed by data from nearly 100 sugar co-operatives in the Indian state of Maharashtra over the period 1971–93.

Based on his extensive work on dairy co-operatives in Gujarat,

Tushaar Shah suggests that the actual performance of any village co-operative is determined by the performance of five components: 1) Governance structure; 2) Critical linkages with federal co-operatives; 3) Patronage system; 4) The micro environment; and 5) Operative systems.[17]

However, there is a perception that the Amul model of co-operative has been less successful outside Gujarat. Scholten refers to the difficulty in replicating the Anand pattern across India, outside its home state of Gujarat.[18] This suggests that flexibility and sensitivity to local conditions are crucial to success.

A less recognised fact is that the co-operatives in other states are organised differently than the GCMMF co-operatives.[19] Evidence from the World Bank revealed that the Anand principles of democratically run co-operatives employing professional managers, had maximised gains to farmers and consumers and, by raising farm incomes, stimulated employment, and generated investment in education, nutrition and sanitation, thereby improving the quality of life.[20]

Role of co-operative legislation

One of the main barriers to the effective functioning of co-operatives is a restrictive legislative environment. At the state level, co-operatives continue to be governed through a number of state-specific acts. This legislation typically endows governments with draconian powers, which have, in many cases, militated against the very concept of a co-operative.[21]

The character of the co-operatives in the 1950 to 1990 period changed from member-centric to state-centric. The 1990s witnessed attempts at unshackling the co-operative sector from the bondages of the government and restoring their democratic character. The Ardhanareeswaran Committee (1987) on law for democratisation and professionalisation of management in co-operatives recommended (a) the deletion of those legal provisions in State Co-operative Societies Acts, which militate against the democratic character and the autonomy of co-operatives and also (b) the incorporation of several provisions in the said state acts which activate the democratic processes for infusing professional management into co-operatives. As a follow-up of its recommendations, six committees were appointed during the last two decades. All these committees made a number of valuable suggestions to turn co-operatives into self-reliant, autonomous and democratised institutions while strongly advocating the need to replace the existing government dominated co-operative laws with a new member-centric legislation.

The Government of Andhra Pradesh took the lead and passed the Andhra Pradesh Mutually Aided Co-operative Societies Act of 1995 which was followed by similar enactments in eight other states. The Multi-State Co-operative Societies (MSCS) Act which was enacted in 1984 was replaced by a fresh consolidated statute MSCS Act 2002, for co-operative societies having jurisdiction over more than one state. The Vaidyanathan Committee on the Revival of Short-term and Long-term Co-operative Credit Structure suggested that a model co-operative law is to be enacted by the states.

The Government of India selected a committee led by Dr Y.K. Alagh, to make recommendations with regard to (a) framing a legislation enabling incorporation of co-operatives as companies and (b) proposed legislation to accommodate the unique elements of co-operative business within a regulatory framework. On its recommendations, a new section was inserted in the Companies Act of 1956 which came into force in 2003. The legislation combines the institutional and philosophical strengths of co-operatives (ownership limited to users; limited interest on shares; absence of equity trading, patronage and not capital-based) with the flexibility and autonomy of company law.

These sets of legal reforms have laid the foundations for re-engineering and re-moulding the co-operative societies. However, much more still remains to be done, particularly in states where there is reluctance to move ahead.

Most recently, the High Powered Committee of 2009 was of the opinion that 'the root causes appear to converge upon the common problem of governance, which in turn is to a major extent determined by the laws that govern co-operatives'. It was of the view that co-operative autonomy could only be ensured through appropriate amendments to the Indian Constitution. As a result, it was decided by the government to amend the Constitution.[22] The Parliamentary Standing Committee on Agriculture which examined this Constitutional Amendment Bill in August 2007 was unanimous that an amendment to the Indian Constitution on co-operatives was not necessary. Instead, it proposed that the Amendment Bill be converted into a central model law. There would be incentives and disincentives for the states that did or did not implement the model law. The states would then be able to enact their own laws which are compatible with the Central Model Law. The Committee recommended that a new Article 43B on empowerment of co-operatives be added in Part IV of the Constitution that contains the Directive Principles of State Policy which states that 'The state shall endeavour to promote voluntary

formation, autonomous functions, democratic control and professional management of the co-operatives.'

Bhat agreed with the view of the Standing Committee and suggested
that no regimentation through uniform law shall be attempted or
thrust upon states.[23] He further suggested that legislation was simply
not enough by itself and should be followed up or accompanied by
building up of a strong and wide base of popular and active participation by citizens. He also suggests that co-operative autonomy needs to
accommodate the human rights of individual members, and incorporate mechanisms to prevent breaches of accountability and mismanagement, to protect the interests of the members and the society. An
active and engaged membership is thus seen as essential for co-
operative stability and success; without this, new regulatory
approaches will almost inevitably atrophy over time.

At the same time, we need to rethink approaches to co-operative
deregulation. The deregulation or more accurately, a *deregulatory
mindset* was an important source of the financial crisis (2007–9) – a
mindset that, to a very significant extent, grew out of profound
changes in academic thinking about the role of government. But as we
think about regulatory reform – including both enactment and implementation – it is important that we correctly diagnose the causes not
only of the financial crisis itself but also of the regulatory failure that
paved the way, both for the bubble and the subsequent crash.[24] This
analysis sounds a note of caution to those who argue that government
control on co-operatives should simply fade away. Further, it cautions
against viewing the government as being incapable of doing anything
constructive for co-operatives.

Role of co-operative policy

In the post-independence period, the national policy on co-operatives
was first enunciated by the National Development Council Policy
Resolution of 1958, followed by the National Policy on Co-operation,
1977, and the National Policy on Co-operatives, 2002. The 1958
policy observed that co-operation was developed as a people's
movement organised on the basis of village community. The National
Policy on Co-operation, 1977, aimed to minimise poverty, to generate
employment within the co-operative sector, to enhance productivity of
the economy and to improve the overall quality of life of the people in
general and members of co-operatives in particular.

The objectives of the National Co-operative Policy of 2002 were to
(a) facilitate all-round development of the co-operatives in the country,
(b) provide necessary support, encouragement and assistance to allow

co-operatives to function as autonomous, self-reliant and democratically managed institutions accountable to their members and (c) enable co-operatives to make a significant contribution to the national economy, particularly in areas which require people's participation and community efforts. The new National Co-operative Policy and modified Multi-State Co-operative Societies (MSCS) Act of 2002 were strongly influenced by the International Labour Organisation (ILO) Recommendation on the Promotion of Co-operatives 193, adopted in 2002. The ministerial task force constituted by Government of India in 2002 prepared a sector-wise 'plan of action' for the implementation of national co-operative policy.

Towards a paradigm shift – government to governance
An analysis of the three dimensions of management, legal and policy context is critical for understanding the success and failure of co-operatives. A 'governance deficit' emerges as a common factor across the three typologies identified for this study. The role of legislation in the poor performance of co-operatives has been over-emphasised by the High Powered Committee and by many co-operative practitioners, while the weakness of governance has been under-emphasised. The analysis in this chapter suggests that in government-controlled and government-supported co-operatives legislation in fact adversely influenced raising/sustaining performance, but that this was not the case in member-controlled co-operatives. With regard to policy changes over time, vast differences seem to exist in declared intent and action on the ground.

Therefore, co-operatives urgently need a complete paradigm shift from 'government to governance'. At the same time we need to convince co-operative practitioners and policy-makers that effective regulation is necessary to address the systemic threats.

This analysis of evidence on the sugarcane co-operatives of Maharashtra, the Primary Agricultural Co-operative Societies and the dairy co-operatives builds a strong case for rolling back the state both as a stakeholder and a regulator in the co-operative sector. The recent legal reforms are indicative of a directional change i.e. from government-dominated to member-oriented co-operative legislation. In order to accelerate this transformation, a sound co-operative governance model must be in place. The co-operative sector as a whole remains poorly understood and its specific governance challenges remain as yet largely unexplored despite their considerable presence in many developing countries including India.

Dimensions of co-operative governance

The studies confirm that good governance is central to the success and sustainability of co-operatives in the developing as much as the developed world. Improving board performance and accountability remains a central issue, together with improving engagement from the wider membership. However there are some issues and challenges in terms of corporate governance that are specific to co-operatives in developing countries.[25] The reality that co-operatives exist for their members and need to work in their interest brings a different perspective to issues of accountability and governance. There is a need for better understanding and precision in measurement of accountability and governance with regard to co-operatives. The other key concerns which need to be addressed through good governance in the Indian context are bureaucratisation and government control and the politicisation of co-operative leadership.

'Member-centricity' and democratic control

Remaining relevant to members is key to member-centricity. Members want their co-operatives to be commercially successful, and to be run in their interest. This requires good quality governance which depends on three broad principles closely linked to each other, namely, (i) transparency in operations, (ii) transparency leading to accountability and democratic governance and (iii) accountability for the stakeholders (primarily members) in terms of providing value. The key question is whether co-operatives are being governed in a way that is fully aligned with member interests and democratic control. The central challenge for co-operative governance remains how to balance the principle of democratic control and retain the role of professional management.

The study of milk co-operatives within Amul indicates the presence of a complex but complementary relationship with limited frictions between different stakeholders including different managerial classes – whether technical or political. Both these classes are involved in managerial activity where problems of jurisdiction and control in decision-making can make or mar the success of an organisation. Both these classes in their actual operational involvement, despite some lapses, have shown a remarkable degree of accommodation, need for concessions and foresight in terms of what will ultimately benefit the average milk producer.[26]

The role of political influence in co-operatives has also hindered the development of a member focus in co-operatives. We have seen how this has been the case with the sugar co-operatives of Western Maharashtra. The broader role of influence in governance structures has been documented.[27] Influence costs arise in any organisation when individuals or groups attempt to influence the decision to their benefit with regard to distribution of benefits among members and is a major source of inefficiencies in agribusiness co-operatives. Further, the high heterogeneity of member preferences makes co-operative decision-making cumbersome, by boosting member influence attempts in multi-product co-operatives. Such co-operatives tend to incur higher influence costs as compared to single-product marketing co-operatives with less heterogeneous members.[28]

High-influence attempts due to bureaucratisation of co-operatives and the politicisation of co-operative leadership in India lead to factions in the board, conflicts in governance and management and lack of consensus in decision-making. Co-operatives require good governance to emerge as effective democratic structures for economic development with a human face, and to protect them from the adverse influence of vested interests as observed in the Amul study.

Participative leadership and good governance

Mannle notes that responsible leadership draws its strength from the understanding and co-operation of the people involved, tapping the wisdom of the group for a collective goal.[29] The consistent growth of Amul over six decades indicates that a visionary leadership that is in constant pursuit of expansion, aligned to its mission of 'serving the farmer', can achieve extraordinary results through mobilising collective action.[30] Mannle goes on to suggest that participative leadership is ideal for the co-operative business model. Participative leadership is defined as leadership that involves employees across levels of the hierarchy in decision-making.[31] When both ownership and responsibilities are equitably distributed amongst employees, there is the possibility to develop a more sustainable business and committed workforce.

The problem of developing participative leadership in India, where politicians have dominated boards for many years, can be addressed by a determined campaign to build a cadre of young co-operative leaders with outstanding capabilities and knowledge of the function of governance, and how it operates within the co-operative business structure. The HPC observed that leadership is not just an inherited trait but is dependent on exposure, education, training and grooming.[32] This is not a common practice in co-operatives and it was recommended that this should be considered as an important responsibility of the board and management.

Learning to compete

Co-operatives remain an important 'instrument for development' and have long been mooted as organisations enabling smallholder producers to compete in settings of profound market and institutional failure.[33]

Of over half a million co-operatives in the country at different levels, a large number today are not viable and on the verge of sickness, while many are practically dormant.[34] Considering the wide-scale sickness of co-operatives in India, consolidation at sectoral level and adopting a stronger business model seems to be a priority in meeting market challenges.

Re-visiting the co-operative domain – expansion to consolidation

A huge gap has emerged between expectations and performance, undermining trust in co-operatives.[35] There is anecdotal evidence to suggest that competitive pressure is the main cause of co-operative mortality.[36] This brings us to a more fundamental question: whether the co-operative form of business can be adapted to all sectors of the economy and more specifically to all products/services in various sectors of the economy.

In this context, it becomes necessary to scrutinise the existing domain of non-viable co-operatives more carefully and challenge unexamined assumptions, false dichotomies and ideological biases that get in the way of seeing 'what is actually there'. The restoration of trust in co-operatives requires consolidation and not expansion in order to bridge the huge gap between expectations and performance.

Improving performance: sound business model

The analysis in this section focuses upon agricultural and allied sector co-operatives which dominate the co-operative landscape in India. How does increasing product market competition affect the technical efficiency of producers' co-operatives? Can it provide them with the incentives to improve their own performance? With emerging market trends, producers are required to deliver a specific product, at a specific quality at a specific place and time. However, the agribusiness sector in India suffers from long and fragmented supply chains. A long supply chain can also mean that each level of the supply chain is unaware of the requirements of the next level and thus there exists disconnect between farmer and processor.[37] With the liberalisation of India's economy and market entry by the private sector, new competitive dynamics have emerged in the dairy industry. Consequently, co-operative organisations have to adjust their structure and operations to these new demands.[38]

In response to these challenges, many co-operatives have started to integrate their operations in areas such as procurement of supplies, logistics, manufacturing, distribution and inventory management. This is hampered by political interference, and also excess staff which adds to the administrative costs thereby creating operational inefficiencies and resultant losses.[39] This requires a reconfiguration of linkages with its members and a move from mere 'exchange' to 'organised exchange'. In other words, co-operative members have to enter into more organised and regular supply arrangements with their co-operative as against the current practice of unplanned occasional transactions.

The other relevant aspect that needs to be addressed is the sheer difference in economic size between farmers and retailers making power imbalanced towards retailers. The main consequences of these imbalances are a relentless downward pressure on farm-gate prices. These market pressures can be countered by integrated supply chains owned and controlled by co-operatives, extending from the farm gate to retail outlet.

Amul was founded on a sound business model: providing quality products to consumers at an affordable price. The entire Amul model dairy value chain from procurement to marketing along with the associated brands remains the sole and exclusive domain of the farmer. Kurien, one of the founders of Amul, comments, 'As a co-operative, our faith requires that we safeguard the interest of both our major stakeholders – the farmers – and the consumers whose loyalty is essential to our continued success.'[40]

By contrast, the government controlled co-operatives such as the State/National Co-operative Marketing Federations act as higher tier organisations of their constituent members. They frequently source from the private sector and also compete with their member societies for retail trade.[41] A comparative study of Amul and Punjab State Supply & Marketing Federation Ltd., (MARKFED, in which the state owns 72% of the equity) for the period 1995–96 to 1999–2000 revealed that Amul scored higher than MARKFED in terms of: organisational effectiveness with no functional overlaps between different organisational levels; well-defined business portfolio in relation to the needs of the membership; value addition and sharing the benefits with the membership; and in the scope and relevance of services offered to members.[42]

'Co-operative advantage' through member commitment
Member commitment is a critical dimension to the success of co-operatives but is a complex issue in the context of the developing

world. The most obvious reason farmers join co-operatives is to satisfy economic goals. Many studies have observed that members place greater weight on economic gains than on non-economic benefits. When it comes to collective gains co-operatives are similar to an organised behaviour system 'wherein the organizing element is the expectation of the members that they as members of the system will achieve a surplus beyond what they could attain through individual and independent action.'[43]

The prerequisite for successful co-operatives is that the farmer-members are willing to supply the co-operatives with raw products, capital and managerial inputs. The commitment is also needed for members to abstain from opportunistic (or free rider) behaviour in their (transactional) relationship with the co-operative. A recent study observed that the development of quality assurance systems along production chains is dependent on the quality of intermediate goods supplied by the farmers.[44] When the quality is observable, a co-operative is able to overcome the free-rider problem. With unobservable quality, co-operatives cannot overcome the free-rider problem (as it requires investment of additional cost in quality testing) and it becomes more serious as the number of members in the co-operative increases.[45]

The declining member commitment can be a result of a perceived lack of connection between members' efforts and co-operative success. On the other hand, member commitment and participation is enhanced by trust.[46] The other important dimension of trust is 'transparency in transactions' as a means to minimise influence activities (when individuals or groups attempt to influence the decision to their benefit) resulting in orderly distribution of benefit among members.

The agricultural co-operatives can differentiate themselves from other organisations or business entities by making 'added value', through a large portfolio of need-based services to membership as important as 'value addition' in raw materials supplied by members. This co-operative differentiation can be achieved through a unique member-co-operative interface to serve the interests of the members beyond business transactions.

The horticulture co-operatives in Valsad (Gujarat), apart from production and marketing-related services, provide many other services such as consumer stores, textiles, stationery, medical stores, flourmills, construction materials and cattle feed. In the Amul model, members are engaged in developing the Vision, Mission and Strategy (VMS), helping members to manage their dairy business efficiently, and projects such as the Women Dairy Education Programme, Clean

Milk Production and Fertility Improvement Programme (FIP). The local base of co-operatives gives them an advantage when building a strong member–co-operative interface which can differentiate them from other business entities.

In successful co-operatives, the bonds between co-operatives and their membership revolve around three major factors, namely strong backward integration through provision of services, benefits of collective marketing and transparency in the process of market transaction.[47] In order to offer higher levels of co-operative advantage, the marketing co-operatives have to undergo considerable 'member orientation' by focusing their activities around the best interests of their memberships.

Conclusions

The strong appeal of the underlying ideology and principles along with the potential advantages of co-operation has led to a huge proliferation of agricultural co-operatives in India between the 1960s and the 1990s, both in size and coverage.[48] However, excessive government intervention and poor management have led to the growth of a large number of poorly functioning co-operatives. A huge gap created between expectations and performance has resulted in a poor image of and general lack of trust in co-operatives. The gradual withdrawal of the state from many economic and social domains is creating new space and opportunities for the co-operatives. The foremost requirement for co-operatives is that of redefining their domain rather than being present in many sectors of economy without any well-defined competitive advantage.[49] There is a need to develop models for managing the process of change and to reposition co-operatives in India.

However, even the High Powered Committee over-emphasised the importance of an enabling legal environment as a factor leading to good governance. The Committee completely ignored reasons for current sickness in Sugar Co-operatives in Maharashtra and the continuing success of the Amul model. In this context, the stand taken in this chapter is that the reform of corporate governance practices needs to precede the reform of corporate law.

It is time to focus on improvements in quality of governance as well as weakening the links between the government and co-operatives along with interventions to encourage greater autonomy for co-operatives. This chapter has argued that it is necessary to develop a better 'co-operative governance' framework which should include ways of promoting member-centricity and democratic control, better accountability of management, and the promotion of a cadre of young co-operators with no interest in mainstream politics and a belief in participative leadership. At the same time, the continuous improvement of governance mechanisms that serve member interests will be of great value.

Secondly, co-operatives need to become more competitive. Considering the wide-scale sickness of co-operatives in India, there is a need for sectoral-level consolidation rather than expansion and the adoption of sound business models for each sector. Lastly, the co-operatives must build upon their inherent 'co-operative advantage' through member commitment and move to a new phase of member relationship by making 'adding value' to membership as important as 'value addition'. The paradigm shift from 'government to governance' combined with other related interventions is likely to restore the image and trust in co-operatives by bridging the existing gap between expectations and performance.

Notes

1 Government of India, Second Administrative Reforms Commission. 'Ninth Report: Social Capital – A Shared Destiny' (2008).
2 D. Shah, 'Working of Cooperative Marketing Societies in India: Some Emerging Issues', *Productivity,* 49:2,3 (2008), 214–219.
3 S. Sawant, B.N. Kulkarnik, C.V. Achuthan and K.J.S. Satyasai, *Agricultural Development in Maharashtra: Problems and Prospects* (Mumbai: University of Mumbai & NABARD, 1997).
4 N.R. Khekale, *Pressure Politics in Maharashtra* (Mumbai: Himalaya Publishing House, 1990).
5 S.J. Kamath, *The Political Economy of Suppressed Markets: Controls, Rent Seeking and Interest Group Behaviour in the Indian Sugar and Cement Industries* (Bombay: Oxford University Press, 1992).
6 M. Lalvani, 'Sugar Co-operatives in Maharashtra: A Political Economy Perspective', *Journal of Development Studies* 44:10 (2008), 1474–1505.
7 M. Punjabi, 'India: Increasing Demand Challenges the Dairy Sector', in Nancy Morgan (ed.), *Small Holder Dairy Development : Lessons Learned in Asia* (Bangkok: Rap Publications, 2009).
8 P. Chandra and D. Tirupati, *Business Strategies for Managing Complex Supply Chains in Large Emerging Economics: The Story of AMUL* (Ahmadabad: Indian Institute of Management, 2003).
9 National Dairy Development Board, *National Statistics*. Available at www.nddb.org/statistics.html.
10 H.C. Triandis and D.P.S Bhawuk, 'Culture Theory and the Meaning of Relatedness', in P.C. Earley and M. Erez (eds), *New Perspectives on International Industrial/Organizational Psychology* (New York: The New Lexington Free Press, 1997), pp. 13–52.

11 D.P.S. Bhawuk, S. Mrazek and V.P. Munusamy, 'From Social Engineering to Community Transformation: Amul, Grameen Bank, and Mondragon as Exemplar Organizations', available at www.humiliationstudies.org /documents/BhawukMrazekMunusamyBeyondSocialEngineeringinPeacea ndPolicy.pdf.

12 W. Candler and N. Kumar, *India: The Dairy Revolution* (Washington DC: The World Bank, 1998).

13 B.S. Misra, *Credit Cooperatives in India: Past, Present and Future* (Oxford: Routledge, 2010).

14 Ibid.

15 B.S. Baviskar and D.W. Attwood, *Finding the Middle Path: The Political Economy of Cooperation in Rural India* (Boulder and London: Westview Press, 1995).

16 A. Banerjee, D. Mookherjee, K. Munshi and D. Ray, 'Inequality, Control Rights and Rent Seeking: Sugar Cooperatives in Maharashtra', *Journal of Political Economy* 109:1 (2001), 138–190.

17 T. Shah, *Making Farmers' Co-operatives Work: Design, Governance and Management* (New Delhi: Saga Publications, 1995).

18 B. Scholten, *India's White Revolution: Operation Flood Food Aid and Development* (London: Tauris, 2010).

19 Misra, *Credit Cooperatives in India*, p. 168.

20 Ibid.

21 Ministry of Agriculture, Government of India, 'Report of the High Powered Committee on Co-operatives' (2009).

22 Department of Agriculture and Cooperation, Government of India, 'Annual Report 2009–2010' (2010).

23 P. Ishwara Bhat, 'Revitalizing the Co-operative Societies through Constitutional Means', *International Journal of Civil Society Law* 8:3 (2010), 8–41.

24 D. Moss, 'Reversing the Null: Regulation, Deregulation, and the Power of Ideas' (Working Paper no. 10–080, Harvard Business School, 2010).

25 L. Shaw, 'Overview of Corporate Governance Issues for Co-operatives' (Discussion Paper, Global Corporate Governance Forum, 2006).

26 A.H. Somjee, 'The Techno-Managerial and Politico-Managerial classes in Milk Cooperatives in India', in Y.K. Malik (ed.), *Politics, Technology and Bureaucracy in South Asia* (Brill Academic Publishers: Netherlands, 1983).

27 C. Iliopoulos and G. Hendrikse, 'Influence Costs in Agribusiness Cooperatives: Evidence from Case Studies', *International Studies of Management & Organization*, 39:4 (1996), 60–80.

28 F.R. Chaddad and M.L. Cook, 'Understanding Cooperative Models: An Ownership-Control Rights Typology', *Review of Agricultural Economics* 26:3 (2004), 348–360.

29 A. Mannle, 'Secrets of Collaborative Leadership' cited in B. Rok, 'People and Skills, Ethical Context of the Participative Leadership Model: Taking

People into Account', *Corporate Governance* 9:4 (2009), 461–472.

30 H. Chawla, 'Amul India: A Social Development Enterprise', *Asian Case Research Journal*, 11:2 (2007), 293–326.

31 G. Spreitzer, 'Giving Peace a Chance: Organizational Leadership, Empowerment, and Peace', *Journal of Organizational Behavior* 23:8 (2007), 1077–1095.

32 Government of India 'Report of the High Powered Committee on Co-operatives'.

33 J. Bijman and R. Ruben, 'Repositioning Agricultural Cooperatives in the North and the South: Where do the Twain meet?' (Paper presented at the 2nd Agri-ProFocus Expert Meeting, Deventer, 2005).

34 Government of India 'Report of the High Powered Committee on Co-operatives'.

35 S.K. Datta, 'Cooperatives in Agriculture', in *State of the Indian Farmer – A Millennium Study* (New Delhi: Government of India, 2004).

36 O.M. Maietta and V. Sena, 'Is Competition Really Bad News for Cooperatives? Some Empirical Evidence for Italian Producers' Cooperatives', *Journal of Productivity Analysis* 29:3 (2008), 221–223.

37 KPMG and ASSOCHAM, 'Storage Facilities For Agri Produce Still Fall Short Over 10 Million Tons: KPMG-ASSOCHAM', available at www.assocham.org/prels/shownews.php?id=2128.

38 Bijman and Ruben, 'Repositioning Agricultural Cooperatives in the North and the South'.

39 V. Goel and B. Suku, 'Supply Chain Management in a Private Farming vis-a vis Cooperative Processing and Distribution Environment of Dairy Sector in India', *Journal of Food Products Marketing* 16:2 (2010), 212–231.

40 V. Kurien, Chairman's Speech, Annual General Body Meeting (GCMMF, Gujarat, 2004).

41 National Co-operative Union of India, 'Recommendations' (Congress literature, 15th Indian Cooperative Congress, 2008), p. 12.

42 Datta, 'Cooperatives in Agriculture'.

43 W. Alderson, *Dynamic Marketing Behavior: A Functionalist Theory of Marketing* (Homewood: Richard D. Irwin Inc, 1965).

44 L. Sanxi, Y. Bing and Y. Jianyu, 'Incentives and Quality Provision in Organisations; Cooperative vs. IOF' (2010), available at http://lisanxi.weebly.com/uploads/5/2/6/5/5265509/re-final.pdf.

45 M.H. Hansen, J.L. Morrow Jr. and J.C. Batista, 'The Impact of Trust on Co-operative Membership Retention, Performance, and Satisfaction: An Exploratory Study', *International Food and Agribusiness Management Review* 5 (2002), 41–59.

46 L.K. Vaswani, *Marketing of Horticulture Products – A Case Study of Cooperatives in South Gujarat in Agriculture-Market Linkages: Evaluating and Evolving a Conceptual Framework in Indian Context* (Mumbai: NABARD, 2003).

47 J. Birchall, *The International Co-operative Movement* (Manchester: Manchester University Press, 1997).
48 L.K. Vaswani, 'Co-operatives in Developing Economies: Managing Change', *ICA-Asia Pacific Research Committee Newsletter* 1:1 (2010).

15

Minding the GAAP: co-operative responses to the global convergence of accounting standards and practice[1]

John Maddocks, Elizabeth Hicks, Alan J. Robb and Tom Webb

Introduction

When International Accounting Standard (IAS) 32: *Financial Instruments: Disclosure and Presentation*[2] was issued by the International Accounting Standards Board (IASB) in December 2003, it aroused the concern of co-operatives around the world and appeared to ask them to turn their accounting world (or at least their balance sheet) upside down. In many cases members' shares which had been reported as member ownership (i.e. equity) were to be reported as a liability. Such a shift would not reflect co-operative principles and, it was feared, would reduce access to financing for co-operatives.

In this chapter we will provide some background on the IASB and its financial reporting standard-setting mandate as well as the development of accounting standards addressing the distinction between liabilities and equity. We will also discuss how the co-operative model differs from the investor-owner model and why it is important for financial reporting standard-setters to recognise this difference. In the second half of this chapter we will discuss the co-operative comment letters that were submitted to the IASB during 2004 in relation to the classification of liabilities and equity. In particular we will explore the extent to which co-operatives draw on co-operative values and principles to provide a coherent co-operative accounting perspective, or whether their comments are better understood as a reactive, piecemeal and pragmatic approach to accounting standards development.

The International Accounting Standards Board

General purpose financial statements have historically been based on national standards set by local accounting standard-setting bodies or through legal statutes. The formation of the European Union and economic globalisation in general led to the formation of the IASB in 2001.[3] The IASB is a London-based standard-setting body of the International Financial Reporting Standards (IFRS) Foundation, a Delaware-registered not-for-profit organisation. The Foundation is funded by the major accounting firms and some 200 multinational corporations. The IASB and the IFRS Foundation are overseen by a geographically diverse Board of Trustees. The trustees have substantial financial experience predominantly with public accounting firms, governments, national standard-setting bodies, securities commissions, fund companies and corporations. The trustees report to and are appointed by a Monitoring Board composed of public capital market authorities.[4] However, co-operatives are not represented on the Foundation or the IASB.

The objectives of the IASB include developing a set of globally accepted accounting standards 'to help investors, other participants in the world's capital markets and other users of financial statements to make economic decisions'.[5] There is little or no recognition that accounting in many accounting entities involves reporting stewardship rather than investment performance, nor is there recognition that the application of business-style accounting is not suited to provide essential constitutional safeguards when applied to governmental accounting.[6]

At present approximately 120 countries require or permit the use of International Financial Reporting Standards (IFRSs). The process of setting financial reporting standards is claimed to be open, transparent and seeks input from the public, in particular investors, analysts, regulators, business leaders, accounting standard-setters and the accountancy profession.[7] Critics point out that the IASB is unlikely to receive input from 'ordinary people suffering from dubious accounting' and that 'there is no evidence to show that notice is taken of the views of non-corporate respondents'.[8] There is also evidence that submissions by informed non-corporates for greater disclosure are ignored in favour of the views of major corporations.[9]

Given the composition of the IFRS Foundation Board of Trustees and Monitoring Board, it is not surprising that current international financial reporting standards do not appear to take account of the differences between the co-operative and the investor-owner models.

There is, perhaps, an underestimation of the extent of these differences and a tendency to see investor-owner approaches as applicable in most cases to co-operatives. This is a direct consequence of the idea that accounting standards should be 'sector neutral', that is, transactions should be accounted for on the basis of their economic substance rather than the type of organisation involved in the transaction.[10] Consequently a common set of generally accepted accounting principles are seen as appropriate for all organisations. Since the IASB focuses on the information needs of the investor, 'sector neutral' accounting standards reflect a bias for the investor-owned business model.

As will be shown below, co-operatives dispute that the adoption of IFRSs provides data that meets members' needs. In one case a co-operative noted that the adoption of international standards was estimated to cost in excess of NZ$500,000 'with no perceivable benefit flowing' to its 304 members.[11] The board had determined that it would not change its existing financial management to avoid 'aberrant' results appearing in IFRS-compliant financial accounting reports.

'Sector neutrality' has been criticised for its role in eroding the public sector in favour of investor-owned businesses in health[12] and for its distorting influence on international financial reporting standards.[13] Its irrelevance for co-operatives has also been noted.[14]

Distinguishing between liabilities and equity

Early on the IASB identified the need to provide guidance for distinguishing between liability instruments (i.e. obligations or debts of an organisation) and equity instruments (i.e. ownership of an organisation). The distinction between classifying shares as equity or liability is an important one not only for co-operatives, but for all organisations. In the event that an organisation runs into financial difficulty, liabilities (financing provided by lenders and creditors) generally have priority for repayment over equity (financing provided by owners). As such, the more an organisation is financed by its owners, the lower the risk of non-payment for the lender. In fact, loan agreements commonly specify a minimum level of equity that the borrowing organisation must meet.

Co-operatives were therefore very concerned about IAS 32: *Financial Instruments: Disclosure and Presentation* which for many co-operatives meant that their member shares would have to be reported as a liability rather than equity, resulting in no equity at all for some co-operatives. But does the classification of member shares as a liability reflect the true nature of member shares? Member shares are, after all, the foundation of the co-operative capital structure and identify the owners of the co-operative. The characteristics of member shares are discussed more fully later in this chapter.

The response from co-operatives to IAS 32 has resulted in attempts to address this issue. International Financial Reporting Interpretations Committee, Draft Interpretation 8 (IFRIC D8): *Members Shares in Co-operative Entities*[15] followed and also drew considerable comment from the co-operative sector. Comments from many co-operatives reflected a sense of frustration that accounting standards did not adequately recognise the differences between co-operative membership and shareholders in investor-owned businesses.

Following discussion, IFRIC D8 then led to a finalised interpretation (IFRIC 2: *Members Shares in Co-operative Entities and Similar Instruments*).[16] Though a member may have the contractual right to request the co-operative to repurchase (i.e. redeem) his or her member shares, IFRIC 2 allows the member shares to be reported as equity if the request can be refused unconditionally by the co-operative. While IFRIC 2 at least partly resolved the equity issue for some co-operatives, it is seen by the IASB as a temporary solution, subject to further discussions and proposals on defining equity and liability. It does not constitute a comprehensive solution for all co-operatives nor does it really address the underlying issue raised by some co-operatives concerning recognition of the particular and unique nature and characteristics of co-operative member ownership, risk and reward.

Since the adoption of IFRIC 2 many co-operatives have changed their governing documents to give their boards the discretionary power to refuse redemption (i.e. repurchase) of member shares. In New Zealand for example, where legislation gives exiting members the right to call on a co-operative to redeem their shares, the Foodstuffs (SI) Ltd constitution was amended to specify that redemption of the Retained Patronage Shares is 'any time at the option of the Co-operative in the Co-operative's absolute discretion'.[17]

Co-operative legislation has also been revised in a number of countries – Germany and Spain for example – in order to permit the granting of this power where it was not possible under previous legislation. Does this represent a shift in co-operative values initiated not by the co-operative movement but by the adoption of a speedy partial solution to an inappropriate application of an accounting standard designed with the external investor shareholder in mind?

IFRIC 2 has been described in terms of a successful outcome of co-operative campaigning, consultation and negotiation with the IASB.[18]

However, it is not clear to what extent IFRIC 2 can be justifiably seen as representing a co-operative consensus view on the issue. Furthermore, is it an example of the successful inclusion of a co-operative-specific approach to accounting or rather a 'fix' which rests on co-operative willingness to amend their governing documents and restrict members' rights? Such a 'fix' suggests a lack of appreciation for, if not a latent hostility to, the co-operative model.

Accounting and reporting for co-operatives

The co-operative sector is a major player in the world economy. According to the Global 300 and Developing 300 Database,[19] the top 300 co-operatives were responsible for a total of US$1.1 trillion turnover in 2008, a 14% increase in turnover from 2007. To put this in perspective, this is the size of the tenth largest economy of the world. Co-operatives are owned and controlled by 800 million people and employ 100 million people.[20]

Co-operatives are often however 'quiet achievers', not actively seeking media publicity. Few business education programmes include the co-operative business model in their curriculums. Since co-operatives do not generally seek financing from the public, that is, they are not publicly listed, they are usually invisible to the financial sector.

Business-style accounting has been promoted to governments worldwide by a number of international organizations including IFAC, the World Bank and the IMF.[21] Even though co-operatives are different from the investor-owned business model, the IASB does not appear to take these differences into full account. According to IFRS *Framework for Preparation and Presentation of Financial Statements*, 'The objective of financial statements is to provide information ... that is useful to a wide range of users in making economic decisions.'[22] While it recognises that financial statements cannot meet all of the information needs of users (identified as investors, employees, lenders, suppliers, customers, government and the public), the IASB asserts that financial statements that meet the needs of investors will also meet most of the needs of other financial statement users.[23] Thus it is clear that 'its focus is on the financial reporting practices of businesses for financial market participants'.[24]

Birchall and Ketilson[25] caution policy-makers that failing to consider how regulations and standards affect co-operatives may limit their growth and development. IAS 32 *Financial Instruments Disclosure and Presentation* is one such example of international accounting standards failing to take the unique co-operative business model into consideration.

What therefore is a co-operative and how does it differ from investor-owned businesses? According to the *Statement on the Co-operative Identity*, 'A co-operative is an autonomous association of persons united voluntarily to meet their common economic, social, and cultural needs and aspirations through a jointly-owned and democratically-controlled enterprise.'[26] Co-operatives are not investment vehicles with the purpose of maximising profits. Co-operatives are guided by seven principles: voluntary and open membership; democratic member control; member economic participation; autonomy and independence; education, training and information; co-operation among co-operatives; and concern for community.[27] According to Birchell and Ketilson[28] the first four principles are what identify co-operatives as distinct from other organisations. Member share characteristics reflect these four principles.

Member shares are purchased as evidence of membership. When members no longer use their co-operative, they will normally cease their membership by surrendering their member shares to the co-operative for redemption. This follows the principle of voluntary and open membership. Unlike investor-owned corporations, co-operatives are democratic organisations controlled by their members. Members have equal voting rights (one member, one vote). Members participate economically in their co-operative. They contribute equitably to the capital, part of which is common (i.e. indivisible) property of the co-operative. By designating a portion of the equity as indivisible, member shares do not therefore necessarily entitle members to a pro rata share of the organisation's equity. Member benefits are tied to their use of the co-operative and return on invested capital is limited. In contrast, corporate shareholder benefits are tied to the capital invested entitling them to their pro rata share of the value of the equity of the corporation. As autonomous, self-help organisations controlled by their members, co-operatives ensure they maintain their autonomy and democratic member control when raising capital from external sources. This is unlike investor-owned organisations where, for example, control may change when capital is raised or shares traded on the equity markets.

Prior to IAS 32, member shares were classified as equity. Member shares are risk capital; they have no priority over any other claims to the assets of the co-operative and they entitle members to vote, control and benefit from the use of the co-operative. However, if members have the right to surrender member shares to the co-operative for redemption, IAS 32 requires the member shares to be classified as liabilities. IFRIC D8 and IFRIC 2 that followed it provide some relief by enabling member shares to be classified as equity if the co-operative can unconditionally refuse to redeem the member shares. However, removing the right of redemption from member shares is contrary to the co-operative organisational model and, more specifically, co-operative principles. While co-operative autonomy and independence may be strengthened by the limited transferability of member shares, members must have the ability to leave the co-operative at their option as part of voluntary membership. Thus the ability of members to redeem their shares is an important part of the co-operative identity. Arguably the removal of the right to redeem member shares could also weaken member control and governance. The right of redemption can be viewed as an important check on management. The ability to attract and retain co-operative members is an indication of management performance in a co-operative. If members lose their ability to redeem their shares at will, then member retention no longer provides the same check on management.

Given the common characteristics of the co-operative organisational model, is there consensus among co-operative responses to the International Financial Reporting Committee Draft Interpretation 8 (IFRIC D8), *IAS 32: Members' Shares in Co-operative Entities*? Do co-operative comment letters on the classification of member shares as debt or equity reflect the co-operative values and principles or do they reflect an acceptance of a pragmatic solution to the classification of member shares as equity?

Methodology

We sought answers to the foregoing questions by conducting a content analysis of co-operative comment letters to the IASB during 2004 regarding IFRIC D8, *IAS 32: Members' Shares in Co-operative Entities*.[29] This particular co-operative discourse with the IASB and the subsequent issue of IFRIC 2 are significant as they represent a rare component of co-operative dialogue with standard-setters. This discourse is also unique in IASB history in that the comment letters came predominantly from co-operatives rather than investor-owned businesses.[30] We examined the comment letters to determine whether there was a consensus among co-operatives on IFRIC D8 and whether the comments from co-operatives reflect co-operative values and principles. Therefore we looked solely at comment letters sent by co-operatives and co-operative apex organisations. In particular we examined the sources of the comments submitted (i.e. country and type of co-operative organisation), looking at whether the organisation supported or disagreed with the interpretation of IFRIC D8 along with reasons, references to the unique characteristics of co-operatives, and any recommended co-operative approaches to classifying member shares as debt or equity. The responses from the IASB and any subsequent amendments were also examined to determine the effect, if any, on the development of this accounting standard.

The comment letters were classified by the following four co-operative types: co-operative apex organisations (those that represent co-operatives and their development); 'consumer' (owned by consumer-members of the co-operative); 'worker' (owned by worker-members of the co-operative); and 'business' (owned by other co-operatives and/or investor-owned businesses for the purpose of buying, processing and/or marketing their goods and services through the co-operative). Analysis by type of co-operative is useful in relation to discussing any variations in accounting outlook.

Observations, analysis and findings

Of the ninety-six comment letters responding to the IASB draft interpretation on member share classification (D8), we identified sixty-nine from co-operatives and co-operative apex organisations. The other twenty-seven comments were submitted by various organisations including a number of national accounting bodies and international public accounting firms. We have included in the co-operative apex organisations two agricultural bodies that have both co-operative and other farming organisations as members. Although these two are not exclusively co-operative bodies, they do recognise their co-operative membership as significant and are, in this case, representing co-operative views to the IASB.

Co-operative organisations from nineteen countries responded together with nine international co-operative bodies. Five of the international bodies represent European co-operatives, three are global and one represents the Asia and Pacific region. An analysis of support for or disagreement with D8 by country and type (see Table 15.1) indicates that the majority of co-operative responses (58%) were from co-operative apex organisations and while a number of consumer and business co-operatives also sent comments, only one worker co-operative commented, albeit the substantial Mondragón Co-operative Corporation.

An initial analysis of the co-operative comment letters to the IASB indicates that co-operative opinion was divided regarding the proposed interpretation, with 59.4% (41 comment letters) supporting the interpretation, and 40.6% (28 comment letters) indicating partial or total disagreement with the draft interpretation. Partial disagreement includes those respondents who accepted that the interpretation allowed some co-operatives to classify their member shares as equity but also recognised that it did not resolve the continuing problem of recognition of co-operative member equity in general. As such they saw it as one step along the way to addressing the wider accounting problem of recognition of differences in co-operative member ownership, and not the complete solution. A common objection to the interpretation D8 was its emphasis on the right to redeem member shares as the sole criterion for classifying member shares as debt or equity.

Table 15.1 Co-operative comment letters in support of or in total/partial disagreement with D8 by country and co-operative type

Country	Type of Co-operative				Support for/ disagreement with D8	
	Consumer co-op	Business co-op	Worker co-op	Apex co-op organisation	Support	Disagree (total or partial)
Australia		5		4		9
Bulgaria				1		1
Canada		1		1	2	
Denmark				1		1
Finland		1		1		2
France	5			2	7	
Germany		1		6		7
Hungary				1	1	
Italy				2	2	
Japan	1			2		3
Kenya	1				1	
New Zealand	1			1		2
Slovakia				1	1	
Spain			1	1	2	
Sweden				1		1
UK	11			1	12	
Ukraine				1		1
Uruguay				1	1	
USA		1		3	4	
International				9	8	1
Total	19	9	1	40	41	28
Total (%)	27.5	13.1	1.4	58.0	59.4	40.6

Support for or disagreement with the proposed interpretation was divided along national lines. Perhaps as a strategy to strengthen their position with the IASB,[31] some countries appear to have co-ordinated their responses. There were a lot of similarities in the content of letters from those countries that presented the largest number of replies. This was most evident in letters sent from co-operative organisations in Australia, Germany, France, Japan and the UK. Of the nineteen countries represented in the co-operative comment letters, ten countries (53%) supported the interpretation and nine countries (47%) disagreed or partially disagreed with the interpretation. This may reflect differing local legislative issues faced in adopting the IFRIC D8 approach. For example, comment letters from German, Australian, New Zealand, Bulgarian and Swedish co-operatives refer to the need to change co-operative legislation in their countries to allow co-operatives to refuse the redemption of member shares and therefore be onside with the definition of member shares as equity. Each of these countries totally or partially disagreed with the IFRIC D8 interpretation. The difference by country may also reflect co-operative organisational and ideological differences between countries in relation to the importance given to the members' right to redeem their shares. A number of respondents, for example Japan, refer to the natural right of members to redeem their shares upon leaving the co-operative, while some link this right to the co-operative values and principles. Indeed the International Co-operative Alliance *Statement on the Co-operative Identity*[32] and in particular the value of openness and the principles of voluntary and open membership and autonomy and independence appear relevant here.

Interestingly all but one of the nine international apex organisations supported the interpretation (see Table 15.2). However, comment letters sent by national co-operative apex organisations were more likely to be critical of the interpretation, with thirteen

Table 15.2 Support or disagreement with the interpretation by co-operative type

Co-operative type	Support	Disagree (partially or totally)	Total
Consumer co-op	17	2	19
Business co-op	2	7	9
Worker co-op	1	0	1
International apex org	8	1	9
National apex	13	18	31
Total	41	28	69

agreeing, and eighteen indicating partial or total disagreement with the interpretation. The variation among consumer, business and worker co-operatives is in all cases aligned with the position of their respective countries.

Since the nature of the co-operative business model is unique, we were interested in determining the extent to which co-operative comment letters drew on these unique characteristics as spelled out in the ICA statement of co-operative identity and the internationally agreed framework of cooperative values and principles to support their position. The following quote from a comment letter on IFRIC D8 to the IASB from the Australian Centre for Co-operative Research and Development (ACCORD) explains the 'co-operative difference':

> A co-operative is a democratic organisation owned and controlled by the people it serves who join together for a common benefit. Co-operatives are based on the values of self-help, self-responsibility, democracy, equality and equity. Unlike investors, co-op members join a co-operative in order to benefit from the goods and services it offers, not to make a substantial return on their initial investment.[33]

Comments from many co-operatives reflected a sense of frustration that accounting standards did not adequately recognise the differences between co-operative membership and shareholders in investor-owned companies. An excerpt from a comment letter by the Canadian co-operative 'The Co-operators', to the IASB reflects this frustration:

> Although co-operatives have been active for over 150 years and are dominant in many marketplaces, including many in the United Kingdom, they are not very well understood. More often than not standards and rules which have been developed for public stock companies are applied to co-operatives with no change to recognize the unique characteristics and purposes of co-operatives.[34]

We identified thirty-two (45%) comment letters that made reference to the unique characteristics of co-operatives, that is, the 'co-operative difference'. Eight concepts relating to this theme were identified. Member democratic control of the co-operative was mentioned in 25 of these comment letters; member benefits based on using the co-operative was mentioned in 17; ICA co-operative values and principles was mentioned in 15; the existence of co-operative goals other than maximising profit was mentioned in 12; the nature of co-operative groups controlled by members was mentioned in 6; differing member rewards was mentioned in 3; differing member risks was mentioned in 2; and the member principle of redeeming surpluses to members was mentioned in 2.

We were also interested in identifying the extent to which co-operative respondents offered alternative approaches to the classification of financial instruments. We reviewed the twenty-eight comment letters of those co-operatives and co-operative apex organisations that had expressed disagreement with the draft interpretation and identified four main themes, with seven suggested approaches within them. The most frequent suggestion, mentioned by sixteen (57%) of the twenty- eight, was to consider all of the financial instrument's characteristics when deciding whether to classify it as equity or liability, the argument being that co-operative member shares mostly exhibit equity characteristics and are therefore more fairly represented as equity. Seven (25%) respondents suggested revisions to the redemption criteria for redeemable share capital to be classified as equity, offering four approaches to the issue:

1. Broaden the criteria for allowing redeemable share capital to be classified as equity where a co-operative has control over the timing and amount redeemed to exiting members.
2. Treat redeemable share capital as equity so long as all claims by creditors can be met from the balance of remaining co-operative funds.
3. Remove the redemption characteristic from the classification decision.
4. Note that no present obligation exists to redeem currently active members. It is only at the point that the member leaves that the obligation to redeem the shares arises. Therefore treat redeemable shares as equity while the member is active.

One respondent suggested that all funds provided by members should be grouped together on the statement of financial position (balance sheet), including items classed as equity or liabilities, the reasoning being that it is important to the co-operative member and others to see the total amount of funds provided by members regardless of their classification as equity or liabilities.

Four respondents did not offer an alternative approach but rather proposed that the standard-setters undertake further research and consultation before putting forward a new proposal for the classification of co-operative financial instruments as debt or liabilities.

The above analysis indicates the extent to which co-operative organisations were willing to offer alternative suggestions; seeking to accommodate standard-setters while also asserting co-operative difference in respect of the differing characteristics of co-operative members' capital. The suggestions include thoughtful and innovative approaches to the presentation of information to members (e.g. the grouping of members' funds on the statement of financial position) as well as a confidence in asserting the need for standard-setters to recognise, understand and accept the differing characteristics of co-operative member ownership as opposed to external shareholder ownership.

A similar confidence and assertion of co-operative difference was found in many of the co-operative comment letters in support of the interpretation. These comments focused however on support for the speedy adoption of the interpretation in order to allow those co-operatives that are able to comply, to treat their member shares as equity.

We reviewed these letters to identify reasons given for supporting the interpretation. We found a range of opinions expressed but the most frequently mentioned referred to the practical consequences of having member shares classed as liabilities, in particular the potential impact on financial ratios, with a possible reduction in access to or increased cost of credit (54.9% of those comment letters that supported the D8 interpretation). Others put forward the view that standard-setters do not fully understand co-operatives (25.4%); that the classification of member shares as debt would misrepresent the financial position or reduce the understandability of the financial position (23.9%); and that member shares are equity from a legal point of view (16.9%).

Those in agreement with the interpretation frequently asserted co-operative difference but did not appear to connect this to any assertion for a broader co-operative accounting approach. They remained focused on the ability of the interpretation to provide a timely solution – encouraging an early adoption of the D8 interpretation; offering their co-operatives a way of continuing to treat member shares as equity. Arguably, they adopted a strongly pragmatic approach resulting in a speedy resolution of the immediate problem but with limited application of co-operative difference to accounting and with little consideration for the impact of the change on co-operative governance and membership.

Conclusions

It is interesting that given the common characteristics of the co-operative member-based organisational model, we found that there was a lack of consensus among co-operative responses to IFRIC D8 with a small majority of the comment letters (60%) supporting the

interpretation. Along national lines, the support or disagreement with
the IFRIC D8 interpretation was almost equally divided, with 47%
of the 19 countries supporting the interpretation. Our comment
letter analysis suggests that this was a reflection of differing national
co-operative legislation and co-operative organisational and ideological differences.

Though many of the comment letters (45%), whether they
supported or disagreed/ partially disagreed with the D8 interpretation,
made reference to the unique characteristics of the co-operative
business model and co-operative values and principles, it is perhaps
surprising that more co-operatives did not do so. More frequently
those that supported IFRIC D8 indicated that they saw it as a practical
solution to avoid reduction in access to credit while those who
disagreed with the interpretation gave a variety of reasons including, in
some cases, reasons linked to perceived co-operative difference. The
wide range of views by co-operatives on this issue is perhaps
unexpected given the often-asserted centrality of member ownership
and control to all forms of co-operative. As such, this example of
co-operative engagement with standard-setters may have resulted in a
compromise which does not have universal acceptance within the
co-operative sector and which has altered a previously accepted feature
of co-operative identity that is the right of redemption.

Given the current IASB emphasis on 'sector neutral' accounting
standards and, at least in this instance, the apparent lack of consensus
among co-operative organisations on the appropriate accounting
treatment, it is likely that the IASB will be reluctant to accept that there
are any deficiencies, and many dangers, in forcing the investor-
ownership model on co-operatives. Rather the IASB will likely attempt
to 'fit' accounting standards designed with the investor-owned
businesses in mind to the co-operative business model.

Prior to adopting IFRS, many national accounting standard-setting
bodies recognised that financial reporting standards designed with the
investor in mind do not provide the information needs of all other
users and therefore set specific standards for non-investor-owned
business such as governments and not-for-profit organisations. Some
national accounting standard-setting bodies are considering whether
the limitations of international 'sector neutral' accounting standards
need to be addressed. For example, the UK Accounting Standards
Board is considering a 'Public Benefit Entities Standard',[35] New
Zealand and Australia have sought to develop financial reporting
standards for government, not-for-profit, educational and heritage
organisations[36] and in Canada not-for-profit entities are permitted to

continue following the previous CICA standards which include special standards for not-for-profit entities, rather than the IFRS.[37]

The issuance of IAS 32 has motivated a more proactive approach toward standard-setting for the co-operative movement. In December 2004 the International Co-operative Alliance set up an ICA/IAS Working Group to liaise and correspond with the IASB and make them aware of the special nature of co-operatives.[38] In his 2007/08 Annual Report the Director-General of the ICA reported that the working group was 'beginning to show real signs of progress in terms of convincing the International Accounting Standards Board that co-operative shares must be accepted as equity'.[39] In 2010 the IASB affirmed their support for classifying member shares as equity even though they may be redeemable when the member ceases to transact with the co-operative.[40]

It would appear that another consequence of the issuing of IAS 32 was the stimulation of research into co-operatives, their performance and their differences from investor-owned firms. This may be seen for example in the publications of The Centre for European Policy Studies.[41]

Initiatives such as those by the ICA and Centre for European Policy Studies have served to educate the IASB about co-operatives and therefore could assist with identifying the co-operative 'place' in the Generally Accepted Accounting Principles landscape. As 2012 has been designated the International Year of Co-operatives it is opportune for co-operatives to stand out as being fundamentally distinct from investor-owned companies.

Notes

1   The authors gratefully acknowledge the support of the Social Sciences Humanities Research Council, Canada and the Centre of Excellence in Accounting and Reporting for Co-operatives.

2   International Accounting Standards Board (IASB), *IAS 32 Financial Instruments: Disclosure and Presentation Financial Statements* (2003). Retrieved 21 July 2006, from Lexis Nexis.

3   The International Accounting Standards Committee (IASC), formed in 1973, was restructured as the IASB in 2001. IFRS, *About the IFRS Foundation and the IASB* (2010), available at www.ifrs.org/The +organisation/IASCF+and+IASB.htm (accessed 31 December 2010).

4   Ibid.

5   IASC Foundation Annual Report 2009, p. 58.

6   A. Robb and S. Newberry, 'Globalization: Governmental Accounting and International Financial Reporting Standards', *Socio-Economic Review* 5:4 (2007), 725.

7 IFRS. *About the IFRS Foundation and the IASB.*

8 P. Sikka, 'There's No Accounting for accountants', *The Guardian (Comment is free),* 29 August 2007, available at http://commentisfree .guardian.co.uk/prem_sikka_/2007/08/no_accounting_for_accounting _s.html (accessed 10 January 2011).

9 P. Sikka, 'Held to Account', *International Accountant* January 2008, 33–35.

10 J. Hooks, S. Tooley/FRRaG, 'Exercising Professional Judgement in an Era of Sector Neutrality: A Study of Choices Made by New Zealand Reporting Entities', *Financial Reporting, Regulation & Governance* 6:1 (2007), available at www.business.curtin.edu/files/FRRaG_2007_6–1 _Refereed_Hooks_Tooley_final.pdf (accessed 4 February 2011).

11 Foodstuffs (South Island) Ltd Annual Report 2008, p. 11, available at www.foodstuffs-si.co.nz/new/annual.asp (accessed 5 December 2010).

12 S. Newberry, '"Sector neutrality" and NPM "Incentives': Their Use in Eroding the Public Sector', *Australian Accounting Review* 13:30 (2003), 28–34.

13 A.J. Robb and S. Newberry, 'Globalization: Governmental Accounting and International Financial Reporting Stands', *Socio-Economic Review* 5:4 (2007), 725–754.

14 A.J. Robb, 'Sector Neutral Stands? Phooey!', *Robb on Cooperation* (2007). Available at http://nz.coop.

15 International Accounting Standards Board (IASB), *IFRIC Draft Interpretation 8 Comment Letters* (2004), available at www.iasbfoundation .org (accessed 21 July 2006).

16 International Accounting Standards Board (IASB), *IFRIC 2 Members Shares in Co-operative Entities and Similar Instruments* (2004). Retrieved 21 July 2006, from Lexis Nexis.

17 Foodstuffs (South Island) Ltd. constitution (Clause 18.2 0).

18 International Co-operative Alliance (ICA), *First Results of the IAS 32 / D8 Consultation* (2004), available at www.coop.org/coop/ias/2004–results-ias.pdf (accessed 21 July 2006); J. Detilleux and C. Naett, 'Cooperatives and International Accounting Standards: The Case of IAS 32', *Revue Internationale de L'Economie Sociale* 295 (Paris: RECMA, 2005).

19 International Co-operative Alliance (ICA), *Global 300 and Developing 300 Database* (2005), available at www.global300.coop/ (accessed 29 July 2010).

20 International Co-operative Alliance (ICA), *Statistical Information on the C-operative Movement* (2010), availble at www.ica.coop/publications /pressreleases/2009–03–g20.pdf (accessed 29 July 2010).

21 Robb and Newberry, 'Globalization'.

22 International Accounting Standards Board (IASB), *Framework for the Preparation and Presentation of Financial Statements,* Section 12 (2001), available at http://eifrs.iasb.org/eifrs/bnstandards/en/framework.pdf (accessed 29 July 2010).

23   Canadian Institute of Chartered Accountants (CICA), *Part I International Financial Reporting Standards, 2011 edition: Framework for Preparation of Financial Statements,* paragraph 10, available at www.knotia.ca /knowledge/Home.aspx?productid=126 (accessed 31 December 2010).
24   Robb and Newberry, 'Globalization', p. 725.
25   J. Birchall and L.H. Ketilson, *Resilience of the Co-operative Business Model in Times of Crisi.* (Geneva: International Labour Organization, 2009), available at www.ilo.org/public/libdoc/ilo/2009/109B09_78 _engl.pdf (accessed 29 July 2010).
26   International Co-operative Alliance (ICA), *Statement on the Co-operative Identity* (1995), available at www.coop.org/coop/principles.html (accessed 21 July 2006).
27   Ibid.
28   Birchall and Ketilson, *Resilience of the Co-operative Business Model.*
29   IASB, *IFRIC 2 Members Shares in Co-operative Entities.*
30   L. Cadiz-Andrion, *Investigating Stakeholder Concerns in Accounting for Co-operative Equity Under International Accounting Standards* (Unpublished master's thesis, University of Canterbury: Christchurch, NZ, 2007).
31   Ibid.
32   International Co-operative Alliance (ICA), *Statement on the Co-operative Identity* (1995), available at www.coop.org/coop/principles.html (accessed 21 July 2006).
33   P. Fitzgerald (ed.), ACCORD comment letter, in International Accounting Standards Board, *D8 Comment Letter: Consultation on IFRIC Draft Interpretation D8, Members' Shares in Co-operative Entities* (2004), available at www.iasb.org/docs/ifric-d08/D8–CL95.pdf (accessed 8 September 2006).
34   K. Bardswick (ed.), The Co-operators Group Limited comment letter, ibid.
35   Accounting Standards Board, Accounting Standards Board August 2009 Consultation Paper: The Future of UK GAAP (2009), available at www.frc.org.uk/images/uploaded/documents/ASB%20seeks%20views% 20on%20proposals%20for%20the%20future%20reporting%20require ments%20for%20UK%20and%20Irish%20entities.pdf.
36   Robb and Newberry, 'Globalization'.
37   Canadian Institute of Chartered Accountants (CICA), Preface to CA Handbook – Accounting paragraph 6, available at www.knotia.ca/ Knowledge/Home.aspx?ProductID=126 (accessed 31 July 2010).
38   The ICA IAS Working Group, available at www.icba.coop/icba-for-co -operatives/the-ica-ias-working-group.html.
39   International Cooperative Alliance Annual Report 2007/08, p. 3, available at www.ica.coop/publications/ar/2007–08–annual-report.pdf (accessed 10 January 2011).
40   International Accounting Standards Board (IASB), IASB February 2010

Meeting Summary, available at www.ifrs.org/Current+Projects/IASB +Projects/Liabilities+and+Equity/Meeting+Summaries+and+Observer+N otes/IASB+February+2010.htm (accessed 3 January 2011).

41 R. Ayadi *et al.*, *Investigating Diversity in the Banking Sector in Europe – Key Developments, Performance and Role of Cooperative banks* (Centre for European Policy Studies, 2010).

16

Resting on laurels? Examining the resilience of co-operative values in times of calm and crisis

Jan Myers, John Maddocks and James Beecher

Nothing wilts faster than laurels that have been rested upon.[1]

Introduction

This chapter responds in part to the economic and financial crises, which we are currently experiencing in the UK and indeed internationally. While this chapter does not focus on the reasons leading to the crises themselves, these events have resulted in – and provide a context for examination of – renewed interest in mutual models of business and service delivery as trust in our financial institutions, public and government agencies, and politicians has been shaken. This interest has been accompanied by re-positioning around principles and values whereby 'cooperatives everywhere are rediscovering their core values as member-owned businesses, and are making these part of their business strategy'.[2]

Operating in a range of industry sectors and under different legislative and regulatory regimes, co-operatives and mutuals take a number of organisational forms, for example: consumer co-operatives, worker co-operatives, building societies, mutual insurers, credit unions and co-operative banks.[3] However, member ownership, economic participation and democratic control are fundamental principles that co-operatives and mutuals hold in common. These principles form part of a statement on international co-operative identity.[4] They are seen to 'guarantee the conditions under which members own, control and benefit from the business' and distinguish co-operatives and mutuals from investor-ownership models of enterprise.[5]

The inherent difference in structure and governance of co-operatives and mutuals in comparison to other legal and institutional forms of service providers and business is often linked to judgements about performance and longevity. Often this causal connection is seen as unproblematic and can lead to assumptions that social justice, democracy in the workplace, wider community accountability and good corporate, social and environmental responsibility are automatically (and unconsciously) embedded in the structures and processes of co-operatives and mutuals. However, in many respects co-operative and mutual values and principles can be likened to metaphorical laurel leaves. Resting on one's laurels – rather than actively developing values and principled-led practice – can lead to multiple problems and specifically the degrading of said laurels over time. Unfortunately, we can point to fractures between espoused values and principles and reported practices of co-operatives and mutuals, particularly in relation to building societies. What is needed, and what this chapter seeks to offer, is an exploration of the relevance of co-operative and mutual values and principles to understanding recent developments in the UK mutual financial sector and in creating effective, robust and socially responsible co-operative and mutual financial institutions.

Co-operative and mutual values resurgence

The resurgence of interest in co-operative and mutual values and philosophy came to the fore with the establishment of the Co-operative Commission (2000–1) advocated by leading members of the co-operative movement. Following a high-profile take-over bid of the Co-operative Wholesale Society (CWS) by Andrew Regan in 1997, two of the Commission's key objectives were to promote a renaissance of the co-operative movement and to re-think and modernise co-operative enterprise.[6] CWS and Regan hit the headlines again, in 2005, when two CWS executives were found guilty and jailed for taking bribes from Regan for preferential dealing.[7] These events provided a springboard for mergers, which created what we now know as the Co-operative Group.

In an attempt to win back consumers and to earn the loyalty of employees, the Co-operative Group undertook a re-branding and repositioning campaign emphasising the 'co-operative difference'.[8] Although the Co-operative Group had made many attempts to build its reputation and brand (see Wilson, Chapter 2, for a useful overview of this), 2008 saw the group begin 'the largest re-branding exercise in UK corporate history' aiming to create a unified identity. This followed the 2007 'revival in the fortunes of the Co-operative Group' and the re-introduction of its members' profit-sharing dividend scheme in 2006.[9]

The Co-operative Bank, for example, now reports on the impact of its ethical lending policy, quantifying value both in terms of the cost in lost business as well as an assessment of business gained as a result of their ethical banking approach. As such, the bank emphasises not only its ethics, but also its 'financial soundness ... principles and profit'.[10] Therefore, the Co-operative Bank has been seen to demonstrate its 'prudent business model and behaviour' and successfully use the co-operative advantage by both identifying itself with the wider co-operative movement while at the same time positioning itself as a smaller but effective member of the banking industry. In 2010, the bank declared a 17.7% increase on its operating result for 2009, even taking into account the bank's commitment to strategic change and reflecting the bank's merger with the Britannia; and pre-tax profits were up by 2.9%.[11]

Re-positioning around principles and values has been given further prominence through the timely and significant development of the Association of Financial Mutuals (AFM) in 2010. AFM aims to provide guidance to help financial mutuals 'identify with, remain committed to and contribute significantly to mutuality' underpinned by organisational values including fairness and democratic gover-nance.[12] This places renewed emphasis on the capacity of co-operatives and mutuals to be 'responsive to the needs of ... customers and employees' rather than submit to the 'demands of investors to take even greater risks in order to extract profits from the business'.[13] Moreover, AFM along with other co-operative/mutual apex and member organisations, has sponsored the first Mutual Manifesto that both outlines the contribution of mutuals and provides practical proposals to government to promote and support the sector.[14]

The capacity to do things differently has been linked to the strength and resilience of mutual models and promotion of the benefits of mutuality.[15] Evidence from Europe[16] outlines a number of key contri-butions of co-operative financial institutions linked to values and practice, including:

- Efficiency – through ownership structures; closeness to customers to achieve superior risk assessment and credit allocation.
- Accessible, high quality services – adaptation of products and services to achieve customer satisfaction; providing access to 'customers in regions which would typically not be served by other players of the credit sector due to decisions based on profitability criteria alone'.[17]
- Local and community-based.

- Strong capitalisation, moderate risk and stable profit levels – including being a buffer against crises in the banking system.

If we look at the building society sector we see similar emphases on conveying the benefits of mutuality to members, vividly demonstrated by the Nationwide building society's 'No but, yeah but, no shareholders' 2010 media campaign and in arguments for and against demutualisation.[18]

The 1986 Building Societies Act paved the way for demutualisation starting with the Abbey National in 1989.[19] This legislation allowed building societies owned by their membership to propose and vote on conversion to a public limited company. If flotation was agreed, members received a cash windfall on conversion. There was a wave of flotations after The Cheltenham and Gloucester became part of Lloyds Bank (now Lloyds TSB) in 1995. The windfalls were quick wins for speculators and this led to many people becoming society members in order to try to vote through demutualisation (known as 'carpetbagging').

The push to demutualise showcased the benefits of becoming a bank: diversification of goods and services; possibilities of earning extra income by entering new markets; and 'greater access to wholesale borrowing, to new investors and to unrestricted use of financial instruments'.[20] In examining the demise of Northern Rock and Bradford and Bingley, Klimecki and Wilmott state that the societies' behaviour could be seen as demonstrating unsustainable lending practices contrary to previous building society ways of working. Such lending practices, collectively identified in the context of credit crunch debates as 'toxic loans', included self-certification or no-proof-of-income mortgages, and the bundling together and sale of high-risk subprime loans and mortgages (loans offered to individuals whose credit rating would mean they would not usually qualify for a loan or mortgage and where there is a high risk of defaulting on debt repayment).

There are several reasons for moving away from traditional building society practice, including changes in legislation and relaxation of regulations. According to Llewellyn and Holmes, where building societies lack 'a substantial efficiency advantage' compared to public limited companies (PLCs) then 'competitive pressures force a convergence of behaviour and remove the major behavioural distinctions between mutuality and PLCs'.[21] Others point to the lure of greater remuneration and bonus packages as well as increased visibility for executives moving from relatively low status building societies to a perceived higher status with conversion to a PLC bank.[22] However, there are more fundamental consequences linked to demutualisation that undermine the foundations of building societies. Before the 1986 Act, 'corporate governance of mutuals had relied on an "identity of interest" between lenders and borrowers. The prospect of demutualization permitted, indeed encouraged, this connection to be severed.'[23]

The push towards demutualisation seems hard to resist. It is a process that only appears to be held in check where member engagement and participation is a robust feature of the organisation and where there is strong board and top management commitment to mutual/co-operative status.[24] For example, in 1999, Leek United survived a hostile conversion bid and Skipton, Portman and Chelsea societies successfully resisted attempts to force votes on conversion.[25] This followed closely on the heels of a narrowly defeated move to demutualise the Nationwide Building Society, which remains the largest society in the sector. Moreover, there is evidence of only one building society voting to demutualise against managerial advice: the Bradford and Bingley building society, which had earlier survived one demutualisation effort only to succumb in 1999.[26]

By 2001, the tide of conversions from mutual to publicly traded organisations started to ebb. Indeed, from the mid-1990s to date, merger rather than demutualisation played the major role in reducing the number of building societies. For those remaining, the notion of mutuality is seen as a key differentiator. Chief executive officers from two building societies were asked to reflect on this experience, stating that:

> What Nationwide worked out ... was [that] there was a nice little niche ... [to] being a building society. This in turn helped to support smaller societies' decisions to remain mutual at this time.

> The whole corporate plan, [the] ethos ... was 'We are a mutual, we are different', very much so – and all the corporate planning was around realising value for members.[27]

However, proposals for a 'new bank' – OneSavings – 'combining' Kent Reliance Building Society with US private equity group JC Flowers, were put forward in 2010. The deal was finalised in February 2011 and saw the transfer of the business of Kent Reliance to the new bank and the set up of a new industrial and provident society – Kent Reliance Provident Society. 76% of savers and 81% of borrowing members voted for the proposal, which has been seen as an opportunity to retain mutuality while providing the opportunity to raise extra, external capital.[28] JC Flowers reportedly invested £50 million and obtains 40.1% of ordinary shares of the new bank into which members' savings, mortgages and investment accounts have been transferred. Existing members will join the new provident society, which maintains a majority ownership of 59.9%. Seen as an innovative player in the building society field (an example given is the outsourcing of back office functions to India), the chief executive officer (CEO) of the former Kent Reliance building society, Mike Lazenby, championed the move stating that, 'members aren't losing their membership; they will own 60 per cent of something bigger, stronger and with better capital'.[29] Since the transfer, Lazenby has stepped down as CEO of the new bank and the interim CEO and chief financial officer is due to depart in June 2011 (at the time of writing, no permanent successors have been announced). While it is considered sensible for a successor to have a building society industry background, there is some concern that this development is potentially a step towards full demutualisation, resulting in part in an undervaluing of mutual principles.[30]

Trust and confidence

Trust and confidence are 'necessarily central to retail financial services'.[31] Yet if we look towards the wider research and academic literature there is lack of consensus on the meaning of trust and the interchangeable concepts of 'trust' and 'confidence' is problematic.[32] If we see these concepts as important to the strength of financial and social (community) relationships, then we need to differentiate between the two.[33]

So, while the general public appears to have lost 'trust' in banks, there has been some evidence of 'confidence' in building societies to be able to take care of individuals' savings. This is evidenced by reported record levels of savings flowing into building societies.[34] However, if we see confidence as instrumental and calculative, as Earle describes, then this has implications for maintaining switches in allegiance and deposits to building societies and co-operative financial institutions.[35] Furthermore, we can see from Llewellyn's analysis, that trust as a relational concept means that customer/members expect 'good behaviour … over and above what is required by law and/or regulation' to work in the interests of customer/members. This implies 'keeping promises, predictable behaviour and not adopting opportunistic behaviour'.[36] This also links with research from the Nottingham University's Financial Services Research Forum that showed that where people do not necessarily feel that institutions actually have their best interests at heart there are reduced levels of affective trust (trust based on relationships, feelings and emotion).[37] This then provides impetus for reduced loyalty to a financial institution over time and the shift to find another that better fits with perceptions of what a 'good' bank or building society should be.

Confidence, for Llewellyn, consists of organisational solvency, integrity and competency. For the consumer, financial transactions in terms of the products and services they access are often of high value and low frequency (such as mortgages and/or long-term savings plans). The relative complexity of the product and, in many cases, the limited experience of the consumer means both trust and confidence in the integrity and the competence of the institution is paramount. This level of cognitive trust is reflected in the degree to which we believe in the reliability and dependability of financial services institutions and may account for some of the reasons why customers prefer to find an organisation they deem satisfactory and stick with it. This is echoed by the comments of a chairperson of a UK building society who explained to one of the authors that:

> [A] relationship with a bank has got many facets. Unlike a normal retail relationship where if you want to go and get a shirt or a suit or a pair of shoes, you'll go into one shop and you'll buy one. If you don't like it well – hey – so what? I'll go somewhere else next time, and it's easy to distinguish between quality and price and environment ... whereas with banking – it's this kind of amorphous mass of institutions all – on the face of it, offering exactly the same type of thing, to exactly the same group of people, and it's very difficult to differentiate ... [But] providing you know the bank provides online service and you can go into a branch and it's regularly well administered then I think for the majority of people ... the relationship is probably there for the rest of their life, providing the bank is sensible about managing that relationship.

Furthermore, while we would expect increased regulation and government intervention in the banking sector to increase trust and confidence by introducing safety checks and increased oversight, this can also work to the detriment of the institution. In this instance, increased regulation leads to reduced levels of trust by the implication that it is necessary to constrain behaviour.[38] In addition, trust and confidence are undermined by evidence of evasiveness and opaqueness regarding information; by the impression of incompetence; and by discovery of problematic incentive structures. The recent focus on declining levels of consumer trust may have been aimed at 'big name' banks, but more generally there are often few distinctions made between banks and mutual financial institutions: building societies and co-operatives risk being tarred with the same brush as banks and investor-owned companies unless they can display differing and better credentials.

It seems there is little room for complacency even though the benefits of 'co-operative difference' and the associated 'co-operative advantage' have been related to the tenacity of the co-operative model in time of economic turmoil.[39] Looking at issues of trust and confidence raises significant questions: does an increasing polemic on 'common good' mark a critical turn away from market to mutualisation? Or are ethics, mutual principles and values seen as resources to be deployed when market mechanisms fail, only to be put away again once the green shoots of recovery are seen and a business-as-usual attitude returns to centre stage? Put another way, is reaffirmation of trust in mutuals merely a reaction to market failure or is it a not-to-be-missed opportunity to reassert co-operative values, ethical conduct and strong participatory governance in these (and other) organisations?

Some societies have undeniably done well, and have placed their business model at the heart of explanations of their performance. However, we need to explore to what extent building societies and mutuals are really doing as well as we think.

Resilience in the co-operative business model

A 2009 report for the International Labour Organization (ILO) looks at the resilience of the co-operative model in times of crisis and suggests that the link between savings and loans acts as a moral barometer.[40] This resonates with the view from the Building Societies' Association (BSA):

> We [building societies] are doing well because unlike our [banking] competitors, we are far less dependent on raising debt on the money markets. If anything, the credit squeeze has reinforced societies' basic model of taking money from savers and lending it to mortgage borrowers.[41]

Yet, through demutualisation and a process of hybridisation,[42] co-operatives and mutuals have sought external (risk-associated) capital and ways around restrictions placed on their conduct and manner of operations. Therefore, we have to question whether it is values or legislative frameworks that provide boundaries around ethical behaviour for mutuals. This concern is echoed in the words of the chief executive of Home Funding who states that while societies are prevented by law from borrowing or securitising more than 50% of the value of their loan books, 'some were exposed by between 20 per cent and 30 per cent' and increasingly, the societies were using the wholesale money markets to fund expansion. The Home Funding CEO further describes some building societies as being 'no different to the banks in terms of their enthusiasm and excitement'.[43]

While this suggests that the moral barometer is not working consistently within and across all building societies all of the time, we need to consider continued and changing responses to the financial crisis. As mentioned earlier, an interesting effect of the recession is the rediscovery of mutual values to differentiate member-owned businesses and one of the ways buildings societies have tried to market their difference is through commitment to the communities in which they work. There have been a number of branch closures through mergers, acquisitions and demutualisation, but in interviews with building society directors carried out by one of the authors, commitment to branch networks and investments in local communities was confirmed as beneficial to perceptions of trust and co-operative difference; as one CEO explains:

> Our commitment to community … doesn't cost us much, [but] we get a lot of coverage … That builds trust. We've maintained and enhanced and increased our branch network since I've been here. That again, I think, gives people a feeling of stability – that we're here for them and we're prepared to invest in being there for them.

In this way, building societies benefit from a 'mutual advantage' – they are potentially more likely to be trusted, and thus more likely to be capable of attracting custom, because of their attachment to membership principles. This attention to locality, place and relationships contributes to the resilience of the business model when times get hard. Yet we need to consider why some institutions have failed, or undergone major change, when the mutual model has been shown to be resilient. Clearly, each institution is different and will vary in its response to a changing economic environment; however there has been one major difference if we compare the mutual model with UK PLC banks.

The preference for mergers over failures within the mutual sector derives from mutual self-interest and the desire to preserve the image of building societies and the stability of the sector. Nonetheless, we can see this as evidence of the continuing benefits of a co-operative principle; that of co-operation among co-operatives, which in turn has wider benefits, as explained to one of the authors by a society CEO:

> '[Building societies have] weathered the storm better in the sense that because they see themselves as a sector, they've looked after their own. And it is absolutely right to say that the only taxpayer losses have been

the Dunfermline. Everything else, Scarborough, Barnsley, Chelsea, Stroud & Swindon ... Derbyshire, Cheshire ... the sector's looked after its own.

However, in other respects, it appears that as building societies and co-operative financial institutions strive to compete in the market, they find themselves adopting similar business practices to those of the PLC banking sector. One reason given has been the necessary adoption of the 'corporate model dictated by the neo-liberal ideology of the time'.[44] This is echoed in the reasoning offered by building society executives, as one of the CEOs interviewed describes:

> [There was] generally a shock wave around building societies getting into trouble, because people just didn't believe that's what building societies should have been doing – but the reality was they were being forced into it, because of competition, driving down prices ... not true for the very small ones ... very simple models, but anybody who was a reasonable size ... they were staring down the barrel of a gun ... saying 'Well, I've no future unless I attract income from elsewhere'. But I just don't think that members, even the [Financial Services Authority], really understood what building societies were getting into, and that's where the shock came from.

The argument that external pressure on larger societies forces a convergence of behaviour is persuasive. However, it is useful to review some of the behaviour and internal decision-making that led up to the need for support from larger societies or organisations external to the sector. For example:

- The Barnsley building society lost £10 million in the collapsed Icelandic banks; merged with the Yorkshire building society.[45]
- The Derbyshire made a loss of £17 million; merged with the Nationwide.[46]
- The Newcastle – £43 million exposure to Icelandic banks and pre-tax loss of £35.7 million for 2008.[47]
- West Bromwich – converted subordinated debt to Profit Participating Deferred Shares (PPDS) in 2009. PPDS are 'perpetual instruments on which the issuer can pay the investors up to a specified percentage of profits in years in which the society is profitable'. The payment amount is at the discretion of the issuer so there is no fixed payment. PPDS also feature a mechanism to enable the write down of the principal amount if the firm suffers losses, enhancing its loss absorbency.[48]

Worthy of attention is the demise of the Dunfermline, which suffered the ignominy of being the first institution to be placed in the Bank of

England's new Special Resolution Regime. Attempts to agree a merger failed due to the size of the capital 'black hole' (estimates vary from £60million to over £100million) after losses in commercial property, and a £9.5 million loss on an IT project. The society also held buy-to-let and self-certified mortgage portfolios purchased from Lehman Brothers and the UK subsidiaries of GMAC (the former finance arm, of General Motors), and had continued offering mortgages in excess of 100% loan-to-value as late as February 2008. Eventually, the society's branches, their good loans and deposits were acquired by Nationwide, who refused to take on the commercial and acquired lending with the result that parts of the Dunfermline's losses are covered by the UK taxpayer.[49]

One might think that the downfall of an institution that many regard as protected from subprime lending and supposedly led by mutual principles would cause more of an outcry than one whose job it is to exploit risk for the benefit of the shareholder purse. However, what we have seen is that popular opinion (and that of some financial commentators) demonstrates support for the UK government bail-out of Dunfermline and the takeover by Nationwide. This is because despite being the 'author of its own mistakes',[50] 'good' mortgages were transferred to the Nationwide and savers protected while providing value for money for taxpayers.[51] Greater concern, however, has been expressed over the rescue by Nationwide of the Derbyshire and Cheshire building societies in 2008 because it left many with reduced protection of their savings under the Financial Services Protection Scheme.[52] The Derbyshire was reported to have bought in poor-quality loans, while the Cheshire reportedly made a substantial £10 million loan to a single property developer, which was unlikely to be repaid in full.[53] The takeover was dubbed by one commentator as one that 'failed mutuals' members' when 'for the sake of expediency [members'] views, interests and rights have been ignored'.[54] Yet despite criticism from members and some sections of the press, the incoming chair of the BSA reiterated the Treasury Select Committee's opinion that building societies are the 'unsung heroes' of the credit crisis. In his inaugural speech to the BSA annual conference, Graham Beale, chair, told members that 'no investor … has lost any of their investment since 1945' and stated his belief that 'building societies offer a real and attractive alternative to banks … offering long term good value, offering great service, treating customers fairly and providing security'.[55]

It would seem that building societies have remained relatively untarnished in recent events. This can be attributed, in part, to the reservoir of trust built up, over time, in relations with customer/members and which remains in place or is more resistant to depletion in times of stress:

> When trust is strong, potentially damaging information can be construed in benign or even positive ways. It takes information with strong moral implications to undermine that trust. The positive emotions associated with the shared-values basis of trust are the main source of its resistance to change.[56]

In contrast, confidence is built on more specific experiences and is deemed more reason-and-performance-based which supports the need for appropriate (government or other) intervention as we saw with the UK government bail-out of banks and the rallying of larger building societies to support smaller ones.[57] We need also to consider, in the case of building societies, that intervention and re-examination of values, has been prompted not because the mutual model is broken, but more by the observation that those organisations that have moved away from a model with no shareholders and no externalised (non-member) interests have suffered in this financial crisis. But is the push towards abandoning mutual principles, as seen in some of the examples above, fully attributable to market pressures and changes in regulatory frameworks?

Historically most financial mutuals formed as a response to market and state failures and locally identified needs.[58] The push for demutualisation in the 1980s and 1990s was fuelled by arguments to adopt efficient business practices through the attraction and retention of the best financial managers and to stretch regulatory boundaries to find ways to access external capital and fund growth.[59] The wave of conversions is supported to a certain extent by studies highlighting improved capital positions of demutualised societies and pointing to improvements in 'organisational efficiency due to the injection of new equity capital, distribution of managerial stock options and decreased risk of insolvency'.[60] However, a more recent UK review suggests that 'a number of societies that have continued to concentrate on a traditional business model focusing on prime residential mortgage lending funded by retail deposits' have remained profitable even into the credit crisis.[61] For example, the Ecology Building Society – established in 1981 – offers mortgage lending and a range of ethical savings opportunities. The ethical and environmental focus of the society's lending practices has contributed to its image as a specialist, small-scale niche provider, which in turn is seen as contributing to the success and longevity of the organisation. Uniting with like-minded European financial institutions through the International Association of Investors in the Social Economy (INAISE), the Society is creating a manifesto for sustainable banking working on the logic that 'much activity of mainstream banking has been socially useless'.[62] Gijselnckx and Develtere also conclude from their case studies that principles and values do not of necessity disintegrate under market pressures. They cite the strength of membership and co-operative and mutual leadership as 'internal mechanisms' that maintain and regenerate goals and identity. They also identify a number of external mechanisms including expectations on the business by members and the public to uphold and publicly demonstrate corporate, social and environmental responsibility and accountability.[63] We can, then, take comfort that isomorphism and demutualisation are not necessary parts of organisational development and economic viability.

Moreover, legislative and regulatory frameworks should and can take account of characteristics that distinguish mutual and co-operative finance models from PLCs, particularly with regard to ownership structures, member participation and control. Ownership and control are key characteristics that distinguish mutuals from banks. Building societies have members, not shareholders. Voting entitlements are limited to one member, one vote rather than based on the size of an individual's or group's investment and there is no automatic right to a share in the profits. Mutuals are therefore not driven to deliver growth in shareholder value and many shareholders will not be customers. As mentioned earlier, the amount of money raised through wholesale money markets – that is sources external to the funds held by the society is, unlike banks, restricted by legislation. Many societies fund the majority if not the whole of their lending through retail deposits. Rather than diminishing the role and status of mutuals, appropriate legislation can support co-operative and mutual difference and, importantly, this has been recognised in calling for building societies to be treated with 'parity of esteem' to banks.[64]

Rather than the business model being flawed, it does seem that mutual financial institutions falter when there is a deliberate move away from their original form and functions. Where advantage is taken in being identified with a broader social movement and with values-led enterprise, there is a sense of identity that helps to differentiate co-operatives and mutuals from investor-owned businesses. Furthermore, we can identify a number of good practice dimensions linked to member loyalty and perceptions of trust: principled business goals and values expressed; espoused member focus and engagement; and connections with communities.

Looking forward: consolidation, super-mutuals and values

The public face of mutualism is changing after the announcement of the 'Butterfill Act': Implementation of the Building Societies (Funding) and Mutual Societies (Transfers) Act 2007 (see BSA's response to government consultation for more details).[65] The Act allows new models of mutuals to emerge without the need to demutualise. In particular this allows the development of the 'super-mutual', the first of which has been the merger between Co-operative Financial Services and Britannia Building Society. This latest mutual development and collaboration is part of what some see as an inevitable and 'sweeping consolidation of Britain's 55 building societies, 33 mutual insurers and 70 friendly societies'.[66] Indeed, as mentioned earlier, the appearance of private equity firm JC Flowers on the mutual landscape could also speed up the pace of consolidation, with the Kent Reliant merger seen as a springboard for targeting other regional building societies in the development of a (rival) super-mutual.[67] Furthermore, the appointment of the ex-CEO of Skipton Building Society as adviser to the private equity firm has signalled further moves in this direction.[68] However, reported targeting of the Principality Building Society – Wales's largest society – by JC Flowers to develop a super-mutual, has raised some alarm at the perceived erosion of the 'culture of mutuality'.[69]

This latest mutation of co-operative financial services could give rise to new forms of organisation with weakened links to the associative, member-oriented mutual model. It is too early to assess these changes. We shall have to await the longer-term embedding and strategic and operational repercussions of such changes in the mutual financial sector in the UK. Even so, we need to ascertain whether the continuing relevance of co-operative and mutual values and principles in creating effective and responsive organisations anchored in local communities can sustain the morphing to super-mutuals and the implications, if any, for other co-operative and mutual organisations nationally and internationally. We can echo the comments of the All-Party Parliamentary Group inquiry into building societies and financial mutuals that while

> The mutual model does appear to be under considerable pressure ... consumers would undoubtedly suffer if the remaining larger building societies gave up the battle as there is considerable evidence to show that mutuals have a positive effect on the overall market.[70]

Banking on mutuals to deliver sustainable financial business models

Many co-operatives have arisen out of individual and collective experiences of austerity and exclusion and we need to build on this history to consider values and principles for the future. As we face increased and multiple crises – climate, energy, water, population – we need to account for the resilience of co-operative and mutual models beyond economic inputs and outputs. As the existing economic model comes under greater scrutiny, we may have to consider what a co-operative and mutual model looks like in a zero growth or steady state economy. This means finding pathways to mutual prosperity outside of the simple economic growth model.

While various reports provide excellent examples of co-operatives and mutuals responding to economic hardship and financial and political crises in different parts of the world, we need to think beyond the 'business as usual' frame that is sometimes offered.[71] This type of argument tends to position co-operative enterprise both as a stop-gap on the one hand and innovative community-led initiatives on the other.

Co-operatives and mutuals provide a historical link to enduring forms of collective enterprise and a platform for development of new institutions. They continually remind us that there are alternatives to the still-dominant investor owned-business model. Many people find these alternatives attractive because of the practical expression of values through co-operative and mutual ways of working which produce benefits aimed primarily at the owner-member rather than the investor-owner. The laurels – trust, transparency and commitment to values-led business – operationalised through organisations owned by, and working for, the benefit of their members, need to be continually reviewed and put to work rather than rested upon. We acknowledge that there is an inherent tension built into co-operatives and mutuals in terms of balancing collective values with business practice. Rather than trying to remove this tension (i.e. to demutualise or become public or privately owned institutions) the task is to both understand its value and manage it creatively in developing sustainable financial and economic co-operative and mutual enterprises.

Note

1   P.B. Shelley, quote taken from Great-Quotes.com, available at www.great-quotes.com/quote/828347.
2   J. Birchall and L.H. Ketilson, *Resilience of the Co-operative Business*

Model in Times of Crisis (International Labour Organization, Sustainable Enterprise Programme, 2009), p. 26.

3. Mutuo, 'Facts about Mutuals' (2008), available at www.mutuo .co.uk/facts-about-mutuals/facts-about-mutuals. Mutuo, a think-tank for 'different wings of the mutual sector,' uses 'mutuals' as an overarching term for traditionally recognised organisations such as building societies, co-operatives and friendly societies as well as housing associations, employee-owned businesses, football supporter trusts and community mutuals.

4 International Co-operative Alliance, 'Statement on the Co-operative Identity' (2007), available at www.ica.coop/coop/principles.html.

5 Birchall and Ketilson, *Resilience of the Co-operative Business;* C. Mills, *Funding the Future: An Alternative to Capitalism* (Elstree, Herts: Mutuo, 2009). Mills provides a useful discussion on differences between investor- and member-owned businesses.

6 J. Monks, *The Co-operative Advantage: Creating a Successful Family of Co-operative Business* (London: The Co-operative Commission, 2001), available at www.uk.coop/sites/default/files/COOP.pdf; J. Birchall, *The Future of Co-operative and Mutual Business* (New Zealand: New Zealand Cooperatives Association, 1998), available at http://nz.coop/docs /johnston.php.

7 Serious Fraud Office, *Historic Cases: The Co-operative Wholesale Society* (2010), available at www.sfo.gov.uk/our-work/our-cases/historic-cases /the-cooperative-wholesale-society.aspx; N. Cope, 'Co-operative Chairman to Step Down', *Independent* (May 2002), available at www.independent.co.uk/news/business/news/cooperative-chairman-to-step-down-653081.html.

8 J. Birchall, *Rediscovering the Cooperative Advantage: Poverty Reduction Through Self-help* (Geneva: International Labour Office, Cooperative Branch, 2003).

9 D. Smith, 'The Co-operative Reaches Re-brand Milestone' (2008), available at www.co-operative.coop/corporate/Press/news/The-Co-operative-reaches-re-brand-milestone.

10 B. Harvey, 'Ethical Banking: The Case of the Co-operative Bank', *Journal of Business Ethics* 14 (1995), 1005–1013.

11 Which, 'Winners 2009', available at www.which.co.uk/about-which/what-we-offer/which-awards/winners-2009; A. Wilkinson and J.M.T. Blamer, 'Corporate and Generic Identities: Lessons from the Co-operative Bank', *International Journal of Bank Marketing* 14:4 (1996), 22–35. Co-operative Financial Services (2010), Financial Statements, available at www.co-operativebank.co.uk/corp/pdf/CFS_Final2010.pdf.

12 Association of Financial Mutuals, 'Constitution' (2010), available at www.financialmutuals.org/index.php?option=com_content&view=article &id=27&Itemid=13.

13 Mutuo, 'Mutuals Manifesto' (2010), p. 3, available at www .financialmutuals.org/images/stories/Mutuals_Manifesto.pdf.

14 Mutuo, 'Mutuals Manifesto', p. 4. Other sponsors include Co-operatives^UK, Building Societies Association and Employee Ownership Association.

15 R. Speer, 'The Co-operative Advantage', *Annals of Public and Co-operative Economics*, 71:4 (2002), 507–23; Birchall, *Rediscovering the Cooperative Advantage*; R. Postlethwaite, J. Michie, P. Burns and G. Nuttall, *Shared Company: How Employee Ownership Works* (London: Employee Ownership Association, 2005), available at www.employee-ownership.co.uk/publications.asp.

16 European Association of Co-operative Banks, *Co-operative Banks: Catalysts for Economic and Social Cohesion in Europe* (Utrecht: EACB, 2004).

17 European Association of Co-operative Banks, *Co-operative Banks in Europe: Values and Practices to Promote Development* (Utrecht: EACB, 2007), p. 5.

18. Nationwide, 'No But, Yeah But, No Shareholders?', Nationwide Building Society Members' *Zone News* (2010), available at www.nationwide-members.co.uk/news/2010/6/23/no-but,-yeah-but,-no-shareholders.

19 Building Societies Association, *Building Societies Act 1986 – a BSA Summary Fifth Edition* (2009), available at www.bsa.org.uk /consumer/factsheets/100003.htm.

20 R. Klimecki and H. Wilmott, 'From Demutualisation to Meltdown: A Tale of Two Wannabe Banks', *Critical Perspectives on International Business* 5:1/2 (2009), 120.

21 D. Llewellyn and M. Holmes, 'In Defence of Mutuality: A Redress to an Emerging Conventional Wisdom', *Annals of Public and Co-operative Economics* 62:3 (1991), 327.

22 Klimecki and Wilmott, 'From Demutualisation to Meltdown.'

23 Ibid., 123.

24 F.R. Chaddad, 'Waves of Demutualisation: An Analysis of the Economic Literature', *Mapping Cooperative Studies in the New Millennium Conference*, University of Victoria, British Columbia, Canada, 28–31 May 2003, 1–32, available at http://web.uvic.ca/bcics/pdf/mapconf /Chaddad.pdf. D. Côté, 'Loyalty and Co-operative Identity – Introducing a New Co-operative Paradigm,' *Revue Internationale de l'Économie Sociale* (RECMA) 295 (2005), 50–69; J. Birchall and Simmons, 'The Involvement of Members in the Governance of Large-scale Co-operative and Mutual Businesses: A Formative Evaluation of the Co-operative Group', *Review of Social Economy* LXII:4 (2004), 487–515.

25 J.N. Marshall, R. Willis and R. Richardson, 'Demutualisation, Strategic Choice, and Social Responsibility', *Environment and Planning C: Government and Policy* 21:5 (2003), 735–760.

26 Klimecki and Wilmott, 'From Demutualisation to Meltdown', 120–140.

27 These quotes are taken from preliminary interviews undertaken with building society staff by one of the authors, James Beecher, as part of his PhD studies into risk and resilience of building societies.

28 S. Morris, 'New Bank for Kent Reliance Savers', *Associated Newspapers Limited* (26 January 2011), available at www.thisismoney.co.uk/savings-and-banking/article.html?in_article_id=5218164in_page_id=7; L. Armitstead, 'JC Flowers and Kent Reliance Promise Customers it Will be a Happy Marriage', *Daily Telegraph* (August 2010), available at www.telegraph.co.uk/finance/personalfinance/building-societies/7925177/JC-Flowers-and-Kent-Reliance-promise-customers-it-will-be-a-happy-marriage.html; A. Steed, 'Firing Line: Mike Lazenby', *Financial Times/FT Adviser* (19 August 2010), available at www.ftadviser.com/FinancialAdviser/Mortgages/Lenders/Features/article/20100819/21abbbee-a54d-11df-a4a8–00144f2af8e8/Firing-Line-Mike-Lazenby.jsp.

29 Armitstead, 'JC Flowers and Kent Reliance.'

30 M. Shoffman, 'OneSavings CEO Agrees to Stand Down', *FT Adviser* (3 March 2011), available at www.ftadviser.com/FinancialAdviser/Mortgages/Lenders/News/article/20110303/2641881e-4020-11e0-9e0b-00144f2af8e8/OneSavings-CEO-agrees-to-stand-down.jsp; CFO World, 'OneSavings Bank CFO Steps Down' (17 June 2011), available at www.cfoworld.co.uk/news/the-cfo-career/3286775/onesavings-bank-cfo-steps-down; P. Gosling, 'Surprise Twist in Butterfill Act Allows Part De-mutualisation', *Co-operative News,* August (2010), available at www.thenews.coop/news/Wider%20Co-op%20Movement/1875.

31 D.T. Llewellyn, 'Trust and Confidence in Financial Services: A Srategic Challenge', *Journal of Financial Regulation and Compliance* 13:4 (2005), 333–346.

32 Speer, 'The Co-operative Advantage'; Birchall and Simmons, 'The Involvement of Members'; T.C. Earle, 'Trust, Confidence, and the 2008 Global Financial Crisis', *Risk Analysis* 29:6 (2009), 785–792, available at www3.interscience.wiley.com/cgi-bin/fulltext/122309286/PDFSTART.

33. M. Siegrist, T.C. Earle and H. Gutscher (eds), *Trust in Cooperative Risk Management: Uncertainty and Scepticism in the Public Mind* (London: Earthscan, 2007).

34 See www.bsa.org.uk.

35 Earle, 'Trust, Confidence'.

36 Llewellyn, 'Trust and Confidence', 336.

37 P. Ennew, *The Financial Services Trust Index 2009* (Nottingham: Financial Services Research Forum, University of Nottingham, 2009), available at www.thefsforum.co.uk/Documents/WhitePapersReports/Public/TrustIndex.pdf.

38 Llewellyn, 'Trust and Confidence', 337.

39 P. Gosling, 'Building Societies are Ready to Ride Credit Crunch', *Co-operative News* (June 2008), available at http://home.coop/news/Wider%20Co-op%20Movement/1344; J. Porritt, 'The Resilience of the Co-op' (2008), available at www.forumforthefuture.org/blog/resilience-of-the-co-op; C. Seib, 'Stable Image Pays Dividends for Co-op in Credit Crunch', *The Times* (September 2008), available at http://business

.timesonline.co.uk/tol/business/industry_sectors/banking_and_finance/art
icle4735669.ece.

40 Birchall and Ketilson, *Resilience of the Co-operative Business Model.*

41 R. Wachman, 'Crunch Forces Societies Together for Mutual Benefit',
Observer (August, 2008), available at www.guardian.co.uk/business
/2008/aug/24/buildingsocieties.

42 W.J J. Van Diependbeek, *Cooperatives as a Business Organisation:
Lessons From Cooperative Organisation History* (Maastricht: Faculty of
Economics and Business Administration, Maastricht University, 2007).

43 Wachman, 'Crunch Forces Societies Together'.

44 L.Talbot, 'Keeping Bad Company: Building Societies, A Case Study',
Northern Ireland Legal Quarterly 66:4 (2009), 443.

45 N. Burridge, 'Building Society Members Could Receive Iceland Windfall',
Independent (February 2010), available at www.independent.co.uk/news
/business/news/building-society-members-could-receive-iceland-windfall-
1885787.html.

46 Derbyshire Building Society, 'Mergers of Nationwide with the Derbyshire
and the Cheshire Building Societies' (2008), available at www
.thederbyshire.co.uk/About_Us.aspx?id=1645.

47 BBC, 'Building Society Makes a Steep Loss' (2009), available at
http://news.bbc.co.uk/1/hi/business/7927798.stm.

48 HM Treasury, 'Building Society Capital and Related Issues' (2010), p. 21,
available at www.hm-treasury.gov.uk/d/consult_buildingsoc_capital.pdf.

49 House of Commons Scottish Affairs Committee, *Dunfermline Building
Society: Fifth Report of Session 2008–9*, HC548 (London: The Stationery
Office Limited, 2009).

50 Gordon Brown, PM in H. Williams, '£1.6bn Dunfermline Sale was "The
Only Option"', *Independent* (March 2009), available at www
.independent.co.uk/news/business/news/nationwide-rescues-troubled-
building-society-1657227.html.

51 S. Johnson, 'Alistair Darling Defends Nationwide Takeover of
Dunfermline Building Society', *Telegraph* (March 2009), available at
www.telegraph.co.uk/finance/financetopics/financialcrisis/5078534/Alist
air-Darling-defends-Nationwide-takeover-of-Dunfermline-Building-
Society.html.

52 H. Williams, '£1.6bn Dunfermline Sale', E. Coleman, 'Savers Lose Trust
in Building Societies: The Rescue of Derbyshire and Cheshire Has Raised
Members' Concerns', *The Times* (13 September 2008), available at
www.timesonline.co.uk/tol/money/savings/article4748028.ece.

53 T. Levene, 'Q&A: Nationwide Merger', *Guardian* (8 September 2008),
available at www.guardian.co.uk/money/2008/sep/08/banks.mortgages.

54 J. Thornhill, 'Mergers that Failed Mutuals' Members: Angry Investors say
Building Society Rescues Ignore Their Opinions – and Rights', *Daily Mail*
(22 December 2008), available at www.dailymail.co.uk/money/article-
1099001/Mergers-failed-mutuals-members-Angry-investors-say-building-

society-rescues-ignored-opinions--rights.html.

55 G. Beale, 'Inaugural Address', The Building Societies Association Annual Conference Dinner, Harrogate, May 7, 2009, available at www.bsa.org.uk/printerfriendly.htm?art=/mediacentre/articles/new_chairman_speech.htm.

56 Earle, 'Trust, Confidence', 787–788.

57 Earle, 'Trust, Confidence'.

58 See K.M.G. Hannafin and D.G. McKillop, 'Altruism in the Economic Evaluation of Credit Unions: A Thought Piece', Journal of Co-operative Studies 39:2 (2006), 5–14.

59 Birchall and Ketilson, Resilience of the Co-operative Business Model.

60 Chaddad, 'Waves of Demutualization', 5.

61 HM Treasury, 'Building Society Capital', p. 13.

62 Ecology Building Society, Building a Sustainable Future (2010), available at www.ecology.co.uk/html/aboutus.htm.

63 C. Gijselinckx and P. Develtere, The Co-operative Trilemma: Co-operatives Between Market, State and Civil Society, Working Paper on Social and Co-operative Entrepreneurship, WP-SCE 08.01 (Belgium: HIVA – Catholic University of Leuven, 2008), available at www.cooperatiefondernemen.be/wp/WP%20SCE%2008–01.pdf.

64 HM Treasury, 'Banking Crisis: Dealing With the Failure of the UK Banks (2009), available at www.parliament.the-stationery-office.co.uk/pa/cm200809/cmselect/cmtreasy/416/41602.htm; HM Treasury, 'Building Society Capital', p. 24.

65 J. Palmer, Implementation of the Building Societies (Funding) and Mutual Societies (Transfers) Act 2009: response by the Buildings Society Association (2008), available at www.bsa.org.uk/policy/response/funding_and_transfers_act.htm.

66 P. Collinson, 'Britannia and Co-operative to Create £70bn "Super-mutual"', Guardian (21 January 2009), available at www.guardian.co.uk/business/2009/jan/21/britannia-cooperative-banks-building-societies.

67 L. Armitstead, 'Kent Reliance and JC Flowers to be Uneasy Partners', Telegraph (14 July 2010), available at www.telegraph.co.uk/finance/newsbysector/banksandfinance/7888632/Kent-Reliance-and-JC-Flowers-to-be-uneasy-partners.html.

68 A. Ellson, 'The Great Windfall Hunt is Back On', The Times (4 November 2006), available at www.timesonline.co.uk/tol/money/savings/article623687.ece; P. Lewis, 'Mutual Boss Tempts "carpetbaggers"', Mike Lazenby interview on BBC Money Box recorded 20 May, 2006, available at http://news.bbc.co.uk/go/pr/fr/-/1/hi/programmes/moneybox/5000724.stm; Building Societies Association, 'News News News: Skipton BS' (2010), available at www.building-societies-members.org.uk/Building%20Societies%20News.htm; J. Quinn, 'JC Flowers Considers Making a Move for Skipton Building Society', Telegraph (September 2010), available at www.telegraph.co.uk/finance/newsbysector/banksandfinance/8025125

/JC-Flowers-considers-making-a-move-for-Skipton-Building-Society.html.

69 Anon., 'Principality is Part of Super-mutual Plans', *Western Mail* (October 2010), availble at www.walesonline.co.uk/business-in-wales /business-news/2010/10/25/principality-is-part-of-us-equity-group-s-super-mutual-plans-91466–27538403.

70 I. Welch, *Windfalls or Shortfalls? The True Cost of Demutualisation. Short Inquiry* (London: The All-Party Parliamentary Group for Building Societies & Financial Mutuals, 2006).

71 Birchall and Ketilson, *Resilience of the Co-operative Business Model*.

17

Shared visions of co-operation at a time of crisis: the Gung Ho story in China's anti-Japanese resistance

Ian G. Cook and Jenny Clegg

Introduction

First set up in 1938, Gung Ho, the movement of Chinese Industrial Co-operatives (CIC), came about at a time of national crisis and within an atmosphere of ferment about the need for social change and economic renewal in China. With Japanese invasion threatening national extinction came the recognition that China's very survival required a united effort to rebuild the nation. Gung Ho (also 'Gong He' which means 'work together') in many ways captured this spirit of the times.

CIC co-operatives were set up to build economic strength in China's hinterland in order to sustain its resistance against Japanese occupation. The organisation came out of a cross-cutting of ideas and aspirations between Chinese patriots and Western internationalists. Co-operative ideals caught the imagination of people in China who saw the potential of participatory enterprise in drawing the wider population in to support the war effort, a necessity if Japan's overwhelming military force was to be resisted. They were joined by a number of progressives from the West who saw China's resistance war as the front line in the fight against fascism.

This chapter sets out to trace the origins of CIC, also known as Indusco, and its role behind the front lines in the resistance war and, at the same time, seeks to highlight the international efforts which rallied to support the movement. Gung Ho operated in both the areas controlled by the CPC (Communist Party of China) and the GMD (the Guomindang or Nationalist Party), and was a creation of their United Front as well as its promoter. Whilst the organisation's momentum grew rapidly in the early war years, once CPC–GMD relations began to deteriorate from 1941, Gung Ho also started to decline and was to dwindle during the civil war of 1946–49. Gung Ho's history is therefore revealing of CPC–GMD relations at this crucial time in Chinese politics, both of their joint efforts as well as the conflicts and tensions within the United Front, offering important insights into the conceptions of a better future to fight for.

The discussion highlights the common motives of the CIC activists, from both the GMD and CPC, as well as their international support- ers, and their shared vision of the potential role of a Gung Ho movement of industrial co-operatives in China's transformation. Such a force for economic democratisation would, in the eyes of the activists, help to open up an alternative path of industrialisation involving rather than marginalising the rural majority. The lessons from this time are still pertinent today.

A time of crisis: Japan's invasion of China

For most Chinese, living conditions became desperate during the 1920s and 1930s following decades of foreign impositions and wars, internal strife, weak government and warlordism. China had become known as 'the sick man of Asia': the countryside beset by periodic floods and famines that caused widespread death and destitution, and the cities dominated by an exploitative elite of Chinese and foreign nationals. Modern industry was concentrated in the coastal areas around the Treaty Ports, concessions gained during the Opium (Anglo-Chinese) Wars of 1839–42 and 1856–60, and included a large share of foreign-owned enterprises.[1] In order to deal with the depth of China's problems, in 1924 the GMD Nationalist Government had set up a United Front with the CPC under the leadership of Dr Sun Yatsen.[2] The GMD was essentially an urban-based party, comprising a left wing committed to a nationalist and social reform agenda and a militarist, anti-Communist wing.[3] After Dr Sun died in 1925, the new leader of the GMD, Generalissimo Chiang Kaishek,[4] unleashed a 'White Terror' war of extermination in 1927 against his erstwhile CPC allies, which spread rapidly from Shanghai to other cities in China, then turning against the Communist base areas in different parts of the country.[5]

China was in turmoil, and in 1931, taking advantage of its neighbour's weakness, Japan moved in to establish a puppet state in the north-east. As Japan then gradually proceeded to extend its power and influence over north China, this galvanised a movement for national resistance with students at its head.[6] In December 1936, against a background of massive anti-Japanese demonstrations, the 'Xian incident' of December 1936 saw one of Chiang's generals, 'the

Young Marshal' Zhang Xueliang, force Chiang to declare a truce with the CPC.[7] Japan was to launch a brutal full-scale invasion of China on 7 July, 1937 and, in response, by September a Second United Front had been formed. This, however, was to prove a somewhat uneasy and sometimes difficult alliance.[8] Whilst CIC came into being in the surge of patriotism that rose to support the United Front in its early stages, it was to suffer as CPC–GMD unity began to fall apart with mutual distrust and tensions deepening after 1941. Following the Japanese defeat in 1945, a full-scale civil war between the GMD and CPC was to break out; by the time of the eventual CPC victory over the GMD that established the People's Republic of China in 1949, China was 'a shattered, ruined land'.[9]

The Japanese armies swept down the Chinese coast in the last few months of 1937 and Shanghai fell in December 1937 after weeks of brave resistance on the part of the GMD troops. The city's miles-long industrialised riverfront was transformed into a scene of devastation as Japanese freighters loaded looted machinery and scrap iron, leaving hundreds of thousands of unemployed factory workers thronging the streets. It was this wanton destruction of China's industrial base that focused the minds of those who were to initiate Gung Ho. Whilst the Japanese continued their advance inland in 1938, the GMD retreated up the Yangtse river: first to Wuhan, then to Chongqing in Sichuan province where it set up its wartime capital. With little industry in the inland provinces, the situation was desperate. It was Gung Ho's idea to set up industrial co-operatives employing the skilled and semi-skilled refugees to produce goods that were essential to the army and civilian population that had fled into China's vast interior – an army, in effect, of economic resistance behind the front lines.

The Gung Ho co-operative vision takes shape

Although there were certain traditions of informal co-operative endeavour among the Chinese peasantry through village-level practices of mutual self-help,[10] as in other developing countries 'the modern co-operative system was one that was imported from abroad from the beginning of the twentieth century',[11] via Japan on the one hand, and via translations of co-operative ideas from Europe. Chinese intellectuals drew on Western thought for modern solutions to China's economic and political problems and ideas of socialism and social democracy were much debated,[12] with co-operative ideas and practices drawing particular interest from those most concerned with issues of social justice. Professor Hsueh Sien Chow at Peking University was an early advocate of the German model of Raiffessen credit co-operatives in China.[13] By the 1920s, the churches and international agencies working in China, such as the China International Famine Relief Commission (CIFRC), had become active promoters of co-operatives.[14] Whilst most of their efforts went into the establishment of credit co-operatives, Liang Shumian's Rural Reconstruction Movement in Shandong province sought to create 'industrialised villages' organised along co-operative lines as a 'third way between capitalism and communism'.[15]

After 1927, the GMD took on the goal of promoting co-operatives, not least to combat communist influence and again with the emphasis on credit co-operatives.[16] However, it was very difficult for outside reformers to penetrate the barrier formed at grassroots level by the local gentry powerholders.[17] Despite these problems in enforcing GMD policies across China, as agricultural and commercial banks extended credit to the countryside, numbers of the various types of co-operatives rose very rapidly to over 130,000 by 1940.[18] Arguably, however, the character of the 'movement', such as it was, shifted away from its largely social and philanthropic role as it fell increasingly under the control of the banks and the government.[19] The CPC also were to establish co-operatives in the areas under their control but, in their case, more as a means of collectivism.[20]

Amongst the founding members of CIC were those who had been involved in the projects of the 1920s and 1930s. Rewi Alley, a factory inspector for the British concession in Shanghai, who was to play the most central role in CIC, gaining him international renown, had worked with the CIFRC in China's north-east in 1929; Lu Guangmian, who was to serve as CIC's organiser in the North-West Region, had been influenced as a student by the ideas of Liang Shumian, and after 1931 became involved in a GMD-led rural reconstruction programme to promote supply and marketing co-operatives among cotton-growers in Hebei province. In his role as a factory inspector, Alley had already drafted some materials on industrial work in China's hinterland and it was these materials that, according to his autobiography, he rewrote 'in line with the idea of setting up a chain of industrial co-operatives extending throughout unoccupied China'[21] to form the basis of the CIC proposal.

A Preparatory Committee for the Promotion of Industrial Co-operatives in Shanghai was formed in April 1938, comprising seven Chinese and four Westerners.[22] This committee of bankers, philan-thropists, co-operative experts and foreign journalists, together with their early supporters, represented a coming together of three very different groups of people: the circle of left-leaning GMD members around Song Qingling, widow of Dr Sun Yatsen, with contact with a number of prominent Chinese bankers; progressive-minded Westerners grouped around the journalists Edgar Snow, his wife, Helen,[we] and Rewi Alley; and a number of committed Chinese co-operators including some Western-trained engineers, known as the 'Bailie boys' owing to their connections with the missionary, Joseph Bailie, pioneer of numbers of flood and famine relief projects in the late nineteenth and early twentieth centuries. The connections between the groups crossed over in Christian (the YWCA) as well as diplomatic and political circles in Shanghai.[24]

With the help of Song Qingling and the British Ambassador to China, Sir Archibald Clark-Kerr (later Lord Inverchapel), the plans for CIC were brought to the attention of the Generalissimo Chiang Kai-shek's wife, Song Meiling. The Songs were highly regarded and had political clout right across the political spectrum, from the sisters Song Meiling on the right through to Song Qingling on the left. Song Meiling overcame the initial resistance of H.H. Kung, then Minister of Finance and Vice-President of China's Executive Yuan.[25] With government authorisation and H.H. Kung as chairman of the board of directors, the Association of Chinese Industrial Co-operatives was officially set up in Wuhan on 5 August 1938, backed by an allocation of five million Chinese dollars from government relief funds and further commitments from the Chinese banking community.[26] Rewi Alley was appointed as Acting Secretary-General, and technical adviser to the Executive Council. Due to the Japanese threat to the city, the GMD organised six trains a day to evacuate whole factories to the north-west behind Chinese lines.[28]

Gung Ho in action

The first co-operative was set up in Baoji in Shaanxi province in 1938 with the assistance of Lu Guangmian, now working for CIC, and comprised seven blacksmiths. Baoji was the terminal of the railway from the east and in a chaotic condition, its streets teeming with refugees; there were no refugee camps and supplies were extremely short. Lu set about drawing up a skills register to divide the refugees into groups for training in co-operative principles and organisation.[28] After two weeks, twelve co-operatives had been established; after two months, around forty were operating successfully, producing foodstuffs, blankets, towels, shoes, surgical cotton and gauze. Regulations governing the setting-up of a co-operative were subsequently drawn up.[29]

From such beginnings, Gung Ho co-operatives rapidly developed in different parts of China where it was safe to do so, spreading also into Communist-controlled areas following the establishment of a CIC depot in Yan'an in Shaanxi province in 1939. The ideas offered shared visions of a society that would combine self-help with mutual aid, thus appealing to rightists who were keen on self-reliance at a more individual level and to leftists who were keen on mutuality at a group level. As Alley puts it, the concepts and practice 'crossed the boundary between the United Front' (between the GMD and CPC)[30] and were 'neither pro- nor anti-Communist'.[31] There were remarkable successes, including for example, the exhibition of more than one hundred industrial products made by co-operatives in the Shaanxi-Gansu-Ningxia Border Region by late 1939. Baoji itself was for a time to become 'a co-operative city' in which products such as shoes or stockings were made and, on the lighter side of a grim struggle there was a restaurant and hostel 'famous for cleanliness and good pork chops'![32]

As a progressive force, within CIC there was a strong emphasis on gender equality, employment of disabled soldiers and opposition to big industrial cities. For example, Madame Chiang Kai-shek donated a not inconsiderable sum of twenty thousand Chinese dollars to the women's work department of the CIC North-West Headquarters. The department not only organised women's co-operatives but ran kindergartens, primary schools, women's literacy classes, and women's clubs which gave advice on a range of matters – from health to family planning, and child welfare to war widows' compensation claims – as well as organising social activities. Staff workers for the department 'tramped the country just like men, scorning the idea that Chinese women were delicate and suited only for home life'.[33]

Even Generalissimo Chiang Kai-shek was to share the Gung Ho vision, arguing for the need to industrialise the countryside, and recognising that CIC had a key role to play. Similarly, H.H. Kung warned of the 'evils of industrialisation',[34] namely desertion of the countryside by the rural population leading to overcrowded cities and unemployment. Chinese people had seen the rise of Shanghai in the 1920s and 1930s to become the major industrial city of China, and one which contained huge inequalities with low wages, a 70–hour week, and contrasting high profits for cotton mills and other industrial activities.[35] As Helen Snow put it, 'The tragedy of Shanghai industry is that it does nothing to improve the economy of the interior.'[36]

CIC set up several training schools and quickly brought together some five hundred fieldworkers, including engineers, accountants and organisers.[37] It was then able to establish a nationwide presence:

Box 17.1 The Gung Ho vision

Song Qingling, Sun Yatsen's widow: 'Industrial cooperatives can maintain the economic stability of our internal market, and thus avoid chaos in the villages even if the Japanese occupy all our cities. They can utilise idle workers, keep our soldiers clothed and fed, avoid famine and other consequences of economic dislocation, support prolonged resistance and make Japanese occupation of our cities entirely profitless. This movement needs the help of progressive people everywhere.'[a]

Lu Guangmian, CIC North-West Regional Organiser: 'The solution for a balanced economy of China lies in decentralised industries organised on a cooperative basis and working side by side with agriculture.'[b]

H.H. Kung, Vice-Premier of China's Executive Yuan, 1935–45, and Chair of CIC's Executive Board: 'The significance of this movement [for industrial cooperatives] ... cannot be overestimated. It points to a new way to China's industrialization.'[c]

Helen Snow, American journalist and the originator of the Gung Ho idea: 'The war emergency makes it possible to create a modern cooperative system in China, for it has broken down provincialism and old prejudices. Every cooperative centre has men and women from many different provinces working together ... in their mutual struggle for livelihood and each group soon develops a new national consciousness and pride in building cooperative industry.'[d]

Chen Hanseng, Marxist economist and Secretary-General of ICCIC: 'As it establishes itself, cooperative industry is bound to take on far-reaching political and social significance ... The present cooperative system, if extended nation-wide to become a coherent part of production in China, will educate the people in individual responsibility as the basis of cooperation. When people are educated to individual responsibility with the habit of mutual cooperation, they cannot help but develop a democratic view of life ... a practical way of bringing (democracy) about is at hand by means of a democratic system of production.'[e]

Sir Stafford Cripps, MP: 'The Chinese Industrial Cooperatives are teaching the people the methods of democratic government. They are building the foundations of a new democracy in China.'[f]

US Admiral Harry E. Yarnell: 'Today the fight for freedom resounds from all corners of the earth. It was the Chinese who struck the first blows for democracy not on December 7, 1941, but on July 7, 1937 ... The Chinese Industrial Cooperatives are an integral part of this world battle for freedom. They give warmth to the freezing, food to the starving, and perhaps most important of all ... hope to the people for the future.'[g]

Mao Zedong: 'I am in favour of the establishment of many small industries in China by means of cooperatives ... If it is possible to build this kind of (cooperative) industries in the guerrilla districts of North China, and in the adjacent war regions in the Northwest, the help would be greatly appreciated and warmly welcomed by the Eight Route Army and my humble self.'[h]

Notes

For full details, see chapter end notes.

[a]   Quoted in Alley, *Rewi Alley*, pp.110–111.
[b]   *Co-operatives*, p. 29.
[c]   'Industrial Co-operatives and the War', p. 2.
[d]   *China Builds for Democracy*, p. 253.
[e]   *Gung Ho!* p. 63.
[f]   Quoted in INDUSCO, *A Nation Rebuilds: The Story of the Chinese Industrial Co-operatives* (n.d. but probably 1944), p. 16. Available from Manchester, Co-operative Archive.
[g]   Quoted in ibid., p. 1.
[h]   Cited in *China Builds for Democracy*, p. 37.

headquartered in the Nationalists' capital of Chongqing in Sichuan province, it organised five regional groupings covering fifteen of China's twenty-eight provinces with over fifty depots, each staffed by a senior organiser and technician.[38] The numbers of CIC co-operatives grew rapidly after 1938, reaching a peak of 1,857 by June 1941, and where numbers allowed, the enterprises were grouped into federations.[39] Formal membership reached around 30,000 with possibly up to 250,000 people connected in some way with CIC work,[40] a small army producing hundreds of different types of products from textiles and foods to chemical and metals trades, and included numbers of transport co-operatives. This was a tremendous achievement, given both the traditional lack of industry within China's countryside, and also the grim wartime situation that faced China.

An account by former Yanqing University professor and CIC field inspector, Ralph Lapwood, of a mass meeting he attended of Gung Ho industrial co-operators in Liuzhou, Guangxi province in 1943, to discuss the establishment of a Supply and Marketing Department of their federation, attests to the vibrancy of the movement:

> The people in the meeting were the skilled workers themselves. There were leather-goods makers who had escaped from Japanese-controlled Shanghai. There were skilled cotton-weavers from Hunan, both men and women. There were local leather-tanners ... There were carpenters who made boats and coffins for which Liuchow [Liuzhou] is famous ...
>
> They had elected their own chairman and committee, and were now listening to the report of the committee on the proposed Supply and Marketing department. When it was finished, questions began. From all the parts of the meeting, from every co-operative society represented, came comments and suggestions. The vitality of it was in startling contrast to all my memories of the miserable and lifeless factory hands of Shanghai. In quick succession came fiery rhetoric from the excitable Hunanese, clever analysis from the Shanghai landers, commonsense queries from the slower spoken natives of Kwangsi. In the give-and-take of debates it was clear that, beneath the veneer of politeness which must surface every Chinese meeting, real problems were being brought out, discussed and solved in a new and thoroughly democratic way.[41]

However, not all the CIC localities were like this. In Ganzhou, Jiangxi province, where the governor, Chiang Kai-shek's eldest son, Chiang Ching-kuo,[42] supported the establishment of Gung Ho co-operatives, the experience was of a very different character. According to Alley, one problem that CIC faced here was the tradition of 'kerosene co-operatives' that were actually dominated by the gentry to make profit for themselves rather than for the peasant members. These 'co-operatives' hoarded kerosene that was needed by most households for lamp-oil; the hoarding resulted in price rises that made a tidy profit but added to the burden of debt that was common in Chinese peasant society in that period. The peasant could have his wife, sons, house or land taken away to pay the kerosene deficit, thus they had to be reassured that the new CIC co-operatives offered profit for themselves rather than the gentry.[43]

The original Gung Ho plan for thirty thousand co-operatives[44] was to prove far too ambitious. The CIC co-operatives faced numerous difficulties: the poverty of the locations, the difficulties of transport, the depredations of wartime inflation and bombing raids, as well as internal shortcomings – the lack of capital and a disproportionate reliance on loans, the inexperience of the co-operative leaders and poor understanding of co-operative principles among actual or potential co-operative members, and the lack of trained engineers and accountants.[45] CIC co-operators had also to deal with the bureaucratic mind-set if not corruption of local officials and other resistance from local elites as well as the suspicions of the refugees from outside on the part of the local populations.[46]

At the same time, CIC began to experience serious political difficulties. Controversy over CIC's institutional independence caused tensions within the organisation itself. On the one hand were the GMD leaders such as H.H. Kung and Song Meiling, in control of CIC's Executive, who saw themselves as the original CIC sponsors and tended to look upon the movement as 'their creation rather than as a co-operative effort by the working membership',[47] and who were concerned primarily with centralised coordination, strengthening the role of the central headquarters with increasing numbers of appointments from the GMD.[48] On the other hand were the fieldworkers for whom democratic self-government was essential to the development of the movement, who sought a decentralised development.[49] US Lieutenant Colonel Evans F. Carlson, who worked with the co-operatives in 1940 and who popularised the expression 'gung ho' in the United States, was to observe 'a vast gap between the bureaucrats and the earnest self-sacrificing men and women who are actually making CIC work in the field'.[50] Whilst the former endeavoured to bring CIC closer under control of the GMD government, the latter thought the movement should not be too closely aligned to any one political party. For the latter, resistant to the infringement of co-operative autonomy on the part of the banks and government, the strength of the United Front and the independence of co-operatives were mutually linked.[51]

The militarist and social reformist wings of the GMD had differed in their attitudes towards mass campaigning to mobilise for the war effort from the outset.[52] The former were deeply suspicious of the Gung Ho activists' commitment to mobilising workers and small farmers, seeing in the movement 'the peril of disguised communism' challenging the existing order.[53] When Chiang Kai-shek turned his troops against his United Front allies ambushing Communist New Fourth Army troops in the Southern Anhui incident of January 1941, several CIC workers were killed and several hundred arrested.[54] Alley himself was eventually dismissed from his post with CIC's Executive for his dealings with the Communists. Fortunately he was able to continue as field secretary of the International Committee that had developed to raise funds for Gung Ho overseas.

Overseas support and the International Committee

With the GMD-led executive keeping tight control over finance, CIC activists, fearing that the movement would be strangled through shortage of funds just at its point of take-off, turned to fund-raising from overseas. On 22 July 1939, with the advice and support of Song Qingling, CIC set up an International Committee (ICCIC) based in Hong Kong to handle overseas donations, the Right Reverend R.O. Hall, Bishop of Hong Kong, serving as Chair, and Chen Hanseng as Executive Secretary. The efforts to raise international assistance became a movement in itself, winning support from across the globe, from Southeast Asia to Europe and the United States. Within a year, overseas donations were nearly one million Chinese dollars, and over the course of the war reached US$5 million (worth one hundred million Chinese dollars).[55]

ICCIC raised funds broadly from three different sources. Early support came from patriotic overseas Chinese communities across Southeast Asia, from wealthy businessmen and bankers as well as from Chinese trade unions. The Chinese Women's Relief Association in the Philippines was amongst the first to raise substantial funds. In the United States, an American Committee in Aid of CIC was set up in 1940, chaired by Admiral Harry E. Yarnell, with Ida Pruitt, a founder member of CIC when in Shanghai, serving as the secretary.[56] The committee gained representation on the United China Relief (UCR) organisation, an umbrella association of the numerous church-and missionary-backed China aid groups formed after the Japanese attack on Pearl Harbor in December 1941. However, whereas United China Relief worked exclusively with Chiang Kai-shek's GMD, the American Committee in Aid of CIC sought to support the United Front as a whole. In its efforts to rally American workers, minorities and women in solidarity with a cause committed to empowering ordinary Chinese people at the grassroots, the committee was, as King argues, pioneering of a non-partisan non-political China-America relationship.[57] Where United China Relief drew the support of Republicans, the American Committee in Aid of CIC found favour among Roosevelt's New Dealers. Indeed, Eleanor Roosevelt, wife of the then US president, was to become Honorary Chair of the committee, although her sponsorship was more of a moral kind since no official American assistance was ever given.[58]

However, it was to Britain that the ICCIC first turned for support due to the strength of the UK co-operative movement. Co-operative societies had been active in the campaigning against the closure of the Burma Road after July 1940, and with a growing interest in the Chinese industrial co-operatives, the Anglo-Chinese Co-operative Development Society Ltd was established in 1941 with Lady Cripps, wife of the popular left-wing Labour MP Sir Stafford Cripps,[59] as Honorary Chair, and Co-operative Party MP Alfred Barnes as Chair. The Society sold withdrawable shares of one pound sterling and started a scheme whereby nine co-operative societies in Britain adopted nine specific areas in China, for example, the London Co-operative Society collected money to go to co-operatives in Chongqing.[60] The Society was also to produce a Gung Ho bi-monthly journal.

Funds raised overseas were allocated to educational and medical projects and used for the purchase of machinery and equipment as well as start-up capital.[61] A hospital in Shandan, Shaanxi Province, was apparently built with funds from the Women's Co-operative Guild in Britain.[62] Foreign support also came in the form of volunteers: veteran British co-operator Professor J.B. Tayler served as a co-operative trainer, while Oxford graduate George Hogg became headmaster of the co-operative Shandan Bailie School before his tragic death in 1945.[63] Despite the efforts to ensure funds were disbursed to co-operatives on a non-political basis, it is unlikely that much overseas contributions got through the GMD blockade to the Yan'an co-operatives in the Communist-controlled areas after 1941.[64]

Why the external interest in Industrial Co-operatives in China? CIC's primary aim to give Chinese refugees from war the skills to rebuild their own lives had a strong humanitarian appeal. Yet CIC also gained support from those who saw the strategic implications of a Japanese conquest of China. Japanese advance throughout Asia would facilitate an alliance with Germany as well as threatening the US across the Pacific. Standing in the front line of resistance against Japan, CIC was then seen not only as an aid to China's poor but as an important part of the struggle against fascism.

Gung Ho as a movement and the legacy of its vision

The industrial co-operative movement in China was essentially a product of wartime circumstances. Whereas the GMD-led pre-war co-operatives had relied on top-down efforts, more of a policy than a movement,[65] CIC came into being at a time of unprecedented mobilisation and politicisation of the Chinese people,[66] in the surge of patriotic solidarity to resist the Japanese invasion. CIC indeed received government backing and its core members were active publicists, promoting the wartime spirit. Its early supporters came from diverse social constituencies: intellectuals and academics, religious groups, social reformers, politicians, bankers and the foreign community. Sharing a view of China's future, these people stepped forward at this time of crisis, pooling their varied skills and expertise to turn the tide of the country's chaotic conditions towards resistance against Japan's occupying armies. Gung Ho took off rapidly between 1938 and 1941 amidst one of the world's largest-ever movements of refugees in the early years of the war. Driven on by the efforts of a core of committed activists, supporters and fieldworkers to rally the people's energies to the war effort, the organisation began to mobilise the educated and worker refugees who had come together under the umbrella of the United Front.

The Gung Ho vision, then, struck a chord across boundaries of politics, class, gender, region and nation. From the anti-fascist viewpoint of CIC, a movement of small-scale industrial co-operatives pointed towards a new way forward for China. It offered a practical and human-faced alternative to the pattern of large-scale industrialisation which was seen to be rooted in the expansion through war of foreign capital into China, at the cost of incalculable human misery. Industrial co-operatives in the rural areas would instead serve as a bridge between the old – the pre-industrial traditional village – and the new – modern industrialisation – introducing new patterns of social and economic organisation, making livelihood possible in the villages. In this vision, CIC set itself up as a symbol of the middle way between the GMD and the CPC, seeking to mobilise a mass participatory industrial co-operative movement as a 'school for democracy' pitted against the spread of fascism, a cohesive force to rally the United Front and keep Chiang Kai-shek engaged in the war of resistance.

CIC was never to realise its goal of a mass movement controlled by producers, falling short of its ideals of self-help and democratic management. Caught up in the hostilities and suspicions between the CPC–GMD especially after 1941, its development was hindered and numbers started to decline. However its problems were also internal. Lacking capital and relevant expertise, the movement soon became over-extended and dependent on external funding,[67] and was limited also by a strong tendency towards centralisation and bureaucratic management in both the GMD- and CPC-controlled areas.[68] The inter-

national publicity surrounding Gung Ho at the time was no doubt
overblown, but nevertheless it represented a remarkable example of
grassroots endeavour in the worst possible circumstances. The most
successful enterprises were those formed by refugees, unencumbered
by traditionalist and localistic ties, and it was in particular in the
CPC-controlled areas, according to Keating,[69] where the power of the
old elites was more effectively destroyed, allowing the refugee resettle-
ment programmes to develop deeper roots in the local communities,
that co-operative efforts at village level were to play a major role in
rural reconstruction. In these areas, co-operatives were less reliant on
loans. Although these enterprises were in fact the chief form of production, CIC co-operatives existed here only in small numbers. However,
local authorities saw to it that they conformed as far as possible with
the self-help and democratic regulations of the CIC constitution.[70]

A particular criticism of CIC emanating from the right wing of the
GMD was that the participation of foreigners in the movement
rendered it artificial.[71] On the other hand, this call to stop 'imperialist
control' was evidently a pretext to bring the movement closer under
government supervision.[72] The independent support from overseas can
be seen as having considerable significance, not just materially, but in
boosting morale within the anti-Japanese resistance and supporting
Gung Ho's non-partisan stance so that it should continue to play a
constructive role in maintaining the United Front. The support from
Britain in particular was an outstanding demonstration of co-operative
internationalism and of the role of 'co-operation among co-operators'
in building a quite different kind of foreign relationship.

With refugees starting to return home as the war drew to an end, the
numbers of co-operatives declined, falling steeply from 1,066 to 335
between March and December 1945.[73] A small number of co-operatives
continued and CIC and ICCIC continued to operate during the period
of civil war between the GMD and CPC. However, following the
establishment of the PRC (People's Republic of China) in 1949, both
organisations were suspended with the setting up of the All-China
Federation of Handicraft and Industrial Co-operatives to realise the
new government's aim of amalgamating China's small-scale, individually run handicraft enterprises. Nevertheless, the Gung Ho experience
was to have a long-term impact. Whilst the co-operative sector
gradually lost its autonomy and became absorbed into the framework
of state planning by the end of the 1950s,[74] the Gung Ho vision was
nevertheless still evident in Mao's ideas in the late 1950s and 1960s to
industrialise the countryside.[75]

Today, as the world's attention is focused on China's recent rapid economic development and progress towards a new future, it is important to recognise that the past experience of wartime remains an essential part of Chinese identity.[76] The spirit of the anti-Japanese resistance remains psychologically integrated into China's self-image and the story of the Gung Ho pioneer co-operators with their vision of a people-centred industrial democracy involving the rural poor of the country's interior, is still popularly known. In the 1980s, after China adopted a new path of economic reform, Rewi Alley gained official endorsement for the revival of ICCIC following the re-launch of CIC. Most recently, with assistance from the Canadian Co-operative Association, ICCIC has focused on training co-operative trainers and has also been working in those areas ravaged by the earthquake which hit Sichuan province in 2008, helping people to set up co-operatives to regenerate the local economy. Today, with PRC plans for mega-city growth and a potential further increase in the urban population of three hundred and twenty million people by 2025, once again fuelling concerns about the rural areas falling further behind, the Gung Ho vision continues to have resonance. Its present-day supporters continue to contribute, so far only in a small way, to the ongoing debates about China's future way forward, promoting the democratic and people-centred traditions of Gung Ho as a source of inspiration to those seeking to drive forward the government's stated aims of a more balanced and participatory development path.[77]

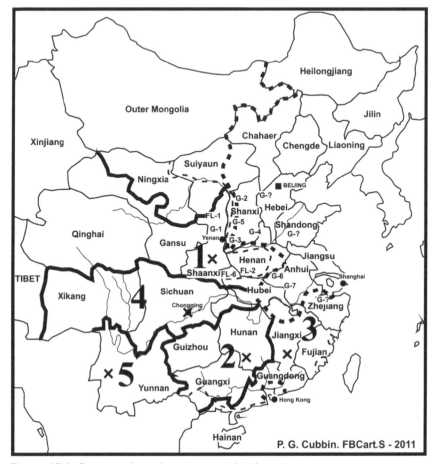

Figure 17.1 Chinese industrial co-operatives headquarter regions

Key: ▪▪▪▪▪▪▪▪▪ᴵ Japanese lines of occupation January, 1940

‒‒‒‒‒‒‒‒‒. Japanese lines of occupation July, 1940

▬▬▬▬▬▬▬ CIC regional boundaries

HQ Regions: **1** North West **2** South West **3** South East

4 West   **5** Yunnan

X = HQ towns **Depots:** (with No.) **FL** - Front-Line **G** - Guerilla

Notes

1 P. Zarrow, *China at War and Revolution, 1895–1949* (London: Routledge, 2006); P. Osinsky, 'Modernisation Interrupted? Total War, State Breakdown, and the Communist Conquest of China', *The Sociological Quarterly* 51 (2010), 587.

2 Zarrow, *China in War and Revolution*, p. 199.

3 J. Gray, *Rebellions and Revolutions: China from the 1880s to 2000*, 2nd edn (Oxford: Oxford University Press, 2003), pp. 246–247.

4 Generally we shall use the modern pinyin version of Chinese names, except for those such as Chiang Kaishek who are known better in the West via the older Wade-Giles system of transliteration.

5 H.J. Van de Ven, *War and Nationalism in China, 1925–1945* (London: Routledge Curzon, 2003).

6 Huang Hua, *Huang Hua Memoirs* (Beijing: Foreign Languages Press, 2008), pp. 3–4.

7 Van de Ven, *War and Nationalism in China*, pp. 186–188.

8 J. Grasso, J. Corrin and M. Kort, *Modernization and Revolution in China: From the Opium Wars to World Power*, 3rd edn (New York: M.E. Sharpe Press, 2004), p. 107.

9 Han Suyin, cited in I.G. Cook and G. Murray, *China's Third Revolution: Tensions in the Transition to Post-Communism,* (London: Curzon Press, 2001), p. 5.

10 Discussed further in P. Hsu, 'Rural Co-operatives in China', *Pacific Affairs* 2.10 (1929), 611–624, and G. Shillinglaw, 'Traditional Rural Co-operation and Social Structure: The Communist Chinese Collectivization of Agriculture', in P. Worsley (ed.), *Two Blades of Grass: Rural Co-operatives in Agricultural Modernization* (Manchester: Manchester University Press, 1971).

11 J. Clegg and I.G. Cook, 'Gung Ho in China: Towards Participatory Co-operatives', *Journal of Co-operative Studies* 42:3, (2010), 4.

12 E. Fung, 'State Building, Capitalist Development and Social Justice: Social Democracy in China's Modern Transformation, 1929–1949', *Modern China* 31:3 (2005), 318–352.

13 P. Trescott, 'John Bernard Tayler and the Development of Co-operatives in China, 1917–1945', *Annals of Public and Co-operative Economics* 64:2 (1993), 212.

14 Ibid., 210–211.

15 Fung, 'State Building, Capitalist Development and Social Justice', 340–341.

16 Trescott, 'John Bernard Tayler', p. 212.

17 Gray, *Rebellions and Revolutions*, p. 241.

18 Clegg and Cook, 'Gung Ho in China', 5.

19 Chen Hanseng, 'Co-operatives as a Panacea for China's Ills', *Far Eastern Survey* 6:7 (1937), 71–77.

20 Cheng-Chung Lai, 'The Structure and Characteristics of the Chinese

Co-operative System: 1928–49', *International Journal of Social Economics* 16:2 (1989), 59–66.

21 R. Alley, *Rewi Alley: An Autobiography*, 3rd edn (Beijing: New World Press, 1997), p. 104.

22 H.F. Snow, *My China Years* (London: Harrap, 1984), p. 305.

23 Edgar Snow's book *Red Star Over China*, which was to introduce Mao Zedong and the CPC's Red base in Yan'an to a wide readership in the West, had just been published by Victor Gollanz. It was Snow's wife, Helen, who first conceived the Gung Ho idea (Alley, *Rewi Alley*, p. 104.)

24 Snow, *My China Years*, pp. 304–306; M. King, *China's American Daughter: Ida Pruitt, 1888–1985* (Hong Kong: The Chinese University Press, 2006), pp. 127–128.

25 The Executive Yuan, literally 'House of Administration' was the Executive Branch of the Nationalist GMD Government; the term is still used today in Taiwan.

26 Chen Hanseng, *Gung Ho! The Story of the Chinese Co-operatives*, IPR Pamphlet No. 24 (New York: American Institute of Pacific Relations, 1947).

27 Alley, *Rewi Alley*, p. 109.

28 Interview with Lu Guangmian's son, 4 June, 2010, ICCIC Offices, Beijing.

29 Alley, *Rewi Alley*, p. 110.

30 Ibid., p. 128.

31 Ibid., p. 145.

32 Lu Kuang-mien (Lu Guangmian), *Co-operatives*, Pamphlet No. 6 (Chongqing: Chinese Ministry of Information, 1946), p. 26. Available from Manchester Co-operative Archive. We are grateful for the help of Gill Lonegran and her staff for facilitating our use of this archive.

33 Ibid., p. 24.

34 H.H. Kung, 'Industrial Co-operatives and the War', *New Defence* 1:1 (1939), 1–2, 8. Available from Manchester Co-operative Archive.

35 N. Wales (Helen Snow), *China Builds for Democracy: A Story of Co-operative Industry* (Beijing: Foreign Languages Press, 2004), pp. 238–239.

36 Ibid., p. 238.

37 R. Barnett, 'China's Industrial Co-operatives on Trial', *Far Eastern Survey,* 9:5 (Feb 1940), 52–54.

38 CIC Association, *China's Industrial Reconstruction: The Story of the Chinese Industrial Co-operatives* (Hong Kong-Shanghai Industrial Co-operatives Promotion Committee, 1938), pp. 49–52.

39 P. Keating, 'Co-operative Visions Versus Wartime Realities: Indusco and the Chinese Communists, 1938–1944', *New Zealand Journal of East Asian Studies* 1:5 (1997), 11–12; and for numbers of CIC co-operatives, see Table 1 on p. 28. A discussion of differing sets of data appears in Members of the American Council Staff, 'Chinese Industrial Co-operatives Marking Time', *Far Eastern Survey* 10:18 (1941), 209.

40 M. Lockett, *From Guilds to 'Gung Ho': Producer Co-operatives in China, 1911–194*, Research Paper MRP87/11 (Templeton College, The Oxford Centre for Management, 1987), p. 5.

41 R. Lapwood, 'Hope for China', *Gung Ho Journal of the Anglo-Chinese Development Society* September 1946, p. 6.

42 Chiang Ching-kuo (Jiang Jingguo) was follow his father in becoming President of the Republic of China (Taiwan) from 1978–88.

43 Alley, *Rewi Alley*, p. 115.

44 Ibid., p. 173.

45 Keating, 'Co-operative Visions Versus Wartime Realities', 18–21; Members of the American Council Staff, 'Chinese Industrial Co-operatives Marking Time', 20.

46 Barnett, 'China's Industrial Co-operatives on Trial', 54.

47 Members of the American Council Staff, 'Chinese Industrial Co-operatives Marking Time', 210–211; King, *China's American Daughter*, p. 147.

48 Members of the American Council Staff, 'Chinese Industrial Co-operatives Marking Time', 212; D.R. Reynolds, *The Chinese Industrial Cooperative Movement and the Political Polarization of Wartime China, 1938–1945* (PhD Thesis, New York: Columbia University, 1975), pp. 318–322. The thesis is available via Xerox University Microfilms, Ann Arbor, Michigan 48106.

49 Members of the American Council Staff, 'Chinese Industrial Co-operatives Marking Time', 210–211; King, *China's American Daughter*, p. 147; Reynolds, *The Chinese Industrial Cooperative Movement*, pp. 346–347.

50 Cited in King, *China's American Daughter*, pp. 147–148.

51 Members of the American Council Staff, 'Chinese Industrial Co-operatives Marking Time', 210.

52 S. McKinnon, *Wuhan, 1938: War, Refugees and the Making of Modern China*, (Berkeley: University of California Press, 2008), pp. 88–92.

53 Barnett, 'China's Industrial Co-operatives on Trial', 52; Members of the American Council Staff, 'Chinese Industrial Co-operatives Marking Time', 210.

54 Members of the American Council Staff, 'Chinese Industrial Co-operatives Marking Time', 210–11; Meng Shouzeng and Yi Ding, 'The Gung Ho Movement in Zhejiang-Anhui', in Editorial Board, *A Collection in Memory of Rewi Alley*, (Beijing: New World Press, 1997), pp. 134–138.

55 Yang Bo, 'Great Ideal and Persistence in Pursuance – In Memory of Rewi Alley's Contributions to Gung Ho', in *A Collection in Memory of Rewi Alley*, p. 147.

56 M. King, *China's American Daughter*, pp. 147–154.

57 Ibid., pp. 150–151.

58 Ibid., pp.144–145.

59 Sir Stafford Cripps, MP was a key figure in forging an alliance between the Western powers and the Soviet Union. A member of Churchill's war

cabinet and for a time Leader of the House of Commons during this period, he later became Chancellor of the Exchequer in the post-war Atlee Government.

60 Snow, *My China Years,* pp. 15–17.

61 Members of the American Council Staff, 'Chinese Industrial Co-operatives Marking Time', 211; A. Barnes, 'This is the A.C.D.S.', *Gung Ho Journal of the Anglo-Chinese Development Society.* September 1946, 4–5.

62 P. Wright, *Passport to Peking: A Very British Mission to Mao's China* (Oxford: Oxford University Press, 2010), p. 347.

63 See J. Macmanus, *Ocean Devil: the Life and Legend of George Hogg* (London: Harper Perennial, London, 2008). The film *The Children of Huang Shi,* starring Jonathan Rhys Meyers, is loosely based on the book.

64 Chen, *Gung Ho!,* p. 36.

65 H.D. Fong cited in Trescott, 'John Bernard Tayler', 212.

66 McKinnon, *Wuhan, 1938,* p. 115.

67 Keating, 'Co-operative Visions Versus Wartime Realities', 5, 13; Members of the American Council Staff, 'Chinese Industrial Co-operatives Marking Time', 213.

68 Keating, 'Co-operative Visions versus Wartime Realities', 18.

69 Ibid., 21–22.

70 Ibid., 22.

71 Barnett, 'China's Industrial Co-operatives on Trial', 53.

72 Lockett, *From Guilds to 'Gung Ho',* p. 6.

73 See Table 1 in Keating, 'Co-operative Visions Versus Wartime Realities', 28.

74 J. Clegg, 'Reforming China's Co-operative Economy: Issues and Experiences', in C. Harvie and B.-C. Lee, *Small and Medium Sized Enterprises in East Asia* (Cheltenham: Edward Elgar, 2008), pp. 178–179.

75 Gray, *Rebellions and Revolutions,* pp. 307–309.

76 D. Lary, 'One Province's Experience of War: Guangxi, 1937–1945', in S. McKinnon *et al.* (eds), *China at War: Regions of China, 1937–1945* (Stanford: Stanford University Press, 2007), p. 332.

77 At the Asia-Pacific regional assembly of the International Co-operative Alliance held for the first time in Beijing in September 2010, the Vice-Premier of the PRC, Hui Liangyu, emphasised that China attached great importance to the development of co-operatives See www.gov .cn/english/2010–09/03/content_1695461.htm (accessed 20 January 2011).

18

The hidden alternative: conclusion

Ed Mayo

If this book were a thriller, or a murder story, then this concluding chapter would be the one to unveil, at the last, the astounding truth of who stands to blame and why various evils have happened. If you share a weakness common in my family, you might even be taking a peek at the end, even before you start the book and read it, as the publisher intended, from front cover to back.

If you have read from the front, or even just dipped in, you will know that the book is indeed not a thriller. There can be no final twists. But there are characters that show their face time and again – Frederick Raiffeissen, the Rochdale Pioneers, the International Co-operative Alliance, Co-operative Colleges – and we have a glimpse over time of how these characters develop. But these are patterns that the reader must pick out, as the book itself is a pick and mix of narrative and analysis. For myself, I have been inspired to read of the Gung Ho co-operative movement in China, bricklayer co-ops in Milan and cigar-smoking co-operators in early twentieth-century Sweden. In these, I can find my own experience as a witness to the inspiration of energetic contemporary co-operatives in business today.

Stories like these are vital. It is important to understand our own history, so that, as a co-operative sector, we don't underplay our sense of ambition or overstate the call of realism. Being part of a co-operative enterprise, particularly a smaller one, is like walking a tightrope. The risks are constant, the challenges unceasing and the interplay of values and commercial decisions is rarely simple. The psychology of dealing with that is to keep moving, to keep momentum. It is easy to forget those that fail and to discount the poker risks of those that succeed. Stories, histories, help to keep our outlook on the world honest.

Coming back to the story of this book though, published on the brink of the United Nations International Year of Co-operatives 2012, we should move to the central plot itself. What is the alternative? And who hid it?

Well, the first question is easier for the reader to answer, because the preceding chapters have painted a rich, multi-layered picture of the practice of the co-operative model. But, then, should we say models? Is it one alternative, or more? There is a case for saying that it is one alternative – diverse, no doubt, but with overlapping dimensions that are common to all: membership, democracy, enterprise. After all, one of the great achievements of recent decades has been the consensus that has been forged around a model of co-operative identity. That identity is written down – though as guidelines rather than as a checklist, as Ian Macpherson reminds us in his earlier chapter. It is also lived out in the way in which co-operatives operate as a movement, coming together through a global association in the International Co-operative Alliance.

Personally, I prefer to think of co-operative practice as about a set of alternatives. Even with a common approach, such as being member-owned businesses, there is a very considerable difference across countries and cultures and depending on which stakeholder is the actual member. Worker co-operatives have helped to create a paradigm for workplace organisation that is quite distinct from the practices of many consumer co-operatives, which in turn have been innovators in relation to goods and services. Arguably, many of the practices of early worker co-operatives are now taken as standard by conventional businesses – staff engagement, worker empowerment, participative models of decision-making and peer review for quality – so that some alternatives have become mainstream. But, as is typically the case with social innovation, it is the easier practices for current power-holders to assimilate and replicate that take off, often stripped of their transformative values, while the true radicalism of engendering a shift of ownership and power itself remains on the outside.

Alternatives do not rest in islands of practice beyond the world of the conventional. There is a constant flux, in which existing models look to adapt what can work from alternatives. Ivan Illich used the term 'tools', reminding us that it is the institutional context and meaning that defines whether tools have radical potential to transform the world around them or whether they simply serve to reinforce it.[1]

The field of corporate social responsibility could be argued to be another alternative that mainstream business has learned from pioneers, including the co-operative sector. It is instructive to see what then happens. When hidden alternatives become visible, it is not a simple story of good and bad, right or wrong. After all, some conventional businesses have taken up the model of social responsibility in new ways that then leave co-operatives that were early adopters looking jaded.

The field of social and environmental accounting, for example, has co-operative pioneers, including VanCity Savings Credit Union in Canada and the Co-operative Group in the UK.[2] Equally, some outstanding work has been done more recently across the corporate sector more widely in delivering frameworks and resources for measuring performance on social goals, such as carbon emissions, water use and waste. For a co-operative to respond to this process of mainstreaming alternatives by claiming its credentials around corporate social responsibility then also carries risks, as the heart of what co-ops are about is different – about 'co-operative' social responsibility – one of our core values – and a model that enfranchises stakeholders through ownership rather than as a voluntary afterthought for the purpose of business reputation.

Corporate social responsibility is a way of framing discussion of an aspect of business life. The conventional frames like this that we use for understanding business life, as Maddocks and team argue in an earlier chapter in relation to accounting, assign a marginal role to co-operatives because of their underlying assumptions on what a business is – however significant or energetic the co-operative sector may be. Like a pair of old spectacles, the frame that you choose – shareholder value, customer service, business growth – focuses on what is in front of you and obscures what is out of sight. To an extent then, we will always be a hidden alternative as long as the language of business and economics remains locked in the freeze-frame assumptions of neo-liberal economic ideologies.

When, famously, Jack Welch, CEO of General Electric from 1981–2001, changed his mind about shareholder value and said in 2009, amidst market turmoil, that focusing on share price was 'the dumbest idea in the world', he failed to pick up on the alternative and say 'now, everybody pile into co-ops instead'.[3] So, it is not enough to be different to the mainstream. After all, you could be a complement to the mainstream as much as an alternative. To be a genuine alternative, you have to offer a distinct and sufficiently coherent option that can be advanced in ways that over time will prove effective.

Let's take the example that Jack Welch prompts. Do co-operatives in fact perform any better than shareholder-owned businesses? If you are involved in co-operatives, or have read enough of the previous chapters, you may have formed your own view (or, in the way of stories, it may simply have confirmed a view that you had before). And at the time of Welch's confession, post-credit crunch, share prices had certainly tumbled and, by definition, conventional businesses were doing badly. But it was not clear that co-operatives were necessarily better placed and the reason was the yardstick that was being used to measure performance. If success equals share prices, then co-operatives will never be an alternative as most are never priced in financial markets, the trades in which are typically based on the opposite of what co-operatives stand for – distant ownership and speculative value. To offer a genuine alternative, we need the model and the measure. We need to promote ideas of co-operative performance and address the question of how one would measure it.

So what, in this example, is co-operative performance? First, we are still talking about value and efficiency. John Roberts, in his book *The Modern Firm*, argues that all business performance is the creation of value, and, in financial terms, that is 'the difference between the maximum that people would be willing to pay for it, less the opportunity cost of the activity'.[4] In terms of economic (Pareto) efficiency, high performance is where there is no other course of action that would make all parties better off. Performance is therefore not primarily about trend improvements over time but whether current activity is the best possible use of resources.

But, second, what the ingredients of value and efficiency are in a co-operative context is fundamentally different. The alternative economist, James Robertson, puts this well. He explains that performance efficiency

> is measured as a ratio between significant inputs and significant outputs; the greater the output in relation to the input, the greater the efficiency. So its meaning depends on what are seen as the most significant inputs and outputs – what inputs are most important to reduce, and what outputs are most important to increase? In farming and every other sphere it has been assumed efficient to reduce labour. Supposedly efficient farms have produced high profits (output) compared with the number of workers employed (input). Ratios between the calorific value of the food produced and the area of land farmed have not been seen as significant. Nor have the externalised costs of water, air and land pollution, soil erosion, impacts on human health, destruction of wildlife and wildlife habitats, and rural unemployment. The meaning of economic efficiency needs rethinking in all sectors of economic activity.[5]

If we put on the spectacles that Robertson offers, co-operative performance is distinct from business performance in that the metrics for success need to reflect inputs and outputs that are in line with co-operative values and principles. While business failure is business failure, whether co-operative or not, forms of co-operative business success will only be efficient if they represent the least costly way of achieving what members value. And this is how I would define co-operative performance – the least costly way of achieving what members value. Even though what members value will vary very considerably, a question one can then ask of any co-operative is how it satisfies itself over time that it knows what members value. There will be metrics of co-operative performance, including democratic process and good governance, which are wholly unlike conventional metrics of shareholder value.[6]

This is one example of the opportunity for the co-operative sector to come to build an alternative paradigm and not just an alternative practice. In this way, one of the challenges in moving from being hidden and heterodox to becoming visible and viable on a wider scale is to articulate a different understanding of economic life. Our job is one of redefining progress.

Luckily, co-operatives are not alone in doing this – we are merely at the business end of social change. There is no shortage of artists, writers, dreamers and activists that are organising to promote a fairer, more democratic and peaceful economy and society. There is a growing school of new economics that is legitimising more rounded ideas of human action and institutions, including co-operative behaviour – and questioning the relevance of market growth in a world of climate constraints and species and habitat loss.

Whether framed in terms of politics or in terms of campaigns and causes, there is and always has been a wider set of social movements that are sisters to the co-operative alternative – and among them are often to be found the next generation of co-operative innovators. What will determine the success of the co-operative model over the next thirty years is whether it can become the business model of choice for those who are building a sustainable, low-carbon economy, those who are growing livelihoods out of poverty or those who are creating new models of open access and democratic innovation and enterprise online.

So, let's return to the narrative threads of the co-operative sector as a hidden alternative. In my view, we are not one alternative but many. This book is a contribution to understanding this diversity. When you are faced with a mainstream economic ideology of market fundamentalism, the complexity of co-operatives is, of course, the point. Culturally shaped, socially varied: the fact that co-operatives represent a series of alternatives, rather than one alone, must be true, and must be something to celebrate. Moreover, some of what has been alternative in the past, such as a commitment to education for all, has already become mainstream through the state (although over 100 million primary school-age children, mainly girls, are still denied that right[7]). The goal of co-operative education is not completed, but it can move on.

So who, finally, is responsible for hiding these co-operative alternatives? It must be someone who has been around for a while. The clues I see suggest that if there were something of the equivalent of an act of hiding, then it dates back to the early years of the twentieth century, because this was the era that appeared to turn its back on the grassroots innovations of self-help, workplace organisation and mutual aid. In the UK, at least, mutuality was on a high at the end of the nineteenth century, with the growth of co-operatives, mutuals, friendly societies and trade unions. These were the forces that had come together into a participative project to reshape the ugly brutality of the Industrial Revolution. For many, a focus on building a 'daily democracy', bottom-up from the workplace, saw the economy as the place to make change and, at the turn of the century, the long-term way to build power.

Within thirty years, though, co-operation and mutuality were hidden, at least as a strategy for wider political change. The key to social progress became capturing the lever of state power. Trade unions, such as the Miners' Federation (that had earlier supported worker control of business – 'mines for the miners') for example, allied themselves to the project of state action and state socialism. If anyone was responsible for tipping the scales away from mutuality over this period, it was probably Beatrice and Sidney Webb, supporters indeed of the co-operative ideals but whose preference was for the vision of the state, professionally managed and democratically appointed. As William Morris warned Sidney Webb, 'the world is going your way at present, Webb, but it is not the right way in the end'.[8]

The twentieth century that followed was an age of mass consumption and mass organisation. From the running of industry through to the triumph of the nation state, big was beautiful. Until large-scale approaches to production and welfare started to break down in its final decades, managerialism and corporate or state-dominated organisation was one phenomenon that the great ideologies of the century all seemed to share. Soviet Russia made an idol of the individual coal worker, A.G. Stakhanov, but only in the name of collectivism. Factory-line Fordism, and the era of mass production, was born in the United States, while one of its most famous beneficiaries, the VW Beetle – the people's car – was conceived in Nazi Germany. The values of the military, based on strong hierarchies and mass participation, won out over the voices that after both world wars called for peace and new models of international co-operation.

So, perhaps the veiling of the co-operative model is simply the sweep of history – the interplay between conflict and co-operation a contemporary version of Tolstoy's grand *War and Peace*. And if models of social organisation are now turning back to more bottom-up and participative models, in line with the drivers of technology and culture, perhaps the co-operative model may be in the process of being unveiled anew. The hiding will come to an end.

Whether that happens or not is now down to those involved in and supportive of co-operative ideals. The strategies that helped to keep the flag flying when the wider world consigned us to the margins may not be the strategies that reconnect us now that the world is waking up to its potential. We should remember that the co-operative narrative, of invention in Rochdale, of values shared worldwide, is a story that should connect us to other member-owned businesses and to longer traditions of community ownership and livelihoods sustained collectively.

We should learn that there are new models of collaborative economic activity emerging online, which warn us not to become stuck in a rear-view mirror interpretation of what is a permissible co-operative form. We should build common cause with the thought leaders who now place co-operation as a vital and overlooked keystone, not just for human evolution and flourishing, but also for contemporary economic health and success.

It is a co-operative value to take responsibility and to share the benefits. The idea of democracy and participation in economic life is a proud one. It has been hidden for these long years. We now … you now, have the wind on our side and the opportunity to change that.

Notes

1 I. Illich, *Tools for Conviviality* (New York: Maryon Boyars, 1973).
2 S. Zadek, *The Civil Corporation* (London: Earthscan, 2001).
3 *Financial Times*, 'Welch Condemns Share Price Focus', 13 March 2009.
4 J. Roberts, *The Modern Firm* (Oxford: Oxford University Press, 2004).
5 J. Robertson, 'Transforming Economic Life', *Schumacher Briefings* 1, 1998.
6 The credit union sector worldwide, for example, has developed a set of performance frameworks, including PEARLS. In the UK, a basket of 'co-operative performance indicators', including financial and non-financial indicators, has been developed for benchmarking and reporting by Co-operatives UK.
7 Unicef UK, *The Right to Education*, 2010.
8 R. Page Arnot, *William Morris: The Man and the Myth* (London: Lawrence and Wishart, 1964).

Index